THE STATE OF THE
EUROPEAN COMMUNITY

Vol. 2

A biennial project of the
European Community
Studies Association

THE STATE OF THE
EUROPEAN COMMUNITY

—| Vol. 2 |—

The Maastricht Debates
and Beyond

edited by

Alan W. Cafruny
Glenda G. Rosenthal

Lynne Rienner Publishers

Longman

Published in the United States of America in 1993 by
Lynne Rienner Publishers, Inc.
1800 30th Street, Boulder, Colorado 80301

Published in the United Kingdom in 1993 by
Longman Group UK Limited
Longman House, Burnt Mill, Harlow
Essex, CM20 2JE, England
and Associated Companies throughout the world

Library of Congress Cataloging-in-Publication Data
State of the European Community : the Maastricht debates and
    beyond / edited by Alan W. Cafruny and Glenda G. Rosenthal.
    Includes bibliographical references and index.
    ISBN 1-55587-359-6 (alk. paper)
    1. European Economic Community. 2. European Economic Community
countries—Economic policy. I. Cafruny, Alan W. II. Rosenthal, Glenda G.
(Glenda Goldstone)
HC241.2.S755   1993
397.1 ' 26 —dc20   93-7665
                                                                        CIP

British Cataloguing-in-Publication Data
A Cataloguing-in-Publication record for this book
is available from the British Library.
ISBN 0-582-22691-0

Printed and bound in the United States of America

The paper used in this publication meets the requirements
of the American National Standard for Permanence of
Paper for Printed Library Materials Z39.48-1984.

Contents

PART 2 NATIONAL INTERESTS AND EUROPEAN UNION

PART 3 TOWARD A EUROPEAN FOREIGN POLICY

PART 4 THE SINGLE MARKET

Preface

Second in a biennial series of "yearbooks" on the state of the European Community, this book, which covers 1991 and 1992, takes up where *The State of the European Community: Policies, Institutions, and Debates in the Transition Years* (edited by Leon Hurwitz and Christian Lequesne) left off. The current volume not only provides a description of key issues and developments in the European Community (EC) during 1991–1992, but also comments on and analyzes events from a variety of conceptual and theoretical perspectives.

This biennial series is one of several projects sponsored by the European Community Studies Association (ECSA). ECSA exists to develop a community of people interested in the EC and to raise the level of knowledge about it. Although there are a number of associations and organizations in the United States that focus on Europe or individual European countries or groups of countries, ECSA is the only organization devoted solely to the EC. It welcomes members from all academic disciplines, as well as the business and public sectors.

ECSA's objectives are to promote study and awareness of the EC by facilitating research projects and other collaborative works among the association's members in order to increase the published literature on the EC; encourage links between the association and European counterpart associations and individuals; publish an informational newsletter; hold conferences and workshops; organize panels on the EC at conferences and workshops sponsored by other organizations; seek and disburse funds to support the association's activities; draw on the membership to speak publicly about EC issues; and undertake other programs, activities, and projects deemed appropriate. The association is fully committed to promoting links with interested individuals and organizations in other parts of the world.

***

In coediting this volume, we and our coauthors have been fortunate to

ix

receive assistance and support from many individuals and institutions. We are especially grateful to the executive committee of ECSA, and to Roy Ginsberg, who originated the idea of a yearbook on the European Community. We would also like to acknowledge financial support from the following institutions: the Department of Government at Hamilton College; Columbia University's Institute on Western Europe; the European University Institute; and the Ford Foundation. Gina Hibbard of Hamilton College and Alasdair Young of Columbia University provided indispensable administrative assistance. Maureen Lechleitner's linguistic and organizational skills were invaluable and greatly appreciated.

Alan W. Cafruny and Glenda G.Rosenthal

1

The State of the European Community: Theory and Research in the Post-Maastricht Era

Alan W. Cafruny & Glenda G. Rosenthal

It has been commonplace for some years now for scholars analyzing the European Community to bemoan the lack of attention paid to major conceptual and theoretical issues. During the 1950s and 1960s, a rich body of literature appeared on both European integration and comparative regional integration. However, as the Community fell into stagnation in the 1970s and idealism waned, this tradition succumbed to a new wave of scholars who deemed the EC ineffectual and unimportant and rejected the normative, teleological approach of many of their predecessors. By and large, those few scholars, mostly European, who showed an interest in EC policies, processes, and institutions in the 1970s and 1980s tended to assume that the EC was a unique organization not susceptible to generalization, and they thus concentrated only on describing selected aspects of its activity. Scholars in the United States, for the most part, preferred to examine the EC in the broader context of the increasingly theoretical study of the international political economy.

We believe that the tide has turned. Since the late 1980s, the contributions in a number of collections on the EC have been placed in a conceptual context.[1] Authors refer now to a "new" European Community, and reviewers call attention to "new thinking" and "fresh perspectives." Journals such as *International Organization,* which paid scant attention to the EC in the 1970s and 1980s, now regularly publish articles that seek to revise old theoretical frameworks or introduce new conceptual lenses. Conferences on both sides of the Atlantic are also now emphasizing theory.[2]

To be sure, scholars of the EC remain preoccupied with the old, time-honored theoretical approaches. Most continue to be guided by concepts such as neofunctionalism and neorealism, federalism and intergovernmentalism, even as they invent new labels for EC processes such as "consociationalism," "liberal intergovernmentalism," or "preference convergence."[3] Moreover, the same time, the EC's external relations continue to affect the nature and pace of economic and political integration.

Part 4, "The Single Market," deals with selected aspects of growing economic integration. The internal market is developing rapidly, but the process of uneven development leads to distributive conflicts. Also, the EC has been unable to formulate a coherent, effective industrial policy.

The Architecture of Europe in the Post-Maastricht Era: Legitimation, Regulation, and Monetary Union

If the underlying logic of the Single European Act was functional and economic, it was ultimately passed because it corresponded to the perceived national interests of Europe's most powerful nations. Governments recognized that international capital mobility had rendered "Keynesianism in one country" obsolete; they saw the SEA as an extension of new domestic strategies of economic and financial liberalization. To be sure, the Commission viewed the single market as a means of accelerating the process of political integration, and not simply as an end in itself. The SEA, for example, called for "the progressive realization of Economic and Monetary Union." Nevertheless, the modest expansion of supranational authority that the SEA introduced, perhaps most notably in the provision of majority voting on single market issues, could be endorsed even by Margaret Thatcher because it was essential to the goal of liberalization.

At Maastricht, the member states debated more fundamental questions about how national and supranational power should be combined and exercised. Of course, not even the most ardent European can claim that the Maastricht Treaty, studded as it is with deliberately evasive passages intended to obscure and finesse sharp conflicts among nations, resembles a genuine constitutional or "founding document." A case in point: the provision for a common foreign policy whereby states can decide (on issues to be determined later) voluntarily to surrender their veto power; or the stipulation that the European Union "might" in the future adopt a common defense policy. As William Nicoll (Chapter 2) writes, "Read as a whole, the Treaty is not about people's Europe, but about states' Europe. The Union citizenship that it inaugurates is a thin veneer"(p. 21).

Power and Legitimation: Implications of the Treaty

Yet, if the Maastricht Treaty can be said to buttress, or indeed consecrate, the nation-state,[5] nonetheless it does transfer a great deal of power from states to EC institutions. This is particularly true in the monetary sphere and can also be seen in provisions for majority voting in the Council on a number of significant issues.

Thus, important symbolic as well as real elements of national power, if not sovereignty, have been surrendered to the Community. The power of the nation-state has been diminished, both as a result of the EC and of global economic interdependence. As power becomes more diffuse and remote from Europe's citizens, Europe has begun to confront a deep crisis of legitimation. Yet, EC institutions and practices retain a decidedly elitist character. The European Community has neither the popular support nor the authority to provide an alternative source of legitimacy. Europe faces a democratic deficit not only at the level of the EC, but also at the national level.

The Maastricht Treaty strengthened the European Parliament and embraced the concept of "subsidiarity." Yet, as Brigid Laffan notes (Chapter 3), despite the acquisition of substantial new powers, the Parliament is still remote from the European mass public. Turnout in EP elections continues to lag behind that in national elections, and the EP elections sometimes gain their significance as de facto referendums on the performance of national governments. Indeed, even the 1992 French referendum on Maastricht was viewed by many to be a vote on François Mitterrand's record.

Wolfgang Luthardt (Chapter 4) analyzes comparatively the causes and consequences of national referendums on the Community. Referendums have been one means by which national governments have sought to legitimize the transfer of decisionmaking power to Community institutions. The results of the French and Danish 1992 referendums clearly show that "integration from above" had met with substantial popular resistance from below.

Strengthening the European Parliament is one means of reducing the "democratic deficit." But greater democracy also requires higher levels of participation at many other levels, including the expansion of interest groups and corporatist structures operating at the EC level. Michael Gorges (Chapter 5) examines the formation and performance of various transnational interest groups in the Community. He finds that interest intermediation at the level of the firm has become well established. However, trade unions are still primarily nationalist in outlook and activity. As high unemployment persists, the implications of different national traditions with regard to labor markets become more problematic for trade unions. "Social dumping" remains a serious issue as firms, aided by SEA reforms, tend to invest and relocate in countries and regions where labor regulations are most favorable to business. During the early 1990s, trade unions did, in selected industries, develop closer transnational links.[6] Nevertheless, at the present time there is little prospect of "macro-corporatism" at the Community level. The Social Charter has encountered stubborn opposition from national governments.

Thus, the development of Community social policy continues to lag far behind the integration of the European marketplace. Robert Geyer (Chapter 6) examines the changing strategies of socialist parties and trade unions toward the Community. Social democrats have hoped that the EC might "rescue" them from the debilitating effects of liberalization; Keynesian strategies might be possible at the level of the Community. Geyer argues, however, that in cutting their links to the national community, these "modernizers" have deprived themselves of a national base of solidarity and tied themselves to a European "community" lacking in class and social solidarity.

Problems of Monetary Cooperation

The power to issue currency is a fundamental aspect of national sovereignty and the most important means by which governments regulate national economies. By providing for one currency and one central bank by the year 2000, the part of the Treaty that deals with EMU clearly constitutes the major achievement of Maastricht. If realized, monetary union would certainly represent an unprecedented and fundamental assault on the nation-state.

David Andrews (Chapter 7) and Wayne Sandholtz (Chapter 8) examine the politics of European monetary cooperation. The ERM was established in 1979 as the nucleus of the European Monetary System. A system of stable exchange rates, it was hoped, would partially insulate Europe's economy from the fluctuations and uncertainties of the dollar. By linking currencies in a relatively narrow band to the deutschemark (DM), the exchange rate mechanism greatly limited the ability of states to intervene in the economy. Most commentators (but not Margaret Thatcher) believe that monetary union is essential to the functioning of the single market.

The disarray in Europe's exchange markets, beginning on "Black Wednesday" (September 14, 1992) and continuing into 1993, indicates vividly the political difficulties of fixed exchange rates in the context of uneven national economic development and unrestrained capital mobility. In September 1992, Britain and Italy (temporarily) withdrew from the ERM; by February 1993, interest rates in Britain had fallen to their lowest level in fifteen years. Throughout late 1992 and early 1993, the French franc came under sharp speculative attack and required repeated intervention by the Bundesbank and Bank of France, despite the fact that France registered a balance of payments surplus for 1992 and a lower inflation rate than Germany.

Recent monetary turbulence casts a shadow over the future of EMU. The process is clearly neither automatic nor irreversible. The attempt to maintain fixed currencies (or establish a single currency) is politically divisive as long as national economies develop unevenly and under conditions of greater interdependence. Moreover, opposition to EMU within Germany becomes more vocal when the Bundesbank is pressed by other countries to reduce interest rates. The crisis of "Black Wednesday" and the subsequent turbulence in European exchange markets may have played itself out by May 1993, by which time the lira, pound, punt, and peseta had been devalued and an effective full-scale realignment was accomplished.

Like the SEA, Europe's monetary crisis invites realist analysis: clearly, the debate over EMU bears the imprint of intergovernmental rivalry and negotiation. At the same time, however, both Andrews and Sandholtz concur that the outcome of the Treaty did not simply reflect a given balance of power in Europe but that it has set in motion norms and practices that are not easily captured in purely intergovernmentalist terms. Andrews argues that, through the Maastricht Treaty, "powerful pent-up structural and neofunctional forces were allowed to assume a particular and distinctive shape" (p. 120) and that a return to the *status quo ante* is unlikely. In the longer run, it is doubtful that Europe will retreat to a lesser form of cooperation than that of the ERM. It seems more likely that a two- or multi-tiered monetary union will be established, with a less ambitious timetable. Such a union would be buttressed by a Franco-German monetary union and perhaps include the Benelux countries, with the others occupying a peripheral role.

National Interests and European Union

The specter of German power cast a long shadow over all events in Europe in the period covered in this book. Germany has been the decisive factor in the Maastricht negotiations and in subsequent economic and political turmoil. Reunification served as a powerful inducement to France to deepen economic and monetary integration. At the same time, both Germany and its partners believed that further political cooperation was desirable. For Germany, cooperation would ease the process of reunification by calming fears of a revanchist Germany; for the rest of the EC, it would guarantee that Germany did not unilaterally establish the terms of reunification and policy toward Eastern Europe. France hoped to recover, in the form of a European Central Bank, at least some degree of de facto political control that it had surrendered to the Bundesbank.

Yet, if German reunification provided the impulse for steps to further unity, the economic and political consequences of reunification have served to undermine that unity. European Political Cooperation was watered down at Maastricht and further weakened by the Yugoslav conflict. As the recession wore on and Germany refused to lower interest rates, the costs of the ERM in France had become painfully apparent. Unemployment in France climbed to 3 million in early 1993, and the franc came under renewed speculative attacks even as the country registered a trade surplus in 1992. Françoise de la Serre and Christian Lequesne (Chapter 9) show that the French referendum exposed deep, underlying antipathy to the Community, particularly among the working class and in rural areas.

A broad consensus within the German government on political cooperation was not matched by similar agreement over monetary union. The Bundesbank had long been wary of the idea of a European Central Bank in which it would have to share monetary leadership. Reunification, however, tilted the balance toward the government as Chancellor Kohl recognized the need to accomplish reunification within the context of a strong EC and close Franco-German alliance. In 1991, President of the Bundesbank Karl Otto Pöhl resigned because of his opposition to monetary union. Kohl nevertheless agreed to EMU—provided France endorse political cooperation in the form of expanded powers for the European Parliament (in which Germany would have the most seats) and a more cohesive foreign policy.

It soon became apparent, though, that Germany's economic strategy for reunification was wildly optimistic. Paul J.J. Welfens (Chapter 10) shows that the policy of moving rapidly toward parity in wages and living standards played havoc with German government finances. Kohl's decision to raise funds on international capital markets rather than through taxation elevated interest rates throughout Europe. Germany played a role in the Community similar to that of the United States on a global level in the mid-1980s. In both cases, a strategy geared primarily to domestic politics raised global interest rates and had deflationary consequences. Ironically, the high successive hurdles that the Germans insisted on at Maastricht are now beyond the reach of Germany itself. By February 1993 Germany's overall budget deficit exceeded 5.5 percent, almost twice the level allowed for eventual membership in the EMU.[7]

Stephen George (Chapter 11) examines the evolution of British strategy in the early 1990s. Under Margaret Thatcher, Britain continued to pursue a strategy of monetary nationalism. Thatcher kept Britain out of the ERM and rejected the concept of a monetary union, which her environment secretary and close adviser, Nicolas Ridley, denounced as "a German racket designed to take over the whole of Europe." In 1990, however, power in the Conservative party shifted decisively to the pro-European faction. Britain entered the ERM and remained in it, at great cost, until September 1992.

The British economy was also crippled by high German interest rates. By September 1992 it was clear to the financial markets, and perhaps also to the Bundesbank, that the pound would have to be devalued. In the end, Prime Minister John Major took Britain out of the ERM, amid acrimonious exchanges with Germany, leaving his economic strategy in ruins and damaging the reputation of the government. Throughout the rest of 1992 and early 1993, the pound floated downward, finally dragging the Irish punt with it in February 1993. Britain registered a negative rate of industrial growth for 1992, and it was unclear if or when it would rejoin the ERM.

Britain prevailed on a number of legal and institutional issues at Maastricht. Still deeply suspicious of monetary or social regulation at the EC level, it was permitted to opt out of both social policy and EMU. It succeeded in removing the word "federalism" from the agreement and ensured that great emphasis was placed on "subsidiarity," although this concept was not clearly defined. Finally, it limited the scope of European Political Cooperation by introducing numerous qualifications to the language of the Treaty. In most areas, British positions and interpretations gained acceptance throughout the

Community during 1992 as popular antipathy to the Maastricht Treaty increased throughout Europe.

In sum, 1992 revealed deep divisions among the most powerful nations of the EC. These divisions were exacerbated by the political and economic effects of German unification and the recession, in itself partly a result of German policy. If the Community is to move forward, it must do so, as in the past, on the basis of renewed cooperation among the big three, and particularly Franco-German unity. At present, however, Germany's preoccupation with its eastern länder has made cooperation very difficult.

Toward a European Foreign Policy

During 1991 and 1992, the Community faced a series of challenges in its relations with the rest of the world: membership for the EFTA (European Free Trade Area) and the Eastern European countries; the Gulf War; civil war in Yugoslavia; and the Uruguay Round of trade negotiations. At the same time, the Community began to confront the issues of citizenship and immigration, with large numbers of economic and political refugees from Eastern Europe crossing into the Community, and racist and xenophobic movements growing. Hans-Georg Betz (Chapter 12) discusses the evolution of national and Community policies toward immigration.

The issue of expansion took on greater urgency after the collapse of the Soviet Bloc. In early 1993, the Community began formal negotiations with Austria, Finland, Norway, and Sweden. John Redmond (Chapter 13) shows that the basic considerations for EC membership have continued to be the net economic benefit to the EC; the GDP of the applicant; and the impact of its agricultural economy on the EC. It is likely that most or all of the EFTA countries will be admitted by the end of 1995. The situation with regard to the Eastern European countries is more problematic.

The inability or unwillingness of the United States to take the lead in the reconstruction of Eastern Europe places a great deal of pressure on the EC and, in particular, on Germany. This raises the question of whether Germany has the means or desire to provide leadership and, even if so, whether the Eastern European applicants could accept it.

In describing Europe's role in the Gulf War, Pia Christina Wood (Chapter 14) shows that its response to the conflict did not reflect new principles of political cooperation, but rather traditional national policies toward the region. Britain steadfastly stood by the United States. France sought to carve out an independent role as mediator, and François Mitterrand repeatedly introduced peace plans designed to provide Saddam Hussein with a means to pull back from Kuwait. Only when these proved unsuccessful and France's lack of power was evident did it reluctantly join the coalition.

The breakup of Yugoslavia has even more starkly revealed the lack of

European political cohesion. As Hans van den Broek, vice president of the commission in charge of external relations and security affairs, acknowledged,

> The Yugoslav drama has traumatized West European people and done more damage to the process of European unity than the hassle about Maastricht. The sad truth is that one year of diplomatic efforts and economic sanctions only helped convince the Serbs . . . that wholesale massacre, rape and ethnic cleansing could go unpunished.[8]

Chancellor Kohl's decision to recognize Slovenia and Croatia in late 1991 in the absence of guarantees for the rights of minorities arguably encouraged Serbs and Croats to take up arms in Bosnia. This action, which constituted a German repudiation of political cooperation and an unprecedented reassertion of German power, directly contradicted French and British policy, although the EC eventually acceded to Germany's wishes and granted recognition. Throughout 1992 the EC was unable to develop a concerted response to the crisis. Summing up the lessons of both crises, Wood argues that "cooperation and coordination within EPC remain viable only as long as they do not undermine national interests, in which case European solidarity disintegrates" (p. 241).

Since the beginning of the Uruguay Round in 1986, the United States and the EC have negotiated over agricultural trade and production within the framework of the General Agreement on Tariffs and Trade (GATT). These negotiations are reviewed by Finn Laursen (Chapter 15). Lack of agreement has precipitated a series of transatlantic trade skirmishes. Believing that it possesses a comparative advantage in many sectors, including grain, the United States seeks to liberalize global agricultural policy. Conflict has centered on Europe's Common Agricultural Policy (CAP), which was conspicuously exempted from the SEA and the Maastricht negotiations. Both sides have provided sizable export subsidies in order to drive each other out of third-country markets.

U.S. policy has aggravated intra-EC conflicts, pitting Germany and Britain against France, the key proponent and beneficiary of the CAP.[9] The central uncertainty for the EC is Germany's willingness to continue to underwrite a generous CAP, especially if this endangers the Uruguay Round. The EC did offer major concessions in 1992 by reducing the increase in spending for agriculture. Moreover, the Community's decision in May 1992 to move from price support to direct subsidies represented a radical change in the CAP and a significant concession to the U.S. position, although it was deemed insufficient by the United States. In October 1992, U.S. Trade Representative Carla Hills announced the United States's intention to impose a punitive import tax on $300 million of annual imports from the EC if further reductions in CAP subsidies were not made.

The EC Commission finally reached agreement with the United States on a further package of cuts, and both sides declared, perhaps optimistically, that the package would make it possible to conclude a Uruguay Round agreement in early 1993. However, despite prodding from Germany, France continued to resist, and even threatened to use its veto power in the Council. As a result, the impasse was expected to continue at least until, and probably beyond, the French elections in March 1993. Once again, the role of Germany will be crucial: it may be compelled to choose between salvaging the Uruguay Round or maintaining the Franco-German special relationship.

Timothy Birch and John Crotts (Chapter 16) concur with Pia Christina Wood that defense cooperation is a prerequisite for effective European Political Cooperation. The Maastricht Treaty calls for the gradual development of a European Defense Identity (EDI) within the Western European Union (WEU), which is to remain distinct from the "Community's political machinery." But EDI is subject to two competing conceptions. For Britain, the WEU should represent the European arm of NATO; France, however, backed by the Commission, calls for a progressive merger between the WEU and the European Union.

Although Britain's outlook prevailed at Maastricht, the debate continues. Birch and Crotts argue that defense collaboration depends, in part, on the establishment of an independent European military-industrial base. The Airbus project provides one example of significant political willingness to collaborate on a European basis; Birch and Crotts present evidence of a more general trend in this direction. They show that the European defense sector is becoming highly concentrated, especially in aerospace and electronics. While much research and production remains national in scope, "the level of bilateral and multilateral cooperation in the developmental stage in conjunction with 'tag-teaming' on bids and contracts is worthy of observation" (p. 279). The Commission is becoming increasingly active, increasing funds for high-technology research with military application and sponsoring programs such as ESPRIT.

The Single Market

By the mid-1980s, it was widely recognized that Europe was lagging behind the United States and Japan in the areas of productivity, investment, and especially, high technology. The SEA was widely heralded as a means of restoring Europe's position. The Cecchini Report confidently asserted that the single market would bring annual growth rates of 6 percent and, in the long run, significantly reduce unemployment.[10] By early 1993, however, these optimistic hopes had been buried by the global recession and high interest rates. The Commission's annual economic forecast predicted that unemployment in the Community would rise to 11 percent in 1993 and 11.5 percent (18 million people) in 1994.[11]

In a number of significant areas, including competition policy, the

Community has begun to play a dominant role. Internal barriers to trade have been largely eliminated, stimulating a wave of mergers. Donald Partan (Chapter 17) shows that merger control policy has become centralized, and the Commission has begun to overrule national governments in this area.

The development of a single market, however, has not been accompanied by a coherent industrial policy. Walter Goldstein (Chapter 18) points to the continuing ideological and political disputes within the EC over the nature of industrial policy. The size and scope of state intervention have consequences for fiscal policies (including the Maastricht convergence targets), industry, and trade. In Italy, for example, three state conglomerates (ENI, EFIM, and IRI) control nearly 500 affiliates and account for a large fraction of GNP and employment. Public subsidies for workers in Italy amounted to $6,000 per capita per year between 1980 and 1986. Similar conditions exist in France, where one-third of all manufacturing and banking is controlled by state concerns. Thus, Goldstein observes, "if these payments were reduced—or eliminated—a major part of the EC workforce would find itself as stranded as the skilled but workless millions in Eastern Europe" (p. 313). The Maastricht Treaty requires that the annual budget deficits of member states should not exceed 3 percent of their GDP. At the end of 1992, forecasts for France's budget deficit ranged from 3 to 4.5 percent; for Germany, 5.5 percent; for Britain, 7 percent; and more than 10 percent for both Greece and Italy.[12] Moreover, most European countries have adopted expansionary budgets for 1993 in hopes of combatting rising unemployment.

Goldstein argues that the SEA left unresolved the key debate between state interventionists, led by France, Italy, and Spain, and free marketeers, led by Britain and the Netherlands. Given the technological deficit with Japan and the United States, should the EC seek to establish a Fortress Europe and develop behind a protective wall and public subsidies? Or should it expose its markets to international competition and force huge cash cows in aerospace, automobiles, computers, and electronics to survive as world leaders or die?

In practice, the option of a Fortress Europe is largely illusory. Anticipating new Community-wide trade restrictions, U.S. and Japanese firms massively entered Europe in the 1980s, building, especially in the U.S. case, on already substantial holdings. It is estimated that the turnover of U.S. affiliates in Europe exceeds by a factor of ten the value of U.S. exports to Europe. At the same time, Europe's largest firms also expanded greatly their own foreign direct investment outside the Community. Europe not only depends heavily on U.S. and Japanese multinationals, but also on its own foreign direct investment.

The Community does not appear eager to abandon the interventionist policy favored by a majority of the Commission (led by Jacques Delors). Goldstein argues that this strategy will not enhance the competitiveness of European companies in the global market. Unless state intervention is greatly reduced, the development of large, world-class European firms, especially in high technology, will be stunted.

The studies of telecommunications by Wilson Dizard (Chapter 19) and of environmental policy by Alberta Sbragia (Chapter 20) indicate clearly that the single market has had an impact on national policy. Europe's telecommunications industry lags far behind that of the United States, accounting for only 15 percent of global trade in communications goods and services. In 1991 the EC had a deficit of $35 billion in electronics trade with the rest of the world even as European firms, spurred on by the breakup of AT&T, have been rapidly penetrating global markets, especially those of the United States. The telecommunications industry did not feature prominently in the SEA because national governments, with the exception of Britain, have opposed the deregulation of their national telecommunications monopolies.

By focusing on advanced services, the Commission has, through a series of directives, been able to introduce some important reforms. It has devised a program of deregulation and encouraged advanced research on a regional basis through subsidies and two major programs, RACE and ESPRIT. But liberalization has, thus far, been extended to only 5 percent of telecommunications, and not to voice telephony. Commission directives reserving government procurement to European firms provoked a new round of conflict with the United States in early 1993.

Environmental policy offers a case in which states have been more willing to surrender authority to the Community. Sbragia shows that a significant amount of legislation is now framed on an EC-wide basis by the Commission, causing a transfer of lobbying activity from national capitals to Brussels. The resulting Commission directives have not, in general, simply accepted the "lowest common denominator." Sbragia does, however, acknowledge that it has been easier to issue directives than to gain compliance.

The Cecchini Report on the impact of the SEA focused on estimated aggregate economic gains and did not seek to assess the relative gains and losses resulting from the single market. In fact, few studies have attempted to do this. Dale Smith and Jürgen Wanke (Chapter 21) present data on the effects of trade expansion for various countries and groups of countries in a range of different sectors. These data show that the benefits of trade liberalization are distributed unevenly. Germany, not surprisingly, is the major winner, but liberalization has had negative consequences for Europe's weaker economies. This analysis has implications for the Community's structural policy, which recognizes that redistribution of wealth is essential to both the single market and monetary union.

The size and composition of the Community budget is obviously the crucial factor in redistributive policy. Through the greatly expanded structural fund, and the newer cohesion fund, the Community has shown a willingness to respond to the needs of the poorer states and regions. Yet, as Michael Shackleton (Chapter 22) points out, neither the Maastricht Treaty nor the 1992 budget provided substantial new commitments to the poorer regions. The overall budget increase (from 1.2 percent of Community GNP in 1992 to 1.37

percent in 1997) is modest in view of the 5 to 10 percent goal that was discussed in the 1970s, and much less than the Commission wanted. In 1992 the Community budget was still less than 3 percent of the total public expenditure of the member states. Shackleton concludes that "for the time being, the Community is seeking to move toward EMU as if it can be done without any effect on a broader budgetary agenda" (p. 388).

Gary Marks (Chapter 23) acknowledges that the budget process itself is dominated by member states, and that the broad parameters of regional policy are established through intergovernmental negotiations and treaties. He argues, however, that the implementation of structural policy is developing according to a logic of neofunctionalism. A great deal of authority has been ceded to the Commission, on the one hand, and to subnational actors, on the other. This has implications for theory, because "treaties are not representative of the ongoing process of institution building" (p. 407). Thus, sovereignty is succumbing, at least partially, to a more complex process of "multilevel governance" in which power is shared among institutions at various levels of competence.

Conclusion

Attempts to draw general lessons or to make predictions about the future of the EC solely on the basis of these essays must be ventured with caution. The future of the EC depends only in part on its internal dynamics; all previous phases of EC institution building have constituted responses to changes in the wider international system as well. What is happening now in Europe is but one component of a very uncertain process of global economic and political transformation.

If the post-Maastricht crisis is ultimately global in scope, it is also an expression of Europe's new German crisis. Germany has expended considerable resources in its single-minded determination to reintegrate and reconstruct its eastern länder. The absorption of Eastern Germany has placed an enormous burden on the whole Community, and particularly on the Franco-German alliance, which has been central to the development of the EC throughout its history. In the long run, Germany will emerge as an even stronger nation, yet still uniquely vulnerable to the instability of its eastern neighbors. In the future, it can only play an even more assertive role in the EC.

Many of the chapters in this volume reflect a growing interest in theory, as noted at the beginning of this introduction. After the strains of 1992, few observers would endorse the optimistic, teleological assumptions of neofunctionalism—the "guarded pessimism" that runs through many of the chapters is hardly surprising. Europe has experienced a severe recession with exceptionally high unemployment. Such factors have always placed great constraints on European cooperation and institution building, and will continue to do so in the future.

Yet, much of the skepticism in the book concerns the tactics of institution building and not the strategic logic of integration. Perhaps few, if any, of our contributors would endorse the realist assumption that all significant events in the Community are reducible to the clash of national interests, however important those interests may be. European integration is a complex process that is not easily captured by the traditional categories of intergovernmentalism and neofunctionalism. If states have successfully defended their sovereignty, the Commission and other Community institutions have also fought tenaciously and successfully to obtain a share of power.

It was the Danish "no" in June 1992, the French referendum in September of the same year, and the ongoing battle in the British Parliament and within John Major's Conservative party in 1992–1993 that have thrown into sharp relief the whole question of the "democratic deficit" in the Community. Sooner or later, national governments and EC institutions will have to come to grips with the question of how much power they are willing to place in the hands of their citizens and how far they are prepared to go in revealing the inner workings of Community decisionmaking. This is yet another of the critical themes running through many of the chapters that follow.

Most of the chapters were written precisely during the time that the European Community was going through a kind of political and economic *crise de conscience*. If we were to characterize the twenty-two chapters in any single way, we would point to the fact that almost every contributor seems convinced that the Community is in crisis but that it will survive and expand, certainly geographically and most probably politically and economically. The underlying assumption appears to be that the Community has carved out a place for itself in the international arena through the strength of some of its policies, the conviction of some of its leaders, and the will of some of its citizens. Above all, the Community gives each member state, large or small, a bigger voice as part of the largest economic entity in the world at the same time that if offers members the prospect of achieving the goals, set out in the Rome Treaty, the Single European Act, and the Maastricht Treaty, of promoting economic and social progress for their peoples.

Notes

1. Robert O. Keohane and Stanley Hoffman, eds., *The New European Community: Decisionmaking and Institutional Change* (Boulder: Westview, 1991); Alberta Sbragia, ed., *EURO-POLITICS: Institutions and Policymaking in the "New" European Community* (Washington, D.C.: Brookings, 1992); William Wallace, ed., *The Dynamics of European Integration* (London and New York: Pinter Publishers (for the Royal Institute of International Affairs, 1990); Gregory F. Treverton, ed., *The Shape of the New Europe* (New York: Council on Foreign Relations Press, 1992).

2. For example, "Economic and Political Integration: The State of the Art" was the theme of the thirtieth anniversary conference (November 1992) of the *Journal of Common Market Studies*; similarly, "European Integration After Maastricht: Uniting Empirical and Policy Research with Revitalized Theory" was the theme of ECSA's Third Biennial International Conference (May 1993).

3. On consociationalism, see Paul Taylor, "The European Community and the State: Assumptions, Theories, and Propositions," *Review of International Studies,* 17, 1991. On liberal intergovernmentalism, see Andrew Moravcsik, "Negotiating the Single European Act," in Robert O. Keohane and Stanley Hoffmann, eds., *The New European Community: Decisionmaking and Institutional Change* (Boulder: Westview, 1991). On preference convergence, see Robert O. Keohane and Stanley Hoffmann, "Institutional Change in Europe in the 1980s," in Keohane and Hoffmann.

4. See, for example, the annual publications of the Centre for European Policy Studies, the *Journal of Common Market Studies,* or the official annual activity reports of the various Community institutions.

5. Alan Milward, *The European Rescue of the Nation State* (Berkeley: University of California Press, 1992).

6. For example, partnership agreements between British and German engineering, printing, and chemical unions have recently been signed. These cover exchanges of information and personnel, joint seminars, and language courses to be funded by the EC. See "GMB in Pact with German Trade Union," *Financial Times,* February 4, 1993.

7. *Financial Times,* February 2, 1993.

8. *International Herald Tribune,* January 18, 1992.

9. Ronald T. Libby, *Protecting Markets: U.S. Policy and the World Grain Trade* (Ithaca, N.Y.: Cornell University Press, 1992).

10. Paolo Cecchini, *The European Challenge, 1992: The Benefits of a Single Market* (Aldershot, UK: Gower, 1988).

11. *Financial Times,* February 4, 1993.

12. *Financial Times,* February 3, 1993.

PART 1

THE ARCHITECTURE OF EUROPE IN THE POST-MAASTRICHT ERA: LEGITIMATION, REGULATION, AND MONETARY UNION

2

Maastricht Revisited:
A Critical Analysis of the
Treaty on European Union

William Nicoll

The Maastricht version of an "ever closer union among the peoples of Europe" took a trouncing within three months of its Europhoric conclusion. In four member states, many citizens decided that that particular European Union was not what they wanted as a political structure. Economically, the law of the market showed that fixed exchange rates could not be held and that the monetary union designed at Maastricht was being built on insecure foundations.

On June 2, 1992, the Danish electorate said no to the Treaty on European Union. The British government shortly withdrew the bill it had submitted to Parliament for ratification. In France, the Treaty had obtained parliamentary ratification at a congress in Versailles on June 22, but the president announced that there would be a referendum on September 20. For fifty days, attention was focused inconclusively on what might be done to persuade Danish voters to think again. In the ensuing fifty days, the Danish question slipped from the foreground as opinion polls began to show that French voters might also say no.

Until the mid-1980s, the governments of the member states of the European Community preferred to follow a low road of constitutional development, adopting nontreaty instruments, such as declarations or agreements, either intergovernmental or interinstitutional. The two formal treaty amendments of 1970 and 1975 were technocratic budgetary affairs—not the stuff of public debate, or even public curiosity. A proposed Act of European Union, the Germano-Italian initiative of 1981, was diluted into a solemn declaration and did not become part of the treaties. It, too, was studded with reservations. With the Single European Act (SEA) of 1987, the member states' governments embarked on the high road of treaty revision. The SEA was both twofold—Community and intergovernmental cooperation—and incomplete. It foreshadowed further treaty amendment to underpin the long-delayed Economic and Monetary Union (EMU), and it provided for a review of political cooperation five years after the entry into force of the SEA.[1]

EMU became the richly prepared material for one-half of the 1991 Intergovernmental Conference. Political cooperation, lightly prepared, formed part of the second half, which also became the receptacle for other matters—interinstitutional relations, amendment of the EEC Treaty, the institutionalization of pre-existing cooperation among law and order authorities, even an abstruse modification of sexual equality law as applied to pensions. The outcome was the Treaty on European Union, signed in Maastricht on February 7, 1992, and proclaimed as setting Europe on its course, especially toward EMU and toward a Common Foreign and Security Policy (CFSP).

If it could no longer be said that Europe was at the crossroads, it was not long before Europe was seen to be at cross-purposes. Chancellor Helmut Kohl declared that with Maastricht, sovereignty had gone out the window, while Prime Minister John Major insisted that British sovereignty was still alive and even reviving.

Within the member states, public support began to slide. Germans worried about the eroding value of the deutschemark. The French worried about the enfranchisement of foreigners. Britons worried about their masochistic membership in the exchange rate mechanism. The Irish worried about abortion on demand. Danes objected to possible conscription into a European army. Spaniards were unsettled by austerity measures taken to pave the way to EMU. Italians were distracted by a wave of internal crises. The peoples of Benelux stood, as always, foursquare for Europe. Portugal, the incoming presidency country, was also imbued with the European spirit; its spokesman said the right things.

Fault lines began to show among the Twelve when the Commission, as requested, presented the spending proposals it believed necessary to fulfill the ambitions of Maastricht (Delors II). It had done the same, with some success, in the wake of the SEA (Delors I), at a time when the Community was out of money and was adopting shifts to keep itself ostensibly solvent.[2] This time around, the Community was underspent and the prospective or actual net budgetary contributors among the member states—now comprising Germany, France, Italy, and Britain—were disinclined to take on higher bills.

The proto-CFSP also faltered. The dispatch of a Community peace-making mission to Yugoslavia on June 28, 1991, on the seventy-seventh anniversary of the assassination of Archduke Ferdinand in Sarajevo, and its success in securing a cease-fire turned sour as umpteen cease-fires were accepted and immediately and even preemptively violated. What was to have been the redemption on European soil of the nonexistence of the EC in the Gulf War stumbled, provoking rifts and unilateral initiatives among the member states.

The prenuptial honeymoon ended in June 1992 with the second Nordic repudiation, by referendum, of the pro-EC stance of a government that had negotiated and signed an EC treaty. It should not have been a total surprise. Eurobarometer, the opinion poll conducted continuously for the Commission, had been showing that a majority among the Danes did not want a common foreign policy or a new international defense organization. Conversely, two

organism with a trunk and branches. The Commission cultivated the tree,[4] but when the Dutch presidency transplanted it into a draft treaty in September 1991, ten member states uprooted it. It was a rare, total rejection of a presidency proposal. In place of the tree, the temple that the Intergovernmental Conference built is a single edifice, although its pillars support different loads—Community, CFSP, and cooperation on Justice and Home Affairs. The detachment of the pillars from the classic Community is the first sign of the predominance of the states. There are three others.

Subsidiarity

Subsidiarity (entrusting to common institutions only those powers required to carry out tasks more satisfactorily than the states acting independently), which determines the relationship between the Community/Union and its member states, is alongside democracy one of the two fundamental principles. To some, President Delors and Vice President Bangemann among them, it is part and parcel of federalism. To others it is the antonym of federalism.[5]

There need be no surprise that a federation is on some cards. The word appears in the Schuman Declaration of May 9, 1950. There is no surprise that it is controversial, being equated with the loss of national standing. This offends notably British Conservatives, on whose behalf Mrs. (now Baroness) Thatcher characterized the Economic and Monetary Union as based on "the willing and active cooperation of independent sovereign states" in her speech at the College of Europe in Bruges in 1988. More recently, her successor differed only in being more openly nationalistic: at his party conference in October 1992, Mr. Major spoke of "voluntary cooperation between independent nation-states."

Subsidiarity seeks to reconcile national and central authority. There is no necessary contradiction between the competing versions of Article A:

> This Treaty marks a new stage in the process . . . [leading gradually to a Union with a federal goal . . . (discarded version)] of creating an ever closer union among the peoples of Europe,[6] in which decisions are taken as closely as possible to the citizen.

According to legal opinion, the principle of subsidiarity creates an overarching obligation on the Community and Union to act only when necessary. Since the principle is in the body of the Treaty, it is in theory justiciable. The most recent president of the Court has said roundly that the Court cannot apply it.[7] But it is clearly intended to "shift responsibility from Brussels to London," as Mr. Major has put it, and counts as one of his famous victories in the Maastricht negotiations.

Four other points are worth noting:

- Subsidiarity works up as well as down. It is likely to be cited to justify the necessity for action by the Community at least as forcefully as it will be used to uphold the prerogatives of the member states. Half of the proposals that the Commission makes are in response to requests from the Council or from one or more of its members.

  ○ It is impossible to write lists of what the member states can do better than the Community. Economic teaching about externalities can help to identify which levels of government can expect to be efficient, but the doctrines are uncommonly difficult to apply to real cases.

- The subsidiarity which the Treaty on European Union consecrates stops at the national capital. Mr. Major has said flatly that it has no bearing on the relationship between Scotland and the United Kingdom.

  ○ Perhaps the subsidiarity extant in member states will help to apply the principle. A member state that has "subsidiarized" a policy area cannot allow the Community/Union to pronounce on it without the consent of the responsible authority that is closer to the citizen.

Intergovernmental Relations

Caveat: In U.S. studies these words refer to relations between the states and the federal government. In European studies they concern how member states work together outside the framework of the Community. There was a consensus among the member states, including the federalists but excluding the Commission, to restrict the scope of supranational authority in the Union and in the new Community.[8] (There is already little supranationalism in the pre-Maastricht Communities.)

The Commission proposes measures and executes them when the Council adopts them and authorizes the Commission to execute. The Commission has some powers of its own under Community law, notably over competition policy and in the ECSC Treaty. As guardian of the treaties, it also verifies whether the member states are fulfilling their obligations. But it has no sanctions of its own against defaulters.

Measures are decided by the Council.[9] For twenty years, outside the budgetary procedure, it acted by consensus or not at all. From the mid-1980s, and especially to secure the completion of the 1992 program, it took many of its decisions by qualified majority voting. This introduced a "minisupranationality" to the extent that up to four member states might see a decision imposed on them. This eventuality was circumscribed. The legal base had to authorize majority decisions. If the Council wanted to change what the Commission was proposing, it needed unanimity. A vote, rarely taken formally, came at the end of a long dialogue in which the participants behaved as if they were striving for consensus. The final voting down of a minority occurred only when the last of a string of compromises had failed and when all delegations and the Commission could say that they had made some effort at accommodation.

There may also be a national veto power. The Luxembourg Compromise of 1965[10] acquired the potency of a single member veto. With the Single European Act and the 1992 program that it backed up, more weight was attached to the efficiency of majority voting than to the sensitivities of the minority. The foreign office minister who piloted the bill through the House of Lords in 1985 said that the veto was still there. The president of the French republic said the same in the Sorbonne TV debate on the eve of the referendum in September 1992.

The Treaty on European Union does not strengthen the powers of the Commission vis-à-vis the member states. It does provide for the Council to be overridden in the new codecision procedure applicable to certain measures if Parliament does not agree with them and if a protracted conciliation procedure has been exhausted. To that extent there is a degree of negative supranationality, justified by the values of participative democracy.

Community Method Not Used

If the Community method is not used, the constraints on the powers of the member states, attenuated in the way that has been described, disappear.

The CFSP and the cooperation on Justice and Home Affairs do not fall under the sway of Community methodology. The Council and the Commission that act in these two areas may be the same people as act in the Community, but they do not interact in the same way. These areas remain intergovernmental. In the CFSP there is a provision for decisions to be taken by qualified majority, provided this has been agreed unanimously (Article J.3.2). It is not apparent why a member state should volunteer to let itself be outvoted, but stranger things have happened in the heat of debate. In the area of Justice and Home Affairs, there is a similar possibility, and measures that implement ratified conventions are to be adopted by a two-thirds majority (Article K.2.c, second indent).

If in these areas majority voting were ever used, which is not an early prospect, it would escape the safeguards of the Community method. The majority could make such amendment as it chose, there being no initiating Commission proposal to limit the scope and purpose of the measure.

The apostle of intergovernmentalism is the British government. According to it, the selling point of Maastricht is that it decentralizes. This is a legitimate overstatement. The Treaty does not centralize much further. To say that it decentralizes for the first time in the history of the Community is a misunderstanding. European Political Cooperation, the precursor of the CFSP, has been intergovernmental since it began in 1969. Cooperation among ministers responsible for immigration, etc., has been intergovernmental since it began, at the suggestion of the British government, in 1986. The Commission attends both, by custom and invitation, but does not attend the intergovernmental Trevi Group on international crime, another British initiative of 1975.

There is another way of weakening the centripetal force of a collectivity. It goes by a number of names, but the general idea is that a member is suffered to exclude itself from the decisions desired by the others.

There have always been derogations from legislation. The rule is that they must be motivated and they must be temporary. They are transitional, and the period of grace is used by the member state with the derogation to prepare itself to join the others. But such temporary derogations might not be enough for a member state that does not want to join in at all, ever. Two of the words used to describe nonparticipation in a Community measure tend to be pejorative. "Europe à la carte" gives the impression of the member states deciding for themselves which Community activities they want to participate in. Such libertarianism could falsify competition. An advantage for the à la carte diner could spell disadvantage for those sitting at the table d'hôte. Willy Brandt invented the expression "two-speed Europe," which has even more negative vibrations in the minds of the slow-movers. The expression that suggests a reputable purpose in a differentiation among the member states is "variable geometry."[11] The salient example of variable geometry is the exchange rate mechanism of the European Monetary System. It is both multi-speed (members have different degrees of latitude in the fluctuations of their currency before they have to defend a rate) and variable (member states can choose to join or not).[12]

Maastricht consecrates the virtues of variable geometry. In the EC, it makes differentiated rules for social measures. It creates an ad hoc Social Community of Eleven and allows it the use of Council, Commission and Parliament to fulfill what the Eleven, excluding—without textual motivation—Britain, have contracted to do. Legal opinion considers that the social measures of the Eleven will be enforceable before the Court, which in principle is concerned with the laws of the Community of Twelve. The monetary union, of which more below, is also geometrically variable and multi-speed. This was stoutly denied after the meeting of the Intergovernmental Conference in Apeldoorn on September 21, 1991, which fixed the main provisions. If/when the monetary union is established, there will be founder members and others. The latter will be known as "member states with derogation," deemed to be temporary until they comply with the convergence criteria. Britain, another "member state with derogation," has not accepted a commitment to join or vouchsafed any intention that it will. Its self-exclusion is again without motivation (protocol on certain provisions relating to the United Kingdom) and without limit of time. Denmark likewise has an option not to join, although it is one of the few that already satisfies the criteria of membership. The notion of two-speed monetary Europe, although plain for all to see, provoked noisy debate when mooted in the changed context of the weakening of the exchange rate mechanism in September 1992. There was speculation—in both senses of the word—about an inner circle of interlinked currencies, clustered around the deutschemark. Denials seem pointless. The monetary union is explicitly multi-speed. Only the member states that meet the criteria can join it. They then run it.

In the CFSP the member states commit themselves to taking common positions and to agreeing, in designated areas, on joint actions. Suppose that discussion fails to produce agreement. Are the member states then condemned to paralysis? The stock answer is that they will try mightily to agree if necessary by fudge and by the wordsmith's art, but there is no sanction against reserved unilateralism except a progressive loss of credibility plus public condemnation by the Commission, which is organizing itself to play an energizing role. In the thin pamphlet that it published in the fall of 1991, the British Foreign Office asserted both that Europe's single voice would be strong in world counsels and that Britain could set its own foreign affairs agenda.

The Treaty on European Union invokes another union, Western European Union (WEU), the unarmed military pact. The references to a common defense policy, mediated through the WEU, are so sketchy that it is impossible to judge what a future European defense arrangement might be.

The only certainty is that there is no procedure for decision-taking. Even the intergovernmental procedures of the CFSP are specifically disavowed (Article J.4.3). What replaces them awaits further work, in a "gradual process involving successive phases" (Declaration on WEU, para. 1). WEU is to become the defense component of the Union (ibid, paras. 2.2 and 3). The relationship is not otherwise defined; neither are the arrangements for the stronger operational role intended for WEU to be made compatible with the defense policy of the Atlantic Alliance and with the dispositions necessary to ensure the collective defense of all allies.

The two NATO and EC members who do not belong to WEU are invited to join. Greece will; Denmark will not. The non-EC European members of NATO, Turkey and Norway, are invited to become associates. The non-NATO EC member, Ireland, is to become an observer.

Nothing in this mosaic suggests that the defense policy of the European Union will be anything but intergovernmental. Where in NATO, in European Union, or in WEU the command structure of the joint European army corps proposed by France and Germany fits in is not explained.

The Treaty on European Union creates or reaffirms a Europe of states. The pillars of the temple—subsidiarity, intergovernmentalism, and variable geometry—sustain the authority of the state. As the later stages of the Uruguay Round may enlighten us, there may even still be a single member veto power in the Community. However, there is one new centralized entity, the monetary part of EMU.

Economic and Monetary Union

Maastricht places the EMU within the Community but gives it such distinctive structures and powers that the monetary union is effectively a fourth pillar. It takes off from Article 102.A.2 SEA, ecumenically entitled "Cooperation on economic and monetary policy (Economic and Monetary Union)."

The report of the Committee chaired by President Delors that prepared for the Intergovernmental Conference described (para. 32) the centralization and collectivization of monetary decisionmaking as falling within "a federative structure which best corresponds to the political diversity of the Community" and considered that it was compatible with the principle of subsidiarity (which had not at the time been fleshed out). The report did not actually recommend a single currency, but fixed exchange rates went in that direction. This is, then, an example of the centripetal effect of subsidiarity. President Delors was refreshingly frank when he said, "Yes, we have to have transfers of sovereignty to achieve economic and monetary union. Why deny it ?"[13] It was precisely this effect that roused Margaret Thatcher when she said that the single currency was the route to a federation that she would never accept. It was an uncharacteristic understatement.

The model of monetary union that the Treaty builds is federative in the limited sense that its governing council includes the presidents of the central banks, but is unfederal and uniate in the sense that it is equipped with a single central and centralizing authority to the exclusion of all subordinate authorities.[14] It is also insulated from the institutions of the Community and from governments of the member states by the iron law of autonomy, which places the monetary authority some distance from the citizen.

The institutions of the Community and the governments of the member states undertake not to seek to influence the members of the monetary authority (The European System of Central Banks) in the performance of their tasks. (Protocol on the Statute, Article 7. The protocol is an integral part of the Treaty). This self-denying ordinance goes further than the protection of the independence of members of the Commission. Neither the member states nor the Parliament has ever undertaken to refrain from trying to influence the Commission,which is their constant endeavor.

The statutory powers of the European System of Central Banks are extensive. They allow it to make regulations which are binding in their entirety and passing directly into Community and member states' law, without the involvement of the Council or of national parliaments. It can impose penalties on undertakings (e.g., credit institutions) for failure to comply with its regulations and decisions (Article 3).

In the monetary union, issues of macroeconomic management—matters that have been the lifeblood of Western politics, determined the rise and fall of governing parties, and affected the fate of national economies—are to be decided by a tribune of central bankers and full-time executives of the European Central Bank. Their decisions on monetary policy are taken by one-man, one-vote majorities. The bank is not accountable to political authority. It sends reports to the Parliament and attends the Council on Economic and Financial Affairs.

This "market oriented authoritarianism"[15] is unlike anything else in the Community or Union. It is the absolutism of Plato's philosopher kings,[16] as to whom Glaucon reminded Socrates that if he made pronouncements of that sort, a large number of decent people would pick up the nearest weapon and come after him. Why did the governments of ten member states opt for a neoplatonic monetary union?

Some may have been impressed by a link between the independence of the Bundesbank and the pre-unification German miracle. Japan offers the contrary example of a central bank that is not independent. Some may have believed that there was no alternative. Whatever they might take as national objectives, their monetary policy and therefore much of the rest of their economic policy would be dominated by the power of the deutschemark (DM), the most stable of currencies and the one most resistant to inflation.

Some had already taken the DM option. The Benelux countries had tied their currencies to the DM. They were subject to decisions over which they had no control and which represented German answers to German problems. An authority in which they would be represented by their own top bankers would be an improvement on alien monetary rule.

Some may have courted the International Monetary Fund (IMF) syndrome. They knew what had to be done, but domestic politics and electoral short-termism stopped them from doing it. In the past, the IMF had been called in, partly for its resources, but partly to shift the onus of unpopular but unavoidable decisions. Monetary union would be a permanent *deus ex machina,* doing the right things for the general good. Some may have subscribed to the reasoning of the Commission's analysis in its report "One Market, One Money," which used modeling techniques to predict gains comparable to those flowing from the completion of the single market. Within monetary union there might also be—although the Commission study declined to forecast "spatial effects"—resource flows towards the poorer member states. Some may have believed that EMU was an essential part of the European Union, including political union of some kind, which was their lasting vision of the future.

In the polarity of the force field of European integration, there are positive and negative currents. The positive is the one in favor of a comprehensive form of European government, usually seen as a federation. The common feature is the transfer of at least some sovereignty/competence/decisionmaking authority from the organs of the member states to the institutions of the federation.[17] The negative force, not synonymous with antimarketeering, opposes centralization in which agencies of the federation poke into the nooks and crannies of national life. Antimarketeers usually call for free trade among European countries but draw the line at further economic integration and political integration. By free trade they probably mean a customs union, and perhaps a single market in goods and services.

Functionalism provides a meeting point between positivists and negativists. The positivists can say that it is a stage on the way to something bigger and will assuredly spill over.[18] Negativists can say that they recognize the interdependence of economies but that the policies they espouse involve no commitment to something qualitatively different. The European Communities of the 1950s to 1980s permitted the two tendencies to cohabit, with the negative in the ascendant. Whatever orators might say about their long-range vision, it is a matter of observation that the member states preferred arrangements in which they held onto their powers and resisted the not negligible integrating forces of the Community they had created. These included the right of initiative of the Commission, which blocks coalition hegemonies among the larger member states; the universality of the budget, which diverts increasing amounts of public funds; the interventions of the Parliament, to which some attention must be paid because the member states conceded direct elections; and the overriding judgments of the Court, which may prevent member states from doing what they want to do.

The single market program was in the functionalist tradition, but with its companion, the Single European Act, the writing was on the wall. Qualified majority voting became widespread, displacing consensus. Political Cooperation was given treaty status, but with a Chinese wall between it and the Community. The Parliament was given more power, including a veto over certain agreements with third countries and over the admission of new members. Economic and Monetary Union was revived and a marker put down for the institutional development it would require.

It could have been the beginning of the end of functionalism. The single market program reached out beyond the treatment of goods and services, to the free movement of people, without travel documents or controls on where they might live. The logic of "One Market, One Money" laid a basis for new thinking about Economic and Monetary Union.

Gravitation toward a center and away from national accountability promoted thoughts about new political organization going far beyond the mere coordination of foreign policy. Nevertheless, the negatavists held on. Subsidiarity could become a new meeting point. Federalists have no difficulty with it and indeed say it is how a federation works. Their opponents give it the same welcome, but as a brake on centralization.

The temple architecture brought new common policies into a loosely defined Union and kept them out of a more tightly drawn Community. For a number of reasons, which may or may not be among those suggested above, EMU went its own way, which is ultrafederal. Its time scale no longer looks realistic, in the light of the market's sustained attacks on a number of currencies.

The British government declined to move on monetary union, on social policy, on open frontiers for citizens, on overstraining the Atlantic Alliance. They succeeded in inserting many of their contentions into the Treaty and opted out of others. The Danes were happy to stay in an Economic Community, but not to join a Community going to a single currency and a Union that has plans for common defense. The French vote produced results only a whisker different from those of the Danish. The Irish electorate took a positive view, possibly influenced—who can say?—by the prominence that its government gave to the cash benefits, past, present, and future, of membership. The British government began an unhappy presidency, in trouble with a faction among its own supporters who think that Maastricht is a treaty too far, unwilling or unable to give vent to the vision thing and obliged to work for the ratification of a treaty on the Hilaire Belloc principle: "And always keep a-hold of Nurse/For fear of finding something worse."

When Axel Krause asked Mrs. Thatcher, President Delors, Chancellor Kohl, and President Mitterrand for their vision of Europe to the year 2000, he was given two polarized answers and two in the middle.[19] Mrs. Thatcher recalled her Bruges speech. What mattered was the reality that there "should remain proud independent nations within a broad framework of cooperation."[20] The chancellor wanted a "United States of Europe," using the language of Monnet's Action Committee. Chancellor Kohl later said—apparently approvingly—that this was not what Maastricht did. President Delors thought that the realistic scenario was President Mitterrand's idea of a loosely structured confederation. Mr. Delors has elsewhere described himself as a federalist. President Mitterrand himself said that his objective was to transform the Economic and Monetary Union into an entity with all the attributes of a union of the states. He acknowledged that we cannot build Europe without delegating more sovereignty, but the European Union of tomorrow will not make the nations disappear.

* * *

The Treaty on European Union is and could only ever be a parcel of compromises. All that can prudently be said about the future Europe to which it addresses itself is that there will continue to be tension between the advocates of a federation with a powerful (but not all-powerful) center, and the defenders of national authority save insofar as demonstrable interdependence requires it to be qualified. If the United States is any guide, the debate has a long run ahead of it.

Let Jean Monnet have the last word. When in September 1960 President de Gaulle poured scorn on the Community and proposed a European confederation, Monnet was not abashed. On November 22, 1960, he wrote to his colleagues in the Action Committee for the United States of Europe:

> If we followed that course we should soon be faced with two methods: the integration method established by the Treaties for the three existing Communities and the method to be adopted for political, defense and education issues will be different. But is that any reason for not seeking unity? I think not. In

the circumstances we must again adopt an empirical approach. I believe and I put it to you that it would be a very good thing to develop different organizations simultaneously within the same European system: a Council of the Six Heads of Government; a Council of Ministers of Foreign Affairs, Defense and Education; and the European Communities with their rules, institutions and responsibilities. I believe that a kind of "European Confederation" could usefully play this role. As I see it, such a body offers, at this point of time, the best means of advancing forward towards a more complete form of European unity. I have no doubt that a confederation will one day lead to a federation. But for the moment is it possible to go further? I cannot say that it is. Meanwhile the confederation would have the very great advantage of assuring public opinion in our countries that they have joined an entity which is not only economic, but political, and that they are therefore part of something bigger than any of their countries alone.

Notes

1. The essential commentary on the SEA is by Jean de Ruyt (a member of the Belgian delegation) in his *L'Acte Unique Européen* (Brussels: Editions de l'Université de Bruxelles, 1987).

2. W. Nicoll, "The Long March of the EC's 1988 Budget," *Journal of Common Market Studies* 28 no. 2 (December 1988), p. 162 ff.

3. The European Council could have been, but was not, given institutional status in Articles 109f.1 and 109k.2.

4. "Intergovernmental Conferences: Contributions by the Commission," Bulletin Supplement, 2/91, Luxembourg: Office for Official Publications of the European Communities, pp. 175–177.

5. For a review of divisions of opinion on the nature of U.S. federalism, see David Beam, Timothy J. Conlan, and David B. Walker, "Federalism: The Challenge of Conflicting Theories and Contemporary Practice," in *Political Science: The State of the Discipline,* Ada W. Finister, ed. (Washington, D.C.: American Political Science Association, 1983).

6. Words taken from the preamble to the treaty establishing the European Economic Community, Rome, 1957.

7. Several times, notably in an article in the *Times* of London, on December 12, 1992.

8. The word "supranational" occurs only once in the founding treaties. It was used in the original ECSC Treaty to particularize the status of the members of the High Authority. When the institutions were merged in the 1965 Treaty, the word disappeared.

9. For commentaries see Robert Keohane and Stanley Hoffmann, eds., *The New Economic and Monetary Union* (Boulder, Colorado: Westview Press, 1991), pp. 133–154 and 158 ff.; and Gregory Treverton, ed., *The Shape of the New Europe* (New York: Council on Foreign Relations Press, 1992), p. 60 ff.

10. William Nicoll, "The Luxembourg Compromise," *Journal of Common Market Studies* 23 no. 1 (September 1984), pp. 35–43.

11. De Ruyt, op.cit., pp. 271–273; Nicoll, "Paths to European Unity," *Journal of Common Market Studies* 23 no. 3 (March 1985), pp. 199–206; Maclay, *Multi-speed Europe?* (London: Royal Institute of International Affairs, 1992); M. Spicer, *A Treaty too Far* (London: Fourth Estate, 1992), p. 4.

12. At one point all save Greece had joined the ERM. Britain and Italy withdrew in September 1992. The Treaty on European Union presupposes that all will join

(Article 109; 1). Britain, which had been invited to join in the preparatory work but did not want to join the ERM, successfully proposed that all member states should belong to the European Monetary System but need not join its ERM. Lord Owen, *Personally Speaking* (London: Pan Books, 1987), p. 117.

13. Quoted in the Commission booklet "Economic and Monetary Union," (Luxembourg: Office for Official Publications, 1992).

14. Sir Alan Walters, "The Changing Role for National Central Banks," in *The European Monetary System and International Financial Markets* (Washington: Friedrich Ebert Stiftung, and Arlington, VA: George Mason University, 1991), p. 22. More generally by the same author, *Sterling in Danger* (London: Fontana/Collins, 1990), chap. 7.

15. Francis Fukuyama, *The End of History and the Last Man* (New York: Free Press, 1992), chap. 10.

16. Plato, *The Republic*, trans. Desmond Lee (Penguin Books, 1987), pt. 7.

17. Koen Lenaerts, "Constitutionalism and the Many Faces of Federalism," *The American Journal of Comparative Law* 38, pp. 205–263.

18. Pierre Uri, "Jean Monnet's Method," in *The Monnet Centenary Symposium* Luxembourg: Office for Official Publications of the European Communities, 1988, p. 54.

19. Axel Krause, *Inside the New Europe,* (New York: Harper Collins, 1992), chap. 10.

20. In her article in *The European* newspaper of October 8–11, 1992, (the week of the Conservative Party Conference), she defederalized further by evoking a Europe of nation-states, based on the idea of cooperation between independent sovereign countries loosely linked in a free trade area.

3

The Treaty of Maastricht: Political Authority and Legitimacy

Brigid Laffan

When representatives of the European Community members signed the Maastricht Treaty in February 1992 after twelve months of formal diplomatic negotiations, it marked the second time in seven years that the member states have engaged in constitution-building. In itself it is an interim step as the new agreement supposes another round of treatymaking in 1996. If we recall the EC's weak institutional and political capacity during the 1970s and early 1980s, this represents a remarkable transformation of its fortunes. In negotiating a new treaty, the EC member states attempted to establish the institutional and legal framework for integration in the 1990s. This chapter addresses the issues that dominated negotiations and follows the Treaty's progress since conclusion of the Intergovernmental Conferences (IGCs) in December 1991.

The Background To Maastricht

Maastricht must be seen in its wider global context. The Treaty on Economic and Monetary Union is a response to changes both in the international political economy and in world politics. The Maastricht negotiations would not have taken place without the success of the 1986 Single European Act which provided the cement for the single market project. The 1992 project gave renewed political impetus to European integration and led in turn to pressures for a deepening of economic integration. Negotiations on Economic and Monetary Union (EMU) followed from the internal market program, yet EMU was more than a deepening of integration because of its consequences for internal economic management within the member states.

Although political integration cannot be divorced from economic integration, the collapse of communism and the rapid German unification provided the main impetus behind the political union negotiations. The transformation of the continent's power relationships has utterly changed the context of European integration. It is no longer possible to talk of Western Europe as a clearly defined region in world politics. German unification has altered the internal dynamics of European integration even as the enlargement of the Community looms ahead. The Treaty of Maastricht was negotiated against the background of an overcrowded EC agenda and considerable turbulence in world politics. By comparison, the Single European Act was negotiated in a far less complex environment.

Political and Economic Turbulence

Political and economic turbulence continued during the Maastricht negotiations and in the aftermath of its signing. Hostilities in the Gulf brought the question of a common foreign policy sharply into focus as the negotiators grappled with establishing a new framework for European Political Cooperation. The breakup of Yugoslavia and the emergence of ethnic and nationalist conflict cast a shadow over the Dutch presidency of the Council in the latter half of 1991. In addition, weak economic performance of a number of member states added the specter of a deep recession. During 1991 and into the first half of 1992, the costs of German unification began to manifest themselves. Budget deficits in Germany led to high interest rates as the Bundesbank moved to protect its reputation for assuring low inflation. High interest rates in Germany, in turn, exacerbated the recession in other member states. In contrast, the Single Act was signed and ratified at a time of economic growth.

Ratification

The ratification of the Maastricht Treaty is proving to be neither smooth nor automatic. The reasons for this lie in the political and economic turbulence outlined above and in the direction that Europe is taking. Ratification of the Treaty required referendums in two countries, Denmark and Ireland. On June 2, 1992, the Danish electorate by a very small majority rejected the Treaty. This marked the beginning of a very real crisis for European integration because Article R.2 of the Treaty of Maastricht and Article 236 of the Rome Treaty state that reform of the Rome Treaty cannot come into force without the consent of all of the High Contracting Parties. If the Danes fail to ratify the Treaty, it is dead. The conclusions of the Lisbon European Council (June 26–27), which took place one week after the Irish electorate endorsed the Treaty, affirmed the decision of the heads of government to press ahead with ratification. President Mitterrand announced a referendum in France in order to give the Treaty renewed political impetus. The strategy almost backfired; opinion polls showed that a no vote in France was possible, but in the event a small majority (51.6 percent) voted in favor of ratification.

The French vote came in the middle of a very serious currency crisis in the European Monetary System. High German interest rates and a weak dollar caused an inflow of capital into the deutschemark, which in turn put pressure on the weaker currencies, forcing the lira and the pound sterling to leave the system and the peseta to be devalued. Sustained support from the Bundesbank kept the French franc within its permitted limits, enabling the system to survive, although considerably weakened by the crisis. The franc, krone, and Irish punt came under renewed pressure in the foreign exchanges during December 1992.

European integration faces one of the deepest political and economic crises since its foundation. There are many facets to the crisis. First, the referendum debates and the Danish no vote highlight tensions between a "Europe of the elites" and a "Europe of the electorates." There are clear misgivings among the mass public about the direction Europe is taking. As the impact of integration spreads throughout the mixed economy, it becomes more visible to the population at large, yet its decisionmaking process seems remote from the mass public. Anti-Maastricht arguments have stressed the dominance of technocracy and the weakness of legitimacy in the Community's political system. Second, the currency crisis undermines one of the central pillars of the Treaty on Economic and Monetary Union. The idea of a two-tier or a two-speed track toward EMU is now commonplace. Third, there is a crisis of political leadership in the Community. Neither President Mitterrand nor Chancellor Kohl is in a strong political position domestically. The goal of a single currency finds no favor with the German public. John Major, presiding over a deeply divided Tory party, finds his government's economic strategy and its policy on "Europe" undermined by the sterling crisis.

The Edinburgh European Council of December 11–12, 1992, appears to have established a framework for dealing with the crisis. The Council reached a decision to enable Denmark to opt out of a single currency, a defense policy, and the aims of political and economic union. A second Danish referendum will be held in the spring of 1993. The Council also agreed to a plan on the future financing of the Community which will run to 1999. Significant concessions were made to the poorer member states.

The Characteristics of Treatymaking in the European Community

Formal interstate treaties play a pivotal role in the European Community's nascent political system. The treaties provide the constitutional basis for the evolving polity at the EC level. There has never been a root and branch overhaul of the Community's institutional system or policy scope. Rather, the process of integration has been gradual, interspersed with infrequent rounds of constitutional bargaining. This bargaining takes place within the Community's well-established negotiating practices.[1] The participants in the negotiating process attempt to simplify the issues by breaking them down into manageable groups. Agreement is reached by moving from the least difficult issues to the most contentious ones. The country holding the presidency of the Council manages the negotiations by preparing draft articles and ultimately a draft treaty. The final text is the product of tortuous negotiations and represents a package deal that is acceptable to all of the participants. The negotiators, both officials and their political masters, attempt to manage the interface between their domestic political arena and the dynamics of Community negotiations. Some negotiators are relatively unfettered by domestic political constraints, whereas others must manage delicate political problems. Community treaties are extremely detailed documents setting out institutional prescriptions and policy scope. They are not classical constitutional documents. Each time the Community has attempted to alter its policy competence, institutional questions have become part of the negotiating agenda. The institutional debate in turn tends to be couched in terms of a tension between advocates of increased powers for the so-called supranational elements of the policy process, notably the Commission and the Parliament, and those political forces favoring a minimalist transfer of sovereignty.

Prenegotiations and the Intergovernmental Conferences

The Maastricht Treaty was the outcome of two sets of negotiations: one on Economic and Monetary Union and the other on political union. The EMU negotiations benefitted from a much longer preparatory phase. The Hannover European Council of June 1988 authorized the president of the Commission, Jacques Delors, to chair a committee of the governors of the national central banks with a view to examining EMU and to making concrete proposals on the subject. The publication of the Delors report in April 1989 was followed by a period of intense political bargaining which led to the decision to convene an Intergovernmental Conference (IGC) to negotiate a treaty on EMU. Even before the formal opening of the conference, the Rome European Council (October 1990) set out the aims of the EMU, the desire for a single currency and the need for a new monetary institution. The member states, with the exception of the UK, agreed to guidelines on the final stage of the EMU.

The preparatory stage for the political union conference only began under the Irish presidency of the Council in the first half of 1990. A report from the foreign ministers that was submitted to the June summit in Dublin established the main issues for the negotiations, namely the scope of the Union, citizenship, political accountability, the efficiency and effectiveness of the Community and its institutions, and the Community's international role.[2] The absence of a lengthy preparatory phase or a committee akin to the ad hoc Committee on Institutional Affairs (Dooge Committee) which preceded the negotiations on the Single Act meant that the negotiators had to process a flood of papers from the member states, the Commission, and other EC institutions. The negotiations were managed during 1991 by the Luxembourg and Dutch presidencies in turn. The presidencies played a pivotal role in steeringthe negotiations through weekly meetings of ambassadors, specialist groups of middle-ranking officials and monthly ministerial meetings. The presidencies were responsible for dealing with substantive and procedural issues. The first phase of the political union negotiations culminated in the publication of a ninety-page paper in April 1991. This ended the analytical phase of the negotiations and opened the way for bargaining between the member states and Community institutions over competing concerns. In June the presidency published a paper on EMU and a draft treaty on political union. The June European Council agreed that the Luxembourg presidency had established "the basis for the continuation of negotiations, both as regards most of the principle points contained in it and the state of play at the two conferences."[3] The Netherlands attempted to alter this by launching a different draft treaty as the basis for negotiations. The Dutch attempt to get agreement on a more federalist document was resisted by the other member states at a ministerial meeting on September 30, known as "Black Monday" in the Dutch presidency. Thus, the Luxembourg draft became the main negotiating text in the final months of the IGCs. The last bargains were struck at the Maastricht European Council in December 1991.

The Heart of the Negotiations

The Treaty of Maastricht represents an attempt to adapt the Community's governance system for the 1990s. The negotiators grappled with three central aspects of governance in the Union:

- The political authority of the Union
- The legitimacy of the Union
- The international role of the Union

Political authority, which we define as the ability to supply governance, is a critical issue in any political system. It is a major issue confronting European integration because the Community, now Union, is an evolving polity. Although the voluntary pooling of sovereignty is the hallmark of European integration, there remains considerable tension between integration and independence, between the advantages of collective policymaking and the costs to national autonomy. Although there is a political system in the Community, it lacks the reservoir of political authority found in mature federal states. In fact, the European Community derives much of its authority from the intermeshing of the national and European levels. The authority of a political system rests on the twin pillars of capacity and legitimacy. Capacity relates to policy competence, the effectiveness of institutions, the possession of adequate policy instruments, budgetary resources, and leadership. Political authority is rendered legitimate by representative parliaments, constitutional norms, and judicial review. A weakness of capacity may undermine the legitimacy of a polity if the system does not deliver what is expected by the citizenry, and likewise a weakness of legitimacy may undermine capacity and hence political authority. Three main issues dominated the debate about the capacity of the Union, namely, its overall shape, policy reach, and the efficiency and effectiveness of its institutions.

The Shape and Goals of the Union

When the Luxembourg paper was published in April 1990, the Union was defined as consisting of three pillars:

- The European Community treaties and EMU
- The common foreign and security policy (CFSP)
- Cooperation in the spheres of Justice and Home Affairs

The imagery used was that of a Greek temple rather than a tree. Each pillar has its own policy scope with different decision rules. Policymaking in the Community pillar rests on the so-called Community method, a form of policymaking that gives an important role to supranational institutions, notably the Commission, the Parliament, and the Court. Cooperation in the other two pillars would be largely intergovernmental in character with some involvement by the Commission and Parliament.

There was strong opposition to this approach from the Commission and a number of member states committed to a unified system of policymaking. In response, the Luxembourg presidency included a reference to a "Union with a federal goal" in its June draft treaty. This in turn met with outright opposition from a British government determined to oppose a treaty that included the word "federal." The Dutch presidency made one more attempt to adopt a unitary system of policymaking in its September draft treaty but met with almost no support from the member states. Consequently, the original Luxembourg approach of three pillars was adopted. Notwithstanding the three pillars, Article C of the Treaty stated that in all areas of policymaking the Union would be served by a single institutional framework.[4] Because of the stipulation that there is a single institutional system as the web that binds the three pillars together, a shamrock is perhaps a better image than a Greek temple.

The Policy Reach of the Union

The policy scope of European integration has expanded greatly since the signing of the Rome Treaty in 1957 in response to socioeconomic changes, the internal dynamics of market integration, and changes in the international political economy. The Maastricht negotiations represented the most ambitious attempt to expand the policy reach of European integration. Article 3 of the Treaty lists a total of twenty-one policy areas that fall within the competence of the Community, together with a separate chapter on foreign policy and judicial affairs. Maastricht brings the union into the heart of contemporary government.

Three policy areas, in particular, dominated the negotiations: money, cohesion (redistribution), and social affairs. In the monetary area, the objective of the negotiations was to design stages two and three of EMU. This required decisions on a system for the management of a common currency, related economic policies, and the timing of stages two and three. In other words, the negotiators had to establish the policy and institutional framework for an EMU. From the outset, the Bonn government wanted to ensure that a European monetary union would be modeled as closely as possible on the German system. This meant that price stability or low inflation would be the main economic objective and that the European System of Central Banks would be independent.

The negotiations presented the British government with major problems because of the sensitive nature of EMU in the internal politics of the Conservative party, the prospect of a general election, and its reservations about EMU on both political and economic grounds. United Kingdom opposition was ultimately solved by a protocol that allowed the UK to sign the Treaty but leaves the decision on participation in the final stage of EMU to Westminster.

***

The length of the transition to the final stage of EMU and the conditions under which a member state could be deemed eligible to join EMU was the subject of intense negotiations in the month before the Maastricht Council. The Treaty is far firmer on this than was anticipated. No later than December 31, 1996, the European Council will decide if the move should be made to the final stage. The Council will base its decision on the degree of economic convergence achieved. Specific criteria are laid down for the convergence test. If no date is set for the beginning of the third stage by the end of 1997, the Maastricht Treaty states that "the third stage will start on 1 January 1999" (Article 109f). The inclusion of a firm date in the Treaty reinforced the political commitment to EMU.

The impact of the currency crisis of September 1992 on the prospects for an EMU by the end of the decade is far from clear. An Ecofin Council that met on September 28 to respond to the crisis stressed the need for early ratification of the Treaty and adherence to the strict convergence criteria laid down in the Treaty. Notwithstanding this, the member states may not be able to adhere to the transitional arrangements in the Treaty because the EMS itself, which is the bridge to a full EMU, has proven to be unstable. The currency crisis raises the specter of a "two-speed" or "two-tier" EMU with a group of member states moving to a full EMU before the dates set out in the Maastricht Treaty.

From the outset, the poorer member states were determined to recreate the link established in the Single European Act between market integration and the politics of redistribution.

The Spanish government, backed by Ireland, Greece, and Portugal, forced a reluctant Commission to take the cohesion issue seriously and subsequently extracted concessions from its richer partners. The Treaty includes provision for a new "Cohesion Fund" that is directed entirely toward the four poorer countries. Although this fell well short of the *Finanzausgleich* (transfer system in Germany among the *länder)* for interregional transfers sought by the Spaniards, it represented a negotiating gain for the poorer countries. The Treaty also included revisions of the SEA articles on economic and social cohesion. The budgetary implications of the Treaty are contained in the Delors II plan which sets out the Commission's budgetary strategy for the next seven years.

***

Social policy proved to be the final contentious issue at the European Council in Maastricht. As the Council came to a close, it became apparent that the UK was unwilling to enter into any negotiations on a strengthening of the treaty mandate in social policy. There was considerable support from the Commission and from most member states for a new treaty chapter on social policy that would allow the Community to decide on aspects of labor law by qualified majority voting. This was anathema to the Conservative government in Britain. Faced with a British determination not to negotiate on the issue, the heads of government reached the extraordinary decision to take the new chapter on social policy out of the Treaty itself and to include it as a protocol. The legal, institutional, and political implications of this are far from clear. The Commission will continue to introduce proposed legislation under the existing social policy provisions and will only resort to the protocol if no progress can be made in the Council. For example, a proposed directive on "works councils" in multinationals is at present stalled in the Council because of UK opposition. This could well be reintroduced under the protocol. A qualified majority vote under the protocol is fourty-four votes out of sixty-six. The "opting-out" clause could well form the basis of a case in the Court because it could be construed that "variable geometry" in social policy matters amounts to unfair competition. Thus the future politics of social policy in the European Community is very much bound up with domestic politics in the UK.

Subsidiarity

The term "subsidiarity" increasingly impinges on all major debates on the future development of the EC. While it is not a new concept in EC parlance, it is only in the last two years that subsidiarity achieved center stage in the debate about constitutional reform. Eurocrats and bureaucrats are attempting to work out the practical application of this rather abstract principle. The term encapsulates a growing debate about the appropriate balance between the policy competences of Brussels-based institutions and the member states. Since its inception the EC has amassed an ever-widening range of policy competences and is today involved in some way or other in most areas of public policy. The transfer or sharing of policy competence has taken place in a gradual and niggardly manner without serious debate about the EC's policy reach and grasp. The EC's capacity as a problem solving arena is impaired if it attempts to do too much.

The concept of subsidiarity originated in Catholic social teaching in the 1930s as a means of restricting the reach of public policy and the role of the state in matters of social policy. As a political or federalist concept, subsidiarity is generally understood to mean that policy competence should be exercised at the lowest effective level. Subsidiarity is thus a principle of federal systems of government designed to maintain as much autonomy as possible at the lower levels of government.[5]

The task of the IGC was to decide on a definition of the principle of subsidiarity and to establish just what role it should play in the politics of policy integration. There was general agreement that the principle should be included in the Treaty, but there were differences between those states that wanted a substantial reference to it and those that wanted it restricted to the preamble. In fact "subsidiarity" is a central theme in the Treaty and will be judiciable. This means that the Court of Justice can interpret the relevant article. The Maastricht Treaty refers to "the scale or effects of proposed action" (Article 3b) and to a Union where "decisions are taken as closely as possible to the citizens" (Preamble). The Commission will have to justify its policy proposals in light of these provisions.

Given the crisis in the Maastricht ratification process, subsidiarity has received renewed attention. The Commission, stung by accusations of technocracy and unwarranted interference in domestic issues, is in the process of translating the objective of the Treaty into reality. A task force was set up to prepare a report on the practical and procedural steps needed to implement the subsidiarity principle. The British presidency sees subsidiarity as a means of assuaging the fears of Maastricht's opponents within the Tory party and as a means of dealing with the Danish problem. Subsidiarity is likely to become a major feature of the governance system. Nonetheless, the division of power and competence will remain politically charged in an evolving polity such as the EC. Invoking the principle of subsidiarity may channel the debate and may induce a more thorough analysis of the Community's policy scope and grasp, but it will not take the politics out of the relationship between the EC and the domestic polities. For individual member states, the principle may well be a double-edged sword: useful to invoke against unpalatable policy initiatives but a problem if used to restrict policy developments in an area of interest.

The Efficiency and Effectiveness of Community Institutions

As the reach of Community policies expands with the management of the internal market, EMU, and the demands of nonmember countries for new relationships with the Community, questions concerning the efficiency and effectiveness of the Brussels legislative process take on a new urgency. The Maastricht negotiations sought to establish the institutional blueprint for the next round of accession negotiations. In the 1980s, the SEA had a dramatic impact on the Community's decisionmaking system, particularly on the operation of the Council. The greater use of majority voting changed the "rules of the game" by removing the psychological barriers to taking votes, and greatly enhanced the speed of decisionmaking.[6] The acceleration of the legislative process had an impact on the other EC institutions as all parts of the legislative process sought to implement the 1992 program. The Maastricht Treaty includes important changes concerning the Community's institutions and makes provision for the creation of a European Central Bank when the final stage of EMU is decided on. The most important changes relate to the role of the European Council, the extension of majority voting in the Council of Ministers, the granting of a right of initiative to the Commission in the area of foreign policy, and changes in the powers of the Parliament.

However, the Treaty does nothing to simplify decisionmaking procedures. Nor does it make institutional powers more akin to those of classical federations. If anything, the Treaty adds to the complexity of the decision rules and institutional responsibilities. Montesquieu's preference for a clear separation between executive and legislative responsibilities did not resound in the negotiating halls of Maastricht. The European Council (heads of government) emerged in the Treaty of Maastricht as the center of political authority in the institutional system. It is responsible for defining "the general political guidelines" for the Union (Article D, Common Provisions) and plays a major role in coordinating the activities of the Union across the three pillars. As such it looks more like a future European government than the Commission, which was regarded as an embryonic government in the 1950s. These periodic meetings of heads of government are now faced with the challenge of providing the Union with sufficient direction to manage a single currency and the Community's international role.

The Council of Ministers and its preparatory committee COREPER also emerged with enhanced authority from the Maastricht negotiations. The

Ecofin Council plays a major role in the management of the EMU, and the General Affairs Council is the locus of decisionmaking on foreign policy matters. Majority voting, a key feature of the Single Act, reemerged on the agenda. The Commission and some member states favored a blanket extension of majority voting with unanimity reserved only for constitutional issues. As this approach did not find favor with a majority of the delegations, there has been an extension of majority voting to some aspects of economic policy, environmental policy, development cooperation, health, consumer affairs, and trans-European networks. There is some provision for voting on foreign policy and in matters of judicial cooperation, but such provisions are extremely limited, and votes may only take place after a series of consensual decisions.

Legitimacy

The legitimacy of governmental action is a key feature of the liberal democratic tradition of government. The rule of law and constitutionalism impose limits on the power of governments. Furthermore, the legitimacy of public authority is based on the involvement of citizens in participatory democracy and their acceptance of the remit of the state. As the EC is a political entity with far-reaching political goals, it must show concern for its legitimacy.

European integration has been an affair of elites, both political and business. The elites have relied on persuading the mass public that European integration is a good thing. Lindberg and Scheingold drew attention to what they called the "permissive consensus" that provided sufficient utilitarian and affective support to sustain European integration.[7] As European integration encompasses more and more areas of public policy, particularly in the economic sphere, the Union could well become the scapegoat for restrictive budgetary strategies. Integration in the past has tended to be somewhat of a fair-weather phenomenon.[8] Two main issues on the agenda derived from a concern with legitimacy, namely, political accountability and citizenship.

Political Accountability

From the outset the European Coal and Steel Community had a representative dimension in the form of an assembly, the precursor of today's European Parliament (EP). Of the four Community institutions, the latter is least satisfied with its powers and influence within the decisionmaking system. After the first direct elections to the European Parliament in 1979, the EP could and did invoke its democratic credentials in its search for more authority and a greater say. The Single European Act, although it fell short of the demands of the EP, strengthened the role of the Parliament in two ways. Provision was made for a cooperation procedure, a second reading of SEA legislation, and an assent procedure for the accession of new member states and association agreements. The Parliament adapted quickly to the new procedures, determined to prove that a greater say for the EP did not undermine the speed of EC decisionmaking.[9] The EP remained dissatisfied, convinced that it alone can overcome the so-called democratic deficit in the Community. Political accountability, or its weakness within the Community's political system, is a perennial issue on the agenda. A "democratic deficit" is highlighted as one of the characteristics of the Community. National parliaments have been weakened by the transfer of policy responsibilities to the EC, responsibilities that are exercised at EC level by the Council of Ministers and not the representative body, the EP.[10] Even after direct elections, the decisive say regarding EC legislation rests with the Council. The SEA redressed the institutional balance, on the one hand, by giving the EP a second reading, but its provisions on majority voting add a new dimension to the "democratic deficit" on the other. Ministers in the Council are now frequently outvoted on legislative matters that become directly applicable in their domestic jurisdictions. On the face of it, then, the EP can marshall weighty arguments in its search for power.

Increased powers for the EP would seem the most appropriate means of strengthening political accountability in the EC. It alone can supervise the Council and the Commission at EC level. There is, however, the dilemma of the dual democratic imperative. Heretofore, EP elections have been characterized by uneven and low turnout in all countries. In 1989, turnout ranged from 90 percent in Belgium (where nonvoters are fined) to 36 percent in the UK. In six member states the turnout was less than 60 percent, considerably lower than in national elections.[11] Because government office is not at stake, EP elections tend to become mid-term tests of incumbent governments, with the result that national political issues dominate in campaigns. The low visibility of the EP is exacerbated by its multiple locations and the sheer distance of the constituencies from Strasbourg, its principal seat. National government office holders meeting in the European Council and the Council of Ministers tend, by and large, to be elected office holders with their own reservoir of authority and legitimacy. The EP saw the Maastricht negotiations and bargaining as an opportunity to press its case for codecision with the Council of Ministers. As the EP did not have a seat at the conference table, it depended on supportive member states to fight its case. Strong support for the position of the Parliament came from its traditional ally, Italy, plus Germany and the Benelux countries.

The powers of the Parliament proved to be a highly contentious issue during the closing stages of the IGC. The Bonn government was unwilling to endorse the EMU project if it were not accompanied by a strengthening of accountability in the sytem. The UK, traditionally opposed to institutional change, did not wish to see any deepening of the Parliament's role. It was supported by Denmark, ever vigilant about the Folketing's role. The new powers conferred on the Parliament by the Treaty of Maastricht represent a compromise between those favoring a greatly enhanced role for the Parliament and the "minimalists."

A new procedure (Article 189b) is to be added to the Treaty. This power of codecision adds a conciliation procedure to the legislative process. If, after two readings by both the Council and Parliament, there is still disagreement, provision is made for conciliation meetings involving the three main institutions.

If this is unsuccessful, the Parliament can use an absolute majority vote to block a decision. This places the onus on the Parliament because it will be seen as a negative force if it blocks legislation too often. Nonetheless, codecision will enhance the Parliament's role in the legislative process.

***

The Parliament's role is enlarged in a number of other important respects. The assent procedure has been extended to new areas of policy, the Parliament will elect an ombudsman, and its right to receive petitions and to set up committees of inquiry has been recognized by the Treaty. The relationship between the Commission and the Parliament has also been altered in the Treaty. The Parliament will now be involved in the appointment of the Commission and must endorse each new Commission with a vote of confidence. From 1995 onward, the life of the Parliament and the Commission will be coterminous, which will underline the accountability of the Commission to the Parliament.

Although the Parliament was dissatisfied with the outcome of the Maastricht negotiations, it is beginning to look like the second chamber of a bicameral legislature. This could well exacerbate the legitimacy crisis in the Community because the Parliament remains a shadowy institution removed from the mass public. National parliaments must be brought into the Community system so as to reestablish the link between the legitimacy of national representative institutions and the Community.

Citizenship

Concern for the legitimacy of the Union led to the inclusion of a chapter on citizenship in the Treaty. This is an attempt to strengthen the attributes of integration pinpointed by Karl Deutsch: loyalty, "we-feeling," trust, and a sense of community.[12] The Community has pursued state-building strategies in the past with the introduction of the Community flag, anthem, and the EC passport.

Maastricht takes this one step further with the introduction of dual, or parallel, citizenship. Three rights of citizenship are included in the Treaty: the right of residence in any EC country, the right to move freely within the Community, and a limited right of political participation. These provide the basis for a body of rights that can be built on as the level of political cohesion increases. The question of citizenship inevitably raises the issue of exclusion. Immigration, which will be dealt with in the third pillar of the Union on judicial cooperation, is set to become one of the most sensitive political issues in the 1990s.

Common Foreign and Security Policy (CFSP)

The challenge of Eastern Europe and German unification provided the motivation for renewed interest in the system of European Political Cooperation (EPC). The breakup of the Warsaw Pact and removal of the threat it posed to Western Europe profoundly altered the security environment for the continent as a whole and for the Atlantic Alliance. The Gulf War added a compelling if complicating factor to the debate on the international role of the EC.

At the outset, it seemed likely that the IGC would concentrate on improving the workings of EPC and extending its scope somewhat. However, it became clear from the initial papers and discussions that a number of member states intended to make these issues central to the negotiations on political union. The Gulf crisis profoundly changed the parameters of the debate on EPC. The appearance of an "out of area" threat lent urgency to the discussions on foreign and security issues. The Rome European Council in December 1990 established the parameters for the negotiators. It concluded that the Union should "deal with aspects of foreign and security policy, in accordance with a sustained evolutive process and in a unitary manner."[13] The final communiqué dealt with the institutional framework for a common foreign and security policy, its scope in terms of common security and the long-term objective of a role for the Union in defense matters.

The outbreak of the Gulf War coincided with the opening of the political union IGC. Despite the inclusion of EPC in the Single European Act, diversity rather than coherence characterized the member states' response to the outbreak of hostilities in the Gulf. The member states were deeply divided on the use of force and on their willingness to be led by the United States. There were two views about the impact of the Gulf on the political union IGC.

First there was the view expressed by British Prime Minister John Major to the House of Commons: Political union and a common foreign and security policy in Europe would have to go beyond statements and extend to action; however, the negotiators should recognize that Europe is not yet ready for this stage.[14]

On the other hand, advocates of a strong role for the Community in international politics argued that the response to the Gulf crisis highlighted the absence of an adequate machinery for dealing with foreign and security policy. Provisions on the common foreign and security policy form a separate pillar in the Maastricht Treaty. When ratified, this pillar will replace European

Political Cooperation, which began in 1969 and was codified in the Single Act. The Treaty of Maastricht, unlike the SEA, sets out in broad terms what the objectives of the CFSP should be. It then establishes the framework for "systematic cooperation" on foreign policy matters. The system resembles the procedures that characterized EPC. Common positions are arrived at on the basis of consensus. However, when the Union agrees to undertake joint action, there is provision for majority voting. A declaration is added to the Treaty by the European Council specifying areas that could be the subject of joint action.

***

The most contentious issue in the negotiations was the policy scope of the CFSP, especially in relation to security. A distinction was drawn between "soft security" and defense. Even before the opening of the IGC, there was agreement that the distinction, found in the Single Act, between the "economic and political aspects of security" and defense would have to go. There was, however, considerable divergence about "hard security," i.e., defense. Toward the end of the negotiations the debate was crystallized by the submission of two papers, a Franco-German proposal on the one hand, and an Anglo-Italian plan on the other. The Franco-German plan involved the creation of a European army under the umbrella of the Western European Union (WEU). The Anglo-Italian plan was far less ambitious: the WEU would be the main vehicle for creation of a European defense identity, but would be mostly geared to "outside of area" threats. Whereas the Franco-German plan sought to downplay the centrality of NATO, the Anglo-Italian plan sought to provide a framework for a European defense identity without undermining NATO. The Treaty of Maastricht is more like the Anglo-Italian plan than is its more ambitious rival. Nonetheless, the states agreed to look at the issue of a "common defense policy" and a "common defense" in 1996, when a new IGC will be convened. The WEU is acknowledged in the Treaty as the arena for European defense cooperation although it maintains a separate organization.

Prospects

The Treaty of Maastricht represents much more than an "SEA Mark II," although it builds on the resurgence of formal integration that began in the 1980s. The Treaty is by far the most important reform and enlargement of the EC treaties since its inception. If ratified, it would enhance the state-like features of the Union and make it much less a hybrid international organization. Maastricht increases the reach of policy integration to include the core areas of state activity. The firm date established for EMU represents a significant deepening of the goals of European integration. The agreement on a common foreign and security policy is much more than an enhancement of EPC.

***

The institutional balance, political accountability, and the extension of the Community's policy scope are part of the continuing debate in the EC about policy competence, authority, and legitimacy. This debate is dominated by a concern for the effectiveness of the EC on the one hand, and the democratic deficit on the other. Here, the outcome of the Maastricht negotiations was more like an SEA Mark II with piecemeal changes to the Community's institutional system and policy scope. The adoption of the three pillars, different variations for majority voting, the social policy protocol, and the codecision procedure, add to the complexity of the Union's decisionmaking rules and do not augur well for the transparency of the Community's business. Power and responsibility are as diffuse as ever in the Community's political system. A far less orthodox approach will have to be taken if the Community is to meet the challenge of enlargement.

The ultimate fate of the Maastricht Treaty remains in doubt because of domestic political issues in a number of states and the currency crisis of September 1992. The Danish government, with the backing of the main opposition parties in the Folketing, presented a memorandum to the other member states on October 30, 1992, seeking declarations and "opt-out" clauses on citizenship, EMU, defense policy, and Justice and Home Affairs. The Edinburgh European Council of December 11–12, 1992 reached agreement on all of the opt-outs sought by Denmark. The agreement has been accepted by the three main opposition parties in the Danish Folketing, which increased the likelihood of a yes vote in the second referendum. This solution to the Danish problem adds to the use of opt-outs and hence variable geometry in the Community. It further underlines the divergence among EC member states about the future direction of integration. The British government also faces formidable problems because of the emergence of a sizeable number of Tory MPs who are opposed to ratification. Once again, "Europe" has become a divisive issue in British politics.

On the other hand, President Mitterrand and Chancellor Kohl appear determined to protect the Community and to press ahead with ratification of the Treaty. The Franco-German motor continues at the heart of the Community. However, both leaders face domestic unpopularity and appear to be nearing the end of their political careers. Their capacity for leadership may be on the wane. Even if Maastricht is ratified, the context within which it will be implemented has changed considerably. First, political leaders in Western Europe can no longer take their electorates for granted. They cannot assume that a "permissive consensus" on integration exists. Second, as integration impinges more and more on sensitive and core issues of national sovereignty and political accountability, the political debate on integration is likely to become more sharply focused. European integration cannot proceed in the 1990s by stealth. The political dimension of integration occupies center stage in this phase of the Community's development. Third, agreements reached in the Community's policy process must be visible and intelligible to the mass public. Fourth, the weakness of political authority in the Community has been highlighted by the manner in which the Community responded to the crises of 1992. Fifth, the currency crisis will at least affect the timing and transition toward an EMU and may have put the policy goal once more beyond the political and economic capacity of the Community.

Notes

1. H. Wallace, "Making Multilateral Negotiations Work," in W. Wallace, *The Dynamics of European Integration.* (London: Pinter, 1990), pp. 213–228.

2. European Community, *Foreign Ministers Report on Political Union,* submitted to the Dublin European Council, June 25–26, 1990.

3. European Council, *Communique* (Luxembourg, June 1991).

4. P. Ludlow, "The Treaty of Maastricht and the Future of Europe," CEPS Working Document no. 68 (May 1992).

5. B. Laffan, "The Governance of the Union," in P. Keatinge, ed., *Political Union* (Dublin: IEA, 1991).

6. Claus Dieter Ehrlermann, "The Institutional Development of the EC under the Single European Act," *Aussenpolitik* 41 (1990), p.138.

7. L. N. Lindberg and S. A. Scheingold, *Europe's Would-be Polity* (Englewood Cliffs: Prentice Hall, 1970), pp. 45–63.

8. L. Tsoukalis, *The New European Economy* (London: Oxford University Press, 1991), p. 295.

9. For an analysis of the cooperation procedure in action, see R. Corbett, "Testing the New Procedures: The European Parliament's First Experiences with its New 'Single Act' Powers," *Journal of Common Market Studies* 27 (1989), pp. 359–371; and J. Fitzmaurice, "An Analysis of the European Community's Co-operation Procedure," *Journal of Common Market Studies* 26 (1988), pp. 389–397.

10. V. Bogdanor, "The June 1989 European Elections and the Institutions of the Community," *Government and Opposition* 24 (1989), pp. 199–214.

11. E. Lakeman, "The European Elections, 1989," *Parliamentary Affairs* 43 (1989), pp. 77–89.

12. K. W. Deutsch, *Political Community in the North Atlantic Area* (Princeton: Princeton University Press, 1957), p. 36.

13. European Community, *Communique* (Rome European Council, December 14–15, 1990).

14. Quoted in the *Financial Times,* January 28, 1991, p. 30.

4

European Integration
and Referendums:
Analytical Considerations
and Empirical Evidence

Wolfgang Luthardt

Introduction

The Problem

This chapter deals with a fascinating aspect of the European integration process: the use of referendums to achieve political legitimation of an enlargement and deepening of the European Community (EC).[1] Especially during 1992, this "magic formula,"[2] which has accompanied the process of European integration since the beginning of the 1960s, has created considerable tension and polarization across Europe and has attracted world-wide attention. The concrete cause of such political turbulence and insecurity within the EC is, first, the deepening of the European integration process that was agreed upon by the heads of government of the EC member countries in the Maastricht Treaty of December 1991 and, second, the speed and nature of the deepening process envisioned in the Treaty. The Treaty, signed on February 7, 1992, provides for the implementation by the end of the 1990s of a political union (EPU) and a European Economic and Monetary Union (EMU). As these obviously touch on crucial issues of national importance, the issue of their acceptance and legitimacy has produced increasing doubts, resentments, and even outright rejection. Is the Maastricht Treaty a challenge to national provincialism or simply a faulty concept?

Organization of the Chapter

The following two problem areas constitute the focus of this chapter. The first part deals with referendums during the 1970s that were intended as political legitimation devices for entry into the European Community (Denmark, Norway, and Ireland), the enlargement of the EC (France), and continued membership in the EC (United Kingdom).[3] The enlargement of the EC continued in the 1980s, when Greece, Spain, and Portugal became members of the EC without holding referendums. The second part examines two treaties that have become cornerstones of an integration process on which referendums have been held: The Single European Act (SEA) and the Maastricht Treaty. To a much greater extent than during the debate over ratification of the SEA, the debate over the ratification of the Maastricht Treaty has been exposed to the threat of, and demands for, referendums. Both treaties deal with the deepening, the speed, and the direction of the EC integration process.

The latest referendums on the ratification of the Maastricht Treaty will be placed in a political and institutional continuum of referendums that accompanied and codetermined the decisionmaking process of European integration. This formal categorization of the latest referendums on Maastricht sheds analytic and empirical light on the complexity and far-reaching implications of the integration process. Thus, this perspective provides an opportunity for interpreting the latest turbulences and insecurities from a comparative angle.[4]

Institutional and Political Choices for the Transfer of Political Decisionmaking Competences

With the exception of the United Kingdom, the member states of the European Community are states with codified constitutions. These constitutions contain differently formulated guidelines concerning the institutional possibilities for the political and institutional transfer of powers. In general, choices can be understood as "choice of rules for a community or group."[5] Legally formulated choices standardize more specifically political options that serve as decision-relevant and legitimate bases for the polity and policy decisions of political actors. Therefore, one can formulate the hypothesis that institutional political patterns codetermine policy outcomes to some extent.[6] Existing decisionmaking rules are the hierarchy and majority principle as well as the unanimity rule which can be identified in the various institutional sets.[7] The process of transfer of decisionmaking powers from national political institutions and actors can take place in two ways. First, the transfer can take place by way of an adjustment through the democratically legitimized institutions of a representative democracy (governments and parliaments). A typical example of this kind of transfer may be found in the EC policy of Germany, Italy, France, Great Britain, Spain, and the Benelux countries. In fact, Italy even precludes the possibility of explicit referendums on laws that deal with international treaties (Article 75 of the Italian Constitution). Germany has the following rule in Article 24 of its constitution (Basic Law): "The Federation may by legislation transfer sovereign powers to intergovernmental institutions." The transfer of decisionmaking powers has so far been based on this institutional principle.

The second method of transfer consists of holding a referendum on the question. Institutionally, one has to differentiate between a prescribed and binding referendum and a consultative referendum. There are three ways in which this can take place: first, there can be a constitutional requirement that a referendum be held (Switzerland is an example of such a strict variant, Article 89, 5, Swiss Constitution); second, the national governments may consider it a good idea to incorporate the population into the decisionmaking process in order to achieve greater political legitimacy; third, considerable intraparty and/or domestic controversy may exist so that the referendum serves the purpose of solution or conciliation.

Especially the latter two political options—pursued based on the strategic calculations of governmental actors—show that holding a referendum is often a product and consequence of group activities, patterns of demands, or systemic resources.[8] Governmental actors who opt for the referendum desire to steer the decisionmaking process with the help of "coordinated policy actions through networks of separate but interdependent organizations."[9] Their aim is to attain a prohegemonical political result that legitimizes the government's policies.[10] These governmental actors appear as "political entrepreneurs"[11] in political markets. Examples for such a strategy are the referendums in Norway (1972), Denmark (1972, 1992), Great Britain (1975), and France (1992). However, the results of several referendums have shown that this political goal is not always realized.

The institution of the parliament can be included in the second approach in three ways: before the enactment, during the decision process, as well as during the final legitimation of the result. Both strategies have been pursued. Denmark even devised a combination: if the accession or the delegation of competencies to a supranational institution is not ratified by a five-sixths majority of the parliament and the government still seeks to pass the treaty legislation, a referendum becomes necessary according to the Danish Constitution (Article 20).

Referendums and Enlargement of the European Community

The Post–de Gaulle Phase: Overcoming Stagnation

In the 1970s a number of referendums were held that were either about membership in, or enlargement of, the European Community. Another referendum was held on continued membership in the EC. A new political drive of requests for membership became possible only when French President Charles de Gaulle resigned from office in 1969 after losing a plebiscite he favored.

The referendums in Denmark, Norway, and the Republic of Ireland were about membership in the EC, while France held a plebiscite on the legitimacy and acceptance of this enlargement. In Ireland the vote on EC membership took place on May 10, 1972.[12] The turnout of 70.9 percent was the highest turnout for any referendum in the history of referendums in the Irish Republic; it was not surpassed in the 1980s. The government, the two big parties, the influential farmers' organizations, the employers' and employees' association, as well as the four relevant daily newspapers were all in favor of EC membership. The presumed advantages associated with the EC by far outweighed the disadvantages; 83.1 percent of the voters were for membership in the EC, only 16.9 percent were against.

In Denmark, the referendum held on October 2, 1972, was also of great interest to the population: the turnout was 90.1 percent. Sixty-three percent of the voters were in favor of entry into the European Community.[13] Since the farmers foresaw advantages from Danish EC membership, the Farmers' party participated in the pro-EC campaign of the Social Democratic and the Conservative parties. In spite of the endorsement of EC membership in Denmark, the referendum led to increased exposure of the anti-EC groups. The national election of 1973, usually characterized as a watershed election, changed the party system and the political landscape in Denmark.

In Norway, on the other hand, the population rejected membership in the EC in a referendum on September 24–25, 1972.[14] The turnout was 77.6 percent and the proponents of Norway's membership in the EC obtained only 46.5 percent of the votes. This meant that membership did not come about. It was a distinctive feature of the vote in Norway that the controversy over EC membership mirrored the character of conflict between center and periphery. The proportion of voters rejecting EC membership increased with distance from the capital, Oslo. In particular, the farmers and the farmers' associations, as well as the fishermen and the fishing industry, saw their economic survival threatened by Norway's possible membership in the EC. As in Denmark, the results of the referendum had considerable impact on the party system. The Liberal party broke up as a consequence of the referendum, and the Workers' party had to deal with a significant loss of support when part of its left wing split from the party after the referendum.

The negative result in the 1972 Norwegian referendum was prefigured in the 1962 attempt to hold a referendum on EC membership. The political leaders of the then-named Norwegian Workers' party did not want to be accused of manipulation as they had been in 1949 when Norway joined NATO by governmental decision. However, Charles de Gaulle's veto of expanding the EC by including the EFTA countries (Ireland, United Kingdom, Denmark, and Norway) precluded this possibility for the Norwegian Workers' party. The referendum was then postponed for ten years. In Denmark the referendum was also put off; however, it was decided that the Danish referendum should be held after the Norwegian vote. The Danish referendum was held on October 2, 1972, the one in Norway on September 24–25, 1972.

In France, the population decided on the enlargement of the EC in a plebiscite on April 23, 1972.[15] The issue was the acceptance of Denmark, Norway, the United Kingdom, and the Republic of Ireland as members of the EC. The turnout was only 60.7 percent; 67.7 percent were in favor of expanding the Community. William Safran has written that this plebiscite, the only one held during the presidency of Georges Pompidou, was not proposed by the cabinet, as Article 11 of the French Constitution prescribes, but was instead initiated by Pompidou himself.[16] Thus, this plebiscite can also be considered part of the French tradition, that is, the president sought to display his independence from the cabinet because the French Constitution does not contain provisions that necessarily prescribe a course of action (Article 11). In fact, Pompidou supposedly sought to strengthen his position vis-à-vis the prime minister, Jacques Chaban-Delmas, to expand the national consensus on important issues, and to affirm France's position for the meeting of the EC heads of state in the fall of 1972.

After two different attempts by the United Kingdom in the 1960s to become a member of the then–European Economic Community were frustrated by France's (de Gaulle's) veto, it finally became a member of the EEC in 1973. Domestic controversies that lasted for several years finally led to a consultative—and in fact binding—referendum on the continuation of Britain's membership in the EEC.[17] During the campaign prior to the referendum, clear controversies and tendencies toward polarization could be detected. One initiating factor for the referendum was a deep divide within the governing Labour party. Harold Wilson, the prime minister and party chairman, was in favor of continued membership in the EEC, while Tony Benn, the speaker of the left wing within the Labour party, supported withdrawal from the Community. The outcome of the referendum was positive, even though the turnout of 64.5 percent and the approval of 67.2 percent were not overwhelming. This is partly due to the traditional British restraint vis-à-vis the EEC and later the EC. The relatively low acceptance of the EC in Great Britain is even more apparent when one looks at elections to the European Parliament: the turnout was 32.8 percent in 1979, 33 percent in 1984, and 36.2 percent in 1989.

The Second Phase of EC Enlargement— The Accession of Spain, Portugal, and Greece

The examples outlined so far could lead one to suspect that there exists some kind of referendum-automatism in those countries that seek to join the European Community. The accession of Spain, Portugal, and Greece in the 1980s, however, points in a different direction. Of these countries, Greece joined the EC first (on January 1, 1981), becoming the tenth member state. The negotiations began on July 27, 1976, and the accession treaty was signed on May 28, 1979. Acceptance into the EC as well as the election of Constantine Karamanlis to the presidency marked the "real" conclusion of the transition period after the end of the military regime in 1974. Both events opened the phase of consolidation of Greek democracy. The negotiations with Portugal and Spain began in October 1978 and February 1979, respectively. The two countries became the eleventh and twelfth members on January 1, 1986. There were no significant anti-EC tendencies in Portugal or in Spain, and referendums on EC membership were not deemed necessary. In both countries, the social democratic parties, the PSP in Portugal and the PSOE in Spain, staunchly supported membership in the EC. The belief that acceptance into the European Community would bolster liberal political institutions domestically played a significant role in that strategy.

In Greece, on the other hand, the politics of the PASOK, the populist socialist party, turned out to be quite ambivalent. From 1977 onward the party advocated a policy of special treatment for Greece within the EC. Furthermore, the party tried to turn the EC issue into a subject for a referendum. However, according to the Greek Constitution of 1975, only the president can initiate such a referendum (Article 44, Paragraph 2). Karamanlis, who was president until 1985, was a clear supporter of continued Greek membership in the EC. Extraordinary conditions were granted by the EC in 1982 and 1983: financial help, as well as Greece's option to block imports from eight EC member states, led to a moderation of the PASOK's policy stance. The PASOK's official rhetorical criticism barely obscured the obvious profitability of Greece's membership in the EC.[18] The incorporation of Greece, Spain, and Portugal into the European Community promoted an important domestic push in two ways: on the one hand, developing liberal democratic institutions were bolstered; on the other, joining the EC meant that the "underdeveloped intermediary organizations [were] pushed forward and led toward a tradition of interest group associations that were focused on particular and collective interests."[19]

The Deepening of the European Community: The Single European Act

SEA: Engine of a New Dynamic?

Renewed political controversies emerged within the arena of the European integration process with the ratification of the SEA.[20] Referendums became necessary prior to the ratification of the SEA in Denmark and in Ireland. The acceptance of the SEA by the twelve member states of the EC put an end to the ten-year "dark period"[21] that lasted from the mid-1970s until the mid-1980s, and set in motion a new political and institutional dynamic in the European integration process. Thus, a period of decision-blockage,[22] which more than once demonstrated the incapacity of the EC's central institutions to act, came to an end. The stagnation was occasionally used in the scholarly literature to interpret the incapacity of the EC institutions as an expression of institutional sclerosis and was thus polemically called "Eurosclerosis."[23]

The SEA envisions, among other things, a gradual shift from the decisionmaking pattern of unanimity (Luxembourg Compromise of 1966) to majority decisions on some policy issues. It also strengthens the consultative role of the European Parliament, whose role can be described as an "'institutional co-player' with limited but real powers and functions."[24] In reality the SEA continued with the traditional EC policy which can be described by the framework of the Rome Treaties, including the package deals,[25] which have a long political tradition within the EC/EEC. Helen Wallace argues that the SEA "marked a recognition of institutional behavior that was already being established as typical."[26] However, the partial move toward majority decisions should not be underestimated. Instead, it should be considered an important streamlining of the process.

Decision-Normality in the Republic of Ireland

The Irish Supreme Court ruled (after a citizen complained that the Irish government's act of ratifying the SEA was incompatible with the Irish Constitution) that a referendum was necessary for the acceptance of the SEA.[27] Consequently, full implementation of the SEA had to be delayed since treaties between member states can only go into effect, according to the Rome Treaties, once all states have ratified them. As a result, the Irish government held a referendum in May 1987. The turnout was low (44.1 percent), but 69.9 percent voted for ratification of the SEA. The positive result was supported by all political parties in the Irish Parliament. Only then could the SEA belatedly go into effect (July 1, 1987).

Political Resistance in Denmark

While the four-party minority government of Danish Prime Minister Poul Schlüter had accepted the SEA, the parliament rejected it. The debate dealt mainly with the general advantages and disadvantages of Denmark's membership in the EC and with the question of whether the SEA was the first step toward a European Union, a concept opposed by a majority of Danes. Moreover, environmental protection played an important role during the debate in the Danish Parliament. From a legal point of view, the European Economic Area (EEA) proposal embodied in the SEA Treaty, was the focus of the debate. In an additional provision of the SEA, the Danish government insisted on the rule that existing Danish laws for the protection of the workplace and the natural environment could not be weakened by EC "harmonization policies."

As mentioned above, the Danish Constitution prescribes a referendum on the transfer of legal authority to international organizations if there is not a five-sixths majority in parliament in favor of such a transfer. Since this was not the case and since the government continued to insist on the ratification of the Treaty, Prime Minister Schlüter set the date for a consultative, but in fact binding, referendum, which took place on February 26, 1986. With a turnout of 74.8 percent, 56.2 percent voted for and 43.8 percent voted against the SEA. Behind the relatively clear yes for the SEA, several relevant aspects emerged that recently affected the June 3, 1992, referendum on the Maastricht Treaty.

There is a relatively strong anti-EC tendency in Denmark, evident in the ratification and the final rejection decision in parliament. Ole Borre notes that public opinion polls during the thirteen years of Denmark's EC membership (1972–1985) regularly displayed a high level of opposition to membership.[28] This opposition shows up among the far left, but also within the social democratic camp, especially among unskilled workers. A comparison of the two EC referendums (1972 and 1986) reveals that there has been a clear increase in anti-EC sentiments. In 1972 there was a turnout of 89.9 percent; 63.4 percent voted for Danish EC membership. In contrast, the turnout for the 1986 referendum sank to 74.8 percent; only 56.6 percent were in favor of the SEA. In both referendums the People's Movement Against the EC, founded in 1965, had a good deal of influence on the outcome.

The anti-EC tendency evident in the referendum on the SEA was also expressed in the low turnout in elections to the European Parliament (1979, 1984, 1989). When one compares the rival groups, it is clear that the Social Democrats, who were moderately in favor of the EC, did relatively badly in comparison with the People's Movement Against the EC (a collection of parties and individuals that also included the Greens in 1989). In 1979 the Social Democrats registered only a slightly better result than the People's Movement, with 21.9 percent against 20.9 percent. In 1984, the Social Democratic party was behind the People's Movement (19.5 percent vs. 20.8 percent), while in 1989 the Social Democrats did better than the People's Movement; the results were 23.3 percent and 18.9 percent, respectively. In both cases (1972 and 1986) anti-EC forces used the referendum as a political weapon. The different political nature of the two referendums in Ireland and Denmark manifests itself clearly. In Ireland, formal constitutional reasons made the referendum necessary, and not, as in Denmark, reasons that were based on principles critical of the SEA.

Opposition to the SEA and the EC continued in Denmark even after ratification of the SEA. The early elections of September 8, 1987, led to the representation of a left-wing populist party (Alliance party) in the Folketing (parliament). This small party has only four seats in the legislature, but it is also a fierce opponent of the EC. For example, it introduced a bill in December 1987 for a referendum on Denmark's withdrawal from the EC. What was remarkable in the first debate on the bill was not only that the governing parties (Social Democrats and Radical Liberals) were against it, but that the

Socialist People's party was also against Denmark's leaving the EC, even though it had traditionally been in favor of withdrawal. The central argument made was that after two unsuccessful referendums, one could only fight against the development of a European Union under existing political conditions.

The Referendum in Italy: A Late Interlude?

A referendum held in Italy in 1989 at the same time as European Parliament elections can be interpreted as more than a reaction to the ongoing controversial debates prior to the ratification of the SEA. The subject of the referendum was whether the EC "should be transformed into an effective Union." The referendum had been initiated by senators and members of the European Federalist Movement in the hope of strengthening the authority of Italian ministers and members of the European Parliament and to give the process of European integration a further push.[29] The draft Treaty on European Union, initiated by Altiero Spinelli in 1979, accepted by the European Parliament in 1984, and passed on to the member states, constituted the basis of the referendum. The draft Treaty included, among other things, decisive steps in the direction of a political-federal union as well as an explicit strengthening of the legislative functions of the European Parliament. The European Union project received massive support from the national parliaments in Belgium, Spain, Germany, and Italy. In Italy the project was approved in the above-mentioned referendum with a large majority. However, the treaty was not accepted by the governments of the EC states. Instead, the SEA, which was less demanding with respect to a political union, was developed further and put into effect on July 1, 1987.[30]

The Referendums on the Maastricht Treaty: Weakening of the Concept or Signal for a Differentiated Design?

Continuity and Challenge

The Maastricht Treaty, signed on February 27, 1992, seemed destined to be the second institutional cornerstone of the deepening process of European integration—at least until the Danish no in the June 3, 1992, referendum.[31] From an internal EC perspective, the Maastricht Treaty delineates the institutional contours of a political union and a European Economic and Monetary Union. The Treaty is to be understood as a continuation of the SEA, a political and institutional reaction, and a strategically directed act with regard to two momentous political events. The president of the European Commission, Jacques Delors, formulated this as follows: "The European development was rejuvenated in 1985 by the Single European Act, without which Maastricht would never have been possible. Then, in 1989, historic events took place: the end of communism and the fall of the Wall."[32] The complete collapse of the Communist regime in Europe and the dissolution of the former Soviet regime have led to the unification of the two German states, formally realized on October 3, 1990.[33] In a number of ways both political events touch upon the EC integration process.

The Referendum in Denmark: Starting Signal for a Rejection?

The first widely visible signal of politically and publicly effective reservation, antipathy, and resistance to the Maastricht Treaty was sent by the referendum that had become necessary in Denmark. The results of the referendum had a shock effect. The Maastricht Treaty was rejected by a small majority of Danes with a vote of 50.7 percent to 49.3 percent; the turnout was 82.3 percent. It was feared, as in earlier referendums, that the proposed political union would structurally undermine the sovereignty of the Danish state and that Danish political institutions would be turned into mere servants of EC institutions. Even before the referendum neither the proponents nor the adversaries of the Treaty could be classified in a simple political schema. In Parliament, the leftist Socialist People's party, the centrist Christian People's party, and the right-wing populist Progress party voted against the Maastricht Treaty.

The Danish results immediately led to considerable speculation about further processes and the medium-term future of the Maastricht Treaty. Amid the hubbub, there were arrogant remarks about the extremely small margin of defeat, implicitly belittling "little" Denmark's effort to stop or at least slow down the train toward European integration. In Switzerland, the Danish result, the French referendum, and the debate in Great Britain were interpreted as massive protests by the people, not so much against the Maastricht Treaty but against the idea of a supranational Europe. The people were thought to have taught the European utopians, in particular Jacques Delors, a painful lesson.

Continuity of Normality in Ireland's Special Circumstances

The referendum that became necessary in Ireland for political reasons was initiated relatively soon after the Maastricht summit. Even though Irish opinion polls occasionally showed a slippage in approval for the ratification of the Maastricht Treaty, the Irish foreign minister insisted that the people should vote for the Treaty. Since becoming an EC member in 1973 (out of economic interests for the most part), the Republic of Ireland (with Spain, Portugal, and Greece) had been among the four poorest countries that had profited most from membership in the EC. The Delors II package established additional financial advantages for the poorest countries, paid for by Great Britain, France, the Benelux countries, and Germany as net contributors. Economic considerations again clearly dominated the referendum of June 18,

1992. The turnout and the results were above average compared to earlier results and contrary to many predictions. The turnout was 57.3 percent, and 68.7 percent voted yes. Not a single electoral district voted against the European integration process. In rural areas, which had clearly voted against partially legalizing abortion, approval of the Treaty was most clear cut. All political parties, except a small leftist party, were in favor of the Treaty. In addition, the unions, the employers' association, the national organization of women's groups, and leading newspapers were in favor. In this sense the Irish referendum represented a continued confirmation of membership in the EC. The fact that there was a clear majority in favor of the Maastricht Treaty in rural areas, as compared to the abortion referendum in which rural voters were mostly opposed, points to another highly troubling issue that has been hotly debated in Ireland: abortion. The almost complete outlawing of abortion was legitimized in the 1983 referendum and consequently included in the Irish Constitution. In 1992, the abortion issue again made waves in Ireland and within the EC. The Irish Supreme Court ruled in a unanimous decision that a fourteen-year-old girl be allowed to travel to London to have an abortion. There were two interesting issues in this case. First, Article 8 of the Irish Constitution, which permits an abortion only if the life of the mother is in danger, has thus become controversial again. Second, in this case there was a serious restriction of freedom of travel within the European Community (one of the four central freedoms of the SEA) by the Irish attorney general, Harry Whelehan, a strong opponent of abortion. The attorney general had threatened prosecution of the parents when and if they returned to Ireland with the girl. The Supreme Court dealt with this single case, but it did not elaborate on the issue.

The crucial feature of the referendum on ratification of the Maastricht Treaty is the broader political context. At the Maastricht summit on December 9 and 10, 1991, a special provision was included in the Treaty, on the insistence of the Irish government, that would allow Ireland to keep women from traveling to other countries in order to have abortions. It was feared then that the Treaty, which was to be the subject of a referendum in June 1992, would be rejected if the abortion issue was made part of the ratification process.

The Referendum in France: The President as Master of Ceremonies?

In France the Maastricht debate opened immediately after the Danish no vote on June 3, 1992. That evening, President François Mitterrand announced a French referendum on the Maastricht Treaty to be held in September 1992. In the public arena, this announcement was interpreted to mean that the French referendum would be a critical moment in the further process of ratification of the Maastricht Treaty; it would thus help determine the future of the European Community. The German press, for example, carried headlines such as "Fate of the EC to be Decided in France," or "Europe's Destiny on a Knife Edge."

At the same time, Mitterrand's announcement was seen to have domestic political motives. First, it was thought that it was intended to split political opposition to the Socialist party with the help of the Maastricht Treaty and thus weaken the opposition before the next election. Second, the decreasing popularity and weakness of the Socialists and Mitterrand would be camouflaged. The Danish vote supposedly fit well into Mitterrand's strategy at the time of the announcement. Constitutional issues did not play a decisive role in the initiation of the referendum. Thus, one can presume that the referendum stands in the tradition of the previous plebiscites used by French presidents in order to get involved effectively in domestic politics. A television debate with Philippe Seguin, the vocal Gaullist spokesman of the anti-Maastricht opposition, which also included the Spanish prime minister and the German chancellor arguing for the Maastricht Treaty, fit very well into this scenario.

The narrow result of the September 20, 1992, referendum (51.05 percent in favor of the Treaty) shows finally that while Mitterrand did not outmaneuver himself politically, he did not achieve his desired confirmation. Given the vigor of the campaign, the turnout was only a disappointing 69.68 percent. From an electoral sociology perspective, voters with higher levels of education and urban voters of higher socioeconomic status voted yes, while workers, farmers, and small-business people voted no. However, the conclusion that France is split and that the middle classes voted for and the lower classes and the farmers against Maastricht, is premature, if not wrong. A differentiated analysis of the referendum results shows a more nuanced picture. "Conservative" Paris was in favor, while "leftist" Marseille was against Maastricht. Most of the farmers in Brittany, who will have to make considerable financial sacrifices, voted for the Treaty, while the rich landowners of the Beauce around Chartres voted against it. In Lorraine, which suffers from high unemployment, a majority opted for the Treaty. These selected data show a much more differentiated picture of the referendum results than the phrase "divided France" would suggest. What was also especially noticeable is that most leading French industrialists, except for Jacques Calvet (CEO of Peugeot) and Pierre Suard (head of the railroad and communications equipment manufacturer Alcatel Alsthom), were explicitly in favor of Maastricht and the continuation of the European integration process.

Referendum Tactics in Great Britain

Debate over a referendum in Great Britain began even before the Maastricht summit of December 1991 and played a role in the subsequent British election campaign. When the Treaty was signed the exact date of the election was not officially known, only that a general election had to be held before July 1992. Prime Minister John Major, a moderate EC proponent, was exposed to heated opposition from a skeptical wing of his own party and its spokeswoman, Margaret Thatcher. She categorically demanded several times that any treaty signed by the prime minister, or any later provisions, be put to a referendum before being ratified by the British Parliament. To these demands Prime Minister Major replied several times: "My view remains that we are a parliamentary democracy, and I see no need for a referendum."

The vote in the British House of Commons following the Maastricht summit resulted in 339 votes for the bill submitted by the government, while 253 voted against it. Norman Tebbit emerged as the new spokesman of a considerably reduced group of EC opponents within the Conservative party. Tebbit announced that he would continue the campaign for a referendum on the EC. Prime Minister Major again rejected such ideas. Thus, not only was the repeated call for a consultative referendum rejected but the British tradition of parliamentary sovereignty was emphasized as well. The demands were renewed after the Danish no to ratification of the Maastricht Treaty. Margaret Thatcher, in particular, continued to call repeatedly for a referendum: Prime Minister Major continued to say that a referendum was not necessary. Instead, he suggested a different strategy: the British government would make its approval of the Maastricht Treaty contingent upon whether Denmark—possibly in a second referendum—reconsidered its position, or whether the EC was willing to make differentiated concessions to Denmark.

Opposition and discomfort also grew somewhat stronger within the Labour party after the Danish no vote. However, at the party conference in Blackpool on September 28–29, 1992, a referendum on Maastricht was rejected. The British government had been able to have an additional provision included in the Treaty to guarantee that the social policy regulations would not apply to Great Britain for the time being. If a majority of voters approved of the Treaty in a referendum, this could be interpreted as an approval of this additional provision. However, the Labour party was strongly against this clause and in favor of the acceptance of social policy regulations in Great Britain as well.

The Beginnings of Referendum Debate in the Federal Republic of Germany

The debates over the different forms of ratification of the Maastricht Treaty, with above all substantive criticism of the European Monetary System with a common currency and a common central bank, also extend to the Federal Republic of Germany. As a result of the Danish referendum, there are more voices now that support the idea of a referendum on the Treaty. In the first comments on the Danish result, as well as the French referendum, politicians from the largest opposition party, the Social Democratic party, made this demand. The Greens have also supported the demand for a referendum. Shortly before the referendum in France on September 20, 1992, the German

EC commissioner, Martin Bangemann (Free Democratic party), dismissed his chief of staff, Manfred Brunner. Many in Germany saw a direct connection between Brunner's dismissal and his call for a referendum. The Bavarian minister of the environment, Peter Gauweiler (Christian Social Union), had also demanded that there be a referendum on the Maastricht Treaty, but his proposal met sharp criticism in his own party as well as in the Christian Democratic Union. The polling organization Forschungsgruppe Wahlen (Mannheim) found in September that 77 percent of Germans thought that a referendum on the Maastricht Treaty would be a good idea.

Conclusions: European Integration, Political Legitimation, and Referendums

The conclusions of this chapter can be summarized as follows:

1. Referendums grow out of concrete historical contexts. In their form and structure, they are political instruments that typically deal with single issues and are oriented toward matters of national interest.[34] A referendum on the stepwise delegation of national competencies implies a dual structure; this differs from the functional properties of other referendums. The institution of the referendum is part of the national political context, but at the same time it legitimizes restrictions on the competencies of institutions that codetermine this national political context and give it its characteristic political and institutional form.[35] This transnational political function qualifies the hypothesis that these referendums can be interpreted as particularly relevant for decisionmaking processes.

2. The referendums on the EC that have been described here confirm the hypothesis that certain decisions are treated according to the criterion of importance of the issue or the issue area. Such referendums signal that there has been and still is considerable political and economic opposition in these countries. In particular, the high predisposition of this issue toward conflict leads to the political mobilization and polarization of the population. This is confirmed by the referendums in Norway and Denmark in 1972, the 1975 referendum in Great Britain, and the one in Denmark on the SEA in 1986, as well as the recent referendums on Maastricht in Denmark and France.

3. Typically, the governmental actors (government and parliament) are those who take the initiative with regard to membership in, and deepening of, the EC. Such a procedure on the one hand demonstrates the dominance of these actors with regard to political initiatives. On the other hand, this initiative is coupled and connected with certain institutional barriers, as the case of Denmark shows. In other countries, it is explicitly regulated institutionally that only governmental actors can initiate, legitimate, and finally approve the transfer of decisionmaking competencies (Italy, Germany, the Netherlands, Belgium, Luxembourg, Great Britain). In Ireland and Greece the president can initiate such a

referendum if it concerns the "national interest"; this is the political rule in Ireland. In France, the president has the option to initiate a referendum in cooperation with the National Assembly and the Senate. Thus, institutional rules encourage, limit, and restrict the political activities of governmental actors.

4. However, these different institutional rules do not imply exact statements about policy outcomes. The governmental actors in favor of the process of integration often feel a need to justify their decisions. This becomes particularly evident in countries that are highly structured by political parties and interest groups that highlight different sets of considerations. Partly, the actors appear to be rational, pursuing their political, economic, and financial benefits according to their individual or collective cost-benefit calculus. Partly, connections and domestic political tactics and strategic political options determine the decisionmaking process. Partly, highly emotional and irrational considerations circulate in the political arenas. The referendum exposes these different dimensions, which together determine the decisionmaking process. The decision itself is then made according to the majority principle. The legitimation and acceptance of the referendum result appears to be greatest when there has been enough of a campaign to explain and discuss the issues under consideration. This process takes the form of a publicly mediated bargaining process. This mediation process between different political elites and public officials on the one hand, and the population on the other hand, is a sine qua non, in particular on a subject as far-reaching as European integration. The debate and the referendums on Maastricht so far have shown that there is still a noteworthy lack of such processes.

5. The decisions made by means of the referendums described demonstrate different lines of conflict between political actors. While the governmental actors usually initiate the entrance into, and the deepening of, the EC, this process often meets significant discomfort, opposition, and rejection in different EC countries. The longest and most explicit opposition against relevant patterns of European integration exists in Denmark. There, the EC integration process has for years been the most pressing foreign policy issue. Like the other Scandinavian countries, Denmark has a very homogenous political culture and a distinct national identity. Obviously, Denmark is not prepared—such is the argument—to sacrifice either one for European integration. The lines of conflict that are connected with the issue of European integration run through all political parties and interest groups. Similar phenomena are discernible in Great Britain and France, as the latest referendum has shown. It is also feared in these countries, albeit for different historical reasons, that national sovereignty would incur losses that would be too great and could not be legitimized. In addition, there are the real financial and economic considerations of the different interest groups. The Federal Republic of Germany, on the other hand, appears to be the country where the opposition against the EC and the process of integration is lowest, for historical as well as current political reasons stemming from unification. Even there, only a small portion of the population is currently willing to

gamble away its own currency for a common European currency.

6. The European process of integration will continue. Nevertheless, on one side it can be observed that in most EC member states an "instrumental idea of Europe" circulates.[36] This idea is used to justify a general approval or rejection of the EC, depending on the tactically assessed domestic political situation and depending on the strategically hoped-for political and economic advantages. On the other side, bargaining processes between EC member states and EC institutions on specific issues will become even more relevant in the future. Different option-out clauses (for Great Britain) or time-limited opt-out clauses (related to the recent Edinburgh summit in December 1992 in the case of Denmark) will arise more often as a result of the shifting policy of deepening and widening the EC.

7. The process of European integration, its schedule (i.e., its deepening), its speed, and its possible enlargement will be more complicated than previously. Past enlargements have "created new problems and challenged institutional development. Future enlargements will certainly carry on that tradition."[37] One thing is clear: How else could so many and such different nation-states arrive at a somewhat workable modus vivendi? The Danish no has again, and with more publicity, put this political reality at the top of the agenda of the European political arena. The recent political developments show again an ambiguous relationship: On one side the various, historically grown political and institutional forms, structures, and specific patterns of decisionmaking in Western European nation-states will continue to exist in there own right.[38] They are confronted on the other side with the gradual establishment and partial acceptance of the European Community as a supranational institution and its institutions as independent, but interrelated, corporate policy actors.[39] A detailed—and serious—debate on the forms, structures, and (especially) their related intermediate goals is necessary.

Notes

1. I would like to thank Glenda G. Rosenthal, Columbia University, and Christopher Anderson, Washington University, St. Louis, for helpful comments.

2. Beate Kohler-Koch, "Optionen deutscher Politik in einer veränderten internationalen Umwelt," in *Staat und Demokratie in Europa,* ed. Beate Kohler-Koch (Opladen: Leske and Budrich, 1992), p. 59.

3. Anthony King, "Referendums and the European Community," in *The Referendum Device,* ed. Austin Ranney (Washington and London: AEI Press, 1981), pp. 113–122; Wolfgang Luthardt, "Direkte Demokratie und Europäische Integration," *Schweizerisches Jahrbuch für Politische Wissenschaft,* 32 (1992), pp. 185–204.

4. Giovanni Sartori, "Comparing and Miscomparing," *Journal of Theoretical Politics* no. 3 (1991), pp. 243–257; Russell J. Dalton, "Comparative Politics of the Industrial Democracies: From the Golden Age to Island Hopping," in *Political Science: Looking to the Future,* vol. 2, *Comparative Politics, Policy, and International Relations,* ed. William Crotty (Evanston: Northwestern University Press, 1991), pp. 15–43; Stanley

Lieberson, "Small N's and Big Conclusions: An Examination of the Reasoning in Comparative Studies Based on a Small Number of Cases," *Social Forces* 69, no. 4, (December 1991), pp. 307–320.

5. Viktor Vanberg and James M. Buchanan, "Interests and Theories in Constitutional Choice," *Journal of Theoretical Politics* no. 1 (1989), p. 51.

6. Fritz W. Scharpf, "Policy Failure and Institutional Reform: Why Should Form Follow Function?" *International Social Science Journal* no. 108 (1986), pp. 179–189.

7. Fritz W. Scharpf, "Decision Rules, Decision Styles and Policy Choices," *Journal of Theoretical Politics* no. 2 (1989), pp. 149–176.

8. Robert H. Salisbury, "The Analysis of Public Policy: A Search for Theories and Roles," in *Political Science and Public Policy,* ed. Austin Ranney (Chicago: Markham, 1968), pp. 159–163.

9. Kenneth Hanf, "Introduction," in *Interorganizational Policy Making,* eds. Kenneth Hanf and Fritz W. Scharpf (London and Beverly Hills: Sage, 1978), p. 2.

10. Gordon Smith, "The Functional Properties of the Referendum," *European Journal of Political Research* no. 1 (1976), pp. 1–23.

11. Robert H. Salisbury, "An Exchange Theory of Interest Groups," *Midwest Journal of Political Science* no. 1 (1969), pp. 11–15.

12. Maurice Manning, "Ireland," in *Referendums,* eds. David Butler and Austin Ranney (Washington: AEI Press, 1978), pp. 193–210; (See voting result, p. 208); Kevin Featherstone, *Socialist Parties and European Integration* (Manchester: Manchester University Press, 1988), pp. 201–204.

13. Sten Sparre Nilson, "Scandinavia," in *Referendums,* op. cit., pp. 169–192; Featherstone, *Socialist Parties and European Integration,* op. cit., pp. 89–94.

14. Nilson, "Scandinavia," in *Referendums,* op. cit., pp. 169–192; Henry Valen, "National Conflict Structure and Foreign Politics: The Impact of the EEC Issue on Perceived Cleavages in Norwegian Politics," *European Journal of Political Research* no. 4 (1976), pp. 47–82; Lars Svasand and Ulf Lindström, "Sliding Towards EC Membership: Norway in Scandinavian Perspective," *Government and Opposition* no. 3 (1992), pp. 330–344.

15. Claude Leleu, "The French Referendum of April 23, 1972," *European Journal of Political Research* no. 4 (1976), pp. 25–46; Vincent Wright, "France," in *Referendums,* op. cit., pp. 139–168.

16. William Safran, *The French Polity* (New York, London: Longman, 1991), p. 144.

17. David Butler and Uwe Kitzinger, *The 1975 Referendum* (London: St. Martin's Press, 1976); Anthony King, *Britain Says Yes: The 1975 Referendum on the Common Market* (Washington, D.C.: AEI Press, 1977), p. 89ff.

18. Richard Gillespie, "The Consolidation of the New Democracies," in *Politics in Western Europe Today,* eds. Derek W. Urwin and William E. Paterson (London, New York: Longman, 1990), p. 231. Thomas D. Lancaster, "Mediterranean Europe: Stabilized Democracies?" in *Modern Political Systems: Europe,* ed. Roy C. Macridis (Englewood Cliffs: Prentice Hall, 1990), p. 273; Kevin Featherstone, "Socialist Parties and European Integration: Variations on a Common Theme," in *The Future of Social Democracy,* eds. William E. Paterson and Alastair H.Thomas (Oxford: Clarendon Press, 1986), p. 245.

19. Kohler-Koch, "Optionen deutscher Politik in einer veränderten internationalen Umwelt," op. cit., p. 58.

20. Emile Noël, "The Single European Act," *Government and Opposition* no. 1 (1987), pp. 3ff; Andrew Moravcsik, "Negotiating the Single European Act," in *The New European Community: Decision Making and Institutional Change,* eds. Robert O. Keohane and Stanley Hoffmann (Boulder: Westview, 1991), pp. 41–84.

21. Stanley Hoffmann, "The European Community and 1992," *Foreign Affairs*

no. 4 (Autumn 1989).

22. Fritz W. Scharpf, "The Joint-Decision Trap: Lessons from German Federalism and European Integration," *Public Administration* 66 (Autumn 1988), pp. 239f.

23. Mancur Olson, *The Rise and the Decline of Nations* (Cambridge: Harvard University Press, 1982).

24. Otto Schmuck, "The European Parliament as an Institutional Actor," in *The State of the European Community,* eds. Leon Hurwitz and Christian Lequesne (Boulder: Lynne Rienner/Longman, 1991), p. 34.

25. Andrew Moravcsik, "Negotiating the Single European Act," op. cit.; Geoffrey Garrett, "International Cooperation and Institutional Choice: The European Community's Internal Market," *International Organization* 46, No. 2 (Spring 1992), pp. 533–560; Thomas Pedersen, "Political Change in the European Community: The Single European Act as a Case of System Transformation," and "Cooperation and Conflict," *The Nordic Journal of International Studies* no. 1 (1992), pp. 7–44.

26. Helen Wallace, "The Council and the Commission After the Single European Act," in *The State of the European Community,* op. cit., p. 21.

27. John Temple Lang, "The Irish Court Case Which Delayed the Single European Act: Crotty v. An Taoiseach and Others," *Common Market Law Review* 24, No. 4 (1987), pp. 709–718.

28. Ole Borre, "The Danish Referendum on the EC Common Act," *Electoral Studies* no. 2 (1986), pp. 189–192; Claus Gulmann, "The Single European Act—Some Remarks From A Danish Perspective," *Common Market Law Review* no. 1 (1987), p. 33f.

29. Neill Nugent, *The Government and Politics of the European Community* 2nd ed. (Durham: Duke University Press, 1991), p. 375.

30. John Pinder, *European Community: The Building of a Union* (Oxford: Oxford University Press, 1991), pp. 40–42.

31. Emile Noël, "Reflections on the Maastricht Treaty," *Government and Opposition* 27, no. 2 (Spring 1992), pp. 148–157.

32. "Was wird aus Europa—und wo liegen seine Grenzen? Mit Jacques Delors, dem Präsidenten der EG-Kommission, sprachen Christoph Bertram und Klaus-Peter Schmid," *Die Zeit,* June 5, 1992, pp. 4–5.

33. Lily Gardner Feldman, "The EC and German Unification," in *The State of the European Community,* op. cit., pp. 313–327; Christopher Anderson, Karl Kaltenthaler, and Wolfgang Luthardt, eds., *The Domestic Politics of German Unification* (Boulder: Lynne Rienner, 1993).

34. Wolfgang Luthardt, "Direct Democracy in Western Europe: The Case of Switzerland," *TELOS* No. 90 (Winter 1991–1992), pp. 101–112.

35. James G. March and Johan P. Olsen, *Rediscovering Institutions* (New York and London: Free Press, 1989); Stephen D. Krasner, "Sovereignty: An Institutional Perspective," *Comparative Political Studies* no. 1 (April 1988), pp. 66–94.

36. Gian Enrico Rusconi, "Was wird aus Europa? Los von Rom. Die Einheit muß aus den Nationen kommen," *Frankfurter Allgemeine Zeitung,* August 29, 1992, p. 25.

37. Alberta M. Sbragia, "Introduction," in *Euro-Politics,* ed. Alberta M. Sbragia (Washington: Brookings Institution, 1992), p. 14.

38. Donald J. Puchala, "Of Blind Men, Elephants and International Integration," *Journal of Common Market Studies* 10, No. 3 (1972), pp. 267–284; Stanley Hoffmann, "Reflections on the Nation-State in Western Europe Today, *Journal of Common Market Studies* 21, Nos. 1 and 2 (1982), pp. 21–37; Robert O. Keohane and Stanley Hoffmann, "Institutional Change in Europe in the 1980s," in *The New European Community,* op. cit.; pp. 1–39; Johan P. Olson, "Analyzing Institutional Dynamics," *Staatswissenschaften und Staatspraxis* 3, no. 2 (1992), pp. 247–271; Philippe C. Schmitter, "Representation and the Future Euro-Polity," *Staatswissenschaften und*

Staatspraxis 3, no. 3 (1992), pp. 379–405.

39. James S. Coleman, *Power and the Structure of Social Theory* (New York: N.W. Norton, 1974), p. 44f.

5

Interest Intermediation in the EC After Maastricht

Michael J. Gorges

Since the coming into force of the Single European Act (SEA), increased use of qualified majority voting and wider authority for Community policymaking have led interest groups and firms to try to improve their ability to participate in policymaking in Brussels. At Maastricht, the members of the Community committed themselves to economic and monetary integration, extended the EC's policymaking authority, and added to the list of issues that fall under qualified majority voting rules. If the disagreements over Maastricht are finally resolved, the extension of the Community's policymaking competence will only prod interest groups to work harder to improve their capacity to influence EC policy elaboration. Effective participation will depend, however, on the ability of interest groups to overcome obstacles to cooperation that have prevented the construction of more influential interest groups since 1958.

In this chapter, I discuss some of the implications of the Maastricht agreements for interest intermediation in the Community. I first review the history of interest group participation in EC policymaking and the development of EC-level interest groups; then I focus on interest intermediation at the macro level, sectoral level, and micro level.[1] I argue that, while it is unlikely that we will see the emergence of EC-level, Scandinavian-style tripartite bargaining, patterns of differentiated sectorallevel and microlevel interest intermediation should persist.

The System of Interest Intermediation in the EC

EC-wide interest groups appeared first in those policy areas for which the Community received responsibility from the Treaty of Rome, establishing horizontal and sector-specific pan-European "federations of federations" in Brussels to participate in EC policymaking. The Luxembourg Compromise directed the attention of interest groups back to the national level. After 1966, an interest group could block legislation in the Council of Ministers if it could convince its government to veto a proposal. Interest groups also devoted more attention to the national level in policy areas over which the Community had no authority, or in which its authority was disputed, e.g., social policy and industrial relations.

The early 1970s saw additional industrial branch and sector committees, national horizontal and sectoral federations, and multinational corporations open offices in Brussels, as well as the founding of the European Trade Union Confederation (ETUC) in 1973. Apart from the ETUC, there was, however, little consolidation of interest groups at the EC level. The SEA, which took effect in 1987, shifted the focus of interest group activity. First, it strengthened the Commission's powers to initiate legislation in a number of areas and expanded the scope of EC policies to include sectors that were previously the responsibility of the national governments. The member states also committed themselves to abolishing the remaining barriers to the free movement of goods, persons, capital, and services by January 1, 1993.

The member states provided themselves with the institutional means to carry out this new task: legislative measures implementing the 1992 project were henceforth to come under qualified majority voting rules. The SEA left the national veto intact in several areas, but the extension of qualified majority voting to new policy sectors has led to an overall reduction in veto use. Within the Council of Ministers, the pressure to compromise has consequently grown much stronger. Policymaking has become far more complex: bargaining and trade-offs are more common, and "staying in the game" is seen as an intrinsic good.[2] These changes have been incorporated into an organizational culture that was already more pragmatic than ideological and valued consensus and technocratic decisionmaking.

The Maastricht Treaty extends the authority of the Community not only in economic and monetary policy, but also in industrial affairs, health, education, trade, the environment, energy, culture, tourism, and consumer protection, as well as in social policy for the eleven signatories of the Social Policy Protocol (SPP). The extension of EC policymaking authority and qualified majority voting should continue to have a significant impact on interest intermediation in the Community. As noted above, a national-level interest group could block legislation if it convinced its government to veto a proposal in the Council of Ministers. There was little need for transnational interest aggregation, and defection from a decision reached through intragroup and intergroup bargaining in Brussels was easy. Reform of decisionmaking processes has significantly weakened the influence of single national governments within the Council of Ministers. With the loss of the national veto, member states can no longer necessarily uphold agreements reached with national-level federations. The SEA and the Maastricht Treaty then, have both increased the appeal of and necessity for rapid, transnational interest definition, aggregation, and coordination, and raised the pressure to improve the effectiveness of EC-level interest associations.

There are hundreds of EC-level interest groups in Brussels, although the membership, resources, status, and influence of these groups vary. Horizontal interest groups include the European Trade Union Confederation (ETUC), the Union of Industry and Employer Confederations of Europe (UNICE), the Committee of Professional Agricultural Organizations (COPA), and the European Center for Public Enterprises (CEEP), representing public employers. Business is represented by twenty horizontal EC-level peak associations, serving industry, public enterprise, crafts, small and medium enterprises, banking, agriculture, and retail trade. There is little transnational aggregation of business interests. The one body established to facilitate contact among horizontal business associations, the Employers Liaison Committee, does not include COPA or the CEEP (although the CEEP is a partner in the social dialogue and did agree to the social dialogue provisions of the SPP), and is an emanation of UNICE. In spite of reforms adopted in 1989, UNICE is still weaker than most of its member federations; much remains to be done if UNICE is truly to become "the voice of European business and industry in Brussels," as it often claims to be.

Sector-specific industry organizations, grouped within the Fédérations Européennes par Branche d'Industrie (FEBIs), outnumber horizontal industry associations. The Commission prefers them as interlocutors; ever in need of information, it has developed close relationships with these associations, as they alone are capable of furnishing the data on which it can base legislation. In addition to the umbrella sectoral federations, there are major subsectoral and product-level associations representing different industries.

National-level associations and individual companies, as well as regional and local governments, also seek to influence the development of EC legislation, both in their national capitals and in Brussels. Practically all EC national-level peak industry and employer federations have offices in Brussels, as do all the former West German länder, several French and Spanish regions, and British local authorities.[3]

Labor, on the other hand, in spite of significant progress in overcoming national, functional, ideological, and religious cleavages, may have sacrificed efficiency for the sake of inclusiveness: forty national-level trade union federations from EC and non-EC countries are affiliated with the ETUC. Although decisions in both its congress and executive committee are taken by two-thirds majority vote, traditions of consensus and solidarity, and a recognition of fundamental power differences within the organization, have led to searches for compromises acceptable to all, resulting in the adoption of lowest common denominator policies. The ETUC lacks resources and depends on the Community to supplement member contributions; the European Trade Union Institute (ETUI), the trade unions' think tank, is heavily subsidized by the Community.

The trade unions are also threatened by a centralization-decentralization process currently taking place in the EC. On the one hand, the institutions of the Community are gaining power at the expense of the trade unions' preferred partners, the national governments. A reasonable strategy would be for the trade unions to concentrate on influencing the development of policy in Brussels, yet the obstacles to a stronger EC-level confederation remain formidable. Rates of unionization throughout the EC are declining, weakening the representativeness of national-level trade unions and their claims to speak for labor, as well as their ability to contribute financially to the ETUC. The logical candidate for leadership of a European trade union movement, the German Trade Union Confederation (DGB), is preoccupied by the problems of German unification, and is not necessarily trusted by other members of the ETUC. Ideological differences among the trade unions persist, and difficulties in reconciling different forms of industrial relations and different social welfare systems and collective bargaining arrangements remain. Although acceptance of different models seems to be growing,[4] implementing decisions taken in Brussels is still a problem. Moreover, the ETUC has always gone to the Commission to obtain, not provide, information, whereas the Commission tends to consult interest groups with the aim of collecting technical information to use in developing legislation.

Nor is the labor movement backed by a strong EC-wide social democratic party. The weakness of transnational party structures and the current disarray of social democracy throughout Western Europe do not bode well for trade union–social democratic party coalitions.

On the other hand, deregulation, the inability of national governments to respond effectively to pressures generated by the international economy, decentralized production and bargaining, employer dominance of industrial relations arrangements, growing differentiation of the working class, and greater use of "flexibility" have become the hallmarks of industrial life in the past decade. Building a strong EC-level organization will not necessarily help trade unions respond to these problems. While proposals for EC-level workers' participation in management (WPM) have existed since 1970, and are also an important component of the Social Charter and the Social Action Program, EC-level legislation has yet to be adopted. Although the Commission, the ETUC, the EP, and the governments of some member states support the development of EC-level WPM, opposition by employers and the British government has blocked any progress on the issue. More recently, concerns about subsidiarity have also played a part in preventing the adoption of legislation. In December 1990, for example, the Commission proposed legislation mandating the creation of European works councils (EWCs) for MNCs in the Community. The Commission has withdrawn this proposal, arguing that a sufficient number of companies had voluntarily established such councils so as to render any legislation unnecessary.

Since the adoption of the SEA, policymaking has picked up speed as the Community has rushed to adopt the 300-odd measures necessary to implement the 1992 project, as well as corollary measures. Both labor and business have attempted to improve their organizational capacity to act at the EC level. In 1989, for example, UNICE undertook a series of reforms designed to strengthen its secretariat, increased its budget by 40 percent, and established direct relationships with single firms. The ETUC, on the other hand, amended its constitution at its 1991 congress and took steps to integrate sectoral-level EC trade union organizations into decisionmaking, established a steering committee with a limited membership in the hope that this would facilitate coalition building and interest aggregation, and increased the ETUC budget. The ETUC also received a bargaining mandate from its affiliates, but there is no guarantee that bargains reached in Brussels with ETUC officials will be implemented at the national or sectoral level.[5]

Both UNICE and the ETUC have been strong supporters of completing the 1992 project, although labor has consistently advocated more and better EC-level social legislation, and both have pushed for rapid ratification and implementation of the Maastricht accords in several joint declarations. Each side, however, continues to stress its favorite themes, subsidiarity and deregulation for UNICE, a stronger social dimension for the ETUC. Thus far, progress on the social dimension and on implementation of the Social Action Program has been stymied by employer and UK resistance.

Corporations, on the other hand, have decided that they can no longer rely on EC-level or national-level interest groups to defend them in Brussels. The "mastodons," i.e., the EC-wide federations of federations, often fail to provide timely information and to respond quickly to Community initiatives. Groups of like-minded industrialists, such as the European Roundtable, have established associations with Brussels offices, and the number of lobbyists (representatives of firms, individual consultants, attorneys, or accountants) in Brussels is estimated to have tripled from 1987 to 1990.[6]

This U.S.-style lobbying, however, is no panacea; the Commission is a small bureaucracy (approximately 3,500 senior officials) and cannot possibly grant a hearing to all those who come knocking at its doors. Interest groups, however, "push against an open door," not least because only they can pull together the arguments of several participants in policymaking and present a more coherent package to the Commission. Moreover, lobbying is expensive, and consultants often lack expertise or credibility with EC officials.[7] As issues of the democratic deficit and accountability have moved closer to the top of the EC's agenda, so have issues surrounding policymaking by "*bureaucrates apatrides*" in collusion with the MNCs' hired guns. There has even been talk of establishing a register of lobbyists who attempt to influence the EP.

Interest groups concentrate their attention on the Commission, which is a small, relatively open bureaucracy that depends on outside experts, either from the national governments or various interest groups, for information on which to base policy. It is crucial for interest groups to be involved early on in the development of a proposal, as it is very difficult to amend a proposal once it leaves a Directorate General (DG) to make its way up to the full Commission. Keeping track of Commission proposals and informing their member about EC-level developments constitute a major part of the work of EC-level interest groups. The Commission is in regular contact with the most important EC- and national-level groups and keeps a list of those groups it officially recognizes.[8] While the Community is hardly a state, it does possess significant institutional and financial resources for structuring the involvement of interest groups in policymaking. Commission representatives in particular have played a significant role in shaping the dynamics of interest intermediation in the major socioeconomic sectors. The Commission, which does not refuse to grant a hearing to representatives of non-EC-level interest groups or individual causes or firms, has made known its *preference* for dealing with the EC-level *organizational* representatives of these groups. In fact, it does grant them something of a representational monopoly by seeking to consult with them first, by including them in the elaboration of policy, by furnishing them with the earliest possible information, and by providing them with the resources necessary to participate in EC policymaking (technical support such as interpreters, meeting rooms, per diem expenses, etc.).

Depending on the treaty provisions under which a proposal falls, the Council of Ministers votes after minimal input by the ESC and EP, or, according to the cooperation procedure introduced by the SEA, adopts a "common position" after proposition by the Commission and a first reading by the EP. The proposal is then referred back to the EP for a second reading. As a result of the Maastricht Treaty, the amount of legislation covered by the cooperation procedure has increased, and the EP has won the right to veto certain Commission and Council proposals. A formerly weak EP has gained enough power to be taken seriously by Commission, Council, and interest groups, which have increased their efforts to influence the EP. Given the probability of further institutional reform in the Community, especially in light of the debate over accountability and the democratic deficit, the EP is likely to become more influential in the future.

Ironically, however, a change in the status of the EP may hinder the institutionalization of corporatist patterns of interest intermediation. Although the EP may prove a useful ally for the trade unions in their attempts to pass stronger EC-level social policy legislation, strong parliaments and competitive party systems in general offer more opportunities for institutionalized opposition and public appeals, while corporatist arrangements tend to limit political competition and conflict. Promoters of Eurocorporatism might want to be cautious about enhancing the role of the EP.

Macrocorporatism in the EC: The Trade Unions and Industry[9]

The Community is endowed with an ostensibly neocorporatist institution, the Economic and Social Committee (ESC), a tripartite body with representatives from business, labor, and consumer and other interests, but it has not developed into an important participant in EC policymaking. The Commission has also taken great pains to establish an ongoing dialogue with the peak organizations of labor and industry, the ETUC, UNICE, and the CEEP, but past attempts to establish EC-level tripartite bargaining, from the tripartite conferences in the 1970s to the social dialogue of the 1980s, have failed.

In early 1991, at the Commission's initiative, the social partners began a review of the social dialogue with the purpose of elaborating a proposal for inclusion in the treaty on political union. After ten months of negotiation, the social partners reached agreement in October 1991.

Unable to convince the United Kingdom to accept the social policy provisions of a draft treaty on political union, the remaining eleven member states signed a separate Social Policy Protocol (SPP) at the Maastricht summit. The social dialogue agreement is included in the SPP. These provisions of the SPP make Commission consultation with the social partners mandatory before social legislation may be proposed. Employers and trade unions must now be consulted jointly before draft legislative proposals are issued, to establish whether they are necessary or appropriate. If need is established, the social partners will be consulted again on proposal content and will give their opinions or recommendations. The social partners have nine months to reach agreement on a proposal, but this period may be extended. During the second consultation, the social partners may decide to adopt an EC-level collective agreement or a joint position on the topic. Any agreement reached may be implemented, with or without amendment, through national agreements according to local procedures and practices, or, for measures falling under Article 118 and with the accord of the social partners, may be forwarded to the Commission and Council of Ministers to become EC law. The Commission, however, must endorse proposals agreed to by the social partners before they can be submitted to the Council and is not obligated to accept an agreement by the social partners as the basis for its own proposals. Proposals forwarded to the Council are voted on according to the rules of Article 118, either by qualified majority or unanimity, depending on the provisions of the SPP, which also extends the Eleven's Article 118 authority to legislate on working conditions, information and consultation (though not codetermination) for workers, equal rights for men and women, and integration of those excluded from the labor market. Decisions on these matters may be taken by qualified majority vote of the eleven signatories. The Community was also granted authority to legislate in matters of social security, protection upon dismissal, representation and collective defense of workers' and employers' interests (including codetermination), employment conditions of non-EC nationals, and financial contributions to employment promotion and job creation, but any legislation in these areas requires a unanimous vote by the Council of Ministers to pass. Wages, the right of association, the right to strike, and the right of lockout are excluded entirely from the protocol.

For the proponents of EC-level macrocorporatism, the social dialogue provisions of the SPP demonstrate the power of both the idea of social partnership and the will to negotiate, as well as establishing a precise legal framework for these negotiations. The change is greatest for UNICE, which has argued for years that it had no mandate to negotiate on behalf of its member federations at the EC level; it seems to have finally received this mandate.[10] Proponents also contend that the SPP establishes the legal basis for a Community model of corporatism and consecrates the role of the social partners in EC-level bargaining.

The protocol's deference to certain national-level preferences could have interesting results, as it allows flexibility in the implementation of agreements between employers and labor wherever national practice demands. It also authorizes the implementation of any agreement at that level; the objections of certain member states to overcentralization are thus seemingly met. The protocol may well promote national-level bargaining; national-level trade unions and employer/industry associations will be obliged to bargain over modifications to a proposal.

The social dialogue provisions of the SPP are open to interpretation. The ETUC contends that the way for EC-wide collective bargaining is now open and that member states will find it harder to veto proposals that labor and management support. For industry, on the other hand, these provisions are intended to keep certain legislation off the EC's agenda.[11] In the end, implementation will depend on the willingness of EC-level business associations to enter into negotiations at the EC and sectoral level. As for social policy legislation, the time seems to have come for the eleven protocol signatories to put their money where their mouths are and stop engaging in what Peter Lange has so aptly called "cheap talk."[12]

Despite the possibilities for macrocorporatism in the new proposals, the EC still does not possess the means necessary for its maintenance. The Community is not a state and is not authorized to use fiscal and monetary policy to alleviate unemployment, the means whereby trade union participation in the national-level macrocorporatist arrangements of the 1970s was normally secured. Only in the Maastricht Treaty has the EC acquired real macroeconomic policymaking authority, yet the monetary policy to which the EC pledged itself at Maastricht is resolutely monetarist and anti-inflationary; there is little the EC can promise labor in return for its cooperation.

One must also ask whether the social partners are capable of fulfilling the functions the SPP assigns them. In the past, both UNICE and the ETUC have negotiated more with the Commission than with each other. Neither association has developed the organizational capabilities necessary to negotiate agreements at the EC level for implementation at the national or sectoral levels. Moreover, the decentralization of collective bargaining implied in the protocol may well reduce the possibility for any effective action at the EC level.

In sum, there are no strong partners to participate in EC-level macrocorporatist bargaining arrangements, nor is there much for them to talk about. Although the social dialogue provisions of the SPP are evidence of the social partners' desire to continue discussions (not necessarily negotiations), and although the SPP establishes the framework within which such discussions may take place, it does not address the organizational problems interest groups face, nor is it a guarantee that the outcomes of EC-wide bargaining will be to either side's liking.

In comparison to tripartite bargaining between the institutions of the Community and representatives of industry and labor, agriculture is highly corporatized. Each year, the Commission, the farmers' lobby, the Committee of Professional Agricultural Organizations (COPA), and the Council of Ministers decide on the level of support to be granted the Community's farmers as part of the Common Agricultural Policy (CAP). COPA is consulted as prices are determined and as policy is implemented. Founded in 1958, COPA is an organization of the agricultural federations of the twelve member states of the EC. In spite of the differences among these organizations, COPA is a relatively well integrated association. It is the Commission's preferred partner in agricultural policymaking; national and sectoral interests must channel their demands through COPA before dealing with EC institutions. COPA is able to reach binding internal compromises during the annual price review, and member federations implement agreements reached in Brussels. Organizational coherence and efficiency are enhanced by a membership limited to organizations from EC member states and by majority voting rules adopted in 1973.

The Community has been attempting to move away from a policy of price supports for farmers to one of direct income support, in order to reduce the proportion of resources devoted to agriculture (by far the largest item in the EC's budget), discourage overproduction, and redress the CAP's bias toward large farmers. COPA has attempted to maintain high support prices and resisted moves toward direct income supports; under such a system, its role in EC policymaking might well be reduced.

Sectoral-level Interest Intermediation[13]

While Maastricht will probably disappoint proponents of EC-level macro-corporatism, the institutionalization of sectoral bargaining patterns is certainly more likely with the expansion of Community competences. Given the emphasis on improving the competitiveness of EC industry, we may, in fact, see the evolution of a supply-side corporatism, with sectoral industry associations and the Commission engaged routinely in policymaking designed to promote the competitiveness of particular sectors and the development of a skilled workforce for those sectors. Directorate General XIII (telecommuni-

cations, information industries, and innovation), for example, already accounts for the second largest portion of Community spending after DG VI
(agriculture).[14] This supply-side corporatism could extend to the micro level
as well.

Although some proponents of the 1992 project aim at a deregulation of
the EC's economy, and concerns about an intrusive, overly ambitious, unac-
countable Eurocracy have been increasingly voiced since the Maastricht
Treaty was signed, it is too early to tell whether the 1992 project and the
principles of mutual recognition and subsidiarity will truly limit the reach of
Community policymaking. At the very least, we should be cautious about
overstating the extent of deregulation. Completion and monitoring of the
internal market, establishment and implementation of a Community monetary
policy, development of Community health and safety standards, and technical
norms for areas currently not covered by any rules will still require EC
regulations, as will the new policy domains opened up by Maastricht. A
Business Week survey,[15] for example, reported that the EC is developing 1,500
safety, health, and quality standards it wants to make consistent throughout
the member states. The Community ultimately wants to establish 10,000 new
standards.

Sectoral Industrial Interests.[16]

Sectoral industry associations, the so-called FEBIs, are widely recognized as
the interest groups most closely involved in EC policymaking. Numerous
studies—of the 1980s' steel crisis, consumer electronics, pharmaceuticals,
biotechnology, chemicals, and telecommunications, among others—have
shown that interest intermediation at the sectoral level is highly differentiated
and cannot be characterized as predominantly pluralist or corporatist.[17]

Why do EC-level sectoral groups form? Although transnational business
collaboration did not begin in 1952 or 1958, EC-level sectoral groups have
historically formed as the Community has extended its policy domain. For a
relatively small investment, an industry can get the Commission to hear its
case, and perhaps to act in its favor. Other benefits, such as status, a listening
post in Brussels, contact with other national-level representatives in one's
sector, and influence within the EC-level interest group also accrue with
participation.

The incentives for sectoral interests to collaborate at the EC level are
certainly present. Whether groups will do so, however, depends on several
factors: the actual extent of EC policymaking authority in the sector, the
degree of internationalization of a sector, the historical legacy of transnational
cooperation, the presence of a national-level sectoral federation or dominant
firm(s) willing to play a leading role, the structure of the market, intercom-
pany relationships at the EC level, ties between a sector and a particular DG,
the presence or absence of competition among sectoral organizations to

represent the same constituency, and national patterns of interest intermediation. Coordination among FEBIs is rare, however; the absence of macrolevel transnational aggregation of business interests is replicated at the sectoral level.

European Industry Committees.

European Industry Committees (EICs) are the sectoral organizations of labor at the EC level. The ETUC officially recognizes fifteen EICs. In theory, they are open to every appropriate trade union affiliated with an ETUC-member national trade union federation. As a result, as many as seventy trade unions may be members of an EIC. However, national-level sectoral federations affiliated to national confederations that are not ETUC members cannot be represented in EICs. EICs send delegates to the ETUC's quadrennial congress, sit on the ETUC's executive and steering committees and vote on all matters except ETUC membership and finances.[18]

The EICs are the trade union bodies most closely involved in the development of Community policy in individual sectors. They cover virtually every sector of the economy, from actors to metalworkers to teachers. Generally, EIC activity focuses on three areas: promotion of cooperation and coordination among members and collaboration with other EICs and the ETUC, protection of sectoral workers' interests in EC policymaking, and creation of a trade union counterweight to FEBIs and MNCs. The first of these goals is paid lip service by all trade unions, but intraorganizational problems continue to plague the EICs: lack of means; lack of leadership; an unwillingness on the part of national-level sectoral federations to follow the line laid down in Brussels; differences among EIC members in terms of power, wealth, and role in the domestic economy; status in the domestic political system; etc. EICs attempt to monitor developments in the Community, but most cannot compete with the FEBIs in terms of resources. They can afford a staff of two or three at most and depend indirectly on the Commission or the international trade secretariats for financial support. Like the national-level trade union federations, national-level sectoral federations have been hit by declining rates of unionization and a corresponding loss of income. EICs hope to negotiate comprehensive sectoral agreements with FEBIs and company-wide agreements with EC-based MNCs, but it is not clear how the relatively few EICs will muster the means to bargain with the myriad better-financed FEBIs.

Generally, EICs support the ETUC's goals of building the social dimension of the internal market and developing Community-level industrial relations. They are also devoting an increasing amount of attention to developing relations with FEBIs and with multinational European firms. Meetings between representatives of EICs and FEBIs have taken place in many industries, but the discussions have centered on the future employment prospects of individual sectors rather than on trade unionists' social concerns.

Several EICs have signed agreements with multinational companies establishing EC-wide consultative arrangements, but these agreements usually grant rights to information and consultation alone, not codetermination. Approximately fifteen MNCs have voluntarily created EC-level group committees, "organs or forums of employee information and, to a lesser extent, consultation."[19] The trade unions have launched a wide-ranging campaign to convince or force more MNCs to create similar committees. Other EC-based MNCs have established informal systems of consultation with their employees. Currently, however, no EC legislation provides a framework for collective agreements, and no MNC has signed a fully binding collective agreement covering several countries in which the group operates. At best, current arrangements can serve as examples of how to achieve agreement on WPM in the future.

It remains to be seen whether the 1992 project will definitively destroy labor's hopes of devising industrial relations regulations with strong roots at both the Community and sectoral levels. Pessimists argue that EC-wide deregulation, coupled with changes in production processes which leave initiative in the hands of the employers, render any attempts to devise EC-level arrangements futile and simultaneously undermine any recourse to a national strategy.[20] Optimists highlight the fact that as practically all member states have some form of works councils, the prospects for EC-level works councils are not completely bleak. Employee participation on company boards or real German-style codetermination is less likely. In only two of the twelve member states (Denmark and Germany) do employees have seats on company boards, while codetermination rights for works councils have been won in only four cases (Denmark, Germany, Luxembourg, and the Netherlands).[21] The trade unions can, however, rely on the backing of two key governments, the French and German, as well as on the support of elements in the Commission, the EP,[22] and the ESC. Before the SPP, EC-level WPM legislation required a unanimous vote in the Council of Ministers and so was bound to fail. As is the case with other social policy legislation, the moment of truth may have arrived; the Maastricht agreement extends qualified majority voting to cover employee rights to information and participation.

Microcorporatism in the EC[23]

At times, the Commission has bypassed EC-level interest groups and developed corporatist arrangements with individual firms or groups of firms. ESPRIT, for example, embodies an agreement among the Community, separate firms, research laboratories, and universities to collaborate on research and share its results in the hope of developing EC capabilities in emerging high-technology industries. Recognizing the Community's problems in international competition with the United States and Japan, the Commission formed an alliance with individual firms to bring pressure on national governments to support its strategy of fashioning a Community industrial policy for these sectors. The budget for the first ten-year program was ECU 1.5 billion.[24] Several other research and development programs, such as BRITE, RACE, BAP, DELTA, and EUREKA are run by the Commission in direct association with individual firms. Alan Cawson argues that the case of the consumer electronics sector "suggests a trend towards a form of microcorporatism where policy is determined and implemented through bargained arrangements between the EC and major firms."[25] These examples serve to demonstrate the variety of government-firm relations possible in the EC; the enlarged policymaking authority of the Community simply leaves the door open to further arrangements of this kind.

Considerations for the Future

The Maastricht agreements are unlikely to change interest intermediation in the EC in the short run. If the past is any guide, we can expect to see interest groups increase their involvement and influence at the policy formulation stage. The Commission will still initiate most legislation, and will therefore remain the most important target for interest groups; conversely, the Commission will continue to rely on interest groups to supply it with timely information. Qualified majority voting will increasingly force interest groups to compromise and form coalitions. This will place a premium on effective decisionmaking within interest groups. If the SEA sent interest groups scurrying to adjust to shifts in the locus of power, the Maastricht accords, if ratified, will only keep them running.

Interest groups, however, will still face the same problems of intraorganizational coordination that have bedeviled them since 1958. They have remained divided along national, regional, ideological, and sectoral lines; to the extent that they have overcome these divisions, they have done so only through compromises fostered by skillful leadership, intragroup bargaining, and learning.

Three issues are likely to determine the future of interest intermediation in the Community: the extent of the EC's policymaking authority, enlargement, and the EC's possible evolution toward federalism. Interest group participation in policymaking has risen as the central institutions of the Community have increased their authority, and institutional change in the Community has *always* given these institutions more power. While it would be a mistake to posit a unidirectional flow of authority to the EC, especially after the post-Maastricht debate over issues of national sovereignty, democratic accountability, and subsidiarity, it seems unlikely that the authority ceded to the Community at Maastricht will be reclaimed by the member states. Sovereignty will continue to be pooled, and the battles between EC institutions and the member states will be similar to those of any federation. In fact, it will probably take a series of cases in the European Court of Justice to sort out the issue of subsidiarity.

Enlargement, regardless of its eventual character or when it occurs, will only increase the need for better preparation, monitoring, coalition-building, and more efficient decisionmaking procedures on the part of interest groups. Fortunately, associations from non-EC countries are already members of some EC-level interest groups; they know how the system works and what it takes to be successful within it. On the other hand, enlargement will accentuate the disparities within the EC and increase competition for Community resources, which in turn will augment pressure on the EC's budget, heighten tensions within interest groups, and pit sector against sector and region against region in more obvious ways than before. This could raise the barrier to intraorganizational coordination even higher. Given differences in welfare state development, however, enlargement will certainly hamper attempts to develop more than skeletal EC-level social policy legislation. If the SPP can lock certain social legislation into place and if new members are required to accept the *acquis communautaire,* then they may have no choice in this regard, although they might insist on "opt-out" clauses in accession negotiations. EFTA countries, with their well-developed welfare states and their traditions of cooperation among labor, industry, and the state, would probably join a coalition supporting more stringent EC-level social policies, if only because they have an interest in raising labor costs in other EC countries. It seems unlikely that they would accept a serious dilution of social policy standards.

For the Commission, however, enlargement means more interest groups seeking access. In response, it may push interest groups to become more centralized, hierarchical, and authoritative, and seek to reward the "most efficient" groups with subsidies, access, etc. Although it has tried to do this in the past, EC-level interest groups have not met Commission expectations, and the Commission has been forced to consult with national- , sectoral- , and regional-level groups as well as with representatives of individual firms. Moreover, the Commission can only provide incentives for interest groups to become more efficient; whether they do so depends on internal interest group characteristics.

Speculation about the future of interest intermediation in the EC also involves speculation about the shape of the future European polity. One debate centers on the possibilities for development of a more federal EC. It is possible that interest groups would develop a decentralized structure to address decentralized targets, that EC-level organizations would remain weak, and that there would be a noticeable absence of hierarchy and monopoly among a wide variety of groups. Interest intermediation in the United States seems to confirm this prediction.

In Switzerland, however, a country with a highly decentralized federal government, the large economic interest groups are organized in influential peak associations. Gerhard Lehmbruch argues that Swiss interest intermediation must be understood as the outcome of "strategic choice on the part of political elitcs in a critical juncturc"; thc cmcrgcncc of strong cconomic pcak associations looks like a case of "political design . . . where the intervention of organized interests . . . is to some extent intentionally created, structured, and institutionalized through state action."[26]

The implications of Lehmbruch's analysis for the EC are clear: federalism does not in and of itself lead to pluralism; the choices of elites and the structure of decisionmaking matter. If the interest intermediation in the EC is unlikely to resemble Scandinavian corporatism, it is equally unlikely to resemble U.S.-style pluralism. Any trend will be uneven, and we will certainly find differences between macro-level, sectoral-level, and micro-level patterns.

Notes

1. For a discussion of the different levels of interest intermediation, see Alan Cawson, *Organized Interests and the State: Studies in Meso-Corporatism* (London and Beverly Hills: Sage, 1985). Interest intermediation at the macro level involves tripartite bargaining among the representatives of the state and peak organizations of labor and business. At the sectoral level, the relevant actors are not peak organizations, but rather, "organizations which close around and defend specific interests of sectors and professions" (Cawson, op. cit., p. 9); at the micro level, firms and state representatives are the key actors.

2. Helen Wallace, "Making Multilateral Negotiations Work," in William Wallace, ed., *The Dynamics of European Integration* (London and New York: Pinter, 1990).

3. Sonia P. Mazey and Jeremy J. Richardson, "British Pressure Groups in the European Community: The Challenge of Brussels," *Parliamentary Affairs* 45, no. 1 (1992), pp. 94–95.

4. See "German example gains fans," *Financial Times,* September 3, 1991; "Co-operation with industry offers way ahead for workers," *The Independent,* September 9, 1991.

5. See *Report For a More Effective ETUC* (Brussels: European Trade Union Confederation, 1991), which was accepted by the 1991 Congress.

6. Mazey and Richardson, op. cit., p. 95.

7. Ibid., p. 100–101.

8. Mazey and Richardson cite a figure of 525 recognized groups. Ibid, p. 94.

9. Macro-level interest intermediation involves negotiations among the state and peak, horizontal organizations of business and labor over issues of importance for the entire economy.

10. Or so it thought. Soon after the signature of the social partners' agreement in October 1991, the Confederation of British Industry questioned UNICE's right to negotiate EC-wide agreements. See "CBI may withdraw from European pact," *Financial Times,* November 25, 1991.

11. See "Business gives some ground on Euro-deals—but with riders," *Industrial Relations Europe,* November 1991; and letters to the editor by the General Secretaries of UNICE and the ETUC in the *Financial Times* of November 12 and 22, 1991.

12. Peter Lange, "The Politics of the Social Dimension," in Alberta M. Sbragia,

ed., *Europolitics: Institutions and Policymaking in the New European Community,* (Washington: The Brookings Institution, 1992).

13. At the sectoral, or meso level, the relevant actors in interest intermediation are representatives of sectors or professions.

14. Alan Cawson, "Interests, Groups, and Public Policy-Making: The Case of the European Consumer Electronics Industry," in Justin Greenwood, et al., eds., *Organised Interests and the European Community* (London: Sage, forthcoming), p. 11.

15. "10,000 New Rules," *Business Week,* September 7, 1992.

16. The extent of sector-specific interest association involvement precludes a detailed analysis of any particular sector here. In-depth studies of various sectors can be found in, inter alia, Thomas Grunert, "Decision-Making Processes in the Steel Crisis Policy of the EEC: Neocorporatist or Integrationist Tendencies?" in Yves Meny and Vincent Wright, eds., *The Politics of Steel: Western Europe and the Steel Industry in the Crisis Years (1974-1984)* (Berlin and New York: De Gruyter, 1987); David Vogel, "Protective Regulation and Protectionism in the European Community: The Creation of a Common Market for Food and Beverages," paper prepared for the biennial conference of the ECSA, May 1991; Cawson, op. cit.; Volker Schneider, "Organized Interests in the European Telecommunications Sector," in Greenwood et al., op. cit.; Justin Greenwood and Karsten Ronit, "Established and Emergent Sectors: Organised Interests at the European Level in the Pharmaceutical and the New Biotechnologies," in Greenwood et al., op. cit.; Stephen Wilks and Maurice Wright, eds. *Comparative Government-Industry Relations* (Oxford: Clarendon, 1987); and Wyn Grant, "Associ-ational Systems in the Chemical Industry," in Alberto Martinelli, ed., *International Markets and Global Firms* (London, Newbury Park, and New Delhi: Sage, 1991).

17. See note 16.

18. *Constitution* (Brussels: ETUC, 1991).

19. "Business gives some ground on Euro-deals—but with riders," *Industrial Relations Europe,* November 1991, p. 2. In January 1991, the Commission approved the establishment of a joint company (Europipe) by Sacilor and Mannensmanröhren-Werke, to be run by a supervisory management board with one half of the seats going to employee representatives. Europipe will thus implement aspects of the draft company law directive on participation before its adoption. "Europipe—the European Company Statute in action?" *European Industrial Relations Review* no. 213 (October 1991), p. 12.

20. Wolfgang Streeck, "More Uncertainties: West German Unions Facing 1992," paper presented at the Seventh Conference of Europeanists, Washington, DC, March 23–25, 1990; Wolfgang Streeck and Philippe C. Schmitter, "From National Corporat-ism to Transnational Pluralism: Organized Interests in the Single European Market," *Politics and Society* 19, no. 2 (1991); Hugh G. Mosley, "The Social Dimension of European Integration," *International Labour Review* 129, no. 2 (1990).

21. European Trade Union Institute (ETUI), *Collective Bargaining in Western Europe in 1989 and Prospects for 1990* (Brussels: ETUI, 1990).

22. Although the left broadly defined holds a majority of seats in the current EP, among rightward-leaning members of the EP are many Christian Democrats, who also support a strong social dimension, including, especially for the German MEPs, EC industrial relations legislation. Moreover, the EP has threatened to hold the completion of the internal market hostage to progress on the social dimension, both for ideological reasons and as a weapon in its fight to gain increased power in its dealings with the Commission and Council of Ministers. See "Le Parlement de Strasbourg accroît sa pression en faveur de l'Europe sociale," *Le Monde,* September 19, 1989; "Cot: Je n'exclus pas la censure," *Libération,* December 8, 1989.

23. The key actors in micro-level interest intermediation are firms and the state.

24. Juliet Lodge, "EC Policymaking: Institutional Considerations," in Juliet

Lodge, ed., *The European Community and the Challenge of the Future* (New York: Saint Martin's Press, 1989), p. 53; Jane A. Sargent, "Corporatism and the European Community," in Wyn Grant, ed., *The Political Economy of Corporatism* (Basingstoke and London: MacMillan, 1985), p. 244.

25. Cawson, op. cit., p. 14.

26. Gerhard Lehmbruch, "The Organization of Society, Administrative Strategies, and Policy Networks," in Roland M. Czada and Adrienne Windhoff-Héritier, eds., *Political Choice: Institutions, Rules, and the Limits of Rationality* (Boulder: Westview Press, 1991), pp. 136–138.

6

Socialism and the EC After Maastricht: From Classic to New-Model European Social Democracy

Robert Geyer

In a recent book on the history of social democracy in the post–World War II period,[1] Stephen Padgett and William Paterson argue that traditional European social democracy[2] is currently experiencing a prolonged period of ideological, organizational, and electoral crisis.[3] For Padgett and Paterson, this period of crisis is based on four general developments: the growth of economic internationalization and interdependence, the decline of the traditional working class and the increased heterogeneity of advanced capitalist societies, the failure of nationally based Keynesian economic policies, and the crisis of the social democratic welfare state. They conclude that all these developments appear to be continuing in the short to medium term. Therefore, the future for social democracy appears bleak.

However, there is one new development that they failed to explore fully: the European Community (EC). For some European social democrats,[4] the EC has the potential to revive radically the flagging fortunes of traditional social democracy. Through the development of the EC, the lost powers of the nation-state could be regained at a European level. Economic internationalization and interdependence could be controlled. Europe-wide Keynesianism could be created enabling the welfare state to be reestablished at the European level. Hence, a major question for both political scientists and European politicians is, can the EC protect social democracy from the international developments that are currently undermining European social democracy? Furthermore, can the EC help individual national social democratic movements[5] to achieve ideological, organizational, and electoral renewal?

Can the EC Protect Traditional Social Democracy?

One way to answer this question is to break it down into the four elements that Padgett and Paterson identify.

Does or Can the EC Protect Social Democracy from the Increasing
Internationalization and Interdependence of the Global Economy?

Historically, the evidence is mixed. Despite the free market rhetoric of the 1957 Treaty of Rome, the early development of the EC was based less on the creation of common markets than on the creation of common protected markets (especially in coal, steel, and agriculture). Protection from the international economy was part of the foundation of the EC. However, this earlier protectionism came under increasing pressure in the 1970s and 1980s.

With the growing economic difficulties of the EC member states, increasing international interdependence, and the ascendence of free market ideology in Europe (especially Britain), the EC's 1992 project was born. This project combined an institutional transformation of the EC ("mutual recognition" and "subsidiarity") with a neoliberal approach to the solution of economic problems (the White Paper's 300 plus proposals, the Cecchini Report) to create a deregulatory dynamic that would encourage a real common market within the EC. This process has undermined (and will continue to undermine) the ability of individual member states to protect and control their domestic economies. Furthermore, despite some fears or hopes about the creation of "Fortress Europe," extensive general protectionism has failed to develop between the EC and external traders.[6] As demonstrated by the recent international trade negotiations, only agriculture has managed to maintain a relatively protected position. The recent Maastricht Treaty negotiations showed no indication of increasing European protectionism. Hence, it is unlikely that the EC would want to or be able to substantially delink itself from the international economy.

Furthermore, with the collapse of communism in the East and the crumbling of the EFTA, the EC has been deluged by a virtual flood of applicants for EC membership. Integrating these new members into some form of unified Europrotectionist policy would be extremely complicated and difficult. Hence, due to the free market orientation of the 1992 project, the current lack of EC-wide protectionism, and the uncertain future EC membership, social democrats should expect little protection from the EC against the dynamics of economic internationalization and interdependence.

Will the EC Affect the Dynamics of Working
Class Decline, Disorganization, and Deradicalization?

It is extremely doubtful whether the EC will be able to limit the effects of working class decline. The EC is in no way directly oriented toward maintaining the traditional working class. Conceivably, the EC's traditional attempts at supporting the coal and steel industries and recent attempts at advanced technology industrial policy (for example, the ESPRIT and EUREKA projects[7]) could support some sectors of the industrial working class.

Furthermore, if the dynamics of the EC were to revive the industrial potential of Europe, the traditional working class might be maintained. However, the inability of the EC to protect substantially European coal and steel industries in the 1980s and 1990s, the limited nature of the EC's industrial policy, and the 1992 project's dynamic of internal EC competition would all appear to indicate the unlikelihood of substantial EC support for the revival of the traditional working class.

In terms of class organization, the EC has more to offer. Through the existence of its corporatist Economic and Social Committee and its attempts at creating and encouraging forms of European corporatism (the "social dialogue"), the EC has been and continues to be a potential arena for the reorganization of European class politics. However, these attempts at reorganizing national class dynamics at a Europe-wide level have, for the present, resulted in few concrete results.[8] Recent attempts at creating Europe-wide collective bargaining and/or industrial relations have continued to flounder. The recent Maastricht Treaty makes virtually no mention of them. In fact, it has been argued by many (including the EC Commission) that the deregulatory dynamic of the 1992 project's "mutual recognition" approach creates a form of "social dumping."[9] By forcing social systems to compete with each other for investment, the generally more organized, high cost systems will lose out to the less organized, low cost systems. Hence, social deregulation will ensue. This deregulation may be encouraged by the likely widening of the EC to include Eastern European nations. Their disorganized working class organizations will act as a further drag on EC-wide class organization.

Finally, as argued by Ronald Inglehart,[10] the EC seems to encourage postindustrial class-deradicalization values. This transformation appears to be most advanced among the young. Therefore, as time goes on, one should expect increasingly postindustrial/deradicalized values. Hence, despite the possibility for the creation of some future forms of EC-wide class organization, working class decline and deradicalization seem to be enhanced by the EC.

Can the EC Save Social Democratic Keynesian Economic Intervention?

At the member state level, the case seems extremely doubtful. As has already been noted, the ability and desire of the EC to create a protectionist arena within which national Keynesianism could be revived seem extremely low, especially in the period of the present 1992 project. Furthermore, the combination of growing internal EC openness between member states and the future creation of a unified currency makes national Keynesian policies a virtual impossibility. At an EC-wide level, there is some potential for an EC-wide Keynesian policy. The European Trade Union Confederation and the Socialist Group of the EC Parliament have argued that with the completion of the

European Monetary Union, the creation of a European currency, and the creation of some form of a European Central Bank, an EC-wide Keynesian policy could be created. This could then be used to form the basis of an EC-wide social democratic economic policy.

However, there are several problems with this argument. First, with the crumbling of the Maastricht Treaty during 1992 under the weight of rejection by the Danish voters in June, near rejection by the French in September, and the mid-September 1992 wave of speculation that forced the British pound and Italian lira to leave the exchange rate mechanism, steps toward European monetary integration have come to a virtual standstill. Further, even without the difficulties over the Maastricht Treaty, monetary union would continue to be on a very rough road in the short term. With the historic divergence between German and U.S. interest rates playing havoc with European currencies and interest rates, the political will to maintain some form of monetary union could easily disintegrate.

Second, even if monetary union succeeds and a functioning EC Central Bank is eventually created, it is unlikely that the bank will be used to promote full employment. The current institutional form of the bank follows the German model, in which an independent central bank concentrates on inflation restraint rather than unemployment reduction as its primary activity. This model virtually precludes attempts to achieve full employment through reflation. The Maastricht Treaty itself stipulates in Article 105 that "the primary objective of the European System of Central Banks shall be to maintain price stability."[11] It also stipulates in Article 104C that "excessive" government deficits are to be avoided and will be subject to financial punishments. Thus, both the monetary and fiscal policies of member states are to be restrained by the future European monetary order.

Third, the EC budget is very small relative to the size of the European economy. The budget would have to be radically expanded if EC fiscal policies were to have any substantial effect of the European economy. As demonstrated by the failure of the attempted expansion of the EC budget by Jacques Delors in early 1992,[12] any dramatic EC budget expansion seems extremely unlikely in the short and medium terms.

Fourth, the likely widening of the EC toward Eastern Europe creates tremendous problems for the creation of an EC-wide Keynesian policy. The needs of these countries are vastly different from the needs of the existing core EC countries. Creating a politically and economically viable EC Keynesian policy would be extremely difficult in such a context.

Can the EC Solve the Dilemmas of the Social Democratic Welfare State?

To answer this question, one must examine the three dilemmas of the social democratic welfare state:[13] its fiscal crisis, bureaucratic inefficiency, and

European development. Regarding the fiscal difficulties of the various national welfare states, it is extremely unlikely that the EC will be able to help due to the limitations on its own fiscal powers. In fact, the EC is a competitor to the fiscal needs of the individual member states. Either new tax revenues need to be found for the EC, increasing the tax burden on an increasingly pressured and resentful European citizenry, or revenues and welfare state responsibilities need to be transferred from the member states to the EC. Neither of these two options appears likely in the near future.

In regard to bureaucratic overlap and inefficiency, the EC seems to be having little effect. The EC may be reducing the amount of bureaucratic overlap between various nation-states. However, it is also adding its own layer of bureaucracy on top of the existing national bureaucracies. Hence, it is difficult to say whether it has reduced or increased the overall level of bureaucracy. Furthermore, there is no indication that the EC is producing new, more efficient types of bureaucratic organization.

Finally, is the EC creating its own European welfare state to replace the existing national ones? There has been some development in this area at the EC level, especially in regard to EC social policy.[14] Following the revival of the EC under the 1992 project, demands for EC social integration began to increase. These demands manifested themselves in the creation of the 1988 Commission working paper, "The Social Dimension of the Internal Market." The central aspect of this "social dimension" was the creation of the EC Social Charter. The Charter contained a list of twelve fundamental social rights and an "action program" for implementing these rights. The Charter was passed in December 1989, but only in a nonbinding form. Hence, the battle over the creation of EC social policy shifted toward a battle over the specific elements of the action program. Since 1989, the Commission has presented to the Council a significant number of social policy proposals in areas such as the regulation of "special types of work" (part-time, seasonal, etc.), different aspects of maximum working hours, rights of pregnant women, employee information, and health and safety. However, only a few of these proposals have been passed by the Council and usually only in a very watered-down form.

The December 1991 Maastricht Treaty increased the consultative powers of the EC Parliament (which has been a strong supporter of increased EC social policy), created majority voting in the Council on some areas of social policy, and encouraged labor-management "consultation" and the elimination of sex discrimination. However, even this seemingly clear advance was complicated by the British "opt-out" clause, which would allow the British to avoid participating in social policies that it did not approve of.

In any case, with the uncertainty over the future of the Maastricht Treaty following the Danish rejection in June 1992 and near rejection by the French in September, and the presidency of the EC Council then in the hands of the Conservative British government, EC social policies have been and should continue to be in a state of stasis throughout 1992 and early 1993.

Clearly, in the near future, it seems extremely unlikely that EC social policies could form the basis of an EC welfare state. The limited financial resources of the EC, the integration of new poor and crisis-ridden members from Eastern Europe, the continued opposition of British Conservatives in the Council, and the weakness of EC-wide social solidarity and corporatistic interest groups makes the creation of a social democratic EC welfare state extremely problematic. EC social policy may be able to encourage the recognition of some European social rights. However, the universalistic implementation of these rights is a long way off. As Wolfgang Streeck and Philippe Schmitter argue:

> For some time to come, whatever will occupy the place of the supranational Single European State governing the Single European Market, will likely resemble a *pre-New Deal liberal state,* with, in Marshall's terms: a high level of *civil rights,* . . . a low level of *political rights,* . . . an even lower level of *social rights,* . . . [and] the almost complete absence of a European system of *industrial citizenship.*[15]

To conclude this section, after examining the impact of the EC on the four general foundations of the crisis of traditional social democracy, one must give qualified support to Padgett's and Paterson's thesis that the EC has only a limited ability to resolve the problems of social democracy. In fact, in many ways it may aggravate those difficulties.

The EC and the Development of British and Norwegian Social Democracy

If the preceding analysis is correct, then one would expect to find that the EC and its 1992 project have had marginal or negative effects on the current ideological, organizational, and electoral crises of nationally based social democratic movements. In order to test this assumption, I will examine the effect of the EC's 1992 project on the development of the Norwegian and British social democratic movements. I will focus on three intervening variables that a comparison of Norway and Britain allow me to highlight: EC membership vs. nonmembership, a stronger social democratic movement vs. a weaker one,[16] and a more flexible, responsive electoral system vs. a less flexible, responsive one.[17]

Both Norwegian society and the Norwegian social democratic movement have been extremely divided over European integration throughout the post–World War II period. Since its first attempt to join the EC in 1962, through its divisive referendum in 1972 (53 percent no to EC membership, 47 percent yes), to its present struggles over the European Economic Area Agreement and its possible future EC membership plans, the Norwegian social democratic movement has had a particularly tumultuous relationship toward the EC.[18]

The Norwegian Labor party (the DNA) and the social democratic movement as a whole can be divided into three major positions in relation to the EC issue: modernizers, traditionalists, and reds/greens. The modernizers are led by Gro Harlem Brundtland (the present prime minister) and have dominated the leadership of the DNA since the early 1980s. They have few links to the traditional working class and represent the right wing of the party. They are primarily white collar professionals who see the party and movement as being stuck in backward and self-destructive ways. They tend to be electorally pragmatic and are determined to keep the party in its electorally dominant position within the Norwegian political system. Due to this emphasis on electoral performance, they reject the traditional ideology and the traditional party/trade union link. They see both of these traditional elements as electorally costly. For this group, the EC represents the future of social democracy. They are the EC's strongest supporters. And, one way or another, they are determined to integrate Norway into the EC.

The traditionalists represent the old industrial working class core of the party and movement. They tend to be critical but basically accepting of the EC. They dislike its free market aspects but support its social policies. Moreover, European socialist cooperation has played an important role in traditional Norwegian social democracy. Hence, despite various rumblings of discontent, the traditionalists have supported the modernizers' pro-EC position.

The red/greens represent the radical and environmental side of the party and movement. The reds tend to be the urban radicals who oppose the capitalistic nature of the EC. The greens are the environmentalists who see the EC as a threat to the Norwegian environment and the rural party members who see the EC as a threat to their way of life. For rural party members, the EC not only threatens them with greater international competition, but also directly endangers the Norwegian state's "districts policy," which provides extensive direct and indirect supports for citizens who work and live in the rural and northern regions. Both reds and greens oppose the centralizing aspects and implications of the EC.

Due to the divisiveness of the 1972 referendum, the EC debate vanished from the Norwegian political scene in the 1970s and early 1980s. With the rise of the 1992 project and the return of the DNA to governmental power in 1986, the debate was revived within the Norwegian social democratic movement by Brundtland and the modernizing leadership. Building on the joint EC-EFTA Luxembourg Declaration of April 1984 in which the EC and EFTA countries agreed to create a new, more cooperative and integrated European Economic Area (EEA), the modernizers began openly to encourage greater links to the EC.

Hence, just as the EC was beginning to revive under the 1992 program, the DNA modernizers attempted to revive the Norwegian relationship to the EC. Recognizing the divisiveness of the issue in Norwegian politics, they sought to keep the issue contained within the elite levels of Norwegian society. However, this strategy was impossible to maintain. The anti-EC, left socialist party (SV) and rural-oriented center party (SP) were determined to criticize any move that the DNA made toward the EC.

With the end of the Cold War and the collapse of communism, the EC and its 1992 project gained immense legitimacy. This encouraged the Norwegian modernizers to push harder for Norwegian integration through the EEA and for eventual EC membership. However, despite these changes Norwegian public opinion toward EC membership hardly shifted in the promembership direction.[19] Furthermore, the EEA agreement did not go as smoothly as planned. Difficulties in the EC Council, Parliament, and Court delayed and distorted it. All the while, anti-EC groups were organizing and gearing up for a new antimembership drive, similar to the successful rejection of the EC in the 1972 referendum.

In the Norwegian local elections in September 1991, the EC (despite the DNA's attempts to minimize its importance and keep the debate at an elite level) and unemployment (at the time a post–World War II high of 6 percent) became the major issues. Both issues combined to hurt the DNA. Since the DNA was in power, it was responsible for unemployment, and the vast majority of voters thought that EC membership would only aggravate the unemployment problem. The election results clearly indicated that opposition to the EC was growing. The SV increased its vote from 6 percent to 12 percent and the SP increased its vote from 7 percent to 12 percent, while the pro-EC DNA declined from 36 percent to 30 percent (its worst result since the 1920s).

Despite these reversals, the modernizing leadership of the DNA has continued to push for greater EC integration and eventual membership. However, with the ongoing difficulties of the EEA agreement, the current difficulties over the Maastricht Treaty, and the failure of the development of EC social policy (a key element in the DNA's justification for joining the EC), support for EC membership has continued to decline in Norway and within its social democratic movement.[20]

For the British social democratic movement (Labour party and Trades Union Congress, TUC)—since the first debates over EC membership in the 1950s and 1960s, to the membership referendum in 1975, to the demand for withdrawal from the EC in the early 1980s—the EC has been a divisive and costly issue.[21] However, since the mid- to late-1980s, Labour and the TUC have been portraying themselves as united, reborn Europeans.

To understand this change, one must explore two main British developments: the transformation of British industrial relations in the 1980s and the electoral collapse and partial recovery of the Labour party during the same period.

The British industrial relations system, until the early 1970s, was based on four main traits: a common law tradition, free collective bargaining, an exclusion of the state from collective bargaining, and a socially acceptable balance of power between capital and labor.[22] However, following the relatively poor performance of the British economy in the post–World War II period, attempts were made in the late 1960s (by the Labour party), early 1970s (by the Conservatives), and mid-1970s (by Labour) to solve these economic difficulties through a transformation of the industrial relations system. These attempts concentrated on increasing state direction and corporatist institutions in the British industrial relations system in order to increase industrial peace and cooperation and to control inflation. However, these early attempts failed to transform the existing system and consequently to remedy its underlying weakness.

With the return of the Conservatives in 1979, the transformation of British industrial relations took a radically new turn. Margaret Thatcher and her followers were convinced that one of the most important causes of Britain's economic difficulties was the power of the trade unions. In order to weaken their power, she concentrated on weakening the statutory immunities that protected the trade unions from the common law. Through various legislative acts (the employment acts of 1980, 1982, 1988, and 1990, and the trades union act of 1984), the Thatcher government drastically weakened the ability of unions to form closed shops, to organize, to be recognized by employers, to regulate their internal activities, and to strike.

How has this development influenced the TUC's relationship to the EC? Until the mid-1980s, the focus of the British unions and the TUC was primarily national; they believed in their ability to prevail under conditions of free collective bargaining and, therefore, to derive benefits from keeping the state out of industrial relations. In general, British labor was either antagonistic or indifferent to the EC.[23]

However, by 1987–1988 the TUC began to become more Europe oriented. This was due to the growing realization of the positive aspects of the EC's 1992 project (especially its social dimension and Social Charter) and the continuing electoral successes of the Conservatives (winning the 1983 and 1987 elections). As Thatcher continued to weaken the unions' legal rights and the Labour party seemed incapable of returning to power, the TUC began to turn to the EC for help. The TUC realized that the EC's Social Charter (a legal charter of basic workers' rights) could be used to create an EC legal floor below which present and future Thatcher-like governments would be incapable of going.[24] Since that time, despite some continuing divisions within the TUC over the EC, the TUC has been strongly pro-EC. Recently, it even supported the Maastricht Treaty on political and economic union.

Not surprisingly, given its close ties to the TUC, the British Labour party has had a very difficult relationship to the EC. Furthermore, like the Norwegian social democratic movement, the Labour party can be divided into pro-EC modernizers, pragmatic traditionalists, and anti-EC leftists.[25] The fluctuations of Labour party policy toward the EC can usually be closely linked to the rise and fall of these groups within the party.

With its defeat in the 1979 election, the power of the left grew substantially within the Labour party. With the election of the left-leaning Michael Foot to the leadership of the party, the growing influence of the left's nationally based economic vision (the Alternative Economic Strategy), and the departure of the pro-EC right wing out of the party to form the Social Democratic party, taking Britain out of the EC became one of the central planks in the Labour party platform.

However, following the disastrous 1983 election (the Conservatives obtaining a massive majority in the House of Commons and the Alliance parties polling almost as much as Labour) the power of the left within the party began to decline with the rise of the more pragmatic and electorally oriented modernizer, Neil Kinnock. Membership in the EC was once again accepted, and the EC began to be seen in a much more instrumental light.

Following the 1987 election, a number of developments occurred that led the party to endorse the EC. First, Kinnock initiated a policy review process in order to modernize the party and make it more electorally viable. The modernization process included distancing the party from the trade unions, weakening the ability of party factions to control party institutions, and increasing the power of the party leadership. These reforms, which weakened the left within the party, strengthened the power of the pro-EC right.[26]

Second, with the rise of Kinnock, the party abandoned its nationally oriented Alternative Economic Strategy. Instead, integration into the dynamic EC and its 1992 project to create a type of German social capitalism became the primary economic goal.

Third, following Labour's disastrous showing in the European Parliament elections of 1979 (winning only seventeen out of seventy-eight seats), the party substantially improved its electoral performance at the European level. In 1984 it won thirty-four seats, and in 1989 it won forty-five out of eighty-one seats, making it the largest bloc of social democrats in the Parliament. This greatly strengthened the pro-Europeans within the party.

Fourth, a pro-EC policy was electorally advantageous for Labour. It undermined the appeal of the pro-EC Alliance parties. Furthermore, as the Labour party's European policy became more positive and unified in the late 1980s and early 1990s, the Conservatives' European policy was becoming increasingly divisive. Since the fall of Margaret Thatcher in November 1990 (partially due to her opposition to the EC), the Conservatives have been strongly divided over the EC. Every pro-EC step that John Major has taken has been opposed by Thatcher and a substantial group of Conservative party backbenchers. Before the April 1992 election, Kinnock presented a united party with a positive EC policy, while the Conservatives presented a divided one. Labour seemed to have improved itself so much that even the *Financial Times* supported it in the election.[27]

Nevertheless, this was not enough to elect a Labour government in the April 1992 election. Since the election, both parties' policy positions have continued on their divergent trajectories. John Smith (Kinnock's successor) has continued to modernize the Labour party and staunchly supports its pro-EC policy. The Conservatives, especially due to the difficulties regarding the Maastricht Treaty, continue to be openly divided over the issue. However, it is important to remember that Labour's unity is one of opposition, not of position. If they had been elected, cracks in EC policy unity would have surely developed, especially over the Maastricht agreement.

Trends in Norway and Britain

In the stronger Norwegian movement, the EC continues to be a divisive and costly issue. Organizationally, ideologically, and electorally the EC creates difficulties for the Norwegian movement.

First, it creates a destructive division within the movement between short- and long-term strategies and goals. For the pro-EC modernizers, the EC provides long-term goals and strategies, but due to the strength of Norwegian social democracy, the short-term costs of integrating into the EC are relatively high. Anti-EC radicals and traditionalists make extensive political gains by stressing these costs. However, they have yet to create a viable long-term alternative to EC membership or integration.

Second, the EC is used by the modernizers to weaken the link between the DNA and the dominant trade union organization, the LO. Arguing that European integration, instead of the nation-state, should be the focus of social democracy, modernizers encourage the unions and the party to delink from each other and build firmer links with their European Union or party colleagues. Further, EC oriented DNA modernizers see the party/union link as out of date and electorally costly. As the EC has developed, modernizers have been strengthened within the movement and the DNA/LO link has been subsequently attacked.

Third, due to the responsiveness of the Norwegian electoral system (proportional) and party structure (composed of a divided right and a hegemonic social democratic party on the left), the issue has badly divided the left and could end the hegemonic electoral dominance of the DNA. The left as a whole (the DNA and SV combined) has continued to do relatively well in the late 1980s and early 1990s, maintaining around 45 percent of the total vote. However, as the dominance of the DNA has continued to decline (from around 40 percent to 30 percent of the total vote) and SV has continued to grow, cooperation between these two parties is essential if a social democratic government is to be formed. Nevertheless, cooperation between these two is virtually impossible given DNA's support for the EC and SV's opposition to it.

Fourth, the EC weakens ideas and organizations of Norwegian class and national solidarity. Traditional Norwegian social democracy was based on a symbiotic idea of class solidarity and Norwegian nationalism. Class solidarity provided the foundation of the specific social democratic organizations (the DNA and LO). Norwegian nationalism directed the social democratic movement toward creating universalistic citizenship rights and benefits within Norwegian society. When modernizers shift their focus from the nation-state to the EC, they are forced to weaken these two foundations. Class consciousness and class-based organizations are extremely limited at the EC level. Furthermore, EC "nationalism" is virtually nonexistent. Hence, social democratic modernizers abandon the basic tools of social democracy without replacing them with comparable forms of EC-wide class and social solidarity.

For the weaker British movement, the EC relationship has provided both costs and benefits for the modernizing leadership. The EC and the 1992 project have been particularly beneficial to the social democratic modernizers within the British movement. They have provided viable short- and long-term goals and strategies. In the short term, modernizers can emphasize the benefits the EC social dimension and social policies would generate if they could be adopted. In the long term, the creation of some type of German social capitalism, based on a more cooperative relationship between capital and labor within a competitive international context, provided them with a more electorally viable strategy than the earlier nationally based Alternative Economic Strategy. It also helped them to change the electorally costly relationship between the party and the TUC. By stressing the need to Europeanize British industrial relations, Labour party modernizers have been able to distance the party from the unions and thus undercut the criticism of union control over the party.

However, this pro-EC strategy also contains negative elements or implications for British social democracy. First, as the 1992 election demonstrated, the electoral advantages of a pro-EC position for the modernizers might not be enough to return them to power within the constraints of the existing plurality-based British electoral system and three-party system. The collapse of the Alliance parties has eliminated one threat to the Labour party. However, the Liberal party and other small, regional parties have been able to attract enough votes such that Labour is not capable of challenging Conservative party hegemony.

Second, current Labour party and TUC unity over the EC is clearly a product of the defensive nature of British social democracy's current position. Within the Labour party, it has been relatively easy to demand party unity over the EC since it provided such obvious political benefits in relation to the divisions within the Conservative party. Recent Labour party debates over Maastricht suggest that if the party had been in power, serious divisions over EC policy might have emerged. Similarly, despite its recent support for the Maastricht Treaty, the TUC is not without divisions.

Third, it is important to emphasize that the central reason why the EC is not a threat to the present British social democratic movement is that its movement has been so weakened in the 1980s that even the few social democratic elements that the EC does offer seem to be an improvement on the current British situation. Lacking the strong, centralized, class-based organizations of the Norwegian movement, the British movement is less disturbed by its integration into the weakly organized, EC-wide class organizations. Moreover, despite its historical strength, confidence in British economic nationalism on the left has virtually collapsed. Linked to this is the success of the Conservatives in the 1980s at strengthening free market ideology and weakening social solidarities. With such a weak position, it is no surprise that British social democracts are more positive toward the EC.

Comparisions

Several interesting points emerge from a comparison of the Norwegian and British cases. First, there appear to be virtually no differences between the effects of the EC on social democratic movements within the EC and outside of it. The EC strengthened the position of the modernizers in both the Norwegian and British social democratic movements. It provided them with a vision and strategy for reorganizing their own movements. Hence, the growing importance of the EC during the 1992 project period has compelled all European social democratic movements to respond to it.

Second, the impact of the EC varies with the strength of the national social democratic movement. In the weaker British movement, support for the modernizers was a key element in the electoral revival of the party. In the stronger Norwegian movement, the increased power of the modernizers split the movement and greatly weakened the electoral position of the DNA. Based on this, one would expect to see growing divisions over entry and integration into the EC in the stronger social democratic movements of the former EFTA states of Sweden, Finland, and Austria.[28] Also, one would expect to see continued support for the EC within weaker social democratic movements.

Third, the form of the electoral and party systems should play a central role in the specific manifestation of the various social democratic movements' responses to the EC. In the rigid British system, anti-EC social democratic voters and activists had nowhere to go once Labour firmly supported the EC. Their only channel for action was to attempt to influence the party internally. In the Norwegian case, anti-EC voters and activists could and did desert to the left socialist and center parties, greatly weakening the DNA.

Conclusion

Let us now return to the original question: Can modernized social democracy linked to a post-1992 EC provide the basis for a revival of traditional social democracy? Despite its successes in the British case, modernized social democracy linked to the EC does not seem capable of recapturing traditional social democracy's golden age of the 1950s and 1960s. As was demonstrated in the first section of this chapter, the EC is incapable of protecting European social democracy from the four main international forces that are undermining it. In fact, in many ways the EC and its 1992 project amplify these forces. Furthermore, modernized social democracy lacks social and class solidarities and organizations and a strong link to the national community. Traditional social democracy derived its power from its ability to motivate and organize progressive social forces within a nation-state. Modernizers ignore or abandon the need for national social organization and solidarity. By cutting their link to the national "community" and linking themselves to a European "community," utterly lacking in Europe-wide class ties and social solidarities, they increasingly weaken the social solidarities necessary to create the organizational basis of traditional social democracy. Thus, neither the EC, modernized social democracy, nor the combination of the two seem to offer a general way out of social democracy's deeper malaise. For the foreseeable future, social democracy will continue to stagnate, caught between the declining abilities and primacy of the nation-state and the socially and organizationally undeveloped EC.

Notes

1. Stephen Padgett and William Paterson, *A History of Social Democracy in Postwar Europe* (London: Longman, 1991).
2. Due to its heterogeneity and its historical evolution, social democracy is inherently difficult to define. Thus, it is necessary to present an ideal-typical example of "traditional" social democracy to use as a reference point. Mark Kesselman does an excellent job of capturing its main principles in the following quote:

> First, an acceptance of a capitalist economy is coupled with extensive state intervention to counteract uneven development. Second, Keynesian steering mechanisms are used to achieve economic growth, high wages, price stability and full employment. Third, state policies redistribute the economic surplus in progressive ways, through welfare programs, social insurance and tax laws. And, finally, the working class is organized in a majority-bent social democratic party closely linked to a powerful centralised, disciplined trade union movement.

See Kesselman's "Prospects for Democratic Socialism in Advanced Capitalism: Class Struggle and Compromise in Sweden and France," *Politics and Society* 11, no. 4 (1982), p. 402.
3. In recent years there has been a growing literature on the crisis of social democracy: T. Koelble, *The Left Unraveled: Social Democracy and the New Left Challenge in Britain and West Germany* (Durham: Duke University Press, 1991); C. Lemke and G. Marks, eds., *The Crisis of Socialism in Europe* (Durham: Duke University Press, 1992); Adam Przeworski and John Sprague, *Paper Stones* (Chicago: University of Chicago Press, 1986).
4. The most well known is, of course, Jacques Delors. However, every major

Western European social democratic party has its EC supporters.

5. I use the term social democratic "movements" to describe the combination of political party and trade union organization that is the basis of classic social democracy.

6. "Europe 1992 and the Developing Countries," Special Issue, *Journal of Common Market Studies* 29 no. 2 (1990); J. Harrop, *The Political Economy of Integration in the European Community* (Aldershot: Edward Elgar, 1989), chap. 9.

7. Articles 130f through 130n of the Maastricht Treaty encourage this type of advanced technology industrial policy.

8. For an overview of these attempts, see Wolfgang Streeck and Philippe Schmitter, "From National Corporatism to Transnational Pluralism: Organized Interests in the Single European Market," *Politics and Society* 19 no. 2 (June 1991).

9. Commission of the European Communities, *The Social Dimension of the Internal Market,* Special Edition of *Social Europe,* Luxembourg, 1988.

10. R. Inglehart, "Changing Value Priorities and European Integration," *Journal of Common Market Studies* 10, no. 1 (1971); and R. Inglehart, *The Silent Revolution: Changing Value and Political Styles Among Western Publics* (New York: Princeton University Press, 1977).

11. Commission of the European Communities, *Treaty on European Union* (Luxembourg: Publications of the European Community, 1992), p. 29.

12. This plan was called the "Delors 2 package" and attempted to increase current EC revenues from 1.2 percent of member state GNP (currently totalling US$ 82 billion) to 1.37 percent of GNP by 1997 (increasing the total to an estimated US$ 112 billion). This plan was flatly rejected at the June meeting of the Council in Lisbon. The latest British proposal (November 1992) calls for a much more modest increase in the budget from 1.2 percent to 1.25 percent by 1999.

13. The term "social democratic welfare state" implies a distinction between the more universalistic "social democratic" elements and more market oriented elements of a given welfare state.

14. Recent works on EC social policy include: P. Lange, "The Politics of the Social Dimension," in A. Sbragia, ed., *Euro-politics* (Washington: Brookings Institution, 1992); H. Mosley, "The Social Dimension of European Integration," *International Labour Review* 129, no. 2 (1990); M. Rhodes, "The Social Dimension of the Single European Market: National Versus Transnational Regulation," *European Journal of Political Research* 19, nos. 2 and 3 (March and April 1991).

15. Wolfgang Streeck and Philippe Schmitter, op. cit., p. 152. Emphasis in the original.

16. The strength of a movement is primarily dependent upon its organizational and institutional structure. Indicators of greater strength include: party and union membership levels, corporatist nature of the industrial relations system, and universalistic development of the welfare state. For all of these aspects, the Norwegian movement is stronger than the British.

17. With a proportional electoral system and six major parties to chose from, the Norwegian system is much more flexible and responsive than the British plurality electoral system with it two and one-half party structure.

18. Some of the major works on the post–World War II history of the relationship between Norway and the EC are: H. Allen, *Norway and Europe in the 1970s* (Oslo: Universitetsforlaget, 1979); Bjørkland, *Mot Strømmen* (Oslo: Universitetsforlaget, 1982); B. Knudsen, ed., *Den Nye Europa-Debatten* (Oslo: Cappelens Forlag, 1989); and N. Ørvik, ed., *Norway's No to Europe,* International Studies Occasional Papers no. 5 (1975).

19. Throughout the early 1990s, public opinion toward the EC has held relatively constant, with 38 percent supporting membership, 38 percent opposing it, and 24 percent uncertain. Opinion within the DNA was divided in a similar way.

20. The public opinion polls of September 1992 show that 36 percent support the EC, 48 percent oppose it, and 16 percent are uncertain.

21. Major works on the British social democratic movement's relationship to the EC include: Kevin Featherstone, *Socialist Parties and European Integration: A Comparative History* (Manchester: Manchester University Press, 1988); Michael Newman, *Socialism and European Unity: The Dilemma of the Left in Britain and France* (London: Junction Books, 1983); L. J. Robins, *The Reluctant Party: Labour and the EEC 1961–1975* (Britain: Hesketh, 1979).

22. Basic works on the British industrial relations system include: Henry P. Brown, *The Origins of Trade Union Power* (Oxford: Oxford University Press, 1986); Ken Coates and T. Topham, *Trade Unions in Britain* (London: Fontana Press, 1988); David Marsh, *The New Politics of British Trade Unionism* (London: Macmillan, 1992).

23. See Paul Teague, "The British TUC and the European Community," *Millennium: Journal of International Studies* 18, no. 1 (1989); Paul Teague, "Trade Unions and Extra-national Industrial Policies," *Economic and Industrial Democracy* 10 (1985).

24. This position can be found in the TUC document, "Europe 1992: Maximising the benefits: Minimising the costs," August 1988, and in the Union of Shop, Distributive and Allied Workers document, "Europe 1992: The USDAW Workbook," 1990.

25. These divisions are similar to the ones used by Stephen George in his work, *Britain and European Integration Since 1945* (London: Basil Blackwell, 1991), p. 73.

26. This policy review process and Kinnock's attempts to modernize the party are reviewed in Colin Hughes and Patrick Wintour, *Labour Rebuilt: The New Model Party* (London: Fourth Estate, 1990).

27. "The Day of Decision," *Financial Times,* April 9, 1992.

28. For example, despite Sweden's current application for membership, recent polls indicate that a majority of Swedes oppose membership.

7

The Global Origins of the Maastricht Treaty on EMU: Closing the Window of Opportunity

David M. Andrews

The December 1991 Treaty on Economic and Monetary Union (EMU) agreed to at Maastricht constitutes a revolutionary agreement on monetary integration between the member states of the European Community.[1] However, recent events have raised serious doubts about the future of the EMU project. The results of the French and Danish referendums (narrow majorities for and against ratification of the Treaty, respectively), together with the dramatic departure of the pound sterling and Italian lira from the exchange rate mechanism of the European Monetary System (EMS) in September 1992, call into question public support for as well as the practicality of monetary union on a Community-wide basis.

It is important to distinguish here among three related but distinct phenomena: the success of the negotiations, problems associated with the ratification process, and the prospects for implementation of the agreement. This chapter focuses on the first of these three issues, with comments on ratification by the national governments. The chapter concludes with a brief summary of contending theoretical explanations of these phenomena, including how the analytical weight assigned to different explanatory factors must vary according to which of these three outcomes—negotiations, ratification, or implementation—is under consideration.

The central argument made here is that the Maastricht Treaty represents a confluence of interests between the French and German governments. Importantly, changes in the international system (not limited to Europe) opened a window of opportunity for France and Germany to come to this agreement on the substance of European monetary union. As this window closes, the viability of the EMU project will increasingly depend on neofunctional variables—that is to say, on the collaborative traditions that have characterized the development of the European Community.

Three important dynamics—two relating to EMU negotiations and one with respect to the ratification process—are examined. First, the French initiative for a single European currency launched in January 1988 and later endorsed by all the major non-German states of the European Community was prompted by de facto reductions in French monetary autonomy. This condition derived from the rapid integration of capital markets (a global phenomenon) and was politically exacerbated by the U.S. dollar's depreciation following the 1985 Plaza Accord. Second, Germany's originally tepid response to the French initiative became revitalized following the collapse of Soviet influence in Eastern Europe and its own impending unification. Strikingly, both these developments—the international integration of financial markets and the collapse of the bipolar balance of power between the United States and the Soviet Union—originated outside of Western Europe. In their absence, European monetary integration efforts would likely have continued to focus on reform of the European Monetary System.

While this conjunction of circumstances proved sufficient to facilitate a Franco-German accord acceptable (in the case of the United Kingdom, only barely so) to the governments of the remaining EC member states, the momentum of 1989–1991 appears to be spent. The effects of international financial integration on monetary autonomy remain in place; the non-German states of Europe, particularly the French, remain concerned about the de facto transfer of European monetary authority to the German Bundesbank. But the diplomatic imperative created by German unification is rapidly receding in importance. Instead, a third dynamic has emerged, created by the costs of financing German unification and exacerbated by a weak dollar policy on the part of the United States. Ironically, while German unification made an elite deal on European monetary union more likely, its economic consequences have reduced the political likelihood that EMU (in the spirit of Maastricht) will be realized. The window of opportunity is closing, leaving the future of European monetary relations in doubt.

International Financial Integration
and French Policy Toward EMU

The immediate institutional predecessors of the Maastricht Treaty on EMU were the European Monetary System organized in 1979 and the capital liberalization directives authorized by the Single European Act (SEA) of 1986. As has been widely noted, successful passage of the SEA was predicated upon the mutual adoption of market-oriented macroeconomic policies by the French, British, and Germans.[2] These governments had been pressured to coordinate their policies because of the constraining effects of heightened international capital mobility (a global phenomenon). The EMS, which in effect institutionalized existing market relations between participating currencies, nonetheless greatly facilitated adaptation to these conditions. By providing a European cast to restrictive policy measures, monetary policy coordination with Germany became politically palatable to the socialist government in Paris.[3] Consequently, the trilateral negotiations taking place among France, Britain, and Germany represented a complex of global economic conditions and European institutions.

This domestic role played by the EMS in France and Europe's other deficit states[4] highlights a long-term political instability in the functioning of the system's exchange rate mechanism (ERM). Austerity programs in these states were linked with the construction of a united Europe in order to prevent leftist constituents from punishing their respective national governments for pursuing essentially right-wing economic policies. In order for this strategy to remain effective, monetary coordination with Germany had to be presented as an interim step toward eventual monetary union. As a consequence, the political expediency of espousing EMU as an objective of foreign and economic policy has been widely accepted by all the major parties within France.[5]

The French government has, as a consequence, been the leading advocate of the Community's eventual adoption of EMU. For example, in 1985 the SEA made reference to "the progressive realization of Economic and Monetary Union." This phrase, suggested by European Commission President (and Frenchman) Jacques Delors, seemed at the time to be more an expression of lofty idealism than a reflection of a pragmatic policy program; political attention was in any event focused instead on the achievement of a unified European marketplace by the end of 1992. (It was perhaps because of the vast chasm that divided EMU rhetoric from reality during the 1970s and early 1980s that British Prime Minister Margaret Thatcher nevertheless consented to the agreement.) But Paris insisted upon the EMU reference; the French feared the impact of still further capital liberalization (as the SEA required) on what remained of an independent national monetary policy.

These fears were not unfounded. As a general matter, whenever it becomes easier for capital to cross international borders—whether because of state deregulation, financial innovation, or technological development—states face a trade-off between pursuing independent monetary policies and enjoying stable exchange rates.[6] Since capital mobility has without doubt greatly increased since 1973, and especially during the past decade, France (as well as the other non-German states of Europe) has been faced with an uncomfortable choice. The balance-of-payments constraints present under conditions of highly integrated financial markets meant that French legal authority or formal monetary sovereignty no longer corresponded with France's capacity to pursue and sustain domestic monetary policies diverging from German practices while at the same time stabilizing the franc's value against the deutschemark. French monetary sovereignty continued to exist as a formal right, but genuine monetary autonomy steadily waned.

French financial liberalization—driven partly by EC directives and partly by the desire to enable French financial firms to compete with their British and German counterparts— further raised the exchange rate costs of pursuing independent policies. Liberalization was largely complete before the 1990 deadline established by the SEA: foreign-exchange controls were relaxed in 1984, 1986, and March 1989; banking liberalization was enacted in 1984; and the French money market was reorganized in 1985, the same year that the Eurobond market in French francs (closed in 1981) was reopened. Studies of covered interest rate differentials find that the last evidence of significant barriers to capital movements into and out of France was in 1986; since then the differential has been close to zero.[7] Of course, not all of capital's heightened mobility is due to public sector initiatives: private sector competition, financial innovation, and technological advances are an important part of the story as well. Nevertheless, the government's decision to promote rather than resist liberalization created an environment increasingly hostile to an independent French monetary policy.[8]

As practical monetary autonomy declined, interest mounted in developing an institutional alternative to the EMS. Of course, the roots of declining French monetary capacity were in the increasing mobility of capital, not the institutions of the EMS per se; indeed, French monetary authorities had originally hoped that the EMS would increase their capacity to sustain temporary divergences from German policy.[9] This did not happen: France was able to use the political cover provided by EMS membership to stabilize the franc's deutschemark value and to fight domestic inflation, but both of these outcomes proved contingent upon convergence with German monetary policy. And while the erosion of French monetary autonomy had been successfully rationalized to the public as a consequence of formal European integration, the subordination of French monetary policy to the Bundesbank continued to irk political authorities in Paris.[10] From this perspective, EMU represented an opportunity for the French to obtain a seat at the table of European monetary policy decisionmaking—entering into decisions that were otherwise effectively under the exclusive control of the Germans.

The End of the Cold War and German Policy Toward EMU

There were essentially three phases to the EMU negotiation process: an initially lukewarm German response to a French initiative of January 1988, a period of heightened expectations precipitated (quite unintentionally) by the actions of the Thatcher government, and the development of a Franco-German consensus on the merits of deeper European integration in light of changes in the international security environment. Whether the Maastricht Treaty on EMU ought to be considered the fulfillment of a specific behind-the-scenes bargain between Paris and Bonn, or simply the consequence of their shared perception of the threats posed by the sudden dismantling of the Soviet empire, is currently impossible to determine. In either event, the collapse of the Berlin Wall in November 1989 and the unification of Germany in 1990 created an elite consensus—a diplomatic imperative of sorts—that the new German republic must be bound irreversibly to the institutions of the European Community. Consequently, beginning in 1989 French support for German unification came to be linked with a deepening of European integration generally and a German commitment to EMU in particular.

* * *

The reemergence of EMU as a major European policy issue was signalled in a major address by French Finance Minister Edouard Balladur in January 1988. Balladur explained his government's continuing objections to the asymmetrical functioning of the EMS, suggesting as an alternative the development of a European Central Bank managing a single European currency.[11] While this proposal was warmly received in France, by the European Commission, and by the governments of Italy, Belgium, and the Netherlands, the German response to Balladur's proposal was initially mixed. Foreign Minister Hans-Dietrich Genscher expressed enthusiasm, but the German finance ministry under Gerhard Stoltenberg was more circumspect. Economics Minister Martin Bangemann eventually endorsed the Balladur position, but Bundesbank President Karl Otto Pöhl argued that EMU could only be a long-term objective and required a politically independent European Central Bank. The German cabinet agreed, accepting EMU as a long-term goal in February 1988. Somewhat reluctantly, Chancellor Helmut Kohl announced in early June that monetary union would be on the agenda for the European Council's upcoming summit in Hannover.[12]

A new phase of EMU discussions was ushered in following the emergence of an ongoing and acrimonious dialogue between European Commission President Jacques Delors and British Prime Minister Margaret Thatcher.[13] Kohl, signalling his solidarity with Brussels in this confrontation, joined with leaders from the other center-right European governments in an October 1988 declaration refuting the Thatcher vision of national sovereignty. Together, these leaders issued a joint statement calling for the convention of an Intergovernmental Conference (IGC) on EMU, dramatically heightening the stakes of the rift between London and Brussels.[14] The following spring brought the report of the Delors Committee for the Study of EMU, authorized at the Hannover summit; Kohl and French President François Mitterrand jointly endorsed its findings prior to the June 1989 meeting of the European Council in Madrid (Thatcher alone expressed dissent). Even during this period, however, German support for monetary union remained heavily qualified. Bonn's endorsement of EMU proposals was intended to contrast with the British position, but was relatively unenthusiastic (compared to the French and Italians) and never failed to mention the pragmatic concerns of the German financial community.

Following the revolutions of 1989, monetary union discussions entered a third phase. Pending unification heightened concerns within the Federal Republic of Germany (and shared by Germany's neighbors) regarding the FRG's future role in Europe. While the unification of East and West Germany had been a consistent aim of the Bonn government since World War II, it had never appeared to be an achievable objective in the near term. This changed suddenly with the fall of the Berlin Wall and the rapid dissolution of the Soviet empire. Consequently, the attention of diplomats and politicians quickly focused on political reform of the European Community, and specifically upon deepening the integration process in order to bind Germany irreversibly to the EC.

In the weeks and months following the dismantling of the Berlin Wall, an informal quid pro quo emerged.[15] European and especially French support for German unification became broadly conditioned upon an accelerated deepening of the Community's institutions. Such deepening was intended to respond to two major foreign policy considerations anticipated in the wake of the Cold War: paralysis in the decisionmaking apparatus of the European Community following the eventual introduction of former Soviet bloc states, and the reemergence of the so-called "German problem."

Formal monetary integration promised to respond to both of these issues and hence was appealing to both French and German authorities. Paris, however, was not originally content to rely upon EMU alone to contain a post–Cold War Germany. In late 1989, France, joined by many of the rest of Germany's neighbors, began to insist upon pledges of further political and especially foreign policy integration within the Community as a condition of its support for unification. In January 1990, Delors, speaking before the European Parliament, suggested that two IGCs be conducted in parallel: one on EMU and one dedicated to institutional reform of the EC. Three months later, in April, Mitterrand and Kohl jointly endorsed this view, calling for twin IGCs on EMU and EPU (European Political Union).

Previously, the political discourse on institutional reform of the Community had emphasized "balancing" certain centralizing provisions of the SEA and EMU in order to address Europe's so-called "democratic deficit." Kohl, indeed, had made a point of calling for enhanced competencies for the European Parliament as early as November 1988. Suddenly, however, the diplomatic imperative created by German unification shifted attention to the development of a common foreign policy for the EC. When the two Intergovernmental Conferences eventually convened in Rome in December of 1990, hopes were high among Eurofederalists for major breakthroughs in the creation of both a foreign policy and a monetary identity for the Community. But the institutional reforms agreed upon at these conferences and included in the Treaty on European Union signed at Maastricht ended up centering almost exclusively on monetary union.

Indeed, the breakdown of the Paris-Bonn axis on political reform of the Community was perhaps the first clear indication that the diplomatic imperative created by German unification had run its course. Mitterrand had earlier joined Kohl in insisting upon enhanced competencies for Strasbourg. But the French president ultimately withdrew his support, declaring at the November 1990 summit that no democratic deficit existed within the Community since "true democracy" was represented in the European Council.[16] With external support at a minimum, Germany's reform proposals languished at Maastricht; for the most part, the Treaty merely codified existing practices.[17] Instead, attention focused on EMU.

The Economic Costs of German Unification and the Prospects for EMU

The diplomatic imperative created by German unification and the end of the Cold War convinced most European elites of the need to bind Germany more deeply into the institutions of the European Community. However, the terms of German unification created economic conditions that have undermined public support across the continent for the Treaty on European Union intended to respond to this imperative. In particular, the one-to-one conversion of East German ostmarks for West German deutschemarks greatly raised the long-term structural costs of German unification. The Bonn government has to date proved unwilling to raise taxes sufficiently to pay these costs; the Bundesbank, in turn, has relied on tight monetary policies to compensate for the inflationary potential created by this fiscal laxity. Given the advanced state of capital market integration within Europe, high German interest rates have been transmitted throughout the Community; in several member states, this has reduced public confidence in elected officials, coming as it does in a time of widespread economic recession. These European-level problems have been further exacerbated by U.S. monetary policy. With short-term U.S. interest rates at thirty-year lows, dollar depreciation has limited the American outlet for European goods and exacerbated the Community's economic downturn. And the dollar's slide against the deutschemark throughout the summer of 1992 increased existing centrifugal pressures within the exchange rate mechanism, eventually leading to dramatic consequences within the currency markets.

* * *

The major impetus behind 1990's rapid timetable for German unification was the acceleration of migration from East to West Germany.[18] The exodus of East Germans, whether via Hungary, Czechoslovakia, Poland, or (after November 9, 1989) directly to the Federal Republic, was crippling the German Democratic Republic's economy. On November 20, 1989, FRG Chancellor Kohl presented a ten-point program envisaging the eventual merging of the two German states. Needing large transfers of West German aid to bail out their struggling state, East German officials were obliged to accept unification terms virtually dictated by Bonn. The March 1990 general elections in East Germany went heavily in favor of Kohl's Christian Democrats and other parties favoring an early economic and monetary merger as well as eventual political unification. By May, the two governments had signed the Treaty on German Economic and Monetary Union, resulting in the replacement of previously nonconvertible ostmarks with deutschemarks effective July 1, 1990.

This agreement was attacked by West German politicians, academics, and the Bundesbank as politically motivated and economically unsound. They argued that a one-to-one monetary conversion would prove costly to West Germany in the short term and would undermine the competitiveness of East German industry in the longer term.[19] Nevertheless, the implementation of German monetary union did prove to be a political success, at least in the short term. The apparent ease of the transition to a unified German economy during the summer of 1990 helped pave the way for the conclusion of the Unification Treaty (August 31) and the Two-Plus-Four Treaty (September 12); the latter agreement lent much needed international legitimacy to what was, in economic terms, a fait accompli. In the run-up to the first all-German general election since World War II, the Kohl government sought to maximize the political gains inherent in this state of affairs. Bonn promised that no tax increases would be needed to finance unification and that no one would be economically worse off while many would benefit from unification.[20] On December 2, 1990, the ruling CDU/CSU/FDP coalition was returned to power on this platform.

In subsequent months, however, as the genuine costs of economic unification became more evident, the Kohl government was hamstrung by its tax pledges. Rather than risking the political ire of its western constituents, it allowed substantial budgetary deficits to accumulate—to the dismay of the Bundesbank. Contrary to the letter of the government's election year promises, social security contributions as well as taxes were in fact raised. The new revenues came at a substantial political cost to the government while remaining insufficient to offset increased transfer payments to the east. Simply maintaining former East German purchasing power (to say nothing of promoting investment in the east) absorbed roughly 5 percent of GDP annually. In the absence of a more solid financing base, Bonn relied upon the capital markets to raise these funds.

Officials at the Bundesbank, wary of the inflationary potential of deficit spending on this scale, felt obliged to compensate for what they regarded as fiscal laxity. Rather than accommodating the expansionary impact of the government's budgetary policies, the German central bank had at its disposal two monetary instruments by which to combat price instability: interest rate policy and the exchange rate. The latter option was somewhat constrained by the deutschemark's participation in the ERM. German monetary officials privately let it be known as early as 1991 that they favored a broad realignment within the exchange rate mechanism, allowing the deutschemark and other strong currencies to appreciate against the remaining EMS participants. These officials broadly hinted that the disinflationary impact of allowing the deutschemark to revalue would enable the Bundesbank to adopt a less rigid stance on interest rate policy.[21] However, most other countries had become almost ideologically committed to a fixed set of parities within the system that had experienced no realignments since 1987.[22] As a consequence, German officials felt obliged to rely solely on domestic monetary policy to combat the inflationary impact of unification.

German interest rates had been steadily rising since 1987. During 1991 and the first eight months of 1992, the Bundesbank increased the Lombard rate (a benchmark for borrowing rates elsewhere in Europe) by 1.5 percent, from 8.25 percent to 9.75 percent. This policy served two important functions: first, by dampening domestic credit creation, the Bundesbank hoped to restrict the growth of the domestic monetary aggregates and thereby fight inflation;[23] and second, the relatively high real rate of return on German assets attracted foreign capital necessary to finance both current account and budgetary deficits.[24] Indeed, the parallels between German macroeconomic policy in the early 1990s and the "Reaganomics" policy mix in the United States during the early 1980s are striking: high interest rates attracting foreign capital to finance large budgetary and trade deficits, resulting in an appreciating currency.[25] Like Reaganomics, however, the German policy proved disruptive to the international monetary system.

The potential for disruption was heightened by the general direction of U.S. monetary policy during this period. The Federal Reserve cut the discount rate eight times over the course of three and one-half years, and reductions in interest rates were increasingly relied upon to stimulate the stagnating U.S. economy in the months prior to the November 1992 election. Short-term U.S. interest rates were just 3.4 percent, their lowest level in thirty years, by September 1992. The international corollary of Washington's loose monetary policy was a substantial slide in the value of the dollar, from 1.67 deutschemark in April 1992 to 1.40 deutschemarks five months later, in early September. This put the dollar's trade-weighted exchange rate at a record low, some 48 percent below its peak in February 1985 (prior to the Plaza Accord).

The summer 1992 slide of the U.S. dollar dimmed hopes for an export-led economic recovery in Europe. Equally importantly, the growing gap between U.S. and German monetary policies was resulting in the overvaluation of several currencies tied to the deutschemark through the ERM. The pound sterling was particularly vulnerable given the importance of Anglo-U.S. trade links. With sterling in the $2.00 range by August, rumors began to sweep the financial markets that an ERM realignment was in the offing. European Community finance ministers sought to quell these concerns at their September 5 meeting in Bath, England, where it was announced that a realignment was unacceptable and, moreover, that no further increases in German interest rates were foreseen. This unprecedented announcement succeeded only in delaying what was increasingly regarded as an inevitable assault by the currency markets on ERM parities. Attentions focused on the upcoming French referendum on the Maastricht Treaty, scheduled for September 20.

In the event, the speculative assault preceded the French vote rather than waiting for it. The Nordic currencies were the first targets, with the Finnish marrka eventually cutting its unilateral peg to the ERM on September 8. The Swedish krona maintained its link to the deutschemark only by raising overnight lending rates to draconian levels: first 24 percent, then 75 percent, and finally 500 percent. Italy's central bank had already raised rates by 1.75 points, to 15 percent, on September 4; by September 10 the lira was nevertheless at its ERM floor once again. On the weekend of September 12–13, German and Italian monetary officials agreed to devalue the lira by 7 percent within the exchange rate mechanism in exchange for a reduction in German interest rates. Again, the Germans broadly hinted (without formally requesting) that if other weak currencies joined in the realignment, there would be greater latitude for interest rate cuts. The British, who had already developed a plan of action intended to help sterling through the following weekend's vote in France, did not volunteer to participate. Frustrated by what they regarded as a refusal to accept the inevitable, Bundesbank officials announced on the following Monday a 0.25 percent reduction in the Lombard rate—an amount widely regarded as the minimum cut possible to fulfill the letter of their agreement with the Italians.[26]

By September 14 ("Black Wednesday") currency traders had focused their energies on the pound sterling. Despite massive intervention in the foreign exchange markets by both the Bank of England and the Bundesbank, and a tightening of British interest rates from 10 percent to 12 percent to, briefly, 15 percent, the pound could not be stopped from falling below its ERM floor of 2.778 deutschemarks.[27] Both the lira (which had fallen below its new ERM floor) and the pound were suspended from the exchange rate mechanism, with sterling slipping below 2.50 deutschemarks in coming weeks. The Spanish and Irish sought to defend their ERM parities by a combination of interest rate hikes and capital controls (the latter a violation of the Commission's single market directives and out of keeping with the existing norms of the EMS). Even the successful defense of the French franc—an undervalued currency on the basis of its purchasing power parity against the deutschemark—required substantial central bank intervention, especially after the *petit oui* of the September 20 referendum. By September 23 intervention had to be supplemented by a rise in benchmark, short-term interest rates from 10.5 percent to 13 percent.

Characterizations of this turmoil varied. English-speaking press accounts regarded the departure of sterling from the EMS as a disaster and a prelude of things to come, whereas continental reports emphasized the endurance of the central or "first-tier" currencies within the narrow band of the ERM. Certainly the events of Black Wednesday did nothing to resolve the sources of the ERM's problems: high German interest rates, the weak U.S. dollar, and the perceived unwillingness of some governments to raise interest rates in the face of general European economic weakness. Consequently, disturbances on Europe's currency markets continued. On November 19 the Swedish government felt obliged to abandon the krona's peg to the ECU;[28] the Spanish peseta and Portuguese escudo were shortly thereafter devalued within the exchange rate mechanism. Further realignments are likely as long as fundamental problems remain unaddressed.

More generally, the events of September 1992 revealed a weakness in the position of most major European governments. The solution they had jointly devised to the problems of reduced national monetary autonomy in an era of relatively open financial borders—namely, the Maastricht Treaty on European Union—has received rough treatment at the hands of both markets and voters. And while the economic and political woes of the Treaty tend to reinforce one another, they are in fact grounded in very different phenomena. Market actors tend to regard the EMU timetable as too lengthy and too tenuous to address adequately the exigencies of highly mobile international capital; hence, rigid European currency parities have once again become, as in the 1970s, an invitation for speculation. Many voters, on the other hand, have come to see the EMU provisions of the Maastricht Treaty as needlessly intrusive into a domain best reserved for national authority.

Support for formal European monetary integration, which had previously been quite high in Germany and especially in France, has rapidly eroded. While factors peculiar to each of these countries have conditioned the shape of national opinion and public dialogue on EMU, changes originating at the global level were what prompted this general erosion of enthusiasm. In brief, national publics across Europe are responding to changes in their situations brought about (politically) by the collapse of superpower rivalry and the unification of Germany, and (economically) by a cyclical downturn of the global economy. The conjunction of these changes has induced reassessments of basic questions of national interest as well as identity.

The irony in this situation should not be missed. European monetary policy coordination, which had been effectively "depoliticized" during the years following the French devaluation of 1983 and the passage of the Single European Act in 1986, has been reintroduced (via the ratification process) as a topic of domestic political discourse under the worst possible economic circumstances: widespread stagnation and rising interest rates. With most of the Community in cyclical decline, non-German publics tend to regard German interest rate policy as nationally motivated and internationally counterproductive; under such circumstances, they are reluctant to institutionalize monetary relations with Germany.

It was the de facto subordination of non-German monetary policy to the Bundesbank that generated official interest in monetary union in the first place, and while the end of the Cold War and the unification of Germany created a window of opportunity for Europe's elite to agree on the fundamentals of monetary union, it has also created circumstances that will make it difficult for these agreements to be acted upon. The emerging schism between public and elite perceptions of Europe's situation, and the appropriate manner in which to move forward, bode ill for the Community's institutional welfare generally. The absence of a frank dialogue on the conditions of national economic life in an environment of integrated capital markets has undermined public confidence in both national leaders and in Brussels, especially now that times are hard. But no such dialogue is likely to emerge until after the Community's current economic downturn has subsided.

Conclusion

Different actors and interests come into play depending on whether one is examining the origins of the Maastricht Treaty, its ratification process, or the prospects for its ultimate implementation by the various states of the European Community. The negotiation of the Treaty itself was largely conducted by governmental elites who sensed that their interests had changed due to extraordinary developments in global economics (in particular international financial integration) and politics (the collapse of the Soviet Union and the end of the Cold War). Put differently, the deals underlying the treaty on EMU were prompted by changes originating outside of Europe itself. Thus, despite a recent resurgence of interest in functionalist integration theory,[29] the successful negotiation of the Maastricht Treaty cannot be understood exclusively in terms of the "inexorable logic of sectoral spillover."[30] While functional and neofunctional arguments of international integration identify elements internal to the process as the critical explanatory variables, it was developments external to Europe that provided the major impetus for the Maastricht accord.

On the other hand, the origins of the Maastricht Treaty cannot be attributed solely to shifts in domestic political coalitions within the European Community. Crossnationally similar changes in ruling coalitions must themselves be explained by references to changes in the political and economic environments in which they take place. Structural changes in both international economics (since the early 1970s) and politics (especially since 1989) have led European states to redefine their conceptions of self-interest, providing opportunities for new political bargains within and between them. Thus, the elite deals underlying the SEA's passage and the SEA's eventual replacement of the CAP as the focal point of political attention within the EC[31] should be regarded as proximate or intervening variables: data to be explained rather than explanations in and of themselves.

Once attention shifts from the origins of the Treaty, however, to the process of its ratification by the various EC member states, the analytical focus does properly shift away from an intergovernmental institutionalist framework[32] to include a greater emphasis on subnational politics. In the domestic politics of Britain, France, and Germany in particular, a pattern of backlash against top-down programs for greater European unity is evident. In more general terms, there is evidence that a schism between elite and public opinion developed during the early 1990s as to the appropriate future course of the Community, especially as the costs of German unification made themselves apparent.

In the late 1980s, confidence in the promised benefits of the Single European Act combined with general economic prosperity and the relative stability of European monetary relations to produce substantial public confidence in EC leaders' further efforts to transform the Community. Global events conspired to dissipate this confidence in the early 1990s. The world economy entered into a period of general slowdown; more specifically, non-German ERM participants found themselves obliged to accommodate a series of German interest rate hikes during a period when domestic economic circumstances seemed to dictate opposite measures. By 1991 and even more by 1992, a significant backlash against greater European integration was evidenced by growing numbers of citizens across the continent.

Interestingly, this public backlash against greater integration was precipitated by the very circumstances that caused many policymakers in Europe's non-German states to favor monetary union. EMU, these officials reasoned, would obviate the problem of adjustment to potentially parochial German monetary policies under conditions of financial integration—exactly the circumstances experienced in the wake of German unification. A European monetary authority, charged with the formulation and conduct of policy for the entire Community, might be more inclined to consider the broader consequences of interest rate decisions.[33] In short, the disruptive effects of Bundesbank policy on the other European states' economies are recognized by most policymakers to be a consequence of European capital market integration, not institutional relations within the Community.

Nevertheless, the absence of effective monetary autonomy under conditions of advanced financial integration is "the one thing which all government ministers know, but which none would ever dare to admit."[34] As a consequence, the public debates in Britain and France (which join Spain as the EC member states with the longest histories of monetary sovereignty) over first passage and then ratification of the Maastricht Treaty were marked by a certain degree of disingenuity. Both the London and Paris governments were held responsible by their respective publics for the poor performance of their economies, and in both cases coordination within the EC was suspected by vocal elements of the opposition to be a primary cause of poor national fortunes. Under these circumstances it was considered impolitic to acknowledge the substantial de facto constraints under which authorities labored. Instead, the public debate during the summer and fall of 1992 degenerated (particularly in the French case) into predictions of economic and political disaster should the Maastricht Treaty fail to be ratified and (particularly in the British case) to insupportable assertions of national autonomy to pursue narrowly defined national interests.

Given the volatility of the ratification process, many analysts have become inclined to downgrade their assessments of the eventual implementation of the Maastricht Treat on EMU. This may prove premature, especially inasmuch as the Treaty itself contains provisions for (among other things) a somewhat flexible, multi-tiered system of European monetary relations. Certainly the prospects for all of the member states moving together toward EMU before the end of the century were diminished by the events of September 1992, but this was never an especially likely outcome in any case. The expected accession to the Community of the EFTA economies, most of whom are likely candidates for inclusion in the inner core of Europe's monetary hierarchy, increases the probability of further institutionalization of European monetary integration. From a political standpoint, the interesting question becomes the relationship of Britain, Italy, and Spain—all large EC members likely to come close to fulfilling but ultimately to fail certain of the Maastricht convergence criteria—with the EMU's so-called "hard core."[35]

It is on the question of implementation that neofunctionalist integration theory is most likely to provide insights. The window of opportunity (however brief) created by the diplomatic imperative of binding Germany to the Community following German reunification has fundamentally altered the terms of political discourse on EMU. Powerful, pent-up structural and neofunctional forces were allowed to assume a particular and distinctive shape, formalized in the terms of the Maastricht Treaty. It will therefore be difficult for dialogue on European monetary relations to return to the *status quo ante,* regardless of the legal fate of the Treaty itself.

Neofunctional integration theory maintains that the integrative lessons learned in other contexts will be applied to monetary unification if the major players, on the basis of their interest-inspired perceptions, desire to do so. The market-driven subordination of the non-German currencies to the deutschemark, institutionalized in the EMS, remains a politically divisive arrangement, demanding some type of institutional adaptation. The motivations of the governments of the non-German states, and especially the French, are relatively unchanged in this regard, while the future definition of German interests remains unclear. Despite this uncertainty, some variety of heightened monetary integration—whether under the terms of the Maastricht Treaty, as a corollary or replacement to it, or under the rubric of a revised EMS—is still likely before the end of the century. The question of who participates in this arrangement, and under what terms, remains open.

Notes

1. The chapter by Wayne Sandholtz included in this volume summarizes the major features of this agreement; they will not be reiterated here.

2. See, for example, Wayne Sandholtz and John Zysman, "1992: Recasting the European Bargain," *World Politics* 42:1 (October 1989):99–100; and Andrew Moravcsik, "Negotiating the Single European Act: National Interests and Conventional Statecraft in the European Community," *International Organization* 45:1 (Winter 1991):29–31.

3. Jeffrey Sachs and Charles Wyplosz, "The Economic Consequences of President Mitterrand," *Economic Policy* 2 (1986):294–295; David Andrews, *From ad hoc to Institutionalized Coordination and Beyond: Twenty Years of European Monetary Integration* (Cambridge, Mass.: MIT Center for International Studies, 1992):19–24.

4. "Deficit states" here refers to states with balance-of-payments deficits, not budget deficits.

5. Witness the unwillingness of either of the two major conservative parties to campaign against Mitterrand's September 1992 referendum in support of the Maastricht Treaty.

6. See for example Robert Mundell, *International Economics* (New York: MacMillan, 1968).

7. Jeffrey A. Frankel and Alan T. MacArthur, "Political vs. Currency Premia in International Real Interest Differentials: A Study of the Forward Rates for 24 Countries," *NBER Reprint No. 1049* (Cambridge, Mass.: National Bureau of Economic Research, September 1988):1096.

8. See for example the discussion by Pascal Petit, "Expansionary Policies in a Restrictive World: The Case of France," in Paolo Guerrieri and Pier Carlo Padoan, ed., *The Political Economy of European Integration: States, Markets and Institutions* (Hemel, Hempstead, Herts., UK: Harvester Wheatsheaf, 1989).

9. In other words, the expectation was that the EMS would function as a crawling peg, allowing for small, periodic realignments. During the period 1979–1983, such conditions did in fact prevail. However, the success of French monetary authorities in achieving their objectives for the real economy under this regime proved to be limited, as inflation continuously eroded whatever temporary competitive advantages were conferred upon domestic industries by devaluations of the franc. Since that time the EMS has greatly limited its initial propensity for parity changes, reflecting a shift in French monetary strategy.

10. This became especially evident in the years following the negotiated decline of the U.S. dollar agreed at New York's Plaza Hotel in September 1985. With the dollar's decline, exports to the United States no longer softened the impact of growing German trade surpluses with its European partners. See Stefano Vona and Lorenzo Bini Smaghi, "Economic Growth and Exchange Rates in the European Monetary System: Their Trade Effects in a Changing External Environment," in Giavazzi, Micossi and Miller, ed., *The European Monetary System* (Oxford: Oxford University Press, 1988); and Marcello De Cecco, "The European Monetary System and National Interests," in Paolo Guerrieri and Pier Carlo Padoan, ed., *The Political Economy of European Integration: States, Markets and Institutions* (Hemel, Hempstead, Herts., UK: Harvester Wheatsheaf, 1989).

11. François Renard, "M. Balladur veut accélérer la construction de l'Europe monétaire," *Le Monde,* January 8, 1988; Philippe Lemaitre, "M. Balladur préconise une stratégie de renforcement," *Le Monde,* January 15, 1988:28.

12. David Buchan and Andrew Fisher, "Curbs on Capital Controls Will Test Finance Ministers," *Financial Times,* June 13, 1988:1. Germany held the rotating

presidency of the European Council, and consequently Kohl had a great deal of influence over the agenda for the June summit.

13. See Stephen George, *An Awkward Partner: Britain in the European Community* (Oxford: Oxford University Press, 1990):192–194.

14. An Intergovernmental Conference is a necessary precondition for amending the Treaty of Rome.

15. Some have argued that an actual backroom deal took place between the French and the Germans linking EMU with the Two-Plus-Four Talks; see for example George Valence, "L'engrenage Européen," *L'Express,* October 19, 1990:19. Wayne Sandholtz, on the other hand, argues that "European integration at present, as in its origins, is motivated by a broad foreign policy goal. . . . Such foreign policy objectives largely explain German support for EMU and account for the rapid steps toward monetary union taken during the period of German unification." ("Choosing Union: The Politics of European Monetary Integration," unpublished, December 1991:22, 24.)

16. "Cardinal differences," *The Economist,* November 3, 1990:56.

17. In the end, the draft treaty on political union produced at Maastricht made some minor adjustments in the legislative terms of representatives of the European Parliament (Article 158 of the Draft Treaty on European Union) and required new Commissioners to submit to a parliamentary vote investiture, the latter being an already-existing practice; See Richard Jacobs and Francis Corbett, *The European Parliament* (Boulder: Westview Press, 1990):261. By contrast, Germany had sought to empower the European Parliament with the authority to elect the president of the Commission, sack individual Commissioners, and initiate legislation.

18. Thomas Mayer, "Immigration into West Germany: Historical Perspectives and Policy Implications," in Leslie Lipschitz and Donogh McDonald, ed., *German Unification: Economic Issues,* International Monetary Fund Occasional Paper no. 75 (Washington, 1990):130–136; Jurgen Kroger and Manfred Teutemann, "The German Economy After Unification: Domestic and European Aspects," Commission of the European Communities, Directorate General for Economic and Financial Affairs, Economic Papers no. 91 (Brussels, April 1992).

19. Even estimates by these critics of the agreement, however, generally fell short of the scale of economic collapse ultimately revealed in the former East Germany; see, for example, *Economic Surveys: Germany 1989/1990* (Paris: OECD, 1990).

20. Indeed, a large tax cut was passed in early 1990. This is only one of several parallels between German macroeconomic policy in the 1990s and U.S. policy during the 1980s, as noted below.

21. Interviews at central banks and finance ministries.

22. For some, like the French, exchange rate fixity was regarded as a necessary step on the road to eventual monetary union. The British were also strong advocates of fixed parities (at least for the pound sterling), though for different reasons. Britain's ERM membership was largely rationalized in terms of its disinflationary consequences, and officials at the Bank of England and HMT believed that these benefits would be lost if the credibility of deutschemark-sterling parity were ever undermined by a formal realignment.

23. The Bundesbank rejected arguments from the OECD and others that singular conditions were responsible for M3's rapid expansion above its target range from the fourth quarter of 1991 onward.

24. A third possible purpose, consistently denied by officials at the Bundesbank but widely suspected outside of Frankfurt, is that such interest rate hikes pressured other governments to accede to the German central bank's requests for a general realignment of ERM parities.

25. Several European officials noted this similarity in interviews.

26. Various press accounts; interviews.

27. Bundesbank President Helmut Schlesinger gave a somewhat ill-advised interview to the press early in the week of September 12, unauthorized (and uncensored) versions of which were immediately leaked to the markets. In the unauthorized version, Schlesinger indicated that a general realignment of ERM parities, including the pound sterling, was in order. This event, which at the very most accelerated events that were already in the offing, nevertheless sparked an angry and virtually unprecedented series of public denunciations between the Bundesbank and HMT; Anglo-German relations briefly fell to post-Thatcher lows.

28. The krona had been pegged to the ECU or European Currency Unit (and hence effectively to the deutschemark) since May 1991, despite the fact that Sweden is a member of neither the EC nor the EMS.

29. For example Robert O. Keohane and Stanley Hoffmann, "Institutional Change in Europe in the 1980s," in Keohane and Hoffmann, ed., *The New European Community* (Boulder: Westview Press, 1991).

30. Ernst B. Haas, *Beyond the Nation-State* (Stanford: Stanford University Press, 1964).

31. Sandholtz and Zysman, op. cit.:100–103; Moravcsik, op cit.:27–44.

32. Moravcsik, op. cit.

33. The notion that EMU represents an opportunity for the inflation-prone states of Europe to seize control of monetary policy and reflate is not supported by the public negotiating record; witness the solid Dutch support for EMU proposals.

34. Interview with British foreign ministry official.

35. Article 109j of the Treaty on European Union specifies four convergence criteria that states must meet in order to participate in the single currency. These criteria concern national inflation rates, the individual government's budgetary position, participation in the narrow (2.25 percent) band of the ERM, and long-term interest rate levels. The hard core of European monetary integration is likely to include Germany, France, the Benelux, and from two to as many as six other strong currency states (including EFTA applicants).

36. Haas, op. cit.:48.

8

Monetary Bargains: The Treaty on EMU

Wayne Sandholtz

The dry elocution and technical wording of the Maastricht Treaty provisions on Economic and Monetary Union (EMU) conceal the intense politics that preceded the agreement. The EMU treaty was a negotiated outcome and its story is therefore one of bargaining and compromise.[1] This chapter explains the shape of the monetary union agreed to at Maastricht by analyzing the bargains it comprises. Even if EMU fails to materialize as foreseen, this analysis can shed useful light on how multilateral bargaining works in the European Community context.

Because the EMU envisioned by the Maastricht Treaty has a German face, it would be easy to conclude that German power explains the bargaining outcomes. Like the Bundesbank, the proposed European Central Bank would have a federal structure, and would be independent of political authorities and committed to price stability. Germany's monetary preeminence might explain the similarities.

However, the explanation based on German power contains both logical and empirical deficiencies. First, if power is the key factor in the motives and behavior of states, then the German desire for EMU is itself puzzling. Why should the Germans favor a change in the monetary regime that will compromise German monetary power? Under EMU, the Bundesbank would no longer set autonomous monetary policies for others to follow if they could; rather, it would be subsumed within the European System of Central Banks (ESCB). Second, the argument based on German power says nothing about the goals of the other EC states. If German wishes had contradicted the objectives of its EC partners, it would have been easy for other states to stall, sabotage, or reject the EMU process at a number of junctures. As I will show, if Germany was pushing its neighbors, it was pushing them in a direction they wanted to go. In fact, there existed a broad consensus among EC governments on many of the fundamental aspects of EMU. The existence of consensus, therefore, explains more than does German power.

Finally, countries that are powerful in terms of traditional, objective measures do not always have their way in international negotiations. Observable power resources do not necessarily convert into bargaining leverage. Much depends on the value that the various actors attach to the potential outcomes, including the "no agreement" outcome. An objectively powerful country that dearly wants an agreement may be in a weaker bargaining position than a supposedly "weaker" country for which an agreement is less imperative. At several points in the EMU negotiations, in fact, the bargained outcome did not match the German position. This chapter suggests a paradox of German power: the presumed advantage was partially nullified by the strong desire of German political leaders for an EMU agreement. The empirical evidence shows that the Germans did not prevail on every issue.

The first section of the chapter explains how a broad consensus on EMU fundamentals created a well-defined area of potential agreement. The most basic issues—central bank independence, the mandate for price stability— simply were not contested. In the second section I posit that failure to make progress on EMU was so unattractive to German political leaders that they were willing to make concessions. The empirical analysis of the EMU bargaining looks at three areas in which the Germans did not get their way entirely: the nature of stage two, the strictness of the convergence criteria, and the deadline for stage three.

Early Consensus

Monetary union in the EC was an idea that caught fire in the late 1980s but that had been smoldering for decades. The Commission had proposed monetary integration to complement the common market as early as 1961.[2] In succeeding years, the monetary union idea flared up occasionally, only to subside when the member states failed to take the necessary substantive steps toward it. The 1969 summit at the Hague committed the Community to achieving monetary union, and the Werner Report of 1970 outlined a three-stage plan. Aspirations for EMU were stifled by divergent national responses to the economic and monetary turmoil of the 1970s (the end of Bretton Woods, the first OPEC crisis). The best the Community could manage were the "snake" and the "snake in the tunnel," through whose revolving doors countries seemed to exit and reenter at their convenience. Establishment of the European Monetary System (EMS) in 1979 revived the EMU ideal. The EMS was supposed to evolve into a monetary union in three stages. Again, in the absence of concrete measures, the idea of EMU subsided.

Finally, in early 1988, memoranda from French Finance Minister Edouard Balladur and German Foreign Minister Hans-Dietrich Genscher fanned the embers. Chancellor Helmut Kohl ensured that EMU would be on the agenda for the Hannover summit in June 1988, at which the heads of state charged the Committee for the Study of Economic and Monetary Union (the

Delors Committee) with assessing how EMU might be realized. The Delors Report emerged in April 1989 and was approved by the European Council at Madrid in June 1989.

- In fact, the Madrid summit formalized a broad consensus, from which only British Prime Minister Margaret Thatcher dissented, that the Community would move decisively toward EMU. The heads of state not only approved the Delors Report but declared that stage one of the three-stage plan it outlined would begin on July 1, 1990, when capital flows would be liberalized in eight of the twelve member states. The summit affirmed that the Delors Report would be the basis for preparations for an Intergovernmental Conference to define the next steps.

The Commission, Belgium, France, Germany, Italy, and Spain took the most enthusiastic view: that agreeing to stage one meant a commitment to stages two and three, which would produce a European Central Bank and a single currency. Only the United Kingdom refused outright to commit to monetary integration. The most striking feature of the Madrid summit was the solid consensus of eleven states in favor of monetary integration along the lines of the Delors plan. Indeed, the consensus was so strong that Thatcher recognized that obstructing progress on EMU would only induce the other states to proceed without Britain.[3]

A full explanation of why EC states desired monetary union is beyond the domain of this chapter; I focus rather on the bargains that defined the *kind* of monetary union it would be.[4] Here also, broad consensus prevailed. The scope of that consensus shows up in many of the crucial points that carried over unchanged from the Delors Report to the Maastricht Treaty. These points can be summarized quite simply:

1. *Price stability* would be the overriding mandate of the monetary union; support for general economic policies of the Community was subordinate to maintaining price stability.
2. The European System of Central Banks (ESCB) would have a *federal structure;* that is, the common monetary policy would be determined at the center, and national central banks, as branches of the System, would be responsible for day-to-day operations.
3. The ESCB bodies would be "*independent* of instructions from national governments and Community authorities."[5]

A few concepts from negotiation analysis can help to explain why this consensus had an important effect on the bargaining. The "zone of possible agreement" is the set of potential negotiated outcomes which each party sees as better than no agreement.[6] The optimal outcomes are those on the Pareto frontier, where the sum of the payoffs for all parties is maximized. But there is an area below the Pareto frontier in which a variety of negotiated agreements would still be better (of higher value) than no agreement. Agreements below the Pareto frontier will have distributional consequences because some parties can benefit more than others. One of the dilemmas of negotiation is that parties compete in that "distributive dimension" by trying to obtain a negotiated outcome that favors them the most.[7] One of the major problems in negotiations is to reduce the number of possible solutions, thus confining the bargaining to a limited portion of the zone of possible agreement and reducing the scope for distributive conflicts.[8] In the EMU process, though in principle many options might have been perceived as superior to the status quo (including even a somewhat reformed EMS), the clear preferences of eleven states were such that many kinds of alternative agreement were ruled out.

The question then becomes, why did national preferences converge on that part of the zone of possible agreement defined by the basic principles of the Delors Report? Two factors explain this strikingly robust crossnational consensus: the shared interests and ideas of EC central bankers and the consensus among national policymakers on the importance of macroeconomic discipline.

The Central Bankers

The central bankers of the EC countries form a community of common interests and beliefs. They share an aversion to inflation and therefore tend to see the main policy objective as defending the value of money.[9] Central bankers favor independence of central banks from political authorities. This derives in part from bureaucratic self-interest: an independent central bank is more powerful and prestigious than one subordinate to politicians. Independence also insulates monetary policy from politicians who might want to inflate for purposes of electoral gain.

The EC's central bankers had crucial inputs into the EMU discussions from beginning to end. The Delors Committee was in effect a committee of the twelve EC central bank governors, augmented by three independent outside experts and Delors himself. Since the governors sat on the Delors Committee in a personal (rather than official) capacity, they could express their own preferences and not simply those of their (in many cases) political masters. The federal structure of EMU would give national central bank governors seats on the ESCB Council. A single currency would be insulated from national political authorities. Finally, rules on excessive budget deficits would extend the powers of the monetary officials to fiscal matters.

The national central banks (along with the ministries of finance) were also represented on the Monetary Committee, whose studies were important bases for the negotiations. Monetary Committee studies in the first half of 1990 stressed an independent European Central Bank (ECB) committed to price stability and further proposed three principles relating to budget deficits: no monetizing of public deficits, no Community bailouts of insolvent member countries, and "excessive" deficits should be corrected.[10] Finally, the Committee of Central Bank Governors prepared the first draft statutes for the European System of Central Banks and the European Central Bank (ECB).

National Policymakers and Monetary Discipline

However, nowhere was it foreordained that national political leaders would share the views of central bankers concerning the dangers of inflation and the virtues of central bank independence. The traditional view, in fact, is that politicians prefer to have a hand on the monetary policy levers in order to time expansionary policies so as to reduce unemployment just prior to elections, with inflation peaking afterwards.[11] The conventional postwar wisdom had been that governments could take advantage of the trade-off between inflation and unemployment; expansionary policies would stimulate growth and create jobs. The inflationary consequences could be dealt with through the exchange rate (devaluation or depreciation). By the late 1970s, however, both inflation and unemployment remained stubbornly high. In fact, the ability of national governments in Europe to pursue independent, expansionary economic strategies had been greatly diminished by the globalization of capital markets. As financial markets became more integrated, governments faced mounting incentives to disinflate.[12] In response to evident policy failure and changes in the international financial system, national leaders began to adapt. Policymakers and large segments of their populations began to view inflation as the primary economic problem. New coalitions favored anti-inflationary measures, leading either to policy changes within governing parties or new governing parties.[13] The emergent preference for price stability manifested itself in most EC countries by the late 1980s. By the end of the decade, national governments had begun to pursue tight monetary policies so as to drive inflation down to German levels.[14]

One hypothesis might be that German power explains the acceptance by national political leaders of ECB independence and the low-inflation mandate. After all, independence and the commitment to price stability are key features of the Bundesbank; German officials stressed from the beginning that the monetary union would have to incorporate those features. Since German participation was absolutely indispensable for any kind of EMU, the other states were forced to accede to German demands. However, most EC governments had converted to disinflation before the EMU project began in 1988. And, in any case, given EC decisionmaking procedures, governments that seriously objected to central bank independence could easily hold out and, if necessary, kill the project by voting against it. As it happened, Germany did not have to strong-arm its partners into accepting ECB independence and the low-inflation mandate. Those aspects of EMU were never in serious dispute. This consensus was based on the shared interests and beliefs of EC central bankers and on the shift of almost all EC governments to disinflationary programs.[15]

The analytical point I have been trying to establish in this section is that a narrow focus on national interests and power is likely to overlook the crucial role of perceptions in defining the zone of possible agreement. The ways in which the parties define the options can make all the difference. A zone of possible agreement can include widely divergent preferences, especially when it comes to distributional questions (or efforts to "claim value").[16] Alternatively, as in the case of the EMU negotiations, a prior consensus on basic principles can focus bargaining on a more restricted region of the zone of possible agreement. Of course, the existence of a consensus did not mean that every issue was resolved, as the next section will show.

Bargaining on EMU

EC governments agreed on the goal of EMU and its general outlines, but German unification affected the ways in which national political leaders perceived the alternatives to a negotiated agreement. For both Germany and its EC partners, unification made the monetary status quo (the EMS) appear distinctly less attractive than it had been before. By diminishing the perceived value of "no agreement," unification strengthened the desires of political leaders to reach an EMU accord. This would explain the willingness of several states—including France and Germany—to compromise on important issues.

German Unification

The drive for monetary union was not a product of German unification. Indeed, the initial French and German proposals for monetary union in early 1988 came well before unification could even be imagined. The fundamental principles of EMU, articulated in the Delors Report, had been agreed by the summer of 1989 before unification began to look like an immediate prospect. What the uniting of the two Germanies can account for is the acceleration of the EMU process that took place in late 1989 and throughout 1990.

Negotiation outcomes are shaped in part by the parties' perceptions of the alternatives to agreement. As the perceived value of "no agreement" decreases, the motivation to reach an agreement increases. Of course, the valuations involved are subjective; in fact, a party can enhance its own payoff from an agreement by making "no agreement" appear less valuable to other parties, which will then be more willing to make concessions.

For German leaders like Chancellor Kohl and Foreign Minister Genscher, unification without some corresponding increase in the level of EC integration was to be avoided. For the sake of future relations with European neighbors, it had to be clear that unification would not lead to a more assertive Germany. In the view of virtually all German political leaders, the best way to reassure EC partners and win their support for unification was simultaneously to strengthen the EC. In addition, in the view of many Germans, European integration was especially important for the Germans themselves as it would prevent a unified Germany from embarking on a path of destructive self-assertion.

German officials were initially divided over EMU. Genscher was the most enthusiastic supporter of EMU and Bundesbank President Karl Otto Pöhl was the most outspoken skeptic.[17] Chancellor Helmut Kohl seemed closer to the skeptics at first, but later planted himself firmly in the Genscher camp.[18] The following year, as the Eastern European drama unfolded, Genscher joined with French Foreign Minister Roland Dumas in issuing a communiqué urging that "a decisive political impulse should be given in Madrid to the implementation of the Delors Report in its totality."[19] Genscher believed that EMU, by tying Germany to the EC, would reduce anxieties provoked by German unification.[20]

In March 1990, with German economic and monetary union approaching, Chancellor Kohl issued an extensive statement on Germany's goals for unification and integration. He reiterated Konrad Adenauer's affirmation that German unity was only conceivable under a European roof. Kohl assured his partners that Germany had no intention of acting like "a bull in a china shop," but rather, "we wish to be German Europeans and European Germans." He also argued that with unification proceeding, the EMU process should be accelerated and linked to political union.[21] In spring 1990, Kohl joined with Mitterrand to call for rapid movement toward EMU and for a parallel IGC on political union. German Finance Minister Theo Waigel, speaking after a Franco-German economic council meeting, emphasized that German unification, rather than being at odds with European integration, would speed it up.[22]

German unification without progress on integration was unacceptable to the country's political leadership, in particular Chancellor Kohl and Foreign Minister Genscher. The perceived decline in value of "no agreement" made German leaders more inclined to accept compromises for the sake of reaching an accord. Interestingly, the same thing was happening with Germany's partners.

In autumn 1989, as German unification began to appear imminent, other EC states began to push for more rapid progress on EMU. France took the lead. President Mitterrand, speaking in Strasbourg in October 1989, declared that the collapse of the Communist order in Eastern Europe meant that the EC "should accelerate its own construction." He called for a conference to begin in autumn 1990 for the purpose of revising the Treaty of Rome so as to include monetary integration.[23] In November, the French president toured the other eleven EC capitals to marshall support for accelerated progress on EMU.[24] At the same time, Prime Minister Michel Rocard stated that France was determined to attain monetary union "regardless of who the partners might be."[25] After the East German elections of March 1990, Foreign Minister Dumas proposed moving up the conference on EMU given the rapid pace of change in Germany.[26]

Leaders in other EC states shared the French concern. A Danish official involved in the EMU negotiations told me that German unification definitely motivated the Social Democratic party (the largest party in the Danish Parliament) to favor further integration.[27] In fact, German unification led to increased support generally in Denmark for strengthening the Community.[28] A Belgian official said that, from a political point of view, there was increased support for EMU as German unification proceeded.[29] The Dutch supported Mitterrand's call for accelerating EMU; just before the Maastricht summit, Andre Szasz, deputy president of the Dutch Central Bank, asserted that without EMU, it was possible that "the western European country we are so familiar with will be replaced by a central European power, with interests of its own which may differ significantly from ours." It was important to guarantee the further integration of Germany in the EC, for, as most EC countries realized, "if we do not grasp this opportunity there may not be another one."[30] The prospect of German unification reportedly increased for Italian political leaders the importance of a more integrated Europe.[31]

To summarize, for Germany's neighbors in the EC, unification without more integration looked distinctly unappealing. This decreased their perceived payoff should there be no agreement on EMU. As with the Germans, the shrinking value of the "no agreement" option meant that the other countries were more motivated to reach an accord on EMU, and thus more willing to make concessions.

The Bargaining

Commission President Delors, even prior to the Madrid summit, advocated the creation of a common central bank and a single currency promptly after the single market came into effect in January 1993.[32] President Mitterrand became the leading advocate of a fast track toward EMU; at the summit he pushed for a firm commitment to completing the IGC by 1992. Britain was the only member against the EMU project, but Prime Minister Thatcher's bargaining position was weakened by two factors: first, the solidity of the consensus among the other eleven in favor of EMU; and second, the fact that an IGC could be convened by simple majority vote, as happened at the Milan summit in 1985.[33] President Mitterrand had also stated publicly that a monetary union could be established with ten or nine members—though he did not desire that result.[34]

The go-fast position gathered more adherents in autumn 1989 as events began to show that German unification could occur in an astonishingly short time. The demonstrations in Leipzig and the fall of the Honecker government occurred in October; the Berlin Wall came down in November. Chancellor Kohl announced his ten-point plan for German unity in November and paired this initiative with support for rapid progress on EMU. At the Strasbourg summit in December 1989, Kohl took the position that the IGC could convene after the East German elections in March 1990.[35] In the event, the summit called for opening the IGC before the end of 1990.

One of the major issues in 1990 during the preparations for the IGC was that of a deadline for starting stage two. Two camps emerged. The French and the Belgians proposed that it begin on January 1, 1993.[36] Italy and Denmark supported this position, arguing that a deadline would compel governments to tidy up their economies.[37] In a paper prepared for the March 1990 informal meeting of the Ecofin Council (and published in August 1990), the Commission had already proposed the January 1993 deadline. Other delegations argued that stage two should begin only after fulfillment of specific economic conditions, which would result in a slower transition and no deadline. Germany led this camp, which included Luxembourg and the Netherlands. Spain also objected to the early deadline, fearing it would not have had sufficient time to implement its economic adjustment plans.[38] The crucial player, however, was Germany. German opposition to an early deadline and insistence on strict economic conditions might have been expected to carry the day, given Germany's monetary preeminence and its indispensability for any EMU.

As it turned out, the most significant split in the debate over deadlines and conditions was that within Germany. Finance Minister Theo Waigel and Bundesbank President Karl Otto Pöhl led the attack against deadlines. Waigel declared that "ideas about dates are less important than the criteria," which would include lower budget deficits.[39] He also argued against fixing any dates for future stages of EMU.[40] Pöhl's cautious attitude to EMU was reinforced in the wake of problems caused by Germany's experience of economic and monetary union between east and west, accomplished in spring 1990.[41] He suggested that five countries with a high degree of economic convergence (Belgium, France, Germany, Luxembourg, the Netherlands) could go ahead with a monetary union and other states would follow when they could.[42] On the other hand, Foreign Minister Genscher advocated rapid progress toward EMU. Chancellor Kohl, with German elections approaching in December, did not commit himself to either camp.[43]

The issue of a deadline was settled at the Rome summit in October 1990. The groundwork for a bargain was laid by a Dutch proposal in September that stage two begin in January 1994 (a year later than under the Belgian and French plan), but that strict economic conditions (on inflation, budget deficits, and interest rates) be met. The Bundesbank endorsed the Dutch plan.[44] Spanish Finance Minister Carlos Solchaga had also proposed a set of conditions for passing to stage two, but these were somewhat less demanding: free movement of capital in the EC (already being achieved under the 1992 program), a prohibition on monetizing budget deficits, participation of all currencies in the ERM, and national legislation to make central banks independent.[45] What sealed a bargain was Chancellor Kohl's willingness to fix a date for stage two, which he reportedly communicated to Italian Prime Minister Giulio Andreotti days before the Rome summit.[46] Kohl did not press for strict conditions, as Waigel and Pöhl had urged. That left the Dutch as the only country favoring strict economic conditions for stage two. The presidency's conclusions to the summit declared that stage two would begin in January 1994 and that the less demanding set of conditions would be met.[47]

Why did the Germans relent on fixing a date for stage two, and then on the strictness of the conditions? Significantly, the German decision came from the highest political level—the chancellor himself. As shown earlier, the strong preference for progress on EMU meant the Germans were willing to make concessions.

The Intergovernmental Conference began in December 1990 and concluded with the Maastricht accord a year later. In between, a number of difficult issues had to be resolved. The remainder of this chapter will examine three crucial outcomes of the negotiations. These dealt with the nature of the institution to be created in stage two, the strictness of convergence criteria to be met for the transition to stage three, and the procedure for deciding to move to stage three.[48]

At the Rome summit, EC heads of state declared that a "new institution, which will be formed by national central banks and a central administrative body," would be created at the start of stage two. Whether this meant the creation in stage two of a European Central Bank was subject to differing interpretations.[49] Draft treaties from the Commission and from France had the European Central Bank being established at the start of stage two. Belgium and Italy sided with France; Greece, Spain, and Portugal agreed with them provided that the transition period to full monetary integration was long.[50] The Germans insisted that the ECB not be created until stage three. The Netherlands and Denmark supported Germany; the United Kingdom opposed setting up anything like a European Central Bank. The Germans argued that real control over monetary policy would remain at the national level until full monetary integration in stage three. Therefore, an ECB with real powers during stage two would divide monetary authority and thus create a dangerous uncertainty about monetary policy. However, without real powers, an ECB in stage two would not be taken seriously.

Jean-Claude Juncker of Luxembourg, who chaired ministerial meetings of the IGC for the first half of 1991, offered a compromise: the ESCB would be established in 1994, but it would not operate as a European Central Bank until 1996. The Belgian finance minister, Philippe Maystadt, proposed calling the stage two body the European Monetary Institute (EMI) and giving it an outside president and vice-president (that is, not chosen from among the central bank governors).[51] The EMI compromise was accepted by the finance ministers in Apeldoorn in late September.[52] However, the debate then shifted to what duties the EMI would have and what its structure would be.

France, backed by Greece, Italy, Portugal, and Spain, wanted the EMI to be an embryonic central bank with its top officials drawn from outside the circle of central bank governors and with control of some of the member states' currency reserves. The Germans held that the EMI should be essentially a committee of central bankers with no genuine monetary powers. The governors of the Bank of England and of the Dutch Central Bank supported the Germans, though the Dutch sided with France and Italy in preferring an outside president for the EMI.[53] A bargain began to take shape in Franco-German meetings.[54] The final version was not concluded until just before the Maastricht summit: the president of the EMI would be an outsider nominated by the central bank governors and appointed by the member states, and the vice-president (in charge of day-to-day operations) would be chosen by the central bankers from among their number. Member states could voluntarily transfer some or all of their reserves to the EMI for it to manage.[55]

As a Danish official involved in the negotiations told me, the EMI bargain was a true compromise: it pleased no one entirely.[56] The French got an outside president for the EMI but not an embryonic ECB. The Germans were satisfied that the EMI was not in any way a central bank but conceded on the outside president and on the voluntary transfer of reserves. The EMI would therefore be more than the existing Committee of Central Bank Governors but less than an ECB. Again, contrary to what one might expect given German monetary preeminence, Germany did not get its way entirely in the design of the EMI.

A second negotiating topic crucial to the EMU plan was the degree to which economic convergence should be a prerequisite for moving to stage three. Germany staked out its position early in the IGC: EMU would require a prior and comprehensive alignment of economic policies.[57] On the general principle of convergence, virtually every delegation agreed. As Commission officials who were present at all the IGC meetings told me, there was broad consensus on the need for convergence of inflation and interest rates at least; the high-inflation countries realized that they had to achieve price stability before entering EMU or it would cost them economically.[58] In fact, by mid-1991 four of the countries whose economies would require the most drastic adjustments—Greece, Italy, Portugal, and Spain—had announced their intention to submit to the EC finance ministers, as part of the multilateral surveillance program, detailed plans for economic convergence.[59]

What energized the debate over convergence criteria was a formal Dutch proposal that conformance to strict, quantitative criteria be required of every state in order to participate fully in EMU. States not meeting the cutoff levels for inflation, interest rates, budget deficits, and exchange rate stability would not enter the third stage. According to Dutch officials involved in the EMU negotiations, they had favored strict criteria for entering stage two; when that did not happen, the only alternative was tough conditions for stage three.[60] Not surprisingly, the Germans endorsed the Dutch proposal, as did the British.[61] Officials from Denmark and Luxembourg told me that their governments sided generally with the Dutch-German position but were more flexible.[62]

What incited vigorous opposition to the Dutch proposal was suggestion that stage three could begin with as few as six states, with no voting by nonparticipants. Italy rejected the Dutch proposal as unacceptable; Greece, Ireland, and the Commission strongly supported the Italian position. Spain agreed with the need for strict criteria in order to be credible with markets and financial actors but also believed that the criteria could not be applied mechanistically. In the IGC, therefore, Spain sided with Italy, though with less fervor.[63] France did not take a strong position; in order to maintain the credibility of its program of economic rigor, France had to favor strict criteria.

In the face of vehement opposition, the Dutch began to retreat from the tough proposal. Belgian Finance Minister Maystadt produced a compromise proposal that eventually proved the basis for agreement. Maystadt proposed flexible application of the convergence criteria, taking into account the trends in economic performance. For instance, if a country's public debt was over the threshold but steadily declining, that would be acceptable.[64] Greece, Ireland, Italy, Portugal, and Spain favored this approach. The issue was not finally resolved, however, until the last ministerial meeting of the IGC.

German officials explained to me that they accepted the Belgian compromise on the final night of the conference. One key was that the French did not strongly support the German position on strict criteria.[65] It became clear that agreement was possible only along the Belgian lines, that is, including trends in the assessment of a country's economic performance. Consequently, the Maastricht Treaty includes demanding convergence criteria but also states that assessments of the fiscal soundness of member states would include examination of the trends of the deficit-to-GDP and debt-to-GDP ratios.[66] The German "golden rule" of public finance (that the government deficit not exceed public investment) was not included as a convergence criterion but was written into the Treaty as an auxiliary condition to be considered.

The bargain on convergence criteria thus included German concessions. But insistence on inflexible criteria ran the risk of producing a stalemate; and German political leaders, as argued earlier, were strongly averse to a "no agreement" outcome. Hence, once again, they overrode the hardliners within their own camp.

The final issue to be examined in this chapter—the procedure for deciding to move to stage three, with its European Central Bank and a single currency—was closely linked to the question of convergence criteria. Would states with derogations or states deciding to opt out of stage three participate in the decision to begin stage three? Should there be a deadline for commencing the final stage? These questions were not fully resolved until the Maastricht summit itself.

The positions taken by the member states corresponded to their stances on the issue of whether there should be a deadline for stage two. The convergence camp, led by Germany and the Netherlands, argued in the IGC that there should be no dates fixed for stage three, but rather that the transition should occur when sufficient states satisfied the convergence criteria. The Dutch proposal of October 1991 had also implied that as few as six states could decide to move to stage three. The opposing view was that a deadline would induce states to make the necessary adjustments and that the decision on moving to the final stage should involve all twelve members.

On the question of a deadline for moving to full monetary union, there was no agreement until the heads of government met at Maastricht. The working proposal was that there would be an initial vote in 1996. If there were not sufficient votes or not enough countries meeting the criteria, the vote would be repeated every two years thereafter until there was a decision. In the final IGC meeting, the French proposed a two-step procedure that had actually been suggested earlier by the Spaniards.[67] Before the end of 1996, an EC summit, on the basis of reports from the Commission and the EMI, would decide whether a majority of states (namely, seven) met the criteria and could decide by unanimity to begin stage three. If on either count there was no decision to start the final stage, by the end of 1998 another summit could decide by majority vote to begin stage three, whether a majority of states met the convergence criteria or not. Eleven states supported the plan; Britain reserved its position for the summit.[68]

At the summit, the French introduced a new wrinkle: if the two-step procedure did not produce a decision to start stage three, it would begin automatically on January 1, 1999. Perhaps the most surprising aspect of the proposal was that the Germans accepted it. Two German officials involved in the negotiations told me that Kohl's support for the final deadline was "very surprising to all of us." The same officials stressed that it was a personal decision by Kohl, and that nobody knew why he took it. They surmised that the chancellor wanted EMU to be irreversible, and the deadline would accomplish that.[69] A British official shared that interpretation. However, Dutch participants offered another explanation: the deadline was accepted because it was proposed at 3:00 AM and everyone was exhausted.[70]

The automaticity of the 1999 beginning for stage three is quite remarkable. German acceptance of the deadline can be explained in large part by the strongly held belief among German political leaders, especially Kohl and Genscher, that decisive progress on EC integration was an essential counterpart to German unification.

Conclusion

The monetary union provisions of the Maastricht Treaty have a German face. An independent, federally structured central bank committed to price stability would look like the Bundesbank. However, it would be a mistake to conclude that German bargaining power in the monetary realm accounts for this outcome. As I have shown, central bankers and political leaders across the

Community shared a consensus that price stability should be the primary goal of monetary policy and that independent central banks were better equipped to realize that goal. In fact, government policies in most EC countries had shifted toward monetary discipline by the mid- or late-1980s. If German power had been necessary to make central bank independence and price stability the bases for EMU, we should have observed substantial persuasion, arm-twisting, and side-payments on the part of the Germans. Instead, we observed agreement, essentially without debate and from the earliest stages, on those fundamental features of EMU.

The explanation based on German power also fails to account for important aspects of the EMU treaty in which the Germans did not entirely get their way. On the stage-two institution, the German position prevailed in that the ECB would not be created until stage three and the EMI would not be an embryonic ECB. However, Germany did concede an outside president for the EMI and the voluntary transfer of reserves to the EMI. Regarding the strictness of convergence criteria, the German-Dutch hard line did not win out. Assessment of compliance with the criteria would include the overall trends and political judgment—not just hard cutoff numbers. On the issue of a deadline for stage three, Germany surprised everyone (including members of the German delegation) by agreeing to the French proposal for an automatic transition in 1999.

As the analysis of the bargaining showed, the crucial factor in explaining these outcomes is not German power but the perceptions of German political leaders of the zone of possible agreement. Bundesbank officials consistently stayed with the tough German position on stage two, convergence, and deadlines. Finance Minister Waigel tended to side with the Bundesbank. But they were regularly overruled by Chancellor Kohl. Why? As German unification became a genuine prospect and then a reality in 1989 and 1990, Kohl's support for EMU solidified. In fact, he saw it as an indispensable accompaniment to German unification. For Kohl, therefore, the perceived value of failing to agree on EMU declined drastically. The alternative to agreement was so reduced in value that it became an outcome to be avoided. Under these circumstances, Kohl was prepared to make important concessions for the sake of agreement.

Objective power resources do not translate directly into bargaining power. A party's perceptions of the alternatives, and thus of the zone of possible agreement, shape the kinds of agreements it will accept. This analysis of the EMU negotiations shows that these notions might be fruitfully applied to other bargaining in the European Community.

Notes

The research for this chapter was made possible by grants from the German Marshall Fund of the United States and Scripps College. The author thanks those national and EC officials who agreed to be interviewed during the summer of 1992; their participation was indispensable, though they must remain anonymous. The author is grateful to Alexander Italianer and Alan Cafruny for helpful comments on earlier drafts.

1. Though there was not a separate treaty on monetary union, I refer to an "EMU treaty" as a shorthand for those portions of the "Treaty on European Union" that refer to monetary integration.

2. See Alexander Italianer, "Mastering Maastricht: EMU Issues and How They Were Settled," in K. Gretschmann, ed., *Economic and Monetary Union: Implications for National Policy-makers* (The Hague: Martinus Nijhoff Publishers, forthcoming), p. 5.

3. "Thatcher Fails to Halt Moves Towards EC Economic Union," *Financial Times,* June 27, 1989, p. 1; Philip Stephens, "Thatcher Rejects Delors Blueprint," *Financial Times,* June 30, 1989, p. 1; "The Meaning of Madrid," *The Economist,* July 1, 1989.

4. For explanations of why EC governments desired monetary union, see the contribution of David Andrews to this volume and Wayne Sandholtz, "Choosing Union: Monetary Politics and Maastricht," *International Organization* 47 (Winter 1993).

5. Committee for the Study of Economic and Monetary Union [Delors Committee], *Report on Economic and Monetary Union in the European Community* [Delors Report] (Brussels, April 1989), pp. 9, 17–20, 35, 36; emphasis added.

6. This terminology comes from James K. Sebenius, "Challenging Conventional Explanations of International Cooperation: Negotiation Analysis and the Case of Epistemic Communities," *International Organization* 46 (Winter 1992), p. 333. The terms "bargaining set" and "bargaining zone" are sometimes used and refer to the same notion. See, for example, H. Peyton Young, "Negotiation Analysis," in H. Peyton Young, ed., *Negotiation Analysis* (Ann Arbor: University of Michigan Press, 1991), pp. 1–23; Margaret A. Neale and Max H. Bazerman, *Cognition and Rationality in Negotiation* (New York: The Free Press, 1991), chap. 2.

7. Neale and Bazerman, *Cognition and Rationality in Negotiation,* p. 20. Sebenius calls this behavior "claiming value"; see Sebenius, "Negotiation Analysis: A Characterization and Review," *Management Science* 38 (January 1992).

8. See Young, "Negotiation Analysis," p. 4.

9. See John B. Goodman, *Monetary Sovereignty: The Politics of Central Banking in Western Europe* (Ithaca, N.Y.: Cornell University Press, 1992), p. 7.

10. See Peter Ludlow, "Reshaping Europe: The Origins of the Intergovernmental Conferences and the Emergence of a New European Political Architecture," in Centre for European Policy Studies, *The Annual Review of European Community Affairs 1990* (London: Brassey's, 1991).

11. See the contributions to Part 2 of Thomas D. Willett, ed., *Political Business Cycles* (Durham, NC: Duke University Press, 1988).

12. See Wayne Sandholtz, "Choosing Union" and the contribution of David Andrews to this volume.

13. See Leon N. Lindberg, "Models of the Inflation/Disinflation Process," in Leon N. Lindberg and Charles S. Maier, eds., *The Politics of Inflation and Economic Stagnation* (Washington, DC: Brookings Institution, 1985), p. 25.

14. Axel Weber measures the credibility of the monetary policies of EMS countries and finds a clear transition from the soft option within the EMS to the hard option. See his "Reputation and Credibility in the European Monetary System," *Economic Policy* 12 (April 1991).

15. Of course, not everybody in every country favored the Delors report model for a European Central Bank. For example, the Italian treasury thought that an ECB should not concentrate solely on price stability but should also be concerned with growth and employment. The Danish finance minister and the Danish Parliament's market committee took the same view. See "Roman Road to EMU," *The Economist,* February 17,

1990, p. 84; *Foreign Broadcast Information Service,* August 24, 1990, p. 32.

16. The term "claiming value" comes from James K. Sebenius, "Negotiation Analysis." On distributional conflicts in negotiation, see Sebenius; Neale and Bazerman, *Cognition and Rationality,* chap. 2; and Stephen D. Krasner, "Global Communications and National Power: Life on the Pareto Frontier," *World Politics* 43 (April 1991).

17. See for example David March and Andrew Fisher, "Pöhl Doubts Need for EC Bank," *Financial Times,* July 1, 1989, p. 1; Peter Torday, "European Central Bank is Years Away Despite Some New Interest in the Idea," *Wall Street Journal,* March 7, 1988, p. 24.

18. "Les marchés des changes rassérénés par les résultats du commerce extérieur americains," *Le Monde,* January 16, 1988, p. 32; David Buchan and Andrew Fisher, "Curbs on Capital Flows Will Test Finance Ministers," *Financial Times,* June 13, 1988, p. 1.

19. Ian Davidson and Robert Mauthner, "West Germany and France Confront UK on Economic Union," *Financial Times,* June 20, 1989, p. 1. The split among German officials was significant. Those most concerned with international political problems, Kohl and Genscher, favored speeding up the EMU process. Officials whose responsibilities were strictly in the economic field (Pöhl, Finance Minister Theo Waigel) remained skeptical and urged less haste and stricter conditions.

20. "Hold On a Minute," *The Economist,* November 4, 1989, p. 58.

21. *Agence Europe,* March 24, 1990.

22. *Agence Europe,* April 10, 1990.

23. David Buchan, "Mitterrand Urges Early Talks on EC Monetary Integration," *Financial Times,* October 26, 1989, p. 1.

24. Laura Raun, "Dutch Back Mitterrand's Plan to Accelerate EMU," *Financial Times,* November 21, 1989, p. 2.

25. "M. Rocard confirme la détermination de la France de réaliser l'union monétaire européenne," *Le Monde,* November 11, 1989, p. 31.

26. "Dumas Suggests Moving Up Monetary Union Talks," *Foreign Broadcast Information Service,* March 20, 1990, p. 12.

27. Interview, Brussels, July 1992.

28. See Peter Ludlow, "Reshaping Europe," p. 404.

29. Interview, Brussels, July 1992.

30. Laura Raun, "Dutch Back Mitterrand's Plan"; David Marsh, "Dutch Fearful of Germany Going Its Own Way," *Financial Times,* November 28, 1989, p. 2.

31. "Not Such a Splendid Isolation," *The Economist,* May 20, 1989, p. 61; "Roman Road to EMU," *The Economist,* February 17, 1990, p. 84.

32. "Not Such a Splendid Isolation," *The Economist,* May 27, 1989, p. 50.

33. Ian Davidson, "West Germany and France Confront UK on Economic Union," *Financial Times,* June 20, 1989, p. 1.

34. "M. Mitterrand n'exclut pas un traité sans le Royaume-Uni," *Le Monde,* July 28, 1989, p. 5.

35. "Deeper, and Deeper Still," *The Economist,* December 16, 1989, p. 51.

36. *Agence Europe,* July 24, 1990.

37. "Not So Fast, Jacques," *The Economist,* September 15, 1990, p. 61.

38. *Agence Europe,* September 10, 1990.

39. David Marsh, "Bonn Supports Bundesbank on EMU, Warns of Rate Tensions," *Financial Times,* September 21, 1990, p. 1.

40. "Not So Fast, Jacques," *The Economist,* September 15, 1990, p. 61.

41. See Katherine Campbell, "Pöhl Warns of Danger in Rapid Moves to EMU," *Financial Times,* September 4, 1990, p. 1; Andrew Fisher, "Bundesbank Adds a Voice to Bonn's Go Slow Chorus on EMU," *Financial Times,* September 21, 1990, p. 10.

42. Philippe Lemaitre, "La banque centrale européenne pourrait être d'abord formée par cinq Etats," *Le Monde,* June 13, 1990, p. 25.

43. George Valance, "L'engrenage européen," *L'Express,* October 19, 1990, p. 19; "Jawohl, EMU," *The Economist,* October 20, 1990, p. 60.

44. Peter Norman, "Stiff Conditions for Next Move to Monetary Union," *Financial Times,* October 8, 1990, p. 5.

45. *Agence Europe,* October 9, 1990.

46. "In Rome, Lions Are An Endangered Species," *The Economist,* November 3, 1990, p. 55.

47. The conditions were: completion of the single market program, initiation (not completion) of a process that would lead to central bank independence in each country by the start of stage three, no monetizing of budget deficits, and no EC bailouts for member countries. Britain did not join in the summit's conclusions, and the Dutch later criticized the lack of strict conditions in the conclusions.

48. The negotiations covered a number of other issues on which member states held strong differences of opinion. Obviously, this chapter cannot address them all. The three issues I have chosen were certainly among the most contentious and were probably the most significant for the substance of EMU. I have chosen not to assess how the opt-out clauses were handled in the negotiations, even though opting out was a high profile question during the IGC. In fact, there existed a consensus from early on that no state would be compelled to join the EMU and, by the same token, that no state would prevent the others from moving to EMU. It was therefore clear that some sort of opt-out arrangement was in the cards.

49. See Alexander Italianer, "Mastering Maastricht"; *Agence Europe,* March 21, 1991.

50. *Agence Europe,* February 27, 1991; *Agence Europe,* March 7, 1991; *Agence Europe,* May 14, 1991.

51. *Agence Europe,* May 14, 1991; *Agence Europe,* June 12, 1991.

52. David Buchan, "Three-point Consensus Ends Two-Speed Europe," *Financial Times,* September 23, 1991, p. 4; *Agence Europe,* September 24, 1991.

53. Peter Norman, "EC Members Divided Over Monetary Institute," *Financial Times,* October 30, 1991, p. 2; Quentin Peel, "France and Germany Fail to Resolve EMU Row," *Financial Times,* November 6, 1991, p. 2; David Marsh, "Dutch Bank Chief Against Powerful Role for EMI," *Financial Times,* November 20, 1991, p. 3; *Agence Europe,* November 6, 1991; *Agence Europe,* November 13, 1991.

54. Andrew Hill, "France and Germany Closer to EMI Accord," *Financial Times,* November 13, 1991, p. 2.

55. *Agence Europe,* December 12, 1991; David Buchan, "Finance Ministers Confirm EMU Accords," *Financial Times,* December 4, 1991, p. 2.

56. Interview, Brussels, July 1992.

57. *Agence Europe,* February 27, 1991.

58. Interviews, Brussels, July 1992; *Agence Europe,* April 9, 1991; *Agence Europe,* May 14, 1991.

59. *Agence Europe,* June 12, 1991; *Agence Europe,* June 13, 1991.

60. Interviews, Brussels, July 1992.

61. David Buchan, "Germans Back Dutch Proposals on EMU Entry," *Financial Times,* September 4, 1991, p. 1; David Buchan, "Germany Ready To Accept Two-Speed Monetary Union," *Financial Times,* August 1, 1991, p. 1.

62. Interviews, Brussels and Luxembourg, July 1992.

63. Interview with a Spanish official, Brussels, July 1992.

64. *Agence Europe,* September 18, 1992. A Belgian official told me that Belgium could not have accepted anything else; interview, Brussels, July 1992. Of course, though performing with the best on inflation and exchange rate stability, Belgium has

one of the higher ratios of public debt to GDP.

65. Interviews, Brussels, July 1992.

66. The specific criteria are: a ratio of public deficit to GDP of not more than 3 percent; a ratio of public debt to GDP of not more than 60 percent; a rate of inflation not more than one and one-half percentage points higher than that of the three best performing countries; interest rates no more than 2 percent higher than those prevailing in the three best performing countries; and exchange rates that have stayed within the narrow band of the ERM for two years. Non-German participants in those final meetings told me that the German state secretary, Horst Köhler, had opposed including trend considerations in the convergence criteria until the end but was overridden by Kohl himself (Interviews, Brussels, July 1992). I was unable to confirm this assertion.

67. Interview with a Spanish official, Brussels, July 1992; *Agence Europe,* September 23, 1991.

68. *Agence Europe,* December 4, 1991; *Agence Europe,* December 5, 1991; David Gardner and David Buchan, "UK Wins Battle To Drop 'Federal' Goal From Treaty," *Financial Times,* December 4, 1991, p. 1.

69. Interviews, Brussels, July 1992.

70. Interviews, Brussels, July 1992.

PART 2

NATIONAL INTERESTS AND EUROPEAN UNION

9

France and the European Union

Françoise de la Serre & Christian Lequesne

The main focus of French foreign policy in 1991 and 1992 was the issue of German reunification. The transformation of Eastern Europe after 1989 upset a delicate European political balance that had existed since the inception of the European Community. The rapid pace of reunification caught President François Mitterrand, no less than most other European leaders, by surprise. As events unfolded, France responded by endorsing reunification in the context of deepening the EC, culminating in the signing of the Maastricht Treaty.

German Reunification and the European Union

Although welcoming the prospect of German unification on the basis of the right to self-determination and the Helsinki principles, the French government was at first hesitant in dealing with the German problem. Mitterrand initially appeared to believe that, for a long time to come, there would still be two German states, even though they might be members of some kind of confederation. His initial support of the Poles over the question of the German-Polish border further damaged a Franco-German relationship that was already suffering from the go-it-alone policy followed by Chancellor Kohl over the timing of the unification process.

However, the guarantees given by Bonn's leaders, the fact that consultations eventually took place within the framework of EPC, and, above all, evidence of an accelerated unification process after the March elections in the GDR gradually eased the situation. With the launching of the economic and monetary unification plan for the two Germanies, the discussion in Paris on integrating the GDR into the Community progressed rapidly from principles to procedures.

While recognizing that the key institutional issues of ratification (e.g., the choice between Article 23 and Article 146 of the Basic Law, or whether to incorporate GDR länder as a bloc or separately) depended on German responsibility alone, Roland Dumas, the French minister of foreign affairs, noted as early as March 20, 1990, that unification "would be easier to realize if the GDR's länder were integrated into West Germany rather than considering integrating a thirteenth state into the Community."[1] This statement reflected Dumas' determination "to put an end to the Franco-German quarrel" quite apparent in bilateral relationships in spite of official statements.[2] At the same time, the French minister was displaying his eagerness to influence events, to accelerate the economic and monetary union process, and to move further toward political union. By endorsing a conference on Economic and Monetary Union (EMU), the French government reasserted the need for parallelism between European integration and German unification. The return of French diplomacy to a quasi-explicit linkage between these two dimensions became apparent with the Franco-German initiative of April 18, 1990, whereby Chancellor Kohl and President Mitterrand suggested to their European partners that in order to reactivate the integration process a second Intergovernmental Conference (IGC) on political union should be convened parallel to the first conference on EMU.

The principle of a second IGC on political union, agreed upon on April 21 at the end of the European Council, was accepted during the European Council in Dublin on June 26. Both conferences opened in Rome on December 14, 1990. What did the French government expect from these conferences?

The Negotiation of the Maastricht Treaty

In 1991, French European policy was obviously dominated by the two IGCs and the drafting of treaties on EMU and political union. For the French government, the European Union reflected two basic objectives: first, the guarantee of parallelism between German unification and European integration; and second, giving priority to the deepening of the Community rather than its further enlargement. During the whole course of the negotiation, France, along with its German partner, attempted to consolidate a leading role in the process of integration.

However, France also sought to preserve a broad scope for intergovernmental cooperation within the Community structure, an objective that has been pursued by all governments throughout the history of the Fifth Republic. This occasionally led to some divergence between rhetorical appeals to the "federal aim" of the Union[3] and the more moderate positions actually held during the negotiations.

The Architecture of the Treaty

The issue of the architecture of the Treaty clearly revealed current French preferences concerning the construction of the Community. France favored the Luxembourg proposal, which envisioned a structure with three pillars of unequal importance, subject to different procedures but united under a common facade. Although, after some hesitation, the French negotiators agreed that the EMU should be part of the European Community pillar (leading nonetheless a slightly separate existence), it seemed advisable to preserve the creation of two intergovernmental cooperation regimes, one for foreign and security policy, and one for Justice and Home Affairs.

The attempt made by the Dutch presidency in October 1991 to return to a single structure encountered opposition from Paris. Like most of its partners, France thus indicated its reservations toward "communitarization" involving renunciations of sovereignty in such sensitive areas as foreign and defense policy or Justice and Home Affairs.

The Economic and Monetary Union

The creation of an EMU, to be achieved at the end of a three-stage process in 1997 or at the latest in 1999, represents the fundamental contribution of the Treaty of Maastricht and at the same time the fulfillment of one of France's main objectives.

Considered both as the driving force of integration after the achievement of the single market and as a means to balance the power of the deutschemark and the Bundesbank within the present EMS, EMU put into effect most of the demands that France presented in the text submitted to the IGC at the beginning of 1991.[4] On the one hand, the prime aim, the irreversibility of the process, is guaranteed by the fact that a deadline (January 1, 1999) has been set for the passage to the third stage. On the other hand, the creation of the European Monetary Institute—the first element of the future European Central Bank—will take place during stage two. Finally, the convergence criteria—inflation, indebtedness, public deficit, and interest rates—are not now major problems for the French government.

The extension of competences. The political union (as distinct from a common foreign and security policy, which is discussed below) meant both increased scope of authority for the Community and, given the current debate about "democratic deficit," a rebalancing of the institutional system.

On the first point, France favored an increase in Community authority but was also less anxious than some of its partners about a clear division of powers between the Union and its member states. Nonetheless, it did subscribe to the principle of subsidiarity written into the Treaty itself. Later on, in the debate to which this issue gave rise at the national level, the French government continued to emphasize its importance.

Within that context, and in the area of "shared competences" between the Community and its member states, Paris has supported the extension of Community intervention to fields that have hitherto been excluded but from now on will be submitted to a qualified majority vote: consumer protection, education, vocational training, health, culture, etc. French negotiators did not succeed, however, in having industrial policy added to that list. Because it establishes a market economy as a fundamental principle "in an open and competitive system," the Treaty contains only an "industrial competitiveness policy" that will have to be decided unanimously. The determined German and British opposition to any sort of intervention in the industrial sector won out over French wishes. However, as a result of strong pressure exerted by President Mitterrand during the Maastricht European Council, France succeeded in bypassing the United Kingdom's opposition to any kind of social policy. The Social Protocol signed by eleven member states represents a considerable step forward for the French government. In part it achieves the goal of a "European social space" advanced since the beginning of the 1980s as a necessary complement to the single market.

Institutional Arrangements

The need to rebalance the institutional system in favor of the European Parliament was accepted by Paris as a necessary counterpart to German concessions on monetary union. Having ensured that the Treaty will strengthen the predominant role of the European Council, where "genuine decisionmaking power belongs,"[5] France occupied an intermediate position among the various points of view. Being neither enthusiastic nor really reluctant on the issue, French negotiators endorsed both the enlargement of the cooperation procedure set up by the Single European Act and the establishment of a "codecision" procedure. It should be noted, however, that they opposed extension of the assent procedure to the fixing of budgetary resources and to constitutional questions as well as to treaty revision.[6] Similarly, France did not favor increasing the Commission's executive authority; President Mitterrand accused it of "taking on things that are not indispensable, giving the impression of being fussy, and causing irritation to a great number of French people."[7]

Common Foreign and Security Policy

Given the relative absence of a European presence in the Gulf War and the lack of European cohesion, caused mainly by the separate initiatives taken by France in order to avoid escalation to a military conflict, the establishment of a Common Foreign and Security Policy (CFSP) was widely supported by French public opinion.

Even though it was a priority in the Franco-German proposals concerning political union, the issue proved to be highly contentious. Having ruled out any "communitarization" of the CFSP right from the very beginning in accordance with permanent national policy choices, France seemed to be satisfied with a formula that does not go far beyond the provisions of the SEA (Article 30). The result seems to lag behind the wishes expressed in the Franco-German proposals, but it is possible that the Yugoslav crisis, by revealing differences in approach compared to other important Community partners, has moderated officially aired preferences. By resisting the idea of a disintegration of the Yugoslav federation, Paris found itself successively at odds with Rome and Bonn about the recognition of Croatia and Slovenia, and with London about the sending of a European buffer force.

The Issue of Defense

Perhaps the provisions of the Treaty that best satisfy French goals in its quest for European Union are those relating to defense. The Common Foreign and Security Policy, concerning "all questions related to the security of the Union, including the eventual framing of a common defense policy which might in time lead to a common defense," represents for Paris, despite the obvious compromise indicated by the formulation, an important step forward. France intends to transform the Western European Union (WEU), "which is an integral part of the development of the Union," into the Union's armed force. The provisions on the formulation of the objective, the framework within which it will be pursued, and the organic link created between the Union and the WEU clearly indicate that the policy pursued jointly by Germany and France, with Spanish support,[8] was finally adopted. Indeed, the WEU is clearly subordinated to the Union, and at the operational level, the initial stages of a permanent politico-military entity have been provided for: a planning staff, increased cooperation in the field of logistics and strategic supervision, and the creation of units under the command of the WEU.

However, the declaration attached to the Treaty and issued by the WEU member states also indicates the limits of acceptance of the French approach and shows that France also had to make some concessions. Indeed, the text stresses that the Atlantic Alliance remains "the essential forum for consultation among its members and the venue for agreement on policies bearing on the security and defense commitments of Allies under the North Atlantic Treaty." The decisions provided for by the Maastricht Treaty may well provoke the return of traditional cleavages between the various partners when the time comes to turn the WEU into the nucleus of a European defense entity. There will also be problems deriving from the existence of national defense policies, especially in the nuclear weapons field, the specificity of which is indeed recognized by the Treaty, but which will eventually have to be addressed and perhaps "Europeanized."

Cooperation in the Field of Justice and Home Affairs

Having been the first to ratify the Schengen Convention[9] in 1991, France had no specific difficulties over the cooperation envisaged in the pillar on "Justice and Home Affairs." Again, Paris staked out a position between those countries that expected a great deal from the new Treaty (in particular Germany, concerning an asylum policy) and those partners most opposed to any Community intervention, above all the United Kingdom. The French government supported the creation of a second intergovernmental cooperation pillar for dealing with these sensitive issues. But apparently it did not oppose some possible future "communitarization" of these issues, allowed for by the juxtaposition of Article 100 C and Article K.9.

The Ratification of the Treaty of Maastricht

French ratification of the Maastricht Treaty involved two stages. In the first stage, Parliament revised the Constitution in order to make it compatible with some provisions of the Treaty. In the second stage, the actual ratification of the Treaty took place through a referendum.

First Stage: the Revision of the Constitution

The Constitutional Council exerts constitutional control in France. In accordance with the Constitution, President Mitterrand, on March 11, 1992, asked the Constitutional Council to determine whether, given the commitments involved in the Treaty, the Constitution ought to be revised. On April 9, 1992, the Constitutional Council announced its decision.[10] It ruled that three specific points in the Treaty called for a prior revision of the Constitution:

1. The right of vote and eligibility of Community citizens in local elections
2. The setting up, at the latest by January 1, 1999, of a single monetary and exchange rate policy
3. The determination of a common visa policy for third country nationals by a qualified majority vote after January 1, 1996

The president of the republic may use two different procedures to start a constitutional revision: the first consists in putting the issue to Parliament; the second, more exceptional, consists in consulting the citizens by way of a referendum. At the outset, the president of the republic decided in favor of the parliamentary procedure, while indicating that, if the Parliament rejected it, he would not hesitate to address the people directly.[11] To use the parliamentary procedure also involves two stages. The revision draft must be passed by the National Assembly and the Senate in identical terms, whereupon the revised draft must be approved by a three-fifths majority of both the National Assembly and the Senate, in joint session as a Congress for that particular occasion.

The April 22, 1992, constitutional bill added a new section, Title XIV, headed "On European Union," to the Constitution.[12] This title comprises Article 88, according to which:

- France agrees to the necessary transfer of authority for establishment of the European Economic and Monetary Union, as well as to fixing rules dealing with border crossing within European Community member states.
- Nationals of European Community member states living in France have the right to vote and are eligible for local office, but can neither exercise the functions of mayor or deputy mayor nor participate in the election of senators.

Started on May 5, 1992, the parliamentary debate required two readings in the National Assembly and one in the Senate before it was finally adopted at the Congress by a three-fifths majority in Versailles on June 23, 1992. This debate was striking in several respects:

1. Although the Maastricht Treaty implies, as first priority, the transfer of authority to the EMU, Parliament, surprisingly, devoted very little time to debate on this issue. Similarly, the adjustment of the Constitution to a common visa policy did not elicit much comment. Indeed, the article of the constitutional draft relating to these two issues was adopted word for word by the Congress.[13] In contrast, parliamentary debate focused on the right to vote and on eligibility of EC citizens to run in local elections (see below), and on the insertion in the Constitution of guarantees reasserting principles of national sovereignty. At the first reading in the National Assembly, the opposition proposed an amendment specifying that the interested parties in European integration were the governments of the member states of the three European Communities (ECSC, EEC, EURATOM). These amendments introduced the symbolic guarantee, important to key voting blocs—especially within the Gaullist "Rassemblement pour la République" (RPR)—that any future federation for the European Union had been ruled out.

2. Unlike the system in Denmark or the United Kingdom, Parliament's control over the government's European policy in France is traditionally weak. The coming into effect of the Single European Act has, however, led Parliament to open a debate on increasing its control. On May 10, 1990, Parliament passed a law requiring the government to inform both the National Assembly and the Senate about ongoing Community negotiations through their delegations for EC affairs.[14] The revision of the Constitution gave the

members of Parliament, whether they belonged to the majority *or* to the opposition, the opportunity to consolidate those improvements by including them for the first time in the text of the Constitution. A new article, inserted during the first reading in the National Assembly, includes two important provisions: first, that the government submits both to the National Assembly and to the Senate, as soon as they have been submitted to the EC Council, any Commission proposal including provisions of a legislative nature; second, that each assembly may express an opinion about those drafts, either within the context of a delegation set up for that purpose or while sitting. The article, slightly modified by the Senate, which eliminated the reference to "Delegations" in order not to offend its permanent committees and replaced giving advice by voting resolutions, shows that members of the French Parliament care about being more involved with the EC decisionmaking process. Furthermore, it demonstrates that the causes of the so-called "democratic deficit" in the European integration system have to be remedied not only at the Community level but also at the national level.

3. In contrast to the adoption procedure applied to ordinary laws, a constitutional revision does not give the last word to the National Assembly, as the text has to be voted in identical terms by the two assemblies. Therefore, the Senate was particularly eager to make the most of its weight in the debates. This weight turned out to be especially important on the eligibility of European Union citizens to vote and run for office in local elections.

One reason for this is that the senatorial majority differs from the governmental majority. Charles Pasqua, president of the RPR group, took advantage of this difference by supporting the reservations of a great majority of the Gaullist electorate with respect to a right which they feared all foreigners (especially North African migrants) might one day assert. Therefore, a Senate amendment was added to the Constitutional Law specifying that *only* European Union citizens could vote and run for office in local elections.

A second reason is that the Senate is elected through indirect universal suffrage by a college of *grands électeurs,* nominated in part by local councilors. Referring to the Constitutional Council's decision, the constitutional bill from the outset specified clearly that EC citizens cannot participate in the election of Senators. However, the Senate thought it necessary to add that those citizens cannot *nominate the Senate electors.* It also specified that the Organic Law, defining all procedures related to application of the right to vote (including eligibility), ought to be voted *in the same terms by both assemblies,* in order best to insure its ruling parity with the National Assembly.

4. Debates as well as votes underlined the fact that divergences over constitutional revision and, therefore, about the Maastricht Treaty cut across party lines. Cleavages are noticeable *within* virtually all political parties. On the one hand, there were factions that approved the revision because they considered the Maastricht Treaty an acceptable stage on the road beyond the

nation-state. On the left, this included a majority of the Socialists. On the right, it included the whole of the centrists (CDS), a majority of the liberals (Parti républicain)—including former President Giscard d'Estaing—and a minority of Gaullists (RPR), including Jacques Chirac, the party's president. On the other hand, there were factions that rejected the revision because they considered intergovernmental cooperation between sovereign nation-states to be the only viable model for a future Europe and saw the Treaty straying from it. Supporters of this view included all the Communists and a minority of the Socialists, who, led by Jean-Pierre Chevènement, place themselves within the "republican-Jacobin" tradition.[15] On the right, proponents of this view included a majority of the RPR, led by two active figures, Philippe Séguin[16] and Charles Pasqua, and a minority of the UDF, under Philippe de Villiers' leadership.[17]

The RPR party was by far the most torn by internal differences, as Jacques Chirac and the main leaders accepted both the constitutional revision and the Treaty, while a majority of the party's parliamentary members was opposed. Therefore, it is not surprising that the RPR adopted an official line of nonparticipation in the vote in the Congress.[18]

Second Stage: the Referendum on September 20, 1992

A referendum to ratify an international treaty is an exceptional procedure in France: it had been used only once before, in April 1972, by President Georges Pompidou to gain acceptance of the treaty enlarging the European Community (to include Denmark, Great Britain, Ireland, and Norway; this last country later withdrew). There are clear reasons why François Mitterrand decided to submit the Maastricht Treaty to a referendum, even though, after the constitutional revision, Parliament's approval would have been enough. Internal political considerations came into play. François Mitterrand's popularity index had never been as low as in the first half of 1992. After eleven years in power, a referendum could either be a means of obtaining fresh legitimacy with a yes vote or a rationale for resignation if the noes carried the day. Perhaps even more important was the realization by Mitterrand as well as some opposition leaders that the European construction was still a very conflictual issue in France. Thus, the best way to avoid any future rejection was to associate the people with it more closely. It was no accident that the official announcement of the referendum was made on June 3, 1992, one day after the Danes had rejected the Treaty of Maastricht.

The referendum provoked an intense debate about Europe throughout French society. Two indicators show the voters' keen interest. First, the level of participation (69.7 percent) was above the average (64.8 percent) registered during the ten polls since 1988. Also, exit polls indicated that 85 percent of the voters decided for or against Europe, and only 10 percent for or against the president of the republic and domestic politics.[19]

The results of the referendum, held on September 20, 1992, were very close: 51 percent yes versus 48 percent no. Of the 25 million votes cast, the difference represented barely 400,000 votes, which, at first sight, gave credence to the notion of a France split down the middle. However, a more precise analysis of the polls reveals that the yes and no votes did not express the opposite views of two homogeneous factions but were the result of the juxtaposition of several cleavages. According to the political scientists Olivier Duhamel and Gérard Grunberg, who produced an interesting analysis of the referendum results in *Le Monde,* there are in fact five cleavages.[20]

The first is *sociological.* Two of the main determinants were the voter's level of education and sociocultural group. The vast majority of people with a university degree voted yes while the noes included many voters who had none. The majority of managers (65 percent), professionals (65 percent), and engineers (67 percent) voted yes, while the majority of farmers (62 percent), employees (53 percent), and workers (60 percent) voted no.[21] This division indicates that in France, European Union is supported by elites. It also shows that the poorest segments of French society are, on the whole, still deeply suspicious of the EC.

The second cleavage is *political.* There is still, with respect to European Union, a centrist France in contrast with a France of extremes. The center-left (the majority of the Socialist party), and the center-right (the majority of the Union pour la Démocratie Française, or UDF) and the center-ecologists (a majority of the Génération Ecologie party) joined together on the yes side. In contrast, the Jacobin left (Jean-Pierre Chevènement's followers within the Socialist party) answered no, as did the formerly Legitimist right (majority of the "Rassemblement pour la République," or RPR). Many members of extreme protest movements voted no: for example, 92 percent of the National Front on the extreme right versus 81 percent of the Communist Party on the extreme left. Contrary to what most commentators thought after the Single European Act, political orientation as a factor explaining voter choice vis-à-vis Europe has not faded away into some overarching consensus.

The third cleavage is more specifically *ideological.* Although this important dimension has not been much analyzed, a connection does exist in France between partisans/adversaries of European Union and partisans/adversaries of more authority in general. Opinion polls show, for example, that opponents of the Maastricht Treaty also tended to support reestablishment of the death penalty, more severe treatment of immigration problems, and stricter school discipline. Thus, opposition to Europe tends to be strong among those segments of the electorate that favor a more authoritarian attitude toward societal questions. This indicates that the European debate in France also has to be examined in the context of the more general debate over tradition and modernity.

The fourth cleavage is *geographic.* The referendum clearly showed a difference between the cities and the countryside. In ninety-three of the ninety-five departments of metropolitan France, the yes score was equal to or higher in the seat of the prefecture than in the rest of the department. With the exception of Marseille, a National Front stronghold, and of some prefectures in the Paris suburbs where the Communists are well established, the majority of large French cities voted yes: 62.5 percent in Paris, 55.9 percent in Lyons, 56.5 percent in Toulouse, 63.4 percent in Grenoble. The more rural the department, the larger the differences between city and countryside. Thus, in addition to the farmers no to reform of the CAP, a rural no to Europe was also expressed. Here again, the causes are likely linked to the contrast between tradition and modernity.

The fifth cleavage is *historical*. Traditionally Christian-Democratic France diverges from republican-secular France as far as European Union is concerned. With the exception of the Paris region, the yes vote majorities clustered in traditionally Catholic regions where the "Mouvement Républicain Populaire" (MRP) was once strongly entrenched, even though it had often been supplanted by the Socialist party by the beginning of the 1970s. This was the case in Brittany, which voted yes by 60 percent, Lorraine (55 percent) and the Loire region (54 percent). In contrast, regions with an old Socialist or Communist tradition tended to produce a majority of no votes. This was the case in Haute Normandie (55 percent), Languedoc-Roussillon (54 percent), Limousin (54 percent), Picardie (57 percent), and Nord-Pas de Calais (56 percent); the latter, although a Catholic region, was pushed to vote no by the traditionally leftist working-class vote in its industrial suburbs.

Thus, French voters made their decision on the Treaty not only according to their individual relationships to national politics, but also to society, history and regional identity. No single cleavage can explain the results of the referendum.

The Debate on Community Enlargement
and Future European Architecture

Will the deepening of the Community as embodied in the Treaty of Maastricht and desired by France, allow for a softening of the positions initially held by the French government on enlargement?

Faced with this problem because of the Austrian application (1989) and because of the upheavals in the East, France, in sharp contrast with the United Kingdom and Germany, at first tried to postpone consideration of new members. While acknowledging that the European system cannot remain confined forever to twelve members, Paris has repeatedly stressed the need "to protect the Community, which is something very specific that works according to rules and depends upon certain principles" and could not be enlarged, in the near future, without suffering dilution.[22] In this context, the relationship of the EFTA countries to the EC was placed within the framework of the "European economic space." For Central and Eastern European countries, France preferred the establishment of association agreements including the possibility of a "political dialogue." It soon became apparent that, in the opinion of French leaders, this association formula showed aim at governing the relationship between the Community and its neighbors in Eastern and Central Europe long into the future. In June 1991, François Mitterrand's remarks that membership of Central and Eastern European countries in the Community could not be envisaged for "des dizaines et des dizaines d'années" was very explicit in this regard.[23]

Thus, the French proposal for a large European confederation is viewed by those countries as a delaying maneuver, aimed at putting off their membership and not as the model of a new European architecture. According to Paris, such a confederation would aim at creating a framework for bringing together all European countries. It would be provided with light political structures of an intergovernmental type (heads of state summits, meetings of foreign affairs ministers) and would aim at organizing cooperation on concrete projects requiring a multilateral approach: environment, transport, energy, immigration.[24]

Since the signing of the Maastricht Treaty and because it can no longer use the argument of the completion of the internal market and the deepening of the Community, France seems to have softened its position on enlargement. It contemplates the opening of negotiations with EFTA candidates once the negotiations related to the future financing of the Community have been completed (Delors II package). In response to its partners' pressure and the not inconsiderable contribution that the membership of wealthy countries would represent for the Community budget, Paris seems to have accepted the prospect of a Community of fifteen or sixteen member states. This is contingent upon the candidates satisfying the Treaty of Maastricht requirements and accepting in particular the provisions of the CFSP by modifying their neutrality status.

On the other hand, the French position has not softened to the point of agreeing to allow Central and Eastern European countries to become members of the Community in the near future. However, France has formally accepted the *principle* of future membership both within the framework of the "European agreements" signed by the Twelve with Hungary, Poland, and Czechoslovakia (agreements that Paris wants to extend to Bulgaria and Romania) and in the bilateral treaties concluded by Paris with the same countries. However, President Mitterrand's insistence on establishing a list of obstacles to their membership, the obvious reservations on imports of eastern agricultural products, and the emphasis on the "confederation" project as the best possible architecture for the European continent show clearly the persistence of French reticence in this area.[25]

However, given the present state of uncertainty over the ratification of the Treaty of Maastricht by two member states (Denmark and Britain) as well as on the implementation of the third stage of EMU, the question of enlargement is not a priority on the Community agenda. The possibility of evolution toward a "variable geometry," which cannot be entirely dismissed, would fundamentally modify the whole approach to enlargement.

Notes

1. *Agence Europe,* January 22, 1990; *Le Monde,* January 23, 1990.
2. See the article by Claire Trean in *Le Monde,* March 21, 1990.
3. R. Dumas's statement in the National Assembly, November 27, 1991.
4. Draft Treaty presented by France on EMU, *Le Monde,* January 30, 1991.
5. President Mitterrand's interview, *Antenne 2,* December 11, 1991.
6. Roland Dumas's press conference, *Bulletin d'information du ministère des Affaires étrangères,* November 12, 1991.
7. President Mitterrand's interview, *Antenne 2,* December 11, 1991.
8. Statement by the ministers of foreign affairs of Germany, Spain, and France, *Le Monde,* October 11, 1991, and statement published after the French-Spanish summit, *Le Monde,* October 27–28, 1991.
9. On June 4, 1991, by 495 votes to 61, the National Assembly approved the Implementation Convention of the Schengen Agreement.
10. Decision no. 96–308 DC. A detailed summary of that decision was published in *Le Monde,* April 16, 1992.
11. See the radio-TV broadcast interview on April 12, 1992, published in *Le Monde,* April 14, 1992.
12. Document of the *National Assembly,* no. 2623, April 22, 1992.
13. Constitutional Law no. 92–554, June 25, 1992, in *Journal officiel de la République française,* June 26, 1992.
14. Law no. 90–385, May 10, 1990, in *Journal officiel de la République française,* May 11, 1990.
15. See Max Gallo, *L'Europe contre l'Europe* (Monaco: Editions du Rocher, 1992).
16. See Philippe Seguin, *Un discours pour la France* (Paris: Grasset, 1992).
17. See Philippe de Villiers, *Notre Europe sans Maastricht* (Paris: Albin Michel, 1992).
18. See *Le Monde,* June 24, 1992.
19. Le Figaro-TF1-RTL poll, September 20, 1992, in *Le Monde,* September 25, 1992.
20. Our discussion of the five cleavages is directly based on Olivier Duhamel and Gérard Grunberg, "Référendum : les dix France", in *Le Monde,* September 25, 1992.
21. See the BVA poll, September 20, 1992, in *Libération,* September 22, 1992.
22. President Mitterrand's press conference at the Rome European Council, December 15, 1990.
23. President Mitterrand's interview on *Radio France Internationale,* June 12, 1991; see *Le Monde,* June 14, 1991.
24. See Elisabeth Guigou's interview in *Politique Internationale,* no. 51 (Spring 1991).
25. See François Mitterrand's important speeches in Berlin, *Bulletin d'information du ministère des Affaires étrangères,* September 24, 1991.

10

The New Germany in the EC

Paul J. J. Welfens

On the eve of unification in October 1990, the Bonn government was optimistic about the prospects of integrating the former German Democratic Republic into West Germany's politico-economic framework. Most EC partners had supported Germany's unification. There was a widespread expectation that closing the east-west income gap in Germany would take less than a decade.[1] In July 1990 financial resource transfers for East Germany were estimated to reach about DM 40 billion annually ($25 billion or 1.5 percent of West Germany's GNP). Moreover, few changes were expected with respect to Germany's pro-integration policy stance in the EC. However, German unification has turned out to be a very costly, difficult, and complex process during which nominal and real interest rates have increased, public deficits have sharply increased, conflicts over income distribution have intensified, and traditional policy stances of the Federal Republic of Germany have been questioned. While the Helmut Kohl government officially continues to endorse EC integration, Germany's poor economic policy has actually undermined it by causing disappointments and imposing unnecessarily high transition costs. Consequently, the German public is less supportive of EC integration than it was in the early 1980s.

The FRG was strongly linked to the EC and the Atlantic Alliance. EC integration enjoyed broad public support despite the fact that Germany—along with France and the United Kingdom—was a net contributor of funds for the EC. West Germany benefited greatly from rising intra-EC trade, rising German exports, and gains from trade and foreign investment in the form of rising real income.

The FRG was also a reliable political ally of the United States and an effective supporter of policy coordination in the G-7 meetings. Reluctance to allow Germany to join in UN military actions had diminished by 1992, although no new consensus has since been established. The Gulf War showed that a united Germany cannot replace the UK as the United States's most important political ally in the EC.

On the eve of unification, Germany enjoyed an economically stable and prosperous economy with a broad social consensus—including social and income policies—that were complementary to the systemic emphasis on competition, entrepreneurship, and a limited role of government in resource allocation. Germany neither embraced industrial policy strategies favored in France, nor did it establish a wide network of state-owned firms typical of France, Italy, Spain, and the UK (before the Thatcher era). Rather, German policy was characterized by a liberal economic stance and anti-interventionist macroeconomics. The politically independent Bundesbank (central bank) was responsible for price stability, while the federal government, in cooperation with the state governments, typically adopted supply-side as well as demand-supporting measures during recessions. Along with the Netherlands, Denmark, and the UK, Germany strongly defended principles of free trade in the EC. Moreover, the "old FRG" together with France, the UK, and Italy contributed to an intra-EC political equilibrium that was further anchored in special Franco-German politico-economic relations.

The Bundesbank's low-inflation policy, in combination with high intra-EC flows of German exports and direct investment, not only made Germany and the deutschemark the anchor of the European Monetary System (EMS) but stimulated two developments: a downward convergence of inflation rates and a move toward an Economic and Monetary Union (EMU) in the EC. EMU implied adjustment pressure for Italy, France, and some other countries, because they had to lift all capital controls, but it also offered prospects for all major EC countries to influence monetary policy and not be permanently subjected to the Bundesbank's policy. Eleven years after the creation of the EMS and the exchange rate mechanism (ERM) as a system of fixed exchange rates, the abolition of capital controls in all major EC countries in July 1990 marked the first stage of EMU, tighter intra-EC monetary policy cooperation and increasing economic convergence. In turn, the Maastricht summit of 1991 brought consensus among EC governments over a new stage two in EMU: as of 1994, creation of the European Monetary Institute, basically a refined EC council of central bankers, with national central banks keeping responsibility over monetary policy. Maastricht also offered a potential switch to absolutely fixed exchange rates in 1997 or 1999; this could then lead some or all EC partners to a common EC currency. However, the turbulent week of realignment in mid-September 1992 (immediately before the French Maastricht referendum) raised many doubts that progressive monetary integration would be feasible. The UK government decided to leave its wide (plus or minus 6 percent) exchange rate band in the EMS in order to let the British pound float.[3] Another devaluation of the peseta and the escudo in November indicated intra-EMS tensions; these are likely to grow during the 1990s if sustained inflation differentials (in need of remedy via devaluation) coincide with a revival of nationalism (discouraging to timely devaluations).

In 1990 the new Germany had a population of nearly 80 million and a labor force of 32 million; in 1991, the labor force had fallen some 300,000, and average per capita income was $21,009. Western Germany recorded net growth through immigration of more than 977,000 (zero natural population growth) in 1990 and some 900,000 more in 1991. Population growth supported economic growth, but per capita output grew, of course, much more slowly between 1987 and 1992. In 1993, West German per capita GNP was expected to decline.[2] While it is West Germany that has to absorb both rising immigration and rising financial costs of German unification, the 16 million people in East Germany face the psychological problems of systemic transformation and unification: the erosion of career patterns, the loss of some 2.5 million jobs (out of 10 million in 1989), the imposition of West German laws and institutions, and the rapid rise of rents in a situation in which many former property owners from West Germany and abroad want to reclaim their housing and industrial property.

As a result of reunification, East Germans no longer proudly claim to be the best in a socialist peer group of CMEA countries but feel that they are at the bottom rung of the all-German society. Nevertheless, although East Germans' economic weight amounts only to some 8 percent of West Germany's national output, at the ballot box in the new Germany the former GDR population represents the equivalent of 25 percent of West Germany's population.

In the following analysis, I examine the politico-economic dynamics of the new Germany and analyze how Germany's role in the EC is changing. The EC itself faces major challenges in the fields of completing the single market program, proceeding toward further monetary integration, and opening up the EC for EFTA countries as well as for Eastern European economies. If for economic or political reasons Germany, France, or Italy become weaker supporters of EC integration in the 1990s, the EC could face another period of stagnation. The close result in the French Maastricht referendum shows that popular support for the EC is diminishing; opinion polls in Germany also show declining pro-EC percentages.

German unification is crucial in terms of the relationship between Germany and its EC partners. It also throws into sharp relief the enormous problems that must be faced in confronting the east-west gap in income and wealth in the whole of Europe. If the EC were actively and substantially to support economic transformation in the former CMEA countries, the problems faced would be even bigger than those faced by West Germany in its attempt to modernize the former GDR economy.

Problems of German Unification

The burden of German unification could erode traditional principles of the FRG's policy, change its role in the EC and the whole of Europe, and contribute to major changes in the relationship between North America and Western Europe. As the German state intervenes more deeply in the process of East German economic restructuring, traditional liberal (nonintervention-ist) policy commitments are weakening. Other EC countries could justify their interventionism and new industrial policies (part of an aggressive EC trade policy) by pointing to Germany's shifting policy stance: East German indus-try will receive huge state and EC subsidies.

Total financial transfers have been even higher—by a factor of four in 1991, or 5 percent of West Germany's GNP. The expected time frame for closing the intra-German income gap is now two decades. While the Bun-desbank and some economists had clearly warned that eliminating the intra-German income gap would be quite costly in view of the obsolescence of 50 percent or more of the GDR's capital stock, the Kohl government promised at first a relatively easy transition to economic restructuring.[5]

The West German economy enjoyed internal politico-economic stability, prosperity, and low inflation rates between 1960 and 1989. An impressive economic record certainly contributed much to the legitimacy of the politico-economic order in the FRG, but whether the new Germany can maintain stability and prosperity in a period of economic and political strains caused by German unification is an open question. Unification, however, brought a widening of the party spectrum, both on the left and on the right, where the "Republicans" have, to some extent, been able to set the agenda of political discourse by emphasizing nationalist issues and anti-EC attitudes. Neither the SPD nor the CDU can expect to reach more than 40 percent of the electorate unless exceptional conditions favor one or the other of these two big parties. This implies that more complex coalitions—and perhaps even a grand coali-tion—need to be formed.

Given the huge pent-up demand in East Germany, most observers ex-pected that German unity would benefit Western European countries as well as Eastern European countries in their role as suppliers of consumer and investment goods as well as intermediate goods. Indeed, German imports rapidly increased in 1991, while exports remained virtually constant, so that the all-German economy recorded a current account deficit: West Germany's high current account surplus, which had hovered between 3 to 5 percent of GNP in the period 1982–1989, suddenly switched to a negative position that could be aggravated during 1992–1993 if other EC economies do not rebound. Germany is no longer a net exporter of capital but increasingly uses foreign savings; indeed, by the mid-1990s it could join the United States in having twin budget and current account deficits. Therefore, the internal problems of Germany will affect the global economy, above all the EC countries. Higher German interest rates have reduced investment, GNP growth, and tax reve-nues not only in Germany but in the whole EC. The intra-EC imbalance of power created by the enlargement of West Germany on October 3, 1990, reinforced this macroeconomic conflict of interests.

Internal Problems of German Unification

Unification raises new problems for a new Germany. Taxes were increased in early 1991, and actual and anticipated transfers for East Germany sharply increased: 140 billion deutschemarks (DM) in 1991 and an estimated 180 billion deutschemarks in 1992; the order of magnitude for transfer payments was wrong by a factor of four at least, and many policy changes became necessary when new problems in East Germany became evident. East Germany's GNP (DM 193 billion) was only 7.4 percent of that in West Germany (DM 2.615 trillion) in 1991. The East German export sector collapsed, reaching sales abroad of only DM 1 billion in May 1992 as compared to the 43 billion of West Germany. Imports increased sharply. East German "imports" from West Germany reached DM 13.5 billion in the first quarter of 1992, while deliveries to West Germany amounted to only 2.4 billion. East Germany's net import GNP ratio was a staggering 87 percent in 1991, while West Germany recorded a net export GNP ratio of 7.2 percent. East German imports from West Germany were six times higher than imports from abroad in May 1992.[6] Thus, unification has turned out to be far more difficult than expected—and promised—by most politicians. The government imposed a surcharge on income taxes in 1991 and planned to raise the VAT rate in 1992. However, these measures are still not sufficient to cope with the financing needs of unification. There is already a visible conflict over burden sharing for financing unification: West German workers have become increasingly reluctant to accept reduced net real wage increases. Facing a rising tax burden and an accelerating inflation rate (which might be temporary), public sector employees went on strike in early 1992. If the expected recession occurs in 1993, wage demands will moderate as a result of higher unemployment, but recession will also make it harder to finance East German reconstruction.

At the end of 1992 wage rates in East Germany had already reached 60 percent of those in West Germany, so productivity must be raised quickly if financial transfers from the west are not to last forever. GDP in East Germany fell from DM 58.4 billion in the third quarter of 1990 to 42.5 billion in the first quarter of 1991 and then increased to 50.1 billion in the fourth quarter of 1991. Productivity in the first quarter of 1990 was DM 6,700 per person, DM 5,500 in the first quarter of 1991, and 7,500 in the fourth quarter of 1991, while gross monthly wages continuously increased from DM 1,290 in the first quarter of 1990 to DM 2,220 in the fourth quarter of 1991. Net real income per worker in East Germany was expected to reach 80 percent of the West German level in 1992.[7] Thus, East Germany has virtually accomplished in three years what took West Germany thirty years. However, this process of catching up has been politically determined. From the standpoint of economic rationality, the divergence between productivity and incomes is likely to narrow over the years.

East German exports stagnated between the third quarter of 1990 and the fourth quarter of 1991 (DM 16.4 billion), but imports jumped from DM 36 billion to DM 61 billion in the period between Economic and Monetary Union and the fourth quarter of 1990. Real GDP fell by 11.4 percent between the second half of 1990 and the second half of 1991, while employment dropped by 18.7 percent so that labor productivity reached one-third of the West German level. In 1992 there was no significant growth of industrial output and productivity in East Germany, and prospects for 1993–1994 are only slightly better.

It will take at least a decade to close the intra-German gap in productivity. Moreover, the gap between east and west is even bigger in terms of per capita wealth. Overall monetary wealth amounted to some DM 2.7 trillion in West Germany in 1990, while private households in East Germany had DM 130 billion.[8] While the East German population represents 20 percent of the all-German population, the output of the former East Germany reached only 8 or 9 percent of West Germany's production in 1990. Even more striking, monetary wealth was just 4.8 percent of that in West Germany. It will take at least a generation to close the intra-German wealth gap which, indeed, might be even higher—when evaluated at market prices—than suggested by the official statistics.

Official unemployment rates in East Germany can be expected to decline to between 10 and 12 percent in 1993–1995. With new factories (e.g., Opel/GM, Volkswagen) becoming operational in 1992, productivity will increase, but whether additional employment will be created to a significant extent is doubtful; increasing local output could create new opportunities for local suppliers, but with the creation of the single EC market—as of January 1, 1993—firms from all over the EC could target the East German markets and producers. The first wave of investment in East Germany benefited West German producers of capital equipment and machinery; the implied increase in West Germany's GNP and tax receipts was not explicitly transferred back to East Germany (federal government expenditures account for only 40 percent of government expenditures in West Germany, so the Bonn government cannot fully control the growth of public expenditures).

In the short term and medium term, a major concern is not about the survival of East German firms but about saving and creating jobs in East Germany. Excessive wage pressure is part of the problem. Wage growth must not consistently outpace productivity growth; otherwise the privatization of the remaining 40 percent of the former state industry would entail massive layoffs without significant opportunities for new employment elsewhere. Wage bargaining accords for East Germany have established an automatic link with the development of West German real wage increases—disregarding the development of productivity in the former East Germany and the question whether the intra-German productivity gap of three to one in favor of West Germany can rapidly be closed. High unemployment rates in East Germany are expected to stimulate westward migration. It is predicted that by 2010 some 2 million people will have left the east, intensifying the competition for jobs and housing in the west, which, of course, is also the preferred place of immigrants, war refugees, and asylum seekers. East German productivity will remain relatively low for some time, partly because in 1991 per capita investment (of private firms) in East Germany was only two-thirds of those in West Germany. State investment in the infrastructural links to West Germany and the whole EC indirectly improves productivity, but at the same time it facilitates the access of external competitors to East German markets and thereby threatens the survival of privatized firms that already face higher unit labor costs than West German firms. Thus, there are only modest prospects for a small economic miracle in the former GDR. Firms facing high wage pressure will be forced to regain price competitiveness not only by upgrading product range but also by increasing imports of intermediate products from neighboring low-wage countries in Eastern Europe. For a successful East German reconstruction, the performance of the West German economy—nine times as big as that in East Germany—is decisive. Strong economic growth in Germany would help EC partners and it would support political stability in Germany. In this context, the deceleration of West German economic growth in 1991/92 is alarming: from 4.5 percent in 1990, economic growth decreased to 3.1 percent in 1991, is expected to reach about 1.5 percent in 1992, and not more than 2 to 3 percent in 1993/94. With the labor force growing at a rate of about 1 percent a year, such growth rates are not impressive; hence, intensified conflicts over income distribution are likely. The social consensus of the FRG is weakening, and extremist parties are gaining support.

Resource Transfers, Budget Deficits, and Privatization

Resource transfers to East Germany in 1991 amounted to almost DM 160 billion, about 60 percent of national income in the former GDR in 1991. While per capita expenditures of the regional and communal governments have almost reached the West German level of DM 7,100, the revenue side looks very different, with a ratio of DM 1,300 to DM 4,600.[9] For West Germany, the other side of the coin is a high budget deficit. There was a change from a balanced budget in 1989 to a deficit GNP ratio of 1.9 percent in 1990, 2.8 percent in 1991, and 3.0 percent in 1992 (from 1991 onward these ratios refer to the all-German GNP). Taking into account as well the borrowing of the railway authorities, the postal system, the Treuhandanstalt (THA), and some special entities set up in the context of German unity, the effective deficit ratio has increased to about 4 percent (still lower than e.g., Italy with 10 percent, or the EC average of 5.5 percent).[10] Although the figures for 1991/1992 are still below the 1975 figure of 6.5 percent, for the world economy it is a new situation in that both the United States and Germany are running high budget deficits. The debt of public authorities could reach DM 1.6 trillion by 1995 (45 percent of GNP), with interest rate payments of some

DM 130 billion annually. If one includes the debt of the Treuhandanstalt (THA)—estimated to reach DM 250 billion in 1995—and the government's commitment to take over old debt in the former East German housing stock (DM 62 billion), the level of public sector indebtedness might even reach DM 1.9 trillion, or 50 percent of 1995 GNP. With highly integrated international financial markets and increasing mobility of real capital, the rising public credit demand in Germany (plus Italy) and the United States will keep global interest rates high.

The desperate state of public administration in East Germany was quickly improved by junior and senior civil servants sent from West Germany. Administrative bottlenecks were thereby reduced relatively quickly. Finally, private business management skills, the crucial factor that is at a premium in all transforming ex-CMEA countries, did not become a sustained bottleneck since younger managers could be motivated to go east and many retired managers from the west were reactivated. Moreover, with almost exclusively West German firms buying into East German industry, firms in the former GDR became part of a functional network of West German firms. Nevertheless, progress in restructuring is slow. While East Germany's output had fallen by one-third in the period 1989–1991, final demand for capital goods and consumption increased by 27 percent.[11] Almost 60 percent of East German incomes were financed by West German income transfers in 1991; similar figures can be expected for several years to come. Public investment plays a decisive role in the former GDR since the ratio of public investment to private investment is about four to one in East Germany, whereas in West Germany the ratio is one to four. After a decade of rebuilding and upgrading the East German infrastructure, the ratio in East Germany should approximate that in West Germany.

With more than 60 percent of the firms privatized in East Germany, the rest obviously face either restructuring, liquidation, or quick privatization. The latter will become more and more difficult, while liquidation will cause political problems; effective unemployment rates will not be allowed to exceed a critical threshold.

With rapid privatization of so many assets in East Germany, there is limited scope for any net revenue from sales proceeds for the Treuhandanstalt and the government, respectively. Legal uncertainties depress the value of industrial property, and many industrial sites have been contaminated.

Sales proceeds from privatization have also been reduced because West German investors absolutely dominate the acquisitions and greenfield investments sector in East Germany. West German savings provide the financial basis for the demand for assets in East Germany. However, increased real interest rates in the German economy have reduced the value of all assets.

The net worth of the THA firms is put at no more than DM 30 billion, and it is quite possible that ultimately liabilities will turn out to be greater than assets. However, the ultimate benefit of privatization is to create competitive jobs, avoid rising future subsidies, and increase future tax revenues. Raising value added by DM 1 billion will generate almost DM 350 million in taxes. Moreover, with a rising number of competitive private firms in East Germany, import competition is reinforced and export capacities are developed such that the all-German economy gradually improves its prospects to build up a current account surplus in the very long term. However, despite the fact that mainly French, Swiss, and Italian companies invested in East Germany and thereby were engaged in the privatization process, the inflow of capital from EC countries, the United States, and Japan has generally been low so far. Xenophobia in East Germany is part of the problem. (Anti-Asian sentiments are, of course, discouraging Japanese investors.)

Immigration Pressure and Xenophobic Reactions

Prior to the 1980s, the integration of immigrants was not highly politicized. After World War II, 10 million refugees and expellees were integrated into the West German economic and political system. During the 1960s, immigrants ("guest workers") were attracted in response to a labor shortage in the FRG. The share of foreign workers in the labor force reached a peak of 11.9 percent in 1973 and had fallen to 8 percent in 1990 in the FRG. By contrast, the percentage of foreigners in the population has increased, namely from 5.4 percent in 1976 to 8.2 percent in 1990.

Foreigners in East Germany represented just about 1.5 percent of the population in the ex-GDR. However, people in the "new länder" lack the West German experience of international mass tourism, multinational firms operating in the country, and high international trade and investment flows. These factors, coupled with the collapse of established rules and authorities, the sharp rise of unemployment, and the perception of many East Germans that they are losers in the process of unification, might explain the violent xenophobic reactions observed in the ex-GDR in 1991 and 1992. Although foreigners in the GDR represent only about 1.5 percent of the population, migrants from other parts of Eastern Europe are increasingly coming to Germany via East Germany. The unification treaty contains a provision that new asylum seekers be assigned on a per capita basis to all länder; thus, East Germany receives about 20 percent of these migrants. There is a common misperception that recent immigrants are, in economic terms, simply competitors in the labor and housing markets. In fact, they have actually been net contributors to financing public households and the social security funds. The widely held belief that immigrants place a strain on public finances is also incorrect. The wave of asylum seekers has, to be sure, led to enormous housing shortages and resulting social conflicts in both East and West Germany. The liberal German asylum rules partly explain why 80 percent of all asylum seekers in the EC came to Germany in the late 1980s, including some 500,000 from the former Yugoslavia.

The main political parties are seeking a new consensus on the question of asylum laws and a possible change of the constitution. Even the liberal FDP has changed its stance and has suggested changing German asylum laws even before a common EC legislation has been agreed upon. In December 1992 the SPD essentially abandoned its resistance to constitutional changes affecting immigration.

Relations Between Germany and the EC

German Inflation Problems and the Bundesbank's Monetary Policy in a Post-Maastricht Perspective

In order to fight inflation, which had reached 4 percent in 1990/91, the Bundesbank raised the discount rate and Lombard rates from a preunification level of 6 and 8 percent, respectively, to post-1948 record levels of 8 percent and 9.5 percent on December 20, 1991, and further raised them in mid-July 1992 to 8.75 and 9.75 before interest rates were reduced in late September. High German interest rates and the demonstrated reluctance of Italy, Spain, and the UK (among other countries) to consider devaluations consistent with cumulative inflation rate differentials vis-à-vis Germany, as well as the nervousness of financial markets immediately before the French referendum, created extreme ERM tensions. When the Bundesbank and other central banks had to intervene massively in the market, the Bundesbank conceded a modest interest rate cut in return for devaluation of the Italian lira; the pound and the peseta were also devalued, and the British government declared that its currency would float until German interest rates came down. Interestingly, the European Parliament's report on German unification had anticipated the problem when it stated in 1990: "Should there be a drastic appreciation of the DM, due for example to a rapid increase in interest rates, then tensions will arise in the Exchange Rate Mechanism of the EMS, in the critical, preparatory phase of the European Monetary Union."[12]

The West German inflation rate (change in the cost-of-living index) had increased from 1.3 percent in 1988 to 2.8 percent in 1989, 2.7 percent in 1990, and accelerated in 1991/92 to 3.5 and 4.5 percent in West Germany, respectively, while the Bundesbank long-term target is to keep the inflation rate below 2 percent. This target was not temporarily increased in the aftermath of German unification. Growth of the broad money aggregate M3 in the first half of 1992 greatly exceeded the 1992 target range of 3.5 to 5.5 percent, which explains why in the context of an almost stagnating German production potential the Bundesbank maintained its anti-inflationary policy stance and raised interest rates until the lira depreciation (September 1992) induced the Bundesbank to reduce the discount rate. The Bundesbank fell victim to an "exchange rate trap" that it had partly created with its high interest rate policy in the first place. The high interest rate policy was designed to reduce the growth of the money supply, but when rising German-EC interest rate gaps—paradoxically partly fueled by disinflation in some EC countries and thereby falling interest rates—attracted huge amounts of speculative capital inflows and forced the Bundesbank to support ERM parities with interventions (buying up the weak currencies against DM), the German money supply rapidly increased. High interest rates became self-defeating for monetary restraint policies.

In view of the Maastricht Treaty, the Bundesbank apparently was eager to regain its leadership in price stability in Western Europe and maintain the anchor role in the EMS that the Bundesbank insists is beneficial for all EC partners. One entry criterion for stage three of Economic and Monetary Union, namely, that inflation rates must not exceed by more than 1.5 percentage points the rate of the three countries with the lowest inflation, gives the Bundesbank and Germany some leverage in indirectly fixing the initial level of EMU three. This of course assumes that Germany again records the lowest EC inflation rate and that the Netherlands and Austria (an EC candidate with good prospects for membership) continue to follow German monetary policy. An additional criterion for EMU is that two years before the Commission reviews pre-entry performance, no devaluation must have been allowed and parity has been maintained in the standard plus or minus 2.25 percent band. Germany's main partner countries are already reluctant to allow a devaluation, even in a transition period in which German monetary policy and sustaining inflation differentials create pressure for devaluation. The high interest policy adopted by the Bundesbank in 1991/1992 is also creating problems in another area of the EMU three entry criteria. EC partner countries with deficit-GNP ratios and debt-GNP ratios of more than 3 percent and 60 percent, respectively, will find it difficult to move toward entry levels if high interest rates slow down economic growth and raise debt growth in the process of rolling over the stock of public debt at increasing interest rates.

The Bundesbank policy drove nominal and real interest rates in EC partner countries to record levels, and short-term rates even exceeded long term rates. This resulted in a slowdown of economic growth in EC partner countries, sharper problems with respect to reducing deficit-GNP ratios in high public debt countries, and great tensions in the EMS. The pound, the French franc, and the Italian lira faced devaluation pressures in the market as many investors rushed into deutschemark deposits whose yield was 6 percentage points higher than U.S. short-term rates. The deutschemark rallied in August 1992, reaching 1.39 to the dollar. Fuelled by the anticipated victory of Bill Clinton in the U.S. presidential race, the deutschemark depreciated vis-à-vis the dollar in late 1992.

On various occasions, most notably at the Bath meeting of EC central bank governors and finance ministers, EC partner countries have criticized the Bundesbank for pursuing an overly restrictive monetary policy whose effects are strongly and painfully reflected in the whole of Europe. The

Bundesbank might indeed have been too restrictive as measured by its own inflation rate target: one may doubt the relevance of an excessive growth rate of M3 (sight deposits, time deposits and savings deposits at statutory notice). Had the Bundesbank's policy indicator been M1 (cash plus short-term deposits), whose growth rates were falling in 1992 and almost within the corridor of 3.5 to 5.5 percent, the Bundesbank might not have maintained a high interest rate policy. Moreover, the sharp appreciation of the deutschemark will indirectly reduce inflation since imported goods will become cheaper. However, German exports will be further slowed down such that Germany's economic growth is reduced, and since EC partners' exports to Germany will strongly rise only if Germany's GNP is increasing, there are reduced prospects for France, Italy, the UK, the Netherlands, and other EC partners to stimulate output expansion by increasing exports to Germany. However, Germany could no longer serve as an economic locomotive as it did in 1990–1991. Moreover, the transmission of Germany's high interest rate policy to EMS partner countries was a particular drag on expansion in EC partner countries with inflation rates below the West German rate.

Trade and Investment Links

The pent-up demand in East Germany strongly stimulated Germany's imports for which the most important sources are the EC partners, Austria, Switzerland, Japan, the United States, and the Asian tigers. Thanks to higher exports to Germany, EC partners could achieve higher economic growth rates. The Bundesbank has suggested that unification-induced changes in net exports to Germany brought half a percentage point of extra economic growth in the EC partner countries in 1991/1992 (see Table 10.1). In 1990/1991 the German import pull amounted for Belgium and France to a growth rate impulse of 1.2/2 percentage points and 0.4/1.7 points, respectively. More than half (54 percent) of French economic growth in 1991 was accounted for by Germany's import pull. For Italy and the UK the figures were 0.4/0.4 and 0.4/0.7 percentage points, respectively; for the whole EC the impact was 0.4 and 0.6 percentage points. However, all EC countries experienced tremors, to varying degrees, as a result of Germany's real interest shock. It is unclear to what extent the growth stimulus was offset by higher interest rates caused by German monetary and fiscal policy (it is clear that countries with a high debt-GNP ratio suffer strongly from the interest rate shock).

German industry is concerned with the strong rise of imports and the stagnation of exports in real terms because this suggests that Germany's international competitiveness is weakening. At the microeconomic level German firms have often maintained their position, but production abroad has increased at the expense of production in Germany (a phenomenon similar to that observed in the case of the U.S./U.S. firms in the 1970s). Only if

Table 10.1 Contribution of German Import Pull to GDP Growth in Selected European Countries (in 1989 prices, billions of currency units).

Country		Change in Bilateral Trade Balance with the DM Area (in national currency)	Contribution of the Change in the Balance (in percentage points)	Share of the Change in the Balance in Overall Growth (in percent)
B**	1990	+ 75.1	+ 1.2	31
	1991	+132.6	+ 2.0	137
FR	1990	+21.6	+ 0.4	59
	1991	+40.8	+ 0.7	96
DK	1990	+7.8	+ 1.0	59
	1991	+8.3	+ 1.1	96
IR	1990	+0.3	+ 1.3	18
	1991	+0.2	+ 0.9	59
IT	1990	+4,226.9	+ 0.4	16
	1991	+4,522.3	+ 0.4	27
NL	1990	+5.3	+ 1.1	28
	1991	+6.5	+ 1.3	63
SP	1990	+85.1	+ 0.2	5
	1991	+27.6	+ 0.1	3
UK	1990	+1.9	+ 0.4	38
	1991	+3.5	+ 0.7	*
P	1990	+11.5	+ 0.2	4
	1991	-57.5	- 0.8	•
GR	1990	-7.9	- 0.1	•
	1991	-4.4	- 0.1	•
(ECU)	1990	+14.4	+ 0.4	33 EC
(ECU)	1991	+21.0	+ 0.6	88 EC

Source: Deutsche Bundesbank *Monatsberichte der Deutschen Bundesbank,* vol. 44 (July 1992).
* Entry not meaningful as change in GDP (gross domestic product) or in the bilateral trade balance was negative.
** includes Luxembourg.

Germany's inflation rate falls under the average of the most important trading partners would its industry enjoy the stimulus of a silent real currency depreciation (as long as no offsetting realignments take place).

Foreign direct investment outflows have reached new record levels, while inflows remain very low. On balance, foreign direct investment creates new jobs abroad, not in Germany. With the new wave of xenophobic reactions in East Germany, the part of the new Germany that needs foreign investment most is now unlikely to record significant inflows for many years.

Berlin vs. Brussels?

German voters and politicians are more inward-looking than before unification. In a period in which the Community seeks to establish greater powers and a rising share of supranational public expenditures, Germany's focus on domestic budgetary priorities leads to potential conflicts of interest between the German government and the EC Commission. It is also questionable whether the traditional Bonn-Paris consensus can hold if the Bundesbank continues its high interest rate policy while France faces more than 2 million unemployed.

Higher EC Budgets as a Problem for Germany

As a by-product of the Maastricht agreements[13] on a new cohesion fund, EC expenditures will rise. The Delors II medium-term budget proposal adds further expenditures growth: EC expenditures were expected to increase by about one-third by 1997 in order to provide the funds for doubling structural adjustment programs in the EC; Spain, Portugal, Greece, and Ireland mainly called for increasing regional policy funds that would help them catch up with the leading EC countries (while not resorting to devaluations).

For Germany rising net contributions are an acute problem, especially in the context of the high cost of German unification. Under the terms of Maastricht, Germany's net contribution would have to rise from DM 19 billion to about DM 30 billion annually. This is not much relative to total German expenditures, but the additional EC contribution has to be carved out of a budget with almost no financial room to maneuver. One may recall the enormous problems that Economics Minister Möllemann had when he pledged in 1991 to reduce subsidies by DM 10 billion—a goal that he almost failed to attain (and indeed attained only with some innovative accounting). With taxes already increased after German unification, accelerated inflation that reduces real income gains and erodes the real value of savings and, finally, with prospects for slow economic growth in the early 1990s in West Germany, every interest group will fight hard to defend its respective income position. Wage bargaining in 1991 and 1992 already showed signs of sharper conflicts. More than 2 million restitution claims create additional conflicts over wealth. Germany is likely to accept a higher EC budget only if its net contribution rises much less than its gross payments to the EC. Increasing the EC structural funds for East Germany could lead the way to a political compromise. A compromise might be difficult to achieve because France—looking for funds to compensate its farmers for losses associated with the GATT-related EC-U.S. agricultural trade package—will also fight hard to avoid rising net contributions.

Declining EC Cohesion?

Traditionally EC integration has been built along the political Bonn-Paris political axis. Franco-German tensions are likely to increase as an enlarged Germany becomes preoccupied with internal problems. However, given the rise of anti-EC sentiments in the UK, there are few alternatives to the axis between Bonn and Paris, and it is notable that German defense of the French franc was openly welcomed in autumn 1992. Divergent policy approaches might also be pursued vis-à-vis Eastern Europe to whose dynamics Germany is most exposed. Indeed, conflicting views became apparent as early as 1990 in the Yugoslavian crisis. While Germany has emphasized the principle of self-determination—not least because this principle helped to restore German unity—other EC countries, especially those with centrifugal ethnic or regional forces, will prefer other political principles. The balance of power in EC institutions, such as the Parliament or the Council of Ministers, will change as a result of the FRG's increased population, and this might lead to intra-EC conflicts.

Problems in East Germany could profoundly change the policy stance of the Federal Republic. First, Germany might become more protectionist vis-à-vis non-EC countries, in particular vis-à-vis Eastern Europe. Capacities built up by foreign investors in Eastern Europe will someday be targeted toward Germany (and the EC), and Germany could find it difficult to expose a weak East German industry to the competitive pressure from Eastern Europe. Moreover, the Bonn government might have to support French or Italian style industrial policy on the level of the EC Commission in order to get approval for state subsidies and to obtain EC funds for restructuring the former GDR. While the Paris-Bonn axis remains intact, the crisis of the British pound in September 1992 has revived some old British-German animosities. British anti-EC resentments, anger over the Bundesbank president's remarks about an overvalued British pound, and fear that the united Germany could undermine the politico-economic status of the UK as a leading power interact here in various ways. The September 22, 1992, Franco-German summit showed that Bonn and Paris want to translate the weak French yes vote into new initiatives to reduce the EC bureaucracy, strengthen EC integration, and reinforce the principle of subsidiarity (commonly embraced at the Birmingham summit).

German Unity, the EC, and the Eastern European Transition

In the absence of the military and political threat from the USSR, Germany will enjoy a higher degree of freedom in Europe. At the same time, however, the absence of a common fear of the USSR reduces the incentive to cooperate in Europe. If nationalistic tendencies gain ground in Germany in the 1990s, the EC will become less attractive as a supranational institution for framing Germany's policies. Industrial rivalries between Germany, France, and the UK could also lead to conflicts (e.g., Renault versus Volkswagen in the Skoda deal in the Czech and Slovak Federal Republic): foreign direct investment and trade in a gradually prospering Eastern Europe could become fields of fierce competition. However, as a result of privatization policies in all major EC countries, the influence of state-owned or state-dominated firms has been greatly reduced, thereby decreasing the danger that state-owned or state-dominated firms from major EC countries will be the main players in commercial rivalry in Eastern Europe and thereby translate business rivalry into political conflicts. Moreover, the emergence of "Euronationals," relatively new phenomena related to the formation of the single EC market, might provide new opportunities to exploit jointly investment and trade options in Eastern Europe.[14]

Between September 1990 and January 1992, Germany contributed almost ECU 36 billion of a total of 63 billion in international financial support for the Commonwealth of Independent States (CIS). During this period other EC countries gave ECU 12 billion, while the United States gave 4.1 billion, Korea 2.2 billion, and Japan 2.0 billion for the CIS.[15]

Strong support for the CIS gives Germany a disproportionate influence in Eastern Europe. The very uneven burden sharing in the EC also indicates diverging commercial and political interests of the leading EC countries. Here Eastern European developments and dynamics could lead to increasing intra-EC conflicts and to declining EC coherence. After the collapse of the CMEA, the borders in Eastern Europe have become open, and the rising east-west income gap is likely to channel most migrants into Germany—often entering it through East Germany. Germany could support EC membership for Poland, Hungary, and the states of the former USSR in order to induce these countries more effectively to control borders and prevent rising migration from the ex-USSR, Romania, Bulgaria, and Albania, but also to arrange a more even (maybe bureaucratically organized) spread of the migration wave into the whole EC.

The united Germany is naturally intensely involved in the Eastern European transition.[16] The transition to the market economy requires the modernization of the capital stock and West Germany is Europe's major producer and exporter of capital equipment. Moreover, the transition has broken up the CMEA, which lost its most Western member country, the GDR, to the united Germany. To be sure, the new Germany's trade orientation will continue to be dominated by the OECD countries for quite some time; East Germany's share in total German exports is only 3 percent. In the long run, however, Germany can be expected to expand trade with the former Eastern bloc. Because of its geographical proximity, East German industry is poised to benefit greatly from the transformation and modernization of Eastern Europe.

The united Germany will be different from the old Federal Republic of Germany. There will be a bigger, but also a more fragile, economic and political power in Central Europe. Its economy and its political system will be exposed both to EC dynamics and to the impulses from Eastern Europe. Germany could be a bridge between east and west in Europe, but whether the FRG could really play such a role is an open question.[17]

With the widening of the EC, Germany could become more influential, assuming that Eastern European countries are and will be highly dependent on Germany. However, the EC itself could become weaker as a Community of sixteen or nineteen-plus; an eastward enlargement would be particularly conflict-prone (for example, more than 4 million Hungarians live outside Hungary, and this would become a problem for the whole EC if Hungary became a member state). EC member states could adopt a more risk-averse strategy on the global level, implying that the EC would be unable to join the United States in providing global leadership. The difficulties in the final stage of the Uruguay Round in GATT already indicate a lack of leadership in the EC.

The Maastricht Treaty—much criticized in academic circles and the Bundesbank—has received overwhelming support in the Bundestag. However, while the parliamentary vote may be understood as a support for anchoring the new Germany in a strong EC, the public (preoccupied with East German restructuring) has become less supportive of integration. Illusory economic policy approaches have created disappointment, weakening credibility and exacerbating political instability. With the unification of Germany, the eastward enlargement of the EC already has begun, but in both Bonn and Brussels there is limited knowledge about problems and opportunities of systemic transformation in the ex-CMEA. Austria's EC membership—supported strongly in Germany—could favorably correct this deficit in EC institutions. Whether Germany will remain firmly integrated in the EC will largely depend on the political will in EC countries to spur economic growth and to restrain economic nationalism.

The growth of nationalism provokes discussions about tangible costs of EC membership and the risk of German dominance of the EC economy, but nationalistic perspectives tend to overlook the intangible benefits enjoyed by the countries under the supranational framework of EC institutions. As the narrow Swiss referendum on membership in the European Economic Area and the declining support for EC application in Scandinavian countries shows, the EC's attractiveness has weakened since the late 1980s. If Western Europe wants to avoid a recurrence of the problems encountered in the interwar period (or even a politico-economic disaster as in Yugoslavia), Germany and its partner countries need to develop a new vision of different stages of integration and prosperity in the whole of Europe.

Notes

1. Some German economists shared this optimistic view. Chancellor Kohl was apparently eager to believe those economists who were inclined to suggest a (false) analogy to the West German economic miracle of 1948–1952, a miracle built upon a functional set of market economy institutions and a continued memory of the market economy. Since the ratio of industrial capital to GNP was close to four in the old FRG, the reasoning went, an East German gross domestic product of DM 500 billion (the value needed if East Germans were to have per capita incomes similar to those of West Germans) would require an industrial capital stock of DM 4,000 billion. The GDR's actual GDP in 1990 reached some DM 180 billion, which would suggest an existing capital stock of some DM 600–800 billion. If one assumes that the switch to a market economy renders 50 percent of East Germany's capital stock obsolete, the capital building gap was easily close to DM 3,000 billion ($ 2,000 billion), which exceeded the West German GDP of DM 2,415 billion by some 20 percent in 1990. It is clear that this capital gap can be closed only over fifteen to twenty years; and equally obvious that catching up in per capita output will take decades rather than years.

2. P. J. J. Welfens, "Umweltprobleme und Umweltpolitik" in *Mittel und Osteuropa,* Heidelberg: Physica/Springer, 1990.

3. There are some obvious analogies to the interwar period in Europe; e.g., the UK returned to the pre–World War I parity in 1925 but devalued the pound in 1931 by 30 percent; most countries of the sterling group followed suit. The big EMS realignment of 1987 was followed by five artificially calm years until 1992 brought a 15–20 percent devaluation of the pound and the lira. More frequent, but smaller devaluations are less likely to force other countries to devalue as well for competitive reasons, because other adjustment mechanisms can cope with minor nominal adjustments of nominal exchange rates.

4. To think in terms of per capita figures is adequate in an economy with a growing population; this is relatively new for the FRG, and policymakers have not yet fully realized the implications of these changes.

5. H. Siebert, *German Unification: The Economics of Transition,* Kiel Working Paper no. 468a, May 1991; International Monetary Fund, *German Unification: Economic Issues,* Occasional Paper no. 75, (Washington, D.C., 1990).

6. These figures are from *Statistisches Bundesamt* (1992), "Zur wirtschaftlichen und sozialen Lage in den neuen Bundesländern," Wiesbaden, August 1992. In the second half of 1990, the import GNP ratio stood at 83 percent in East Germany.

7. IWD, "Arbeitsplatze gefragt," *IWD Mitteilungen,* vol. 18, no. 10, 1992.

8. DIW, "Die Vermogenseinkommen der privaten Haushalte in der Bundesrepublik Deutschland 1990," *DIW Wochenbericht,* vol. 58, no. 31, 1991.

9. DIW, "Zur Entwicklung der offentlichen Haushalte 1992/93," Finanzpolitik am Scheideweg, vol. 59, no. 37: 443–452, 1992.

10. For these and related figures see "Germany 1991/92,"*OECD Country Report,* (Paris: OECD, 1992).

11. IWD, "Arbeitsplatze gefragt," *IWD Mitteilungen,* vol. 18, no. 10, 1992.

12. European Parliament, *The Impact of German Unification on the European Community,* (Luxembourg: DG for Research, European Parliament, 1990), p. 9.

13. Welfens, *Umweltprobleme,* op. cit.

14. M. Klein and P. J. J. Welfens, eds., *Multinationals in the New Europe and Global Trade,* (Heidelberg and New York: Springer, 1992).

15. IWD, "Deutschland gibt am meister," *IWD Mitteilungen,* vol. 18, no. 10, 1992.

16. P. J. J. Welfens, *Market-Oriented Systemic Transformations in Eastern Europe,* (New York: Springer, 1992).

17. Ibid.

11

The British Government and the Maastricht Agreements

Stephen George

Ever since Britain became a member of the European Community (EC) in January 1973 it has been regarded as something of an awkward partner.[1] This reputation has been based on less than cooperative behavior on the part of British governments, which in turn has been the result of a combination of factors. Important among these have been a different and less federalist view of the direction that the EC ought to take from that held in some of the original member states, and the effect of domestic politics on the attitude of the governments.[2] Both of these elements can be seen to figure prominently in the attitude taken by the British Conservative government to the Maastricht agreements.

In order to understand that attitude, it is useful to go back to 1984 and the Fontainebleau meeting of the European Council at which the dispute over Britain's budgetary contributions was finally resolved. The British government also submitted to that meeting a paper on the future of the EC that proved to be an accurate guide to the positions subsequently taken up on the single market program, the Single European Act (SEA) and the Maastricht Treaty.

Europe—The Future

The paper, which was undoubtedly intended as a serious contribution to the debate that was then taking place on the revival of the EC, stressed the need to tackle the high levels of unemployment in Europe, to make the EC "relevant to the lives of our citizens," to tackle pollution, and the importance of closing the technology gap with the United States and Japan. It also recognized a need for Europe to emerge as an independent actor on the world stage and supported the strengthening of the European arm of NATO.[3]

The solutions suggested to these problems fitted the traditional British preference for intergovernmental rather than supranational solutions, and for free market measures rather than measures of positive economic integration.

177

For example, the proposed solution to the first two problems was to open the internal market; to the problem of allowing citizens to identify more with the Community, it was to simplify customs and border formalities and to dereg-ulate air services, so introducing more competition and allowing ticket prices to fall. The package was weak on institutional reform, reasserting the import-ance of the national veto and suggesting that all that was needed for the European Parliament was "to work out ways of keeping it better informed, responding to its suggestions, and bringing it to work in greater harmony with the main decision-making institutions of the Community."[4]

This document formed one of the texts around which debate on the future of Europe revolved over the next few years; but it was only one document, and others were considerably more federalist, particularly with regard to the institu-tional aspects of the process.[5] Nevertheless, the launch of the single market program in 1985 seemed initially to move the debate in the British direction.

The Single Market Program

Lord Cockfield's white paper on the freeing of the internal market was music to British ears. It embodied the idea of a deregulated, free-market Europe that had been the British view of what the EC should be since at least the election of the Thatcher government in 1979. However, a dispute soon emerged between the government and President of the Commission Jacques Delors, who was there apparently speaking on behalf of several of the other member states, over to what degree the freeing of the market was an end in itself and to what degree it was only the first step in an extended view of what "1992" was about. In particular, under Margaret Thatcher the British government took exception to two proposed further developments of the program: the addition of a social dimension and the need for a monetary union.

Thatcher's infamous Bruges speech of October 1988 was a particularly strong statement of the British position.[6] It caused a furor among the other member states because it was couched in very forthright terms. There were reports at the time that the British Foreign Office had tried to tone down the language because it would risk unnecessarily antagonizing those other mem-ber states that were strongly in favor of a social dimension to the program.[7]

Contrary to some reporting of the issue, though, her rejection of the social dimension to the 1992 program was not just an expression of a personal prefer-ence; it represented the view of the government as a whole. Similarly, it is noticeable that although Thatcher in other forums was to reject monetary union quite clearly and strongly, in the Bruges speech she only asserted that before discussion of a European Central Bank made any sense it was necessary to implement the commitment to the free movement of capital, to establish a genuinely free market in financial services, and to make greater use of the ECU.[8]

Eventually, though, it was Thatcher's strong line against the idea of monetary union that led to her downfall. Although the British government had always negotiated around a certain conception of the nature of the

Community that it wanted to see, it had also generally been prepared to be pragmatic in the interests of the British economy. There had also been a recognition on the part of the Foreign Office that diplomacy does not mean always getting your own way: compromises have to be made. Thatcher was not a compromiser, and she firmly believed in certain principles on which she was not prepared to move. One of these was her resistance to monetary union.

Money is a sensitive issue of national sovereignty. First, it has a symbolic importance. Second, monetary policy is a key element in determining the level of economic activity in a country. On both grounds Thatcher was not prepared to see the pound superseded by a European currency that would be controlled from outside of Britain. Some of her doubts were presumably shared by other members of the government, but as Sir Geoffrey Howe pointed out in his resignation speech of November 13, 1990 (an attack on Thatcher's European policy from which she never recovered), if the other EC states were intent on proceeding with monetary union, Britain could not afford to be excluded.

Although it was the monetary issue that was her undoing, Thatcher also got out of line with what other members of the government considered to be the realities of the situation on the question of extending the existing political cooperation procedures to give the EC a security and defense dimension. Her view had always been that the surest guarantee of world order was for the United States to give strong leadership. This Atlanticism had led her to resist extending political cooperation beyond intergovernmentalism and to deny the need for any security or defense dimension. This was the thinking behind the proposal in the Fontainebleau paper for the European wing of NATO to be strengthened, a solution to demands for a clearer European defense identity that would not undermine the Atlantic Alliance.

Unfortunately for Thatcher, the Bush administration was also in favor of a stronger, independent European role in security and defense and was prepared to see this role subsumed under the EC. The reason for the U.S. desire that Europe should play such a role was simply to share the burden of policing an increasingly turbulent world; the preference for an EC umbrella perhaps reflected the influence of Germany on thinking in the administration, and in turn the influence of France on Germany. Whatever the reasons, the resistance of Thatcher even to the idea that the Western European Union (WEU) should be developed as a bridge between NATO and the EC ran squarely into the problem that the United States was supportive of such moves, which made it very difficult to sustain the argument that they would undermine the Atlantic Alliance.

The Single European Act (SEA)

After she left office, Thatcher became a vocal critic of the Maastricht Treaty, yet she was the prime minister who signed the SEA, which was arguably the first step on the road to Maastricht. It was the SEA that first abandoned the principle of the national veto in the Council of Ministers. It also gave new powers to the European Parliament, wrote a new chapter into the founding treaties on cooperation in economic and monetary policy (with the subtitle in parentheses of "Economic and Monetary Union"), and brought the intergovernmental procedures of European Political Cooperation into a treaty for the first time.

Why did Thatcher sign this treaty? Almost certainly it was because she recognized that the single market program could not be achieved without majority voting. Although all the governments were agreed on the desirability of the single market, on every one of the 300 measures identified by Cockfield there would have been an objection from some vested interest in some member state. With a veto system in operation, nothing except the most anodyne measures would have been passed, and certainly there would have been no chance of meeting the 1992 target for completion.

Whether the prime minister realized that the SEA went further than being a mechanism for implementing the single market program is difficult to say. Certainly this is how it was presented to Parliament by Sir Geoffrey Howe, then deputy prime minister, when he proposed the second reading of the bill to ratify it on April 23, 1986. Although one or two voices were raised warning of the implications of the measure, relatively little attention was paid to this rather far-reaching treaty, and it was rushed through Parliament by the government in a very short time.

Like all treaties, the SEA was a compromise, and it was a compromise that gave more to the British position than it did to the more advanced federalist positions within the Community. However, for the federalists it was seen as only another step on the road to European Union, whereas for the British government it represented an episode completed. What undermined the British position was the rapid pace of events in Europe in the years that immediately followed the signing of the SEA. German unity and the collapse of communism in Eastern Europe put both monetary union and political union back into sharp focus and convinced the federalist tendency that more needed to be done. Events put impetus behind the moves for further changes to the treaty, and despite British objections, further Intergovernmental Conferences were set up on both monetary union and political union. These led to the Maastricht Treaty.

Negotiating Maastricht

Soon after John Major came to office in November 1990, there was a marked change of tone in British pronouncements on matters connected with the EC. Chancellor of the Exchequer Norman Lamont let it be known that on monetary union the British scheme for a "hard ECU," which had been seen as a spoiling proposal designed to prevent monetary union, was not sacrosanct, and that the government would accept any approach that was evolutionary. On the social dimension, Employment Secretary Michael Howard appeared alongside Social Affairs Commissioner Vasso Papandreou at a press conference at which he stressed that the government could accept fully 50 percent of the Commissioner's proposed legislation on social matters. On a defense identity for the EC, Foreign Secretary Douglas Hurd made it known that the government had no objection to the WEU developing as a bridge between the EC and NATO, something that Thatcher had rejected and continued to reject in speeches in the United States after she ceased to be prime minister.

Major himself visited Germany in March 1991 to repair the damage that had been done to Anglo-German relations in the final months of Thatcher's premiership. Nicholas Ridley, then the environment secretary, had been forced to resign for describing monetary union as "a German racket designed to take over the whole of Europe," and a memorandum of a seminar at Chequers to discuss the German issue was leaked to the press revealing that qualities such as "aggressiveness" and "bullying" had been attributed to the German people—charges not well received there, especially coming from Margaret Thatcher.

During this visit, Major spoke to Chancellor Kohl's Christian Democratic Union, stressing the extent to which they had common traditions with the British Conservative party. This can be seen as a prelude to an attempt to get the British Conservative members of the European Parliament admitted to the Christian Democratic group in that institution, but also to an eventual move to get the Conservative party accepted as a member of the caucus of Christian Democratic leaders that met prior to important Council of Ministers and European Council meetings. The Major government was clearly aware of the need to find allies in the new political game that was emerging in Europe.

Such overtures, however, glossed over certain fundamental differences between the British Conservatives and the European Christian Democrats. First, the Christian Democrats had a strong commitment to federalism as a general principle of government and to European federalism as a specific expression of that general principle; the British Conservative party was hostile to federalism. Second, although the Conservative party had a Tory tradition of paternalism, the Thatcher governments had established a policy of weakening trade union power and reducing employers' obligations that interfered with the working of the labor market, whereas German economic success was based on a social contract with labor that institutionalized workers' rights.

Both of these difficulties emerged in the course of the negotiation of the Maastricht Treaty. When the Luxembourg presidency in June 1992 proposed a draft treaty that incorporated a commitment to a "European Union with a federal goal" in the preamble, there was a political outcry in Britain. Although Major at one point suggested that the phrase might be acceptable to the British government were federalism clearly defined, pressure from within his party led ultimately to the British pressing their demand that the phrase be with-drawn. Ironically, it was replaced by the original phrase that had been used in the Treaty of Rome, "an ever closer union," which was arguably even more dangerously open-ended than the term "federal." A federal system has clearly demarcated spheres of competence for authorities at the different levels, whereas an ever closer union could end up with a unitary European state. So much for the subtleties of political science; prejudice more often carries the day.

Incompatibility of the Conservative concept of social order with conti-nental concepts proved just as intractable. Here, domestic political opposition extended beyond the boundaries of the Conservative party. British employers' federations were adamantly opposed to the provisions of the social legislation proposed by the Commission. Ultimately the British government could not square this particular circle, because the provision of a social dimension to the Community was as important to the European Christian and Social Democrats as it was anathema to the British. In the event Major achieved a surprising victory on this at Maastricht. It was agreed to remove the social chapter from the Treaty altogether and to replace it with a social protocol attached to the Treaty, with Britain excluded.

Although this was a solution to the problem for Britain, it caused severe problems for the rest of the EC. First, it posed a serious problem for those countries that dare not oppose the social chapter for domestic political reasons, but might have hoped that the British would block it for them. It would have been very difficult, for example, for the Spanish Socialist gov-ernment to oppose the social chapter; yet there was no doubt that some of the provisions would make Spain less attractive as a site for investment. Although no government would admit to occupying this position, there was little doubt in the minds of British officials that there were such disappointed govern-ments who had expected to be able to go on hiding behind the British veto as they had done so often in the past on specific items of legislation. Second, the solution caused a tremendous legal headache for the Community because it was by no means certain that such a protocol could be legally binding.

In many other respects the negotiation of Maastricht went remarkably well for the British government. The more extreme federalist positions that had been advocated at times by various actors in the game were not pushed. It seemed as though when the chips were down, the British view of the EC was nearer than the federalist view to a consensus position. The extent of disappointment of federalist aspirations was clearly indicated by the strength of an attack that Delors launched on the draft treaty in a speech to the EP on November 21, 1991.

On political union, the British representatives had the great satisfaction of being able to accept the French government's proposals for a new European Union with three pillars, of which the pillars devoted to internal security and external policy were avowedly intergovernmental. From the viewpoint of the

British government, modest increases in the use of majority voting in the Council of Ministers to cover matters such as environmental protection, international transport policy, and development cooperation; a small further increase in the powers of the European Parliment; and a largely symbolic commitment to a concept of European citizenship were small concessions to make in return for keeping political cooperation and internal security matters outside of the EC framework altogether.

It was the Germans who had pushed most strongly for these areas to come under the EC. Chancellor Kohl was concerned that the united Germany that had been his great achievement should not become a monster, and he go down in history as the Frankenstein who created it. He had therefore advocated a much more federal structure in the hope that it would act as a restraint on his own country. His acceptance of the idea of the three pillars was reluctant and provisional. The agreement to review the working of the structure by 1996 was seen by the British as giving them five years in which to prove to the German chancellor that the intergovernmental pillars could actually work effectively.

On monetary union, a consensus soon emerged in the relevant Intergovernmental Conference on the importance of convergence, and although a timetable was incorporated into the Treaty, it was qualified by a requirement that participating states should meet stringent criteria on economic and monetary convergence. This opened up the prospect of a two-speed Europe so far as Economic and Monetary Union was concerned, but it satisfied the concern that an institutional straitjacket would be placed on divergent economies.

Here, though, domestic politics intervened in a particularly stark form. Thatcher's personal opposition to monetary union led her publicly to attack the concept, and in order to defend himself, Major felt obliged to give a commitment that Britain would not enter a monetary union without first obtaining the explicit consent of Parliament. This meant that Britain could not sign up to the timetable and had to be granted an opt-out clause, or rather what Major described as an "opt-in" clause, allowing the decision on proceeding to stage three of the monetary union to be made by Parliament at the time when it was imminent. There was no doubt in the minds of most commentators, though, that the government had every intention of ensuring that Britain could meet the convergence criteria and would be one of the first states to proceed to monetary union.

Defending Maastricht

In presenting the Maastricht agreements to Parliament on December 11, 1991, and again when introducing the debate on the agreements on December 18, the prime minister stressed the extent to which he had refused to accept what for many Conservative politicians was the unacceptable. Pressure to take foreign policy decisions by majority vote had been successfully resisted, and the social chapter had been taken out of the Treaty at British insistence. He explicitly linked the Treaty with the question of further enlargement of the Community, suggesting that this was imminent and would serve to dilute what elements of federalism had crept in; and he stressed that the principle of subsidiarity—that decisions should only be taken at the Community level where a compelling case could be made that they were more appropriately taken at that level than at the national level—had been written into the Treaty as a legally binding principle.

In the debate on December 18, the Labour party chose to place a great deal of emphasis on the failure of the government to accept the social chapter, which it saw as a denial to British workers of the rights that would be granted to workers in the rest of the EC. In response, the government stressed the extent to which the social chapter would have led back to the pattern of industrial relations that had existed in Britain before 1979 and had resulted in strikes and economic inefficiency. It was clearly the government's strategy to stress the extent to which it was continuing the Thatcherite legacy of isolating and marginalizing trade unions. This also had the advantage of diverting attention away from concessions that had been made.

The biggest concessions were in the area of monetary union. Here, Chancellor of the Exchequer Norman Lamont made a great deal of the way in which he had refused to be pushed into a commitment to abandon sterling and attacked the Labour party for having committed themselves irrevocably to a single currency. However, Labour leader Kinnock scored a debating point here by asking the chancellor under what circumstances he would recommend to the House that Britain should *not* join a monetary union. Lamont declined to reply, which Kinnock described as "deeply disturbing." From the Conservative side of the House, Norman Tebbit, a former close ally of Thatcher, argued that a single currency would lock the poor into permanent poverty, fuel Nazi movements, and destroy the EC. Thatcher herself listened to the debate but did not speak.

While members of the British government were stressing in Westminster that the Maastricht Treaty was a very limited document, Delors was telling the European Parliament that the same Treaty had relaunched the Community, and was predicting that monetary union would force deeper political union. These differences of presentation were representative of the different audiences and of the fact that Maastricht was a compromise in which neither side wanted to admit its concessions. Thus, Delors tried to talk up the federalist aspects of the Treaty not just to the European Parliament but to the media throughout Europe. This, though, proved to be a big mistake.

Delors' emphasis on the federalism of the Treaty caused alarm bells to start ringing in several member states in the new year. Opinion polls showed doubts in Ireland and Denmark, but also in France, and in Germany, where monetary union was very unpopular. In May the British government began to gear itself up to taking over the presidency in July with an offensive to demonstrate its firmness of purpose behind Maastricht. Tristan Garel Jones, the Foreign Office minister with responsibility for Europe, made a speech in Bonn giving a most positive view of Britain in Europe, saying that the British government stood firmly by the Maastricht Treaty and warning against the dangers if it were not ratified. Also in May, the Queen made her first speech to the European Parliament, an event of some symbolic significance that served to underline British seriousness about its role in the EC but served to annoy the British Eurosceptics.

At the same time, efforts were being made on the domestic front to ensure that Conservative backbench rebels did not embarrass the government by forcing it to rely on opposition votes for ratification. As part of the process of reassurance, John Major assured the House of Commons on May 12 that "the sovereignty of this House is not a matter that is up for grabs."

When the ratification debate opened in Parliament on May 20, Major said that the Treaty marked a turning point away from EC centralization, a move that would be enhanced by the imminent enlargement of the Community from twelve member states to twenty. He knew that many people feared the creation of a strong central government in Brussels with some powers devolved to the member states, but the agreement to go for cooperative arrangements outside of the framework of the EC on foreign and security policy, justice and internal matters reflected a steady diminution of "the old tendency among some of our partners to think that action by the Community was always the answer."

A strategy was emerging in the defense of Maastricht. The government was pressing the view on its own supporters that Maastricht enshrined intergovernmentalism, and where it did not, the British had managed to opt out. At the same time, it was taking advantage of the unpopularity in other parts of the EC of Delors' federalist interpretation to impose its own minimalist interpretation. As the British presidency approached, the rejection of the Treaty by the Danish electorate in a referendum on June 2, 1992, appeared to strengthen the British hand.

Denmark's narrow referendum defeat of Maastricht (by 50.7 percent to 49.3 percent) sent a shock wave throughout the Community. Although the Treaty could only come into effect if ratified by all twelve member states, the others decided to press ahead with ratification. In Britain, however, Parliament decided not to proceed with the committee stage of the ratification bill, and in France, President Mitterrand immediately announced that he would suspend parliamentary ratification and hold a referendum as well. An emergency meeting of foreign ministers was held on June 4 on the fringes of a NATO meeting in Oslo, following which it was announced that the other states would proceed with ratification and that there could be no renegotiation of the terms of the Treaty. Nevertheless, this unity hid a resentment among the smaller member states aroused by a joint statement of France and Germany the previous day to the effect that progress would continue with or without Denmark. The statement was issued without prior consultation and seemed to dismiss Denmark as unimportant.

Denmark's action provoked a strengthening of anti-Maastricht sentiment elsewhere in the EC. Seizing on this to reinforce the British interpretation of the Treaty, Foreign Secretary Douglas Hurd told the House of Commons on June 8 that it was vitally important to allay fears throughout Europe that Maastricht would turn out to be a centralizing move, a comment that was made against the background of press reports that Britain was advocating an addition to the Treaty, a declaration removing any ambiguity about it being a reversal of moves to centralization. Such an interpretation of course ran against the view that had been expressed by Delors to the European Parliament and the interpretation that had been put on the Treaty in some of the other member states, but the outbreak of public concern even in the core countries of France and Germany had given the initiative to the British to press their minimalist view.

At the same time as the Danish result strengthened the hand of the government in the politics of the EC, it caused it problems in domestic politics. Between seventy and eighty Conservative and Ulster Unionist MPs signed a Commons backbench motion calling on the government to use its presidency of the Council to make a new start on the development of the EC; but the prime minister told the Commons that renegotiation was not a practical proposition "at the present moment." Clearly he was constrained in this by the unwillingness of the Germans and French to consider any change in the terms of the Treaty, although his own interpretation of it as a decentralizing document, as in fact a new start in itself, also made it unlikely that he would embrace the idea of renegotiating.

Just how far it had at least contributed to a change of mood in the direction of traditional British concerns was indicated by the hostile reception given at a meeting of finance ministers on June 9 to Commission proposals to increase the size of the budget of the EC. German Finance Minister Horst Köhler told the press that after the Danish referendum the EC needed to show it was going in the right direction by restraining spending.

The following day Delors came under attack in the European Parliament for allegedly wishing to take power away from the smaller member states. When a Dutch member accused him of this, Delors angrily replied that he had never said any such thing; but a Danish member reminded him that when he had spoken to the European Parliament in April he had talked of shocking the member states at the Lisbon summit when he unveiled plans to deal with the institutional implications of future enlargement. Delors was believed to be opposed to further enlargement because it would enhance the forces favoring intergovernmentalism. His statement had therefore fed fears in Denmark of the emergence of a European super state in which national identities would be submerged. There seemed little doubt that the federalist tendency was on the defensive and even in retreat.

Even Chancellor Kohl felt it necessary to tell the Bundesrat (the federal upper chamber) that Germany rejected a centralist Europe, and that a future European Union was not to be a melting pot in which national identities would be lost. In a country that had always been among the strongest supporters of a federal Europe, in theory if not consistently in practice, this change of language was particularly significant. Kohl also indicated that all of the powers of the Commission needed to be re-examined to see whether some of them could be better handled at the national level. In other words, some of the existing powers might be repatriated.

An agreement was reached on this issue at the Lisbon meeting of the European Council in late June, when it was decided that all existing legislation should be examined to see whether it could be modified or scrapped. This was obviously an important victory for the British view that centralization had already proceeded too far, although there were dangers in reopening the question of the Commission's powers. For example, the French appear to have wanted to repatriate competition policy because they were unhappy with the way in which the British Commissioner Sir Leon Brittan was using the powers that he had acquired to vet large-scale mergers. Nevertheless, the British did seem to have gained something here.

There was also agreement at Lisbon that work would start immediately on negotiating mandates for the EFTA countries that had applied to join the EC (Austria, Sweden, Finland, and Switzerland) and that dialogue with the countries of Eastern and Central Europe would be stepped up in preparation for their membership. Again there was an apparent gain here for the British view that there should be rapid progress toward enlargement.

Usually in the EC gains are accompanied by concessions, and perhaps the concession that Major had made was agreement not to undermine the Treaty or to support its amendment. He told Parliament on June 25, immediately before leaving for the Lisbon European Council:

> The Maastricht Treaty was negotiated in good faith by all member states. I have no intention of breaking the word of the British Government that was given on that occasion, neither do I have any intention of compromising what we agreed on that occasion and wrecking this country's reputation for plain and honest dealing and good faith.

What else was happening behind the scenes is difficult to say, but there were also interesting developments at the Commission. At the end of June, the member states agreed unanimously to appoint Delors as president for a further two years. This was to cover the interim between the end of his Commission's term of office and the inauguration of a new Commission on the timetable laid down at Maastricht for the terms of the Commission and the EP to run concurrently. At the same time, the Commissioner who had most frequently clashed with the governments of the member states, Italian Environment Commissioner Carlo Ripa di Meana, resigned. There was widespread speculation that he had been pushed by Delors, and that there was also influence brought to bear on the Greek government to replace another combative high-profile commissioner, Vasso Papandreou. It looked as though the Commission was being neutered so as to lower its profile and make it appear less threatening to the electorates of the member states. Coincidentally, the moves would make it less irritating to the governments of the member states, and particularly to the British government, which had frequently found itself in conflict with both the outgoing commissioners.

As Britain assumed the presidency at the beginning of July, the domestic problems concerning the Treaty continued. Margaret Thatcher, now Baroness Thatcher of Kesteven, in her maiden speech in the House of Lords, repeated her call for a referendum in Britain on Maastricht and made it clear that she would vote against ratification. This gave an unequivocal lead to her many supporters within the party. She also said that Britain ought to use the presidency to restate the Luxembourg Compromise and rejected comments by the prime minister that the SEA (which she had signed when she was prime minister) was a more centralizing document than Maastricht. This attack on her former protégé received a strong reply only an hour later (although clearly it was not a reply in the sense that Major could have been responding directly to Thatcher's comments).

The prime minister told the 1922 Committee of Conservative backbenchers that the government wanted more power to remain with national governments, and for some powers to be repatriated; but this had to be done by negotiation. He added that if Britain had been negotiating from the center of Europe throughout the previous twenty years, it might have had more influence on the development of the Community than had been the case. This seemed to be a swipe at his predecessor's negotiating style. The domestic political contest was becoming heated.

Lady Thatcher attacked the prime minister again in a television interview with David Frost on June 28. She said that Major had been wrong to agree to reappoint Delors, whom she described as a man who had increased bureaucracy and who had chosen to go for majority voting wherever he could rather than unanimity. Major was also wrong on Maastricht, which she described in a ringing phrase as "a treaty too far," and on maintaining the value of the pound within the exchange rate mechanism (ERM) of the European Monetary System, because a policy of high interest rates that was right for Germany was causing high unemployment in Britain.

Major counterattacked on Lady Thatcher's call for a referendum when he reported to the Commons on the Lisbon European Council on June 29. He vigorously defended the Treaty, dismissed calls for a referendum, and repeated the line that he had given to the 1922 Committee before leaving for

Lisbon, that he was not prepared to see Britain standing on the sidelines of the EC with other countries making the decisions that affected the livelihood of British people.

At this stage, the British government was conducting very successful diplomacy within the EC, taking advantage of the concerns in other member states about centralizing tendencies to move the Community further in the direction that it wished to see; but it was also itself suffering from the same domestic problems that afflicted the other governments. These might have been kept in check, though, had it not been for the monetary crisis that erupted in the run-up to the French referendum.

Indications that the French might vote against Maastricht in the referendum on September 20 led to a loss of confidence by the financial markets in the ability of the ERM to hold together. The lira first came under speculative pressure, and even a devaluation of 7 percent did not restore confidence. The pound was next. On September 16 it was forced out of the ERM amidst recriminations against the Bundesbank for not being prepared to give adequate support to maintaining the parity. An attempt by the British to get a general realignment of currencies within the ERM had failed, and the decision to float the currency was subsequently taken unilaterally by the British government.

This whole episode caused a considerable setback to John Major's strategy. First, it ruined his economic strategy of combating inflation by tying the pound into a high parity against the deutschemark. Second, it appeared to vindicate Lady Thatcher's strictures against that policy and so strengthened the position of her and her supporters in the internal debate within the Conservative party. It also temporarily caused a cooling of the good relations with Germany that were essential to success in EC diplomacy.

After the French referendum produced the smallest of votes in favor of Maastricht (50.6 percent to 49.3 percent), Major called a special European Council meeting for October 15 and said that Britain itself would not bring the Maastricht ratification bill back to Parliament until the Danish problem had been solved. The German government continued to insist that the Treaty must be ratified without any changes, and after suggesting publicly that the time might be right for a pause for reflection and some possible amendment of the text, Hurd accepted this position following a consultation of foreign ministers in New York in the interstices of a UN session on September 21.

The French result, however, put new momentum behind the opponents of Maastricht within the Conservative party, and at the party conference on October 6, Lord Tebbit, the former cabinet minister Norman Tebbit, launched a stinging attack on the government, demanding that they press home their advantage against the federalist tendency in Europe and force a renegotiation of the Treaty. He received a standing ovation from about one-third of the audience, and the reply of the foreign secretary, although politely applauded, was much less enthusiastically received.

Subsequently, on November 4, the government scraped a victory by only three votes in the House of Commons on a motion to reintroduce the bill to ratify the Treaty. The Labour party, despite having proclaimed itself pro-EC, decided to vote against the government on the grounds that this was in effect a vote of confidence in the government, and Conservative backbench rebels were apparently bought off with a commitment that the final ratification would not take place until after a second referendum had been held in Denmark.

The Record of the British Presidency

In the face of these domestic political problems, it was difficult for the British presidency to take a strong line in Community affairs, and there was some criticism from other member states of self-absorption and failure to address any concerns other than those of Britain. However, by the end of the six-month presidency, there were certain achievements that could be claimed.

The first was the settlement of a disagreement with the United States over agriculture that had been holding up an overall agreement in the Uruguay Round of trade negotiations under the General Agreement on Tariffs and Trade (GATT). The second was to broker agreement at the European Council meeting in Edinburgh in December on the intractable issues of how to get Denmark into a position where it could hold a second referendum on Maastricht with some prospect of getting a positive result, and the future size and distribution of the EC budget.

The GATT agreement was actually negotiated by the Commission, but the British presidency did make an important contribution by throwing its weight behind Agriculture Commissioner Ray MacSharry, who was negotiating seriously to get a settlement and at one point appeared to be undermined by a lack of support from the Commission president, Jacques Delors. Although French farmers reacted angrily to the agreement, and the French government was highly critical of it, there was a feeling that this was all predictable, and that the cost of sinking an overall trade agreement would be too high for the French economy for a veto actually to be used. In any case, that would come only after the end of the British presidency.

The special European Council meeting in Birmingham in October failed to come up with any solution to the Danish problem, but the regular biannual meeting in December, which was held in Edinburgh, did approve a series of opt-out clauses for the Danes that would allow them to hold a second referendum with some reasonable prospect of a successful outcome for the government.

The issue was linked to that of the future size and distribution of the EC budget. Spain was insisting on an increase in the existing structural funds and a substantial cohesion fund to help the poorer member states, while the net contributors to the budget, including Britain itself, were anxious to keep the increased cost as low as feasible. Again a compromise was brokered at the meeting, leaving the British presidency able to claim a success despite its problems during the six months.

Conclusion

Democratic politicians always have to perform in two arenas: the arena of power where they must make decisions that they believe to be in the national interest while still satisfying the demands of powerful interest groups; and the arena of support where they have to satisfy the electorate, members of their own party, and in cases where there are coalition governments, the members of parties to which they are allied.

Where foreign policy is concerned, the arena of power is especially complex because of the presence of other states whose governments are also pursuing their national interests. These may conflict with those of the first state, with all the states also trying not to fall foul of powerful domestic interest groups and also having to keep an eye on their own arenas of support.

At least the traditional field of foreign policy is relatively insulated from domestic interests and is usually a matter of some indifference to electorates and most party members. The EC, though, offers a particularly difficult field because it both contains other states whose legitimate interests have to be accommodated, and is an area of policy that impinges directly on domestic politics, so it is of considerable concern to the electorate and to party members. In the case of the British government, the biggest problem over Maastricht has been satisfying the concerns of other states while retaining the support of Conservative party members.

Maastricht was a compromise document, but it gave much less to the federalist view than it did to the British view of the future of the Community. Skillful diplomacy, combined with a reluctance of allegedly federalist governments to support the concept in practice, produced a better result than might have been achieved had Thatcher's blunter approach still been dominant. The federalist elements that were in the Treaty were thought to be necessary to allow those governments who believed that they had pro-federal electorates to sell the package to their domestic audiences. In fact, as events showed, several European publics were even less enamored of federalism than their governments. The reaction to Maastricht killed the myth that most Europeans wanted to live in a European federal state.

Events allowed the British to press home their advantage and gain agreement on a strengthening of the subsidiarity principle and on opening negotiations for a further enlargement of membership that would bring in more states that were suspicious of federal and centralizing tendencies. Unfortunately, they also strengthened the hand of those elements within the

Conservative party that were opposed to any form of European federalism, however weak and circumscribed.

While the German and French governments desperately argued against reopening the whole package, which was already far weaker on the federal front than Chancellor Kohl had wanted, British opponents of Maastricht attacked their prime minister for not using the problems that the Treaty had revealed to destroy it, thereby challenging the Germans and French to a confrontation. Such a confrontation would undoubtedly have torn the Community apart and could have led to the emergence of a little Europe grouped around the German-French alliance, which however tenuously was still holding together. It was a dangerous line, and one that the government had no choice but to resist, but the gap between the requirements of the arena of support and those of the arena of power was uncomfortably wide.

In this respect, John Major was suffering from the legacy of his predecessor's approach to the problem, which was to put the arena of support first by playing up to long-held prejudices within the Conservative party against loss of sovereignty. This worked during the circumstances that prevailed for much of Thatcher's premiership, but when the point was reached where the threat of exclusion from a European monetary union put British economic interests at risk, a change of approach became necessary. However, reconciling the requirements of compromise in the arena of power with the requirements of sustaining support within the party proved very difficult for Major and his cabinet colleagues, and left them in an extremely uncomfortable position.

Notes

1. Stephen George, *An Awkward Partner: Britain in the European Community* (Oxford: Oxford University Press, 1990).

2. On the first of these factors see Stephen George, *Britain and European Integration since 1945* (London: Blackwell, 1991), chap. 2, "The Policy of the British State." On the second set of factors see Stephen George (ed.) *Britain and the European Community: The Politics of Semi-Detachment* (Oxford: Clarendon Press, 1992).

3. "Europe—The Future," *Journal of Common Market Studies* 23 (1984) pp. 74–81.

4. Ibid., p. 79.

5. The main "federalist" document that informed the debate was the European Parliament's Draft Treaty Establishing the European Union. On the genesis, acceptance, and content of this document, see Juliet Lodge (ed.) *European Union: The European Community in Search of a Future* (London: Macmillan, 1986).

6. Margaret Thatcher, *Britain and the European Community* (London: Conservative Political Centre, 1988). Speech at the opening of the academic year, College of Europe, Bruges, Belgium, October 17, 1988.

7. Ibid.

8. Ibid.

PART 3

Toward a European Foreign Policy

12

Fortess Europe or Promised Land?

Hans-Georg Betz

The Future of Immigration in a United Europe

In the 1980s the affluent, advanced industrial countries of Western Europe have become the destination of growing numbers of would-be immigrants and refugees. Fleeing poverty, social and political turmoil, civil war, and environmental catastrophes, they arrive in Western Europe at an increasingly rapid pace. Since most Western European countries closed their doors to new immigrant workers two decades ago, new arrivals are forced to claim political asylum if they want to find haven in Western Europe. The response of the Western European public has been quick and straightforward: the majority regard immigrants and refugees with growing hostility, which at times has erupted in violent assaults by right-wing extremists, hooligans, and Nazi skinheads on foreigners and their dwellings. At the same time, there has been a surge of support for radical right-wing populist parties, which have been quick to capitalize on the political climate of fear and resentment. Both developments are the clearest signs of growing xenophobia and racism in Western Europe.

Their revival presents a particularly critical challenge to the EC, not least because it goes against the EC's fundamental values and political vision. Since one of the EC's main objectives is the free movement of people within a common labor market, the EC has contributed to, if not outright caused, the creation of a two-track status of residence and citizenship in its territories. Whereas it is relatively easy for the citizens of a member country to move across borders as tourists or in search of employment, citizens of non-EC states (especially if they happen not to come from one of the advanced, non-EC industrial countries in Europe, East Asia, or North America) find it increasingly difficult both to enter the EC and to find employment there. As a result, the "Fortress Europe" that "Americans, Japanese and other outsiders fear when the European Community finally becomes a tariff-free, continent-wide market at the end of [1992] is already being built. But its walls are intended to keep out people, not commodities."[1] The likely extension of EC membership to the countries that currently comprise EFTA will very probably aggravate the problem. In a majority of these prospective member states, xenophobic sentiments are riding high. Parties that appeal to these sentiments are among the most successful of their kind in Western Europe. Thus, extension of membership to these countries can be expected to strengthen the political front opposed to immigration and a generous policy on asylum.

***

In 1987, roughly 13 million foreign citizens lived in the EC. This amounted to about 4 percent of the EC's overall population. Of those, about 60 percent were citizens of non-EC countries. Germany, France, and Great Britain accounted for almost three-quarters of all foreign nationals from member countries, and more than 80 percent of all foreign citizens from non-EC countries. Among non-EC Western European democracies, Switzerland (with roughly 1 million foreigners), Sweden (400,000), and Austria (280,000) were hosts to relatively sizeable foreign populations.

Three factors primarily explain the presence of immigrants in Western Europe: the scarcity of labor during the years of the economic miracle in Western Europe, which caused governments to recruit what they considered to be temporary immigrant workers; a policy of family reunification that started in the 1970s with the objective of integrating resident foreign populations into host societies; and a growing influx of political and economic refugees from Eastern Europe and developing countries in the late 1980s.

Postwar labor migration in Europe was a response to the labor shortage experienced in the northern European industrial countries in the late 1950s and 1960s. Responding to the economy's rising demand for fresh labor, Western European governments actively recruited foreign workers first in southern Europe and then also outside Europe. Germany, for example, concluded the first such treaty (with Italy) in 1955. Treaties with Spain, Greece, Turkey, Morocco, Portugal, Tunisia, Yugoslavia, and even South Korea quickly followed. Between 1960 and 1973, the number of foreign workers grew from 280,000 to roughly 2.6 million. The situation was similar in other countries. In Switzerland, the number of foreign residents with at least a one-year residence permit almost doubled from 330,000 in 1960 to 600,000 in 1973; in Austria, it increased tenfold, from 21,000 in 1963 to over 220,000 in 1973.

Oil crises, world wide recession, and mass unemployment in the 1970s caused a majority of Western European governments to adopt stringent measures to prevent further immigration. Germany ordered a halt to recruitment in 1973; France closed its borders to foreign workers in 1974; Norway adopted annual limits on foreign labor in 1974; Sweden passed a comprehensive immigration policy in 1975. As a result, the size of the foreign work force stabilized or even decreased. In Germany, for example, the number of "guest workers" declined from 2.3 million in 1973 to a little more than 1.5 million in 1985 after the government created a program giving foreign workers financial incentives to return home. However, by 1991, the number of foreign workers had grown to roughly 1.9 million.

The continued, relatively large immigrant presence in Western Europe is an indication that the policies of the 1950s and 1960s were based on wrong assumptions and false expectations. Generally, Western European governments assumed that immigrant workers were only attracted by economic gains. If these economic gains were "reduced or ceased altogether, for example through unemployment," or "if their expectations of work and saving failed to materialise" they would return home. However, despite recessions, despite the fact that foreign workers have generally been more affected by unemployment than the native work force, and despite efforts by Western European governments to encourage repatriation, they "are showing every sign of settling as permanent members of their new countries."[2] As one survey found, in 1990, two-thirds of foreign residents living in France would stay in France even if they could find employment in their home countries. In fact, in 1990, almost half of Germany's foreign population had lived in the country for fifteen years or more, more than two-thirds of all foreign children and youth had been born in and had grown up in Germany.[3]

The response of a number of Western European countries to the failure of earlier policies has been an effort to integrate into the host societies those foreigners who were already there while strictly controlling the influx of new arrivals. Integration measures include the facilitating of family reunification, efforts to improve the education and professional training of foreign youth, and the extension of social and political rights to immigrants including, in such countries as Sweden and the Netherlands, the right to vote in local elections. As a result of this new policy, the composition of immigrant populations has in most cases changed quite dramatically. The proportion of those gainfully employed has decreased considerably, while the number of their dependents increased. Thus, in 1973 two-thirds of the resident foreign population in Germany were employed; in 1990 the figure was not more than one-third. This trend is also reflected in the presence of a growing number of foreign women as a percentage of the entire foreign population. In 1974, only a third of the foreign population in Germany over sixteen were women. In 1987 women made up 42 percent, exemplifying the success of family reunification.[4]

If these and similar policies have generally advanced and improved the status of resident foreigners in Western Europe, they have also closed the door for new immigrants. Many would-be immigrants have thus been forced to seek entrance in Europe as political refugees, since the right to asylum is one of the last cracks in the walls. Since its asylum policy was largely a response to postwar resettlement in Europe and to the Cold War, Western Europe was rather unprepared for the rush of asylum seekers in the late 1980s. Official statistics speak a fairly clear language: in 1983, the total number of refugees seeking political asylum in Western Europe amounted to about 70,000 persons. By 1989, with almost 320,000 cases, that number had more than quadrupled. In 1991, Germany alone received more refugees (256,000) than all Western European countries together in 1988; Switzerland and Austria together received almost as many as Western Europe as a whole did in 1983.

***

Xenophobia and racism are hardly new phenomena in postwar Western Europe. During the 1960s, economic recession and growing unemployment provoked a wave of hostility against immigrant labor in Germany, France, Great Britain, and Switzerland. In the 1980s, what has come to be seen as an "invasion of the poor" gave rise to a considerable increase in xenophobia throughout Western Europe. As early as 1986 the European Parliament warned (in the so-called Evrigenis Report) of growing xenophobia and racism. EC-wide surveys on attitudes toward non-EC citizens support the report's findings. In 1988, more than one-third of EC citizens polled thought there were too many people of another nationality or race and that the presence of people from outside the EC was bad for their country's future. One in five thought outsiders rights should be restricted. By 1991, half of those polled thought the number of non-EC nationals was too high, and a third thought their rights should be restricted. More than a fifth were opposed to accepting people from countries south of the Mediterranean or Eastern Europe who wished to work in the EC. About 60 percent wanted to restrict immigration from other countries. Most alarming of all, only a quarter was willing to accept without restrictions people seeking asylum in Western Europe even if they were "suffering from human rights violations in their country." Nineteen percent advocated refusing to accept them at all.[5]

German surveys show that the pronounced hostility toward refugees is closely related to the dramatic increase in their number. Confronted with a wave of refugees, East German emigrants, and ethnic German resettlers from Eastern Europe and the former Soviet Union, between March 1988 and February 1989 the number of Germans polled who were willing to accept all political refugees decreased from 32 percent to 23 percent. At the same time the number of respondents supporting a drastic reduction in their number increased from 29 percent to 46 percent.[6] The situation is hardly different in the major EFTA countries. In 1990, for example, more than two-thirds of the Austrian public surveyed agreed completely or in part that there were too many foreigners in Austria. Seventy-one percent thought Eastern European immigrants were seeking an easy life while the better quality people stayed at home to rebuild their own countries. Only a minority thought Austria would gain from the presence of foreigners, while 57 percent thought the continued influx of immigrants and refugees could only provoke an increase in xeno-phobia.[7]

Underlying the recent wave of xenophobia and racism is a social and political climate of anxiety and resentment that has quickly spread throughout Western Europe. Although prompted by the current economic, social, and cultural transformation of advanced Western societies, structural mass unemployment, and the general apprehension associated with them, this climate quickly came to be dominated by the question of immigration. Faced with the destabilization and, in some cases, collapse of the familiar and known, a growing number of Western Europeans have begun to blame foreigners for their problems.

Studies on attitudes toward foreigners speak clearly. Of those surveyed in 1988, 34 percent associated foreigners with an increase in unemployment, 17 percent thought they exploited social security benefits, 15 percent considered them a cause of violence and crime, and 20 percent thought more foreign children in schools would reduce the level of education.[8] These attitudes reflect "welfare state chauvinism," the notion that jobs and social benefits should go first to "our own."[9] It is hardly surprising that these sentiments have grown stronger in times of mass unemployment, soaring national deficits, and painful cutbacks in public services. Despite the fact that the great majority of reasons for xenophobia turn out to be little more than prejudices, xenophobic sentiments are swiftly gaining ground.

Four examples, two from EC countries, two from EFTA countries, reveal the similarity between different societies. In 1991, a poll showed 57 percent of the German population thought foreigners were aggravating German unemployment, 72 percent blamed them for the tense housing situation, and 66 percent thought they were abusing social services. Although Italian society has only recently begun to confront the fact that Italy has become one of Europe's chief countries of immigration, the effects on public attitudes are already becoming visible. A 1991 survey showed 38 percent of the Italian population associated non-EC immigrants with an inevitable increase in unemployment, and 69 percent agreed at least in part that as a result of the presence of non-EC citizens there was an increase in drug dealing. Polls showed that the situation is not much different in some of the smaller European countries that are confronted with a growing number of refugees from Eastern Europe and the developing world. In Austria in 1990, 49 percent thought that foreigners were taking jobs away from Austrians, and 67 percent associated immigrants with increasing crime, violence, and disorder; so did 46 percent of the Norwegian population.[10]

If the Western European public tends to associate immigrants with unemployment, the exploitation of social security benefits, and delinquency and violence, studies on the actual situation of immigrant workers in Western Europe arrive at rather different conclusions. Immigrant workers hardly represent a threat to the jobs held by their German, French, or Austrian counterparts. Generally, immigrant workers are less educated and less well trained, performing jobs that natives often refuse to accept. Because of their lack of education and formal professional training, they are considerably more vulnerable to unemployment. Since success on the postindustrial labor market depends heavily on formal education, training, and continuous retraining, immigrant workers can be expected to be among the main losers during the current modernization process. They might thereby add to unemployment, not by displacing native workers but by becoming unemployed themselves. Studies on the impact of foreign workers on the welfare state arrive at similar conclusions. Generally, immigrant workers have been significant net contributors to social security systems. In Germany alone, foreign workers contributed in the 1980s between 8 and 10 billion deutschemarks annually to the pension system without profiting from it to the same extent as the aging German population.[11] Although it is true that refugees receive considerable financial support from a number of governments, this has to be seen in light of the fact that refugees are still often not allowed to seek employment and thus depend on government payments for survival. Finally, even the fact that foreigners are disproportionately often involved in crimes is rather misleading. A great many of these crimes are foreigner-specific, i.e., illegal border crossings, violations of residence requirements, etc., and thus cannot be committed by natives. Beyond that, foreigners are more likely to be acccused, arrested, and jailed than natives. A valid approach to the question of foreigners and crime first has to confront these biases before it can arrive at cogent conclusions.[12]

These examples suggest that the current wave of hostility toward foreigners in Western Europe is hardly the result of a thorough and objective debate. Rather, it is driven by fears that resist rationality. Possibly the most telling example of these fears is the notion of "invasion" that characterizes much of the current discussion on immigration.[13] Behind this image stands the fear that Europe is being inundated by a wave of people from the developing south fleeing overpopulation, environmental destruction, and the threat of starvation. This image emerged in the late 1970s and the 1980s in response to the growing number of immigrants and refugees from underdeveloped, overpopulated non-European countries rather than from what were until recently the poor regions of southern Europe. This was partly an (unintended) consequence of the immigration stop and return policies of the 1970s that convinced a considerable number of foreign workers from Europe to return to their home countries. As a result, the proportion of non-Europeans steadily increased. In part it were a result of the fact that in the 1980s a growing proportion of refugees were from developing countries. In France, for example, in 1968 more than 85 percent of the immigrant population were Europeans. In 1982, that number had dropped to less than 50 percent. At the same time, the number of immigrants from the Maghreb region increased from 23 to 39 percent.[14]

As a result there is growing concern that Europe is becoming "subverted" by alien cultures, above all by Islam. According to the 1988 special Eurobarometer study on xenophobia and racism, for a sizeable portion of those polled, Muslims represent today the "other" in terms of culture and religion.[15] Increasingly, such alien cultures and life-styles are being perceived as a threat to European culture. In 1990, 45 percent of Austrians surveyed considered immigrants a threat to Austrian life-style and national identity. In the same year, half of the French respondents felt no longer as much at home as before.[16] Surveys like these reveal the extent to which images of threat, subversion, and resulting alienation have been popularized. In their most drastic forms, these fears lead to responses that recall the darker days of Europe's past: In a 1991 poll, 24 percent of the German population agreed that "we should take care to keep the German people pure and to prevent the mixing of peoples."[17]

Questions of immigration and asylum have dominated part of public debate in Western Europe since the early 1980s. Since the late 1980s, they have also come to figure prominently in political debate. In 1990 in France, the question of how to deal with immigration ranked second only to how to confront mass unemployment. At the end of 1991, opinion polls suggested more than two-thirds of the population of former West Germany accorded it top political priority, far ahead of the environment or unemployment.[18] Despite growing inclinations on the part of the established parties to speak out against immigration and to propose new restrictions, for a considerable segment of the population these responses have been too slow and too little. As a result, they have turned to new political parties on the radical or extreme right. This is hardly surprising. As early as 1988, at the beginning of the dramatic increase in the number of asylum seekers, as much as 11 percent of those asked in the member states said they approved at least in part of movements in favor of racism.[19]

Although for the majority of radical right-wing parties the question of immigration and asylum is only one among several major issues, all of these parties owe much of their political success to the spread of xenophobia. During the past several years, much of the debate on the radical right in Western Europe has focused on Jean-Marie Le Pen's National Front in France. Le Pen, who is the head of the Technical Group of the European Right in the European Parliament, is certainly the most prominent representative of political xenophobia in Western Europe. His success in appealing to and manipulating French fears and resentment has shown that diffuse xenophobic sentiments can be translated into concrete political gains. In the regional elections of 1992, almost 14 percent of the French electorate voted for the National Front. It is hardly a coincidence that since the late 1980s radical or extreme right-wing parties proposing similar programs have emerged in a growing number of Western European countries.

Within the EC, politically significant radical right-wing parties (i.e., parties that are represented at least in regional assemblies) exist in Denmark (Progress party), France (National Front), Belgium (Vlaams Blok, National Front), Germany (Republikaner, DVU), and Italy (Northern League). Within would-be EC countries, there are significant similar parties in Austria (Freedom party), Norway (Progress party), Switzerland (Automobile party, Swiss Democrats, Tessin League), and Sweden (New Democracy party).[20] It would be a simplification and grossly misleading to dismiss all of these parties as mere anti-foreigner or protest parties. Only the strongly nationalistic populist parties (National Front, Vlaams Blok, Swiss Democrats, Republikaner, and DVU) concentrate heavily on the foreigner issue. The others propagate a primarily neoliberal, even libertarian program. Its cornerstones are on the one hand the celebration of individual effort and entrepreneurship, on the other vehement opposition to higher taxes and profound hostility to the centralized power of the state and bureaucracy in general. However, even the neoliberal parties, such as the Danish and Norwegian Progress parties (founded in the 1970s primarily as antitax parties), have found it increasingly expedient to ride the anti-immigrant wave. It is hardly a coincidence that both parties recovered significantly in the late 1980s after they had added anti-immigrant rhetoric to their political programs. (The Norwegian party increased its representation in Parliament from two seats in 1985 to twenty-two in 1989.)

The electoral importance of an anti-immigrant position is well-documented for the National Front. In the presidential elections of 1988, 22 percent of all voters, but almost 60 percent of National Front voters, said immigration was among the most important problems determining their vote. However, for neoliberal parties xenophobia has also had vital importance. For example, in the 1991 Viennese election that brought the Freedom party massive gains, 55 percent of its voters said they had voted for the Freedom party because of its (hostile) position on the foreigner question. The situation was similar in the 1991 parliamentary election in Switzerland. The refugee question was of top political priority for 21 percent of Swiss voters, but almost half of the voters of the Automobile party.[21] Founded in 1987 to represent the rights of Swiss drivers against increasing environmental restrictions imposed by the established parties and the Greens, by 1991 the party had become the most significant representative of Swiss xenophobia, improving its parliamentary representation from two seats in 1987 to eight in 1991.

The secret of the radical right parties' political and electoral success is as simple as it is effective. In true populist style, they mirror the concerns, prejudices, and resentment of their voters as faithfully as they can. The Belgian Vlaams Blok's statement of principles guiding its policy on immigration is quite representative of the profound xenophobia that informs the political program of the nationalistic populist parties:

> The number of non-European guest workers, illegal foreigners and so-called political refugees must be rolled back. Their massive presence means that assimilation and integration are impossible. If Flanders wants to remain Flanders, it has to change course drastically. . . . and this even more since

uprooting [i.e., a person's removal from his or her native environment] leads to insecurity and crime. The Vlaams Blok wants to avoid large future ethnic confrontations and preempt mutual xenophobia.[22]

In order to achieve these goals, the large majority of non-European immigrants (the Vlaams Blok program continues) must be encouraged to return to their home countries. In concrete policy terms this means, among other things, that political refugees should be sent back as soon as the political situation in their country has improved; the immediate return of all illegal immigrants; heavy penalties for employers who hire and employ foreigners illegally; and the introduction of a "discouragement policy" against would-be immigrants, e.g., by abolishing social security benefits.

Even if neoliberal parties are less forthright in their hostility towards foreigners, they pursue similar goals: the Norwegian Progress party states that although it supports the free movement of goods, capital, and labor across national borders, this "presupposes that immigrants should not be allowed to benefit from welfare arrangements and other arrangements which are contingent on long-term accumulation of rights through payments or through citizenship": for this reason the party supports a restriction of immigrant labor to short term contracts without an automatic right to family reunification.[23] Umberto Bossi, leader of the Italian Northern League, which in the 1991 elections emerged as Italy's fourth largest party, argues in a similar vein. In his view, work and housing should be guaranteed to those who reside in a country. "All that has a moral significance: the preconditions for survival should be guaranteed in the first place to the families which have contributed to the wealth of a country for a long time."[24] In order to prevent foreigners from what his party views as abusing Italian hospitality and a false sense of solidarity, it demands a drastic tightening of existing entrance requirements, including obligatory visa requirements for all *extracomunitari* (non-EC citizens). Those seeking to work in Italy should not be allowed to enter the country unless they are already in possession of a valid contract with an employer.[25]

Even more drastic are the Swiss Automobile party's demands designed to stop the influx of refugees. The party proposes that Switzerland renounce adherence to the 1951 Geneva Convention on Refugees, which was born of the experience of World War II. "Today's global mass migrations can no longer be accepted with reference to that convention."[26] These examples are an indication of the extent to which questions of immigration and asylum have become radicalized in Western Europe. Although the most radical proposals are still confined to the extremes of Western European politics, the continued success of these parties cannot but influence the direction the dominant parties will take on this issue.

***

The fact that a growing majority of the population of present and prospective EC countries shows increasing hostility toward foreigners from
outside Western Europe makes the task of arriving at a sensible and fair
immigration policy in Western Europe increasingly difficult. The fact that a
growing number of Western Europeans are abandoning the established parties
to vote for radical right-wing populist parties is equally disconcerting. This
development is as much a reflection of growing xenophobia and racism as it
is a sign of growing distrust of the established parties and their ability and
willingness to address pressing issues. It is with regard to the latter issue that
the questions of xenophobia and right-wing radicalism assume their true
significance for the future of the EC.

During the past decade, individual governments, parties, and bureaucracies have increasingly come under attack for being unresponsive to the
concerns, attitudes, and political ideas of the average citizen. The result has
been growing disenchantment with democratic institutions. It has found its
most explicit expression in increasing voter abstention and protest votes.
Because the citizens of the EC have even less influence on the decisions of
the major EC institutions, these institutions are even more vulnerable to the
charge that they are detached from the average citizen and thus cannot be
trusted. The rejection by a majority of Danes of the Maastricht agreement was
symptomatic of the extent to which these sentiments are diffused, particularly
in the smaller countries.

Probably one of the most important reasons for growing disenchantment
and distrust is that there is a significant attitudinal and value gap between the
political class of professional politicians and public functionaries and the
public. Individual country studies show striking differences in attitudes
toward foreigners between public officials and most other relevant social
groups. Generally, civil servants tend more strongly to favor accepting
immigrants, giving them financial support, and allowing them to preserve
their own culture than do the general public. Particularly high level public
officials are among the most liberal on these issues of all social groups. In a
survey conducted in Germany in 1991, 40 percent of those employed in the
public administration, but only 26 percent of the general public, favored
accepting all recognized political refugees; 33 percent as compared to 16
percent came out in favor of accepting all relatives of resident foreign
workers.[27]

One might suspect that public officials are also among the people most
sympathetic to the notion of multicultural society, which recently has assumed a prominent place in the public debate on immigration. The central
point of this debate is whether Western European societies should seek to
integrate their foreign residents without pressuring them to abandon their
traditions and cultures. This implies that the relationship between foreigners
and natives should be characterized by reciprocity and equality rather than

assimilation and exclusion. It also means that the native population should make an effort to understand and tolerate alien cultures and, if necessary, contribute to their preservation. The notion of multicultural society might be the most appealing model for a future united Europe. However, if recent German surveys are any indication, it is unlikely that this model receives much support. In 1992, polls indicated that less than a quarter of the German population favored it; almost half did not even know what "multicultural" meant.[28] If approving of the presence of non-EC foreigners at all, the great majority of Western Europeans, when asked, seem rather to favor assimilation.

It is in this context that the political importance of radical right-wing populist parties for the process of European integration has to be evaluated. Right-wing radical populist parties owe much of their success to their ability to exploit public disenchantment with the political class and present themselves as both true advocates and representatives of the "common people." It is for this reason that a number of these parties are vehemently opposed to the EC. Thus the Swiss Automobile party explains its rejection of Switzerland's proposed EC membership with the notion that the EC is too bureaucratic and centralistic and that Swiss membership would mean a considerable curtailment of Switzerland's model of direct democracy and thus a significant reduction of the rights of the Swiss citizens. Others, while in support of their countries' membership or prospective membership in the EC, equally stress their support for a Europe of citizens rather than large-scale corporations and bureaucracies.[29]

However, upon closer analysis of their programs, it becomes quite clear that radical right-wing populist parties are less concerned about extending the rights of "the people" vis-à-vis the political class than about safeguarding the integrity of the European "peoples" (i.e. ethnically and culturally defined entities) against outside threats. It is hardly a coincidence that the Vlaams Blok campaigned for the 1991 election with the slogan "Out of Self-Defense." Whether under the notion of a "Europe of the peoples" (Umberto Bossi), a "Europe of the regions" (FPÖ), or a "Europe of the Fatherlands" (Republikaner), the main objective of the radical populist right is to prevent a united Europe from turning into a "multiracial, multiethnic, and multireligious" state in which "the forced and uneasy living together of diverse, if not incompatible, cultures and races will lead to social revolts and turbulence."[30] Rather, their vision of a united Europe is a federation of ethnically and culturally distinct peoples that trade with each other for mutual benefits in a free internal market while otherwise jealously guarding their cultural identity and welfare privileges. "Our own people first," "Germany for the Germans," etc., mark the essence of this politics of self-defense.

In their attack on the immigration policies of the established parties, the radical right make it quite clear that in their view the main threat comes from would-be immigrants from developing countries. These immigrants are not only seen as an economic drain on resources that should be reserved for the native population, but also as a threat to the cultural identity of the peoples of Western Europe. To quote Bossi, the leader of the Italian Northern League: "I am convinced that the non-EC foreigners who come from certain regions of the world—particularly Arabs from the Middle East and Maghrebis—have no intentions of integrating themselves and accepting our customs. Therefore, they are a ticking social bomb that creates tensions and hostility. They take a thousand rights while showing no tolerance, while refusing to accept our mode of life." Even more drastic is from the *German Republikaner*: "Stop the advance of aggressive and intolerant Islam in Germany and Europe! Islam wants religious world domination."[31]

* * *

The fact that at the beginning of the 1990s radical right-wing populist parties can once again use a language of xenophobia and hatred for political gain is indicative of the level of acrimony which the discourse on immigration and asylum has reached in Western Europe. Yet it would be a serious mistake to blame the revival of xenophobia and racism exclusively on these parties. The radical right merely expresses the views and attitudes of a growing portion of the population of the most advanced Western European countries. Confronted with a world which threatens to slip into chaos, Western Europe increasingly gives the appearance of being an island of tranquility, peace, and prosperity.

Confronted with the triple crisis of population explosion, poverty, and environmental destruction in much of the developing world, a growing majority of Western Europeans has gone into a defensive stance, seeking to preserve what it has accumulated in material and social security. However, one might suspect that underlying the anxiety expressed in the attitudes of Western Europeans toward immigration is also the realization that Western Europe cannot detach itself from global problems.

The climate of public indifference if not secret approval that accompanied many of the skinhead assaults on immigrants and refugees in Germany in 1992 was possibly the clearest evidence of the extent to which hostility toward immigrants and refugees had penetrated the fabric of Western European societies. The murders of three Turkish citizens by German neo-Nazi skinheads in Mölln in late 1992 had a sobering effect both on German society as well as the citizenry of other Western European countries and led to a growing number of acts of solidarity with foreigners. However, it is rather doubtful that there was a genuine reversal of public opinion in regard to the negative effects of mass immigration into Western Europe.

Xenophobia and racism, together with the strengthening of radical right-wing ideologies and parties, can thus be expected to continue to present one of the most significant political challenges to the EC in the 1990s. The major countries of immigration are also members of the EC. The political challenge to an immigration and asylum policy that is in harmony with Western humanist values is gaining ground in EC member countries and prospective member countries. The agreement between the ruling CDU, CSU, and FDP and the largest opposition party, the SPD, at the end of 1992 to restrict severely Germany's liberal asylum laws was probably the most important signal that Western Europeans would prefer to turn the EC into a "Fortress Europe," at least as far as immigration is concerned, rather than maintain an open policy toward the outside world.

Although entrance requirements are still largely set by national governments, the EC will have to arrive at a comprehensive immigration policy, and not just because a considerable segment of its population looks to the EC for guidance. In 1988, more than a third of the citizens of the EC agreed that EC institutions should work out a common policy that will apply to all member states.[32] A Europe without internal borders, as initiated by the Schengen Agreement, can only become reality if there is agreement on this vital issue. With both xenophobia and disenchantment with democratic institutions running high, this will hardly be an easy task. Whether it succeeds will be an important measure of Europe's political and moral maturity.

Notes

1. Craig R. Whitney, "Europeans Look for Ways to Bar Door to Immigrants," *The New York Times,* December 29, 1991, p. 1.

2. Zig Layton-Henry, "Race and Immigration," in *Politics in Western Europe Today,* Derek W. Urwin and William E. Patterson, eds. (New York and London: Longman, 1990), p. 162.

3. Gérard Le Gall, "L'effet immigration," in SOFRES, *L'état de l'opinion 1991* (Paris: Seuil, 1991), p. 131; Beauftragte der Bundesregierung für die Belange der Ausländer, *Daten und Fakten zur Ausländersituation,* Bonn, July 1992, p. 14.

4. Beauftragte der Bundesregierung für die Belange der Ausländer, op. cit., p. 15; Dietrich Thränhardt, "Die Bundesrepublik Deutschland—ein unerklärtes Einwanderungsland," *Aus Politik und Zeitgeschichte* B24/88 (June 10, 1988), p. 5.

5. *Eurobarometer: Public Opinion in the European Communities,* special issue on racism and xenophobia (November 1989), pp. 42, 68; *Eurobarometer* no. 35 (June 1991), pp. A35–A37.

6. EMNID, Spiegel poll, March 1988, February 1989.

7. Fritz Plasser and Peter A. Ulram "'Die Ausländer kommen!'" in *Österreichisches Jahrbuch für Politik 1990,* Andreas Khol, Günther Ofner, and Alfred Stirnemann, eds. (Vienna: Verlag für Geschichte und Politik, 1991), pp. 314, 321.

8. *Eurobarometer: Public Opinion in the European Communities,* special issue on xenophobia and racism (November 1989), p. 61.

9. Jorgen Goul Andersen and Tor Bjorklund, "Structural Changes and New Cleavages: the Progress Parties in Denmark and Norway," *Acta Sociologica* 33 no. 3, (1991), pp. 195–217.

10. EMNID, Spiegel poll, November/December 1991; ISPES, *L'atteggiamento degli italiani nei confronti dell'immigrazione extracomunitaria* (Rome: November 1991), p. 34; Plasser and Ulram, op. cit., pp. 314, 321; Central Bureau of Statistics,

Survey on Attitudes Towards Immigrants, Oslo, 1988.

11. Regine Erichsen, "Zurückkehren oder bleiben? Zur wirtschaftlichen Situation von Ausländern in der Bundesrepublik Deutschland," *Aus Politik und Zeitgeschichte* B24/88 (June 10, 1988), p. 23.

12. Norbert Kostede,"Die Ausländer als Verbrecher," *Die Zeit* 26 (June 19, 1992), p. 8.

13. Jan Werner, *Die Invasion der Armen* (Mainz and Munich: v. Hase & Koehler, 1991).

14. M. Tribalat, "La population étrangère en France," *Regards sur l'actualité* 118 (February 1986) pp. 3–35.

15. *Eurobarometer: Public Opinion in the European Communities*, special issue on xenophobia and racism (November 1989), pp. 37–41.

16. Plasser and Ulram, op. cit., p. 321; Le Gall, op. cit., p. 123.

17. EMNID, Spiegel poll, November/December 1991.

18. *Le Nouvel Observateur*, November 13–19, 1990, p. 6; Forschungsgruppe Wahlen, "Politbarometer 11/91."

19. *Eurobarometer* no. 30 (December 1988), p. 65.

20. See Hans-Georg Betz, "The New Politics of Resentment," *Comparative Politics* 25 (4), July 1993.

21. Pascal Perrineau, "Le Front national, d'une élection à l'autre," *Regards sur l'actualité* 161 (May 1990), p. 25; Fritz Plasser and Peter A. Ulram, "Analyse der Wiener Gemeindewahlen 1991," in *Österreichisches Jahrbuch für Politik '91*, Andreas Khol, Günther Ofner, and Alfred Stirnemann, eds. (Oldenbourg: Verlag für Geschichte und Politik, 1992), p. 112; Claude Longchamp and Sibylle Hardmeier, *Analyse der Nationalratswahlen 1991*, VOX Publikationen no. 43 (January 1992), p. 23.

22. Vlaams Blok, *Uit Zelfverdediging*, election program, 1991, pp. 14–17.

23. Fremskrittspartiet, *Political Program of the Progress Party (Norway) 1989–1993* pp. 30–31.

24. Umberto Bossi with Daniele Vimercati, *Vento dal nord* (Milan: Kupfer & Sperling, 1992), pp. 144–146.

25. Ibid.

26. Autopartei-Die Freiheitlichen, *Parteiprogramm* (April 1991), p. 9.

27. EMNID, Spiegel poll, August/September 1991.

28. *Allensbacher Berichte* no. 9 (1992).

29. Jürgen Scherrer, chairman of the Automobile party, in a personal letter to the author, April 1992; FPÖ, *FPÖ und EG*, FBW-Dokumentation 2 (Vienna: Freiheitliches Bildungswerk, 1992), p. 8; Bossi with Vimercati, op. cit., p. 202.

30. Bossi with Vimercati, op. cit., pp. 148, 203.

31. Bossi with Vimercati, op. cit., p. 149; Die Republikaner, 'So darf es nicht weitergehen,' election leaflet, 1992.

32. *Eurobarometer,* special issue on xenophobia and racism, (November 1989), p. 84.

13

The Wider Europe: Extending the Membership of the EC

John Redmond

After a period of stagnation, the last few years have seen the momentum toward European integration reaching heights approaching those of the 1950s. One of the major external effects of this has been that non-EC Europe has felt compelled to reassess its relationship with the Community. Most have come to the same conclusion, and the result has been that a queue to join the Community has formed. Turkey applied in April 1987, Austria in July 1989, Malta and Cyprus in July 1990, Sweden in July 1991, Finland in March 1992, Switzerland decided to apply in May 1992, and Norway in November 1992. The Commission has already issued its opinions on Turkey (negative), Austria (positive), Sweden (positive), and Finland (positive), and the outstanding opinions are imminent. In addition, the Community has rebuffed an application from Morocco in 1987, on the grounds of noneligibility, and has accepted (in the preamble of the Europe Agreements) that EC membership is the eventual, although not automatic, objective of its relationship with Poland, Hungary, and Czechoslovakia. Any Europe Agreements with Bulgaria and Romania are likely to state the same, and beyond all these countries are a whole range of smaller European states that may well wish to join the EC in due course.

In the short term, an application from Iceland is possible while, in the longer term, the former Soviet republics (such as the Baltic countries and Ukraine) and Yugoslavian republics (certainly Croatia and Slovenia) and even Albania wait in the wings. The number of applicants could eventually exceed twenty, particularly as the boundaries of "Europe" are not entirely clear. Indeed, in its submission on enlargement to the Lisbon summit in June 1992, the Commission explicitly chose not to define "Europe" by taking the view that it was "neither possible nor opportune" to define what "European" meant in the context of its use as a criterion for acceptance as a member of the Community.[1] The implications of such a comprehensive enlargement for the existing Community are profound and extensive and are taken up in the final section following an examination of those applicant countries that constitute the "frontrunners" in the short and medium term.

However, the actual mechanics of joining the Community are relatively straightforward in principle. A formal application is made to the Council, which then requests an "opinion" from the Commission and, on the basis of this, decides whether or not to accept the application and proceed to negotiating the terms of entry. A decision to proceed must be unanimous, and since the 1987 Single European Act, the approval of the European Parliament is also required. Negotiations then take place at the intergovernmental level, that is, between the government of the applicant state and the Council (normally represented by the presidency), albeit with considerable input from the Commission. The only condition imposed by the Treaty of Rome was that any applicant must be European (Article 237), but in practice, three other requirements also emerged: that new members should be democratic, respect human rights, and accept the *acquis communautaire*. The Maastricht and Lisbon summits formalized these and added several more conditions, specifically that new members must:

1. Accept the emerging *acquis politique*, that is, the common foreign and defense policy both as it already exists and as it will be extended by the Maastricht Treaty.
2. Subscribe to the *finalités politiques*, that is, the long-term objective of European Union.
3. Have a "functioning and competitive market economy."[2] It is not clear to what extent prospective members have specifically to fulfill the conditions (relating to inflation, interest rates, budget deficits, and national debt) required to join fully in Economic and Monetary Union.
4. Have "an adequate legal and administrative system in the public and private sector."[3] New members must be able to implement Community policies.

Clearly there is scope for different interpretations of many of these conditions, and it is not possible to give a clear definition of an acceptable applicant country. Moreover, it is evident that some aspiring members will have difficulties, most obviously, the EFTA neutrals with 1 and the Eastern Europeans with 3 and possibly 4. The operational implication that consequently arises is that the enlargement procedure will be difficult, potentially disorderly, and inevitably contentious. It may also be the case that the Community's criteria may be interpreted more generously for some applicants than for others, with consequent political implications.

At this stage it may be useful to draw briefly on previous experience, not only of the first and second EC enlargements themselves but also from the negotiations for the European Economic Area (EEA) and the Europe Agreements. While there are clearly major differences between the past and forthcoming enlargements, there are still lessons that can be drawn, some of which are confirmed by the later experience of the EEA and Europe Agreements, most notably:

• The primacy of economics in the negotiations and any assessment of net benefit. While political considerations have had some initial importance, particularly in the second enlargement, it is agriculture, the GDP of applicant countries, likely claims on the structural funds, and more general budgetary issues that have quickly become the dominant considerations. Thus the (rich) EFTA countries are currently regarded by the EC as being easy to assimilate, but the Mediterranean and (prospective) Eastern European applications provoke uneasiness.

• The attitude of existing member states can be critical, as shown by the French veto of the British application in the 1960s and, equally, by the French support for the Greeks in the 1970s that enabled a doubtful Commission opinion to be overturned. Most of the current applicants have close links with at least one existing EC member state and can therefore expect some internal support for their membership bids.

• Enlargement of the EC can have important effects on the EC's relations with the rest of the world and those of the new member because it upsets the delicate balance of Europe's external trading relations. For example, the Iberian accession in the 1980s led to a displacement of U.S. exports and a consequent trade dispute. In the current situation, the likely scale of enlargement of the EC is such that it may reawaken fears of a "Fortress Europe."

• The Community drives a hard bargain and its members are adept at protecting their own interests. For example, the agreement of the first common fisheries policy in 1970 shortly before agreeing to accession terms with four countries that had combined fishing interests far greater than those of the EC Six was not entirely accidental. The EC's efforts to push through the Maastricht Treaty, particularly the common foreign and security policy elements, could be construed as an attempt to do something similar on a much larger scale.

Finally, there is a lesson that has become apparent from a comparative examination of the effect of joining the Community on past new members. While EC accession offers an opportunity to attract foreign investment and EC financial aid, and to use this to generate economic development and enhanced growth, this opportunity can only be grasped with appropriate national economic policies. EC accession is not a panacea that will solve everything; rational and appropriate national policies are even more essential within the EC if the opportunities provided by membership are not to be lost. For this reason, the countries that formerly made up part of the Soviet bloc or Yugoslavia, and indeed the Turks, would do well to consider EC accession as a beginning as well as an end.

Turning to the EC's more recent negotiations with the rest of Europe, both the EEA and the Europe Agreements would seem to suggest that the Community continues to drive a hard bargain. Despite strong pressures, the EC was unyielding in its unwillingness to allow non-EC involvement in decisionmaking in the former case, and anything beyond essentially superficial concessions on agricultural imports into the Community in the latter. The EEA experience also suggested, somewhat paradoxically, that it was harder to negotiate and implement a "halfway house" than full EC membership and, consequently, that the EEA is unlikely to be able to play the role of a "waiting room" for aspiring EC members. Lastly, the Europe Agreements lay bare the limited assistance that can be expected from the EC and reinforce the view that the EC is not a cure-all and that prospective new members need to put their own house in order, largely by their own efforts. The limited improvements contained within the Community's recent efforts to "redirect" its global Mediterranean policy[4] would appear to send a similar message to the Mediterranean applicants. Thus, a variety of lessons can be gleaned from the past. However, looking to the future, the next three sections of this chapter examine the problems and prospects of each group of applicants in turn, beginning with the "EFTAns."

***

A close relationship between EFTA and the EC has always been inevitable given their high degree of economic dependence.[5] The central importance of the EC as a trading partner is common to all the aspiring EC members (Table 13.1), but in the case of EFTA the dependency is mutual: EFTA is the EC's major trading partner, accounting for more than the United States and Japan combined. EFTA is also unique in that its membership includes the only European countries[6] that have implicitly (by joining a European free trade area) or, in the case of Norway, explicitly (in a referendum), chosen not to join the Community. Indeed, Switzerland has shown in recent referenda that its population have grave doubts about joining any international organizations[7] (including the European Economic Area). Consequently, these countries differ from the Eastern European and Mediterranean applicants, which have essentially grasped at the straw of EC accession as soon as they felt even remotely able, in that opting to try and join the EC has meant they have actively had to change their minds. Moreover, this volte-face has not been based on a gradual evolution of opinion but has taken place very quickly. In fact, even as late as 1989 when Austria broke ranks, it seemed extremely unlikely that Switzerland, Finland, Iceland, and Norway would seek EC membership even in the medium term. More importantly, this lack of interest in EC accession appeared not only to reflect the view that a satisfactory EEA would provide a suitable framework for future EC-EFTA relations but also deeply ingrained national attitudes, tendencies, and internal structures that were incompatible with the EC membership.

Table 13.1 Basic Statistics of the Countries Applying for EC Membership

Country	Population (millions, 1990)	Total Employment in Agriculture (%, 1989/90)	Exports to EC as % of Total (1989)	Per Capita GDP (US$, 1990)
EC12	327.1	7.1	n/a	16,190
EFTA				
Austria	7.7	7.9	63.9	19,240
Finland	5.0	8.4	43.9	26,070
Iceland	0.3	5.7	56.5	20,598[a]
Norway	4.2	6.5	65.2	23,120
Sweden	8.6	3.3	53.5	23,680
Switzerland	6.8	5.6	56.6	32,790
The Mediterranean				
Cyprus	0.7	13.7	47.0	8,040
Malta	0.4	2.5	69.6	6,630
Turkey	56.1	47.8	46.5	1,630
Central and Eastern Europe				
Bulgaria	8.8	19.2	4.6[b]	2,210
Czechoslovakia	15.7	11.5	18.2[b]	3,140
Hungary	10.6	19.6	25.6[b]	2,780
Poland	38.2	26.4	23.9[b]	1,700
Romania	23.2	27.9	17.6[b]	1,640

Sources: Economist: "A Survey of the European Community," 11 July 1992; and T. Pederson, "Integration and Enlargement: Challenges to the EC in the 1990s," paper presented to the Inaugural Pan-European Conference in International Studies, Heidelberg, September 1992.

Notes: [a]1989

[b]These figures are now outdated and should be regarded as indicative.

The interesting question then becomes, why have the EFTA countries changed their minds? There are a number of factors:

- A fear that the creation of the EEA would not be sufficient to offset the handicap of being outside the EC's internal market. The disadvantages include not only restricted market access for EFTA exporters compared to their internal EC competitors, although this may be the most important, but also the consequent loss of economies of scale and attractiveness to foreign investors and, also, the exclusion from the EC's public procurement market.
- The rapid collapse of the Soviet bloc. This made a closer EC-EFTA relationship more likely, for both political reasons—the neutrality constraint was relaxed for the EFTA neutrals—and economic reasons—the economic chaos in the former Soviet empire has created a hole in the external economic relations of some EFTA countries.
- A growing sense that the EC was "Europe" and nonmembership of the former implied, in some sense, exclusion from the European mainstream.

- There has been a "bandwagon" or "domino" effect which has been accelerated by the sheer pace of change of the political map of Europe.

However, it is clearly the first of these and, in particular, the failure of the EEA to alleviate EFTA fears of exclusion, that has been the driving force behind the wave of EFTA applications to join the Community. The EEA was initially seen as a mutually acceptable means of alleviating EFTA fears about the single market program while simultaneously allowing the EC to delay enlargement in order to concentrate on deepening. Thus the EFTA countries would be able to take part in the single market without having to take part in the common agricultural policy and the common foreign and defense policy. Moreover, the EFTA countries are rich and saw little reason to change their own successful systems. Unfortunately, the EEA proved difficult to negotiate, contentious, and ultimately an unsatisfactory alternative to full EC membership, and so, one by one, the "EFTAns" are turning toward the latter. Indeed, it has been argued that the EEA provides the worst of all worlds for the EFTA countries and that their exclusion from the EC decisionmaking process is "forcing them to lose more independence if they stay outside the Community than if they join it."[8]

The first applicant from EFTA was Austria, in 1989, and the change of heart was in part driven by business interests, although Austrian opinion on EC accession is very mixed, with agricultural and environmental interests opposing it. However, on the Community side, few, if any, member states are against accepting Austria, and the Commission's opinion on the application[9] emphasized the lack of economic problems. The only problems that were raised concern the substantial changes required in the agricultural sector—most of the EFTA countries subsidize their agriculture more that the EC—and Austrian restrictions on the transit of EC trucks, which would become unacceptable if Austria were to join the Community. In fact it is not the economic sphere but the question of Austrian neutrality that creates the biggest potential dilemma. Indeed, the Commission has felt it necessary to suggest that there will be a need "to seek specific assurances from the Austrian authorities with regard to their legal capacity to undertake obligations entailed by the future common foreign and security policy."[10] Fortunately, there are signs that the problem is simply fading away as Austria redefines its neutrality. In mid-1992 the Austrian foreign minister was quoted as saying that "the concept of neutrality, as we understand it, is flexible and has to be adapted to political and military circumstances in Europe. . . . our country's neutrality is no longer what it was in 1955. . . . Austria subscribes 100 percent to the Maastricht Treaty. . . . Austria [is] ready to take part in a common defense policy."[11] If this is the case, then the neutrality issue should cause few problems, although it remains to be seen how representative this view is.

For many years the Swedish welfare model and its neutrality were considered to be incompatible with EC membership. However, opinion began to change rapidly from 1989, partly in reaction to the EC's single market program and also because of the decline in the economy, which made the pursuit of the "Swedish model" seem less essential. Moreover, events in Eastern Europe had much the same effect on the neutrality concept. Swedish neutrality was, in any case, always very pragmatic and was "a self-chosen policy, the interpretation of which is the sole responsibility of the Swedish government."[12] It now seems that it has been redefined to mean nothing more than "nonalignment to military organizations" and may even be taken further to allow Swedish participation in WEU.[13] Finally, business interests, the central trade union, all political parties (with the obvious exceptions of the Communists and the Greens), and public opinion in general all favor EC accession. Even Swedish farmers, faced with internal reforms that mean an end to the traditional Nordic model of heavily subsidized agriculture, are in favor. Swedish accession to the EC is becoming irresistible. The Commission's opinion on the Swedish application was issued at the end of July 1992 and essentially mirrors that on Austria: it anticipates no major problems other than a need for specific assurances that Swedish accession will not impede the pursuit of an EC foreign and security policy.

Finland has fiercely guarded its sovereignty and neutrality for many years, to the extent that any relationship with the EC has been a controversial issue. Thus, in the late 1960s "the debate in Finland about [even] a free trade agreement with the Community took on almost the same dimension as the internal argument in Norway about EC membership,"[14] and, indeed, Finland did not become a full member even of EFTA until 1986. This aloofness reflects various Finnish concerns stemming from the proximity of the Soviet Union, its insularity and consequent aversion to the idea of free movement of labor, and from particular policies; Finnish regional policy, aimed at promoting the viability of its remote areas, and its heavy subsidization of agriculture would inevitably conflict with EC policies. Consequently, the Finns opted firmly for the EEA until public opinion shifted sharply toward favoring EC accession in the early 1990s. The main political parties are more divided (but with a majority in favor), and agricultural interests and the population in the remoter areas are, not surprisingly, opposed to EC membership. This shift has been very sudden and reflected at least four factors:

- The demise of the Soviet Union and the consequent collapse of Finnish-Soviet trade.[15] The collapse of the Soviet bloc also relaxed the constraint imposed by Finnish neutrality.
- The associated decline in the Finnish economy.
- The realization that the EEA was an insufficient response to the EC's single market program, particularly as the "EFTAns" were to be excluded from the decisionmaking process.
- The application for EC membership of Austria and, particularly, Sweden, with which Finland has close links.

Thus Finland is now set to participate with Austria and Sweden in the next wave of EC enlargement. Indeed, the Commission issued a positive opinion on the Finnish application in November 1992.

The final EFTA neutral is Switzerland, arguably the most neutral of all. Five major obstacles to EC membership have been identified:[16]

- Neutrality.
- Federalism: considerable powers are devolved to the cantons which would create institutional problems but, without which, it is feared that Switzerland would disintegrate into its French-, German-, and Italian-speaking components.
- Policies toward foreigners: the Swiss fear being swamped by foreign nationals and, in particular, the selling off of land to foreigners.
- Agriculture: in common with other EFTA countries, the Swiss subsidize agriculture much more than the EC does.
- Direct democracy: this raises the biggest conflict, particularly the regular use of referenda in Switzerland.

To this list should be added EC-Swiss disputes over the transit, through Switzerland, of trucks engaged in intra-EC trade and the associated environmental problems. These drawbacks had led Switzerland to pursue a "third way" between isolation and accession. However, this position has now changed radically in some quarters in the face of dissatisfaction with the EEA, the feeling that full membership is the only viable alternative, and the implications for neutrality of the end of the East-West divide in Europe. Nevertheless, Switzerland remains very divided over any involvement with the EC, with the French speaking Swiss in favor of membership and the German speakers suspicious and cautious. It was therefore not entirely surprising that, in December 1992, the Swiss rejected membership of the EEA in a referendum. This would seem to rule out Swiss accession to the Community in the foreseeable future.

On the face of it, the remaining Scandinavian "EFTAn," Norway, appears to be a relatively uncontroversial applicant for accession. After all, it is a NATO member, so neutrality is not a problem; and it has already negotiated membership once, and so presumably this can be simply reactivated. However, the Norwegians seem incapable of actually deciding that they want to join the Community. The 1972 referendum was an acrimonious affair in which agrarian and fishing interests combined to produce a no vote. The principle Norwegian fears centered on the belief that the newly created common fisheries policy threatened one of Norway's principal resources, farmers' fears that the common agricultural policy offered less support than they already had, and the loss of sovereignty. So bitter was the divide that the EC enlargement issue was thought to be too sensitive to resurrect until very recently. The decision of the present government to espouse EC accession stems from similar factors to other EFTA countries, notably dissatisfaction with the EEA, the collapse of the Soviet bloc, and the desire not to be isolated if Sweden and Finland join the Community. However, public opinion remains sharply divided even though the government eventually did apply for EC membership in November 1992.

Iceland remains the least likely of the EFTA countries to seek EC membership and remains, for the present, content to accept the EEA as an adequate alternative. Of course, Iceland has no problem with neutrality as it is in NATO, but the reliance on the United States for security is indicative of the strong transatlantic links that offset its European connections. More generally, Iceland has a tradition of remaining outside the mainstream of international politics and guards its sovereignty jealously. Iceland is well aware what being a small state within the EC could mean. "They could buy Iceland in an afternoon,"[17] the Icelandic prime minister has said. However, the main obstacle to EC membership is created by the country's economic dependence on fish. Accession would bring free access to the EC market for Icelandic fish but the price of opening up the Icelandic fishing grounds to all EC fishermen is considered to be too high. Nevertheless, there are small signs that opinion is beginning to shift with business interests leading the way. Moreover, Iceland might be swayed by the accession of its Nordic partners, particularly Norway. Most specifically, the open access for its fisheries products that Iceland's main competitor would receive as a full EC member would have extremely detrimental effects on the Icelandic fishing industry. Finally, the seventh EFTA member, Liechtenstein, is presently satisfied with the EEA and has no plans to apply for EC membership in the immediate future.

***

The European Community has a longstanding interest in the Mediterranean and, in the 1970s, created its Global Mediterranean Policy (GMP).[18] Unfortunately, the GMP has fallen well short of nonmember Mediterraneans' aspirations, and those that feel able and are eligible have voted with their feet and applied to join the Community. The three current applicants—Turkey, Cyprus, and Malta—are all poorer than the EC on average (see Table 13.1), particularly Turkey, and all might be expected to be major beneficiaries of the various EC funds, and, indeed, this is one of the major attractions of EC membership. In addition, each applicant is politically divided and the side applying to the EC sees political advantages in membership: the Turks hope that it would confirm their European orientation in the face of Islamic opposition, the Greek Cypriots believe that it would put pressure on the Turkish Cypriots and mainland Turks to resolve the political division of the island, and the ruling Maltese Nationalist party hopes that it would end the specter of a re-elected Labour government turning its back on Europe again. However, it is perhaps the variety of issues that the three applicants present that is more striking. In particular: the sheer size of Turkey, its relative poverty, and its cultural differences; the division of Cyprus that makes it unique as an EC aspiring member and raises unique difficulties; and, finally, the fact that the Maltese application looks increasingly difficult for the EC to reject.

If many of the EFTA countries might be described as reluctant Europeans, then the Turks might be described as rather desperate Europeans. Turkey began to reorientate itself to Europe—its "European vocation" as former President Ozal has called it[19]—in the last century and, more definitively, with the reforms of Atatürk from 1922. Turkey is a member of NATO, but this is really its only trump card, and Turkish accession raises major questions on virtually every front, including new ones like cultural differences: for example, the difficulties relate to economics (Turkey's low GDP per capita and the implications for the EC budget), politics (Cyprus, the Kurds, police brutality, and human rights), EC institutions (the size of Turkey), culture (the place of Islam in Turkey), and specific issues (agriculture and the free movement of labour). The Turks were the first of the current applicants, and the Community delayed the Commission's opinion for as long as it could. Eventually, however, it was issued, in December 1989, and it was negative.[20] The reasons for this rejection were essentially the list of problems given above, and the EC offered an enhanced association agreement as an alternative. However, the Turks regard their rejection as a temporary one, and their application will have to be reconsidered in due course.

The Cypriot application is linked to that of Turkey, to some extent, for obvious reasons, although it is not impossible that Cyprus could be admitted to the EC before Turkey.[21] If it were simply a matter of economics then Cyprus could be considered a very attractive prospective member of the EC: the Greek majority enjoys a per capita income approaching that of Spain, the economy has been booming, and Cyprus is already engaged in creating a customs union with the EC through the second stage of the EC-Cyprus association agreement. Moreover, the impoverished Turkish north is small enough to present a relatively trivial economic problem. However, the central issue is not economic but political. As long as Cyprus remains a partitioned island it is unlikely to be acceptable to the EC as a member. Indeed, it is the Greek Cypriots alone who have applied for EC membership. The official position of the Turkish Cypriots is that they oppose this on the grounds that they were not consulted as they should have been under the terms of the 1960 Constitution, although this opposition has not prevented them from a very active pursuit of EC import quotas for Cypriot agricultural exports. A political divide of this nature and the lack of any solution to this political impasse in the foreseeable future almost certainly precludes Cypriot accession.

Malta lacks resources, has a small agricultural sector, and is dependent on imports and foreign capital; therefore, it viewed the EC's completion of its internal market with some alarm, and it is this, together with the Iberian enlargement, that has pushed Malta to an application for EC membership. Another major factor was the change in government in 1987 from an anti-EC Labour government to a pro-EC Nationalist government (which was re-elected in 1992). This made an application for EC membership inevitable. Nevertheless, an important effect of this internal political disagreement has been that there is a lively debate in Malta about the merits of membership and possible alternatives,[22] although the preferred Labour party alternative of a long-term framework agreement (weighted in Malta's favor) with a periodic review of the membership option is both politically unrealistic and potentially amounts to little more than accession with a long transition period. In economic terms, Malta would simply be a minor addition to the EC's impoverished south, and the main problems would arise in Malta itself. There is the question of Malta's nonalignment, but Malta, like Cyprus, seems willing to compromise in order to get the benefits of EC membership. In any case, this issue will be resolved, with no reference to the Cypriot and Maltese positions, when the EFTA neutrals join the Community. In fact, the major difficulty on the EC side concerns the size of Malta. It would be the first "microstate" to be admitted to the Community and would raise important institutional matters of practice and principle. Small countries have a disproportionate effect on the Community institutions in terms of another commissioner, another seat in the Council, and so on, but, more importantly, the ultimate question is really whether a small country like Malta (or Cyprus) could really take its turn at running the EC (Council) presidency. However, these are institutional questions that the EC is going to have to address in a wider context, and this may delay Maltese accession for some time. Nevertheless, Malta's prospects for EC membership look good, and the possibility of it slipping in with the next wave of EFTA countries is not entirely unfeasible.

***

The final group of aspiring European Community members consists of the countries in Central and Eastern Europe that formerly constituted part of the Soviet bloc or, indeed, in some cases the Soviet Union itself.[23] For many of these, full EC membership is probably a long way in the future unless the Community were to disintegrate into a much looser arrangement. Realistically, the only countries that have much chance of joining within the next ten years or so are Poland, Hungary, and the Czech Republic (although a completely independent Slovak Republic might have to be excluded), with Bulgaria and Romania following them, possibly within the same timescale. However, these are very early days and, although these countries are keen to show their interest in EC accession, this currently amounts to a political aspiration and is not an economic possibility. It is true that the EC has accepted countries on political grounds when the economic omens were not good in the past (Spain, Portugal, and Greece), but the Eastern European economic problems are of a much higher order. Of course, it is precisely because of these problems and, more specifically, the help that EC financial and technical assistance could give to the process of economic development, that makes EC membership attractive. In addition, the former Soviet bloc members want to take part in the single market and, effectively, obtain an EC guarantee for their fledgling democracies. Finally, unlike the EFTA neutrals, they take a very positive view of future EC cooperation in the fields of defense and security.

The Community's response has been a cautious and, some would say, an ungenerous one. The standard trade and cooperation agreement of the type that the EC has with many countries is available to states that are up to it. Many are not, particularly those in the European part of the CIS. Beyond that are the Europe Agreements, which have so far only been negotiated with Poland, Hungary, Czechoslovakia, and (more recently) Romania, and (a long way) beyond that is accession. Another intermediate stage between the Europe agreements and accession may well eventually emerge; membership of the EEA was being widely put forward as a candidate for the EC's "premembership" chamber, although the drawbacks that emerged during the negotiation of the EEA have made this a less likely scenario. Nevertheless, cooperation with the countries of Eastern Europe is very attractive to the EC; such cooperation would enhance European security and is in line with the EC's underlying political values; moreover, there is great potential for trade with Eastern Europe, and, more importantly, economic failure would make many of the new democracies susceptible to a return to a more authoritarian regime and would provoke emigration into the EC, which the Community sees as undesirable and extremely problematical.

The EC is proceeding very carefully and is essentially caught between the political necessity of being very positive toward the countries of Eastern Europe and the economic reality that the same countries are very far from being economically ready for accession. A new form of association, Europe Agreements, have been negotiated with Poland, Hungary, Czechoslovakia, and Romania,[24] and Bulgaria will follow. These agreements include:

- Association institutions
- Political dialogue
- A free trade area in industrial goods and rather more limited concessions in agriculture
- Economic and financial cooperation
- Cultural cooperation

There is also a reference in the preamble of these agreements to EC accession as an ultimate (but not automatic) goal, although the Community was very reluctant to give this. In fact, the five aspiring EC members in Eastern Europe are all at different stages of the same process, and they are so far away from EC accession as to make comments about individual states of limited relevance. Nevertheless, it is clear that the sheer size of the Polish population makes it a more difficult case and that this also applies to Romania to some extent. Similarly, the division of Czechoslovakia may create complications.

However, many of the problems that would arise in any accession negotiations are common to all five and will also arise in the application of the Europe Agreements which might be regarded, like the EEA, as an unsatisfactory half-way house. These include market access for certain Eastern European products, notably steel, textiles, and agriculture; the difficulty is that these commodities represent, at the same time, the products that the East can best produce for export and the sectors in which, for various reasons, the EC wants to protect its own producers. Another major area relates to the movement of labor and, specifically, the need to allay EC fears of massive migration from Eastern to Western Europe. In fact, all four freedoms of movement (goods, people, services, and capital) will be problematic and can clearly not be introduced until significant progress has been made in reforming the economies of the five countries concerned (and of any other prospective Eastern European members). Ultimately, it is political and, especially, economic reform that holds the key to accession to the EC for these countries, but since the EC has a vested interest in such reform, then they can expect to be admitted as members in due course, but not yet.

***

The Community stands accused of a very negative attitude to enlargement: "In essence all policies are aimed at avoiding the question of membership. . . . In a way, the Community is offering bribes to the Eftans and East Europeans not to bother it too much."[25] This is clearly not a viable long-term strategy. There has been no clear strategic thinking about how the Community needs to evolve to maintain its momentum, and because of this, the EC has been unable to formulate a coherent policy toward the aspiring members. This may be partly because the EC's agenda is overloaded. It sought to deal with the enlargement issue initially by stating that the internal market must be completed first. The EC then extended this and said that, in addition, the future financial arrangements of the Community (the Delors II package) must also be settled. However, recognition that difficult decisions have to be taken seems to have begun at the Lisbon summit in June 1992 when an enlargement policy was presented on the basis of a Commission paper[26] that was adopted at that summit. In fact, this did little more than identify the issues and imply the likely order of accession of the applicant states.

The report did, indeed, clarify the criteria that new members would have to meet and went on to look at the potential conflict between widening and deepening, stating categorically the need to "ensure that 'more' does not lead to 'less'" (para. 19). In this connection, the role of subsidiarity and the need to make good the "democratic deficit" by enhancing the role of the European Parliament were stressed. As far as who is first in the queue is concerned, the integration of the EFTA countries "would not impose insurmountable problems . . . although . . . there remain a number of sensitive fields. . . . Likewise, the integration of Cyprus and Malta into the Community system would not pose insurmountable problems of an economic nature" (para. 17). However, Cyprus is later excluded partly because its smallness creates institutional dilemmas but mainly because it is politically divided (para. 30), while Malta is also excluded but, interestingly, only because of the institutional difficulties raised by its size (para. 31). Turkish accession is currently a nonstarter (para. 29), and the Eastern Europeans are currently only "partners" (para. 34–39). Thus there are currently two clear groups: the probables (the EFTA countries) and the improbables (Turkey and Eastern Europe); Malta and Cyprus are somewhere in the middle, with Malta tending toward the former and Cyprus toward the latter.

The report goes on to raise two potential general problems, adopting an inflexible attitude to the first and a flexible one to the second. Firstly, it indicates unequivocally that the embryonic common foreign and security policy that may lead to a common defense policy is sacrosanct. "Applicant countries should be left with no doubts in this respect. Specific and binding assurances will be sought from them with regard to their political commitment and legal capacity to fulfil the obligations" (para. 17). The second issue relates to institutional reforms, and the report simply asks three questions concerning the working practices of the EC institutions, the number of members each institution should have, and how the decisionmaking process should work (para. 23). It seems probable that this difference of approach reflects the fact that there is agreement among the EC Twelve about the need for a common security policy but substantial disagreement over the shape that institutional reform should take. In this connection the Benelux countries have already fired a warning shot in the memorandum that they submitted to the Lisbon summit.[27] This explicitly lays down how EC institutions should be organized in a larger Community (p. 3):

- "The larger countries will have to accept some over-representation of the smaller member countries," for example, in the European Parliament.
- "The Commission must be composed of one member per Member State. This also applies to the European Court of Justice."
- "The six-monthly rota for the Presidency [of the Council] held by each Member State should not be changed."
- As far as majority voting is concerned, the proposal is that the current principle should be maintained by which large countries cannot combine to impose decisions, but small countries cannot combine to block them.

This amounts to saying that the present system should continue. Clearly the scene has been set for a very contentious debate. More generally, institutional reform will be the central issue raised by enlargement within the existing EC, while the main "external" question will revolve around the neutrality issue (although when the Eastern Europeans come to the front of the queue the main concern will relate to their access to the EC market, particularly for "sensitive" products).

However, all these questions are really part of a much wider debate over the form that the Community should take in the future. This raises the specter, if that indeed is what it is, of a multi-tier or multi-speed Europe, the Europe of concentric circles. Given the aspirations of the applicant states, it may be necessary for the EC to grant membership sooner rather than later, and some kind of partial or "outer" membership may be the only way of accommodating those countries that are simply not ready for full membership. After all, a multi-speed Community has arguably already arrived: there are at least three forms of membership of the exchange rate mechanism, the Schengen Agreement covers only two-thirds of the current EC membership, and opt-out clauses were agreed for two members at Maastricht and extended for Denmark at Edinburgh. Moreover, in the run up to the Birmingham and Edinburgh summits, there were dark rumors that, if the ratification of the Maastricht Treaty became impossible, then France, Germany, and the Benelux countries were prepared to go it alone and create their own version of European Union. In fact, in the context of enlargement, a multi-speed EC may have advantages in that it could allow the more peripheral members to play some role in the decisionmaking procedure without taking on the full mantle of membership. In this scenario, every European state has its place in "Europe" (or the Community, which would amount to the same thing) and is basically happy with it, or at least with the involvement in decisionmaking and the incentive of progressing to a higher tier of membership. This latter possibility is important because the problem with being a second rank member of the Community is that it is full membership of the existing EC that the current applicants really want.[28]

This is the optimistic scenario if one accepts the underlying assumption that there exist unrealistic expectations of imminent EC membership in countries that are not yet ready for the responsibilities that membership would bring. The pessimistic assumption is that the Community continues to act negatively with the result that Europe becomes divided, initially on economic lines, but eventually on political lines, as the former Soviet bloc countries turn away from democracy in the face of their failure to be accepted in the Western European mainstream. In this scenario, the EC would absorb only EFTA and become a rich man's club, leaving Eastern and parts of Central Europe together with Turkey and other Mediterranean states impoverished on the periphery, with no prospect of EC membership. The unyielding stance that the Community has been adopting toward new members, particularly with regard to the requirement to accept the *acquis communautaire* plus the

Maastricht Treaty and the common foreign and security policy, suggests that this pessimistic scenario is a real possibility. (Only institutional reform seems open to discussion, and that is arguably not new but part of an evolutionary process that is happening anyway.) This would make for a decidedly unstable Europe and is in nobody's interest. More specifically, there is a real danger that the EC will become totally preoccupied by its own internal concerns and will continue to be ungenerous to the rest of Europe, especially to the East.

In late 1992, the Community finally agreed to begin formal negotiations with Austria, Finland, and Sweden in January 1993, and with Norway a few months later. However, the negotiations will not be easy in the face of hostile public opinion in at least two of those countries. The most recent opinion polls indicated majorities against EC accession, with 33 percent in favor and 50 percent against in Sweden and only 30 percent in favor and 54 percent against in Norway.[29] Moreover, a shadow is cast over the proceedings by the Swiss rejection of the EEA, and, furthermore, the extensive Danish opt-out agreed at Edinburgh may conceivably be viewed as a precedent by the aspiring EC members from EFTA, particularly the neutrals. Consequently, the optimistic scenario also has its problems. Ultimately however, whichever way forward is chosen, it is clear that the widening issue is probably the most important faced by the EC today. It is about much more than enlarging the Community.

Notes

1. "European Commission Report on the Criteria and Conditions for Accession of New Members to the Community," *Europe Documents* no. 1790 (July 3, 1992), paragraph 7.

2. Ibid., *paragraph 9.*

3. Ibid.

4. Commission of the EC, *Communication from the Commission to the Council: Redirecting the Community's Mediterranean Policy* (Brussels, 1990).

5. A more detailed consideration of the EC's relations with EFTA and the prospects for an "EFTAn" enlargement is provided by R. Schwok, "The European Free Trade Area: Revival or Collapse?" in J. Redmond, ed., *The External Relations of the European Community: the International Response to 1992* (London: Macmillan and New York: St. Martins Press, 1992); and H. Wallace, ed., *The Wider Western Europe* (London: Pinter for the Royal Institute of International Affairs, 1991).

6. Malta might also be in this category, although its reluctance to establish close relations with the EC before 1987 stemmed from peculiar local circumstances and did not reflect a general view taken by the major political parties and the electorate at large.

7. For example, it was as late as May 1992 that the Swiss finally voted, very narrowly, to join the IMF and the World Bank, with only 55 percent voting in favor in a turnout of only 39 percent of the electorate.

8. Schwok, op. cit., p. 67.

9. See "European Commission Opinion on Austria's Request for Membership to the European Community," *Europe Documents* no. 1730 (August 3, 1991).

10. Ibid., p. 3.

11. Comments of Mr. W. Wolte, Austrian ambassador to the EC, *Europe* no. 5764

(July 3, 1992).

12. S. Astrom "The Nordic Angle I: Sweden's EC Dilemmas," *World Today* 44 no. 11 (November 1988), p. 191.

13. A. Michalski and H. Wallace, *The European Community: The Challenge of Enlargement* (London: R. I. I. A., 1992), p. 44.

14. K. Sorsa, "Finland and European Integration," *New Europe* 2 no. 1 (Spring 1989), p. 24.

15. Up to 1990 approximately a quarter of Finnish exports went to the USSR.

16. See Schwok, op. cit., pp. 71–72 and, for more detail, R. Schwok, *Switzerland and the European Common Market* (New York: Praeger,1991), pp. 107–115.

17. Maria Romantschuk, "Island är inte till salu (Iceland Not For Sale)," *Hufvudstadsbladet*, October 6, 1990, quoted in Schwok in Redmond, op. cit., p. 70.

18. More detail is provided by J. Redmond, *The Next Mediterranean Enlargement of the European Community: Turkey, Cyprus and Malta?* (Aldershot: Dartmouth, 1993).

19. See T. Ozal, *Turkey in Europe and Europe in Turkey* (Nicosia: K. Rustem and Brother, 1991) for a (very) full statement of this argument.

20. Commission of the EC, *Commission Opinion on Turkey's Request for Accession to the Community* (Brussels: SEC(89) 2290 final/2, 1989).

21. The opposite—Turkey being admitted before Cyprus—is unlikely because Turkish accession is probably impossible until there has been major progress on the Cyprus issue, and such progress would also facilitate Cypriot accession since the partition of the island is the principal barrier to it joining the Community.

22. For a detailed account of the arguments in favor of joining the EC, see Malta Department of Information, *Report by the EC Directorate to the Prime Minister and Minister of Foreign Affairs Regarding Malta's Membership of the European Community* (Valetta, 1990). The arguments against are given in Malta Labour Party, *Malta and the EEC: Economic and Social Aspects* (Valetta, 1990).

23. A useful recent account of the EC's relations with the former Soviet bloc countries is provided by J. Pinder, *The European Community and Eastern Europe* (London: Pinter for the Royal Institute of International Affairs, 1991).

24. These agreements will not be implemented until some time in 1993 after they have been ratified by all the relevant parliaments. In the meantime, interim agreements are applying the commercial elements of the Europe Agreements.

25. J. M. C. Rollo and H. Wallace, "New Patterns of Partnership," in G. Bonvicini et al., *The Community and the Emerging Democracies: A Joint Policy Report* (London: Royal Institute for International Affairs, 1991), p. 64.

26. "European Commission Report on the Criteria and Conditions for Accession of New Members to the Community," *Europe Documents* no. 1790 (July 3, 1992).

27. "The Community's Enlargement: the Benelux Memorandum Submitted to the European Council of Lisbon," *Europe Documents* no. 1789 (June 27, 1992).

28. There is a related issue here: this concerns the possibility that allowing the current applicants to join the Community too quickly would weaken it so much that, by the very act of joining, the new members would cause the Community to cease to be the organization to which they applied to join and to which they want to belong. This problem could be construed as a good argument for having a multi-tier EC and allowing new "members" to progress to full membership gradually.

29. *Financial Times*, December 14, 1992, p. 3.

14

European Political Cooperation: Lessons from the Gulf War and Yugoslavia

Pia Christina Wood

Events over the last five years have pushed the European Community into the limelight and stimulated new debate over the possibilities for political as well as economic union. The newfound enthusiasm of the late 1980s and early 1990s for a common European foreign policy built upon earlier efforts to achieve this objective. The idea for a framework for political cooperation was first introduced at the Hague summit in December 1969 by President Georges Pompidou and was further defined by the Luxembourg (Davignon) Report in October 1970, which called for greater cooperation in foreign policy. The Copenhagen Report of 1973 reiterated the need for concerted action in foreign policy, and the London Report of 1981 established consultative procedures to allow for a faster response to crises. The Single European Act, ratified in 1987, further defined the framework (Title III, Article 30) for European Political Cooperation (EPC). Although all obligations remained voluntary, member states, defined as High Contracting Parties, agreed to inform and consult each other on foreign policy issues before any final positions were taken. Title V, Article J.1 of the Maastricht Treaty signed (but not ratified) on February 7, 1992, states that "The Union and its Member States shall define and implement a common foreign and security policy, . . . covering all areas of foreign and security policy."[1]

These institutional developments have led to a growing debate over how to interpret the record of EPC and predict its future development.[2] There can be little disagreement that a common European foreign and security policy has not yet emerged. Consultations do occur regularly but EPC remains limited in scope, characterized largely by "lowest common denominator" declarations. The inability of EPC to respond in unison has been particularly noticeable in crisis situations such as the Gulf crisis (August 2, 1990–January 15, 1991) and the Yugoslav crisis beginning in 1991. In each case, initial attempts to coordinate a European approach were undermined by the lack of effective EC institutions and the determination of member states to assert national interests. Instead of an emerging "single European voice" in foreign policy, it is more likely that member states will continue to use EPC as an instrument of national foreign policies within an intergovernmental bargaining framework.

The Gulf Crisis, August 2, 1990–January 15, 1991

EPC and the Struggle for Consensus

The Iraqi invasion of Kuwait on August 2, 1990, caught the European Community by surprise. Despite the increasingly acrimonious exchanges between Iraq and Kuwait in July and August and reports that Iraqi troops were massing along the border, the Europeans were preoccupied by problems in Eastern Europe, possible unification of Germany, and discussions over the economic and political union of the EC.

In the immediate aftermath of the Iraqi invasion, the Europeans were able to agree to certain common responses within the EPC framework. The Twelve strongly condemned the Iraqi invasion and managed on August 4 to agree to impose an immediate embargo on oil imports from Kuwait and Iraq, to freeze all Iraqi assets, and to suspend all military, scientific, and technical cooperation with Iraq.[3] The Europeans also unanimously agreed to UN Resolution 661, which called for the imposition of a trade and economic boycott on Iraq and Kuwait. Although some observers hailed the unanimous agreement as an indication of a growing European identity in foreign policy, the outrageousness of the invasion made it easy for everyone to agree on a common response. The EC also sought to coordinate its military response through the Western European Union (WEU). It was agreed at a WEU meeting on August 21 that there would be coordination between forces, sharing of intelligence, and logistical support.[4] Agreement over economic aid to frontline states was also reached on August 31 (the Twelve agreed to send 1.3 million ECU to Jordan), but the members were divided over how to respond to the U.S. request for money. After a long debate, a compromise was reached between those who wanted to maintain a distance from the United States and those who wanted to lend support. EC funds would not be used to pay for the cost of U.S. deployment, but money would be given to those nations financially strained by the crisis, particularly Jordan, Egypt, and Turkey. Finally, the EC was able initially to coordinate its response toward two important issues: the question of embassies and European hostages. The EC resolved that it would not close any embassies in Kuwait despite orders to the contrary from Saddam Hussein and warned that the Community would respond in unison against maltreatment of any EC citizen.

Despite these agreements, cracks in European unity appeared almost immediately. First and foremost, the Europeans were unable to reach agreement to support individual military action.[5] In the initial stages of the crisis,

Great Britain sent six warships, France sent the aircraft carrier *Clemenceau,* and the Netherlands sent two frigates. In September, the British government, without consulting or informing the other EC members, decided to send 6,000 combat troops to the Gulf, a decision that directly contradicted the EC policy of maintaining pressure on Iraq through the embargo and demonstrated the importance Britain placed on the Atlantic link.[6] Eventually each country responded individually. For example, Belgium sent two minesweepers and five ships to the Gulf and jets to Turkey. Italy sent ships and Tornado jets to Saudi Arabia.[7] It soon became clear that the anticipated leadership of the WEU would not materialize. Disagreements between the French and British as well as reluctance by other members to participate in the WEU reduced it to a marginal role in the naval blockade. Coordination during the war itself was carried out on an individual basis between the participating European countries and the United States. Sharp exchanges between national leaders occurred as well. British Prime Minister Margaret Thatcher, on August 30, strongly criticized all the Europeans except France for their lukewarm support for the United States. Spanish Prime Minister Felipe Gonzales, in turn, categorized Thatcher as a hawk who was more anxious to fight than to find a peaceful solution to the problem.[8]

By November, European solidarity was showing further signs of strain from disagreements over how to gain the release of the hostages held in Kuwait and Iraq and, more generally, over EC diplomacy toward Iraq. Saddam Hussein further exacerbated the tension among EC members when he announced on October 23 that he would free all French hostages. This led to numerous charges that France had made a separate deal, directly contradicting the EC decision to deal with the hostage issue as a unified body. The French government immediately announced that Iraq's decision had been unilateral and emphatically denied that it had negotiated with Iraq at any level.[9] The Twelve met in Rome at the end of October and agreed not to send government representatives to negotiate individually with Iraq over the release of the hostages. Despite this agreement, Willy Brandt traveled to Iraq with at least the tacit support of the German government, an action that the Dutch, Belgians, and British condemned.[10] But the lack of European solidarity over the hostage issue was overshadowed by the EC's attempt to avoid a war with Iraq and the French decision to break rank and play "lone ranger."

On November 29, the UN Security Council passed Resolution 678 which not only allowed members to "use all necessary means to uphold and implement" previous resolutions but also set a deadline, January 15, 1991, for Iraq to comply with previous UN resolutions. Immediately European diplomatic activity increased in an attempt to find a solution before the deadline arrived. On December 4, the Twelve announced that they would invite Iraqi Foreign Minister Tariq Aziz to discuss the situation with them after his visit to Washington. However, when Aziz did not go to Washington, the EC met in Rome on December 18 to assess the situation. Under pressure from the United

States not to interfere, a compromise was reached between those who supported a European initiative and those who sided with the United States. The EC agreed to wait and see if a U.S.-Iraqi meeting would materialize on January 3 but promised to meet on January 4 to consider the situation.[11]

It was at the January 4 meeting that the precarious consensus completely broke down. Roland Dumas, the French foreign minister, presented a seven-point plan, including the following steps: the announcement by Iraq that it would withdraw from Kuwait; talks between Jacques Poos, the president of the EC, and Iraq's Foreign Minister Aziz even if the scheduled meeting between U.S. Secretary of State James Baker and Aziz did not take place; and, after the evacuation of Kuwait, the convening of one or two international conferences to consider all the problems in the Middle East.[12] Both Britain and the Netherlands categorically rejected the postcrisis Middle East conference because they opposed any EC actions that might undermine U.S. initiatives.[13] The argument proved moot, as Aziz did agree to meet with Baker in January and then refused any subsequent meeting with the EC. With the failure of the Baker-Aziz talks, France attempted to convince the EC to send an emissary to Iraq for a last-ditch peace effort. This effort failed due to strong opposition from the Netherlands, Denmark, and Great Britain. Dumas succinctly stated: "Europe does not have a common foreign policy."[14] With the EC deadlocked, Mitterrand decided to ignore it and launch a final national initiative on January 14; once again, it was rejected by the United States and Great Britain.

The Gulf crisis demonstrated the elusiveness of a common European foreign policy. The United States not only dominated the political and military arena but also applied pressure on individual European countries to join the alliance, both economically and militarily, against Iraq. This, in turn, exacerbated the differences between Great Britain and the Netherlands, which strongly supported the United States, France (which wanted to cooperate but not too closely), and the majority of the other Europeans, who simply wanted to maintain a low profile.

National Foreign Policies—France, Great Britain, and Germany

During the Gulf crisis, President Mitterrand attempted to strike a balance between maintaining France's reputation as an independent player and coordinating with the U.S.-led coalition against Iraq.[15] In the United Nations, France's preferred forum because of its permanent seat on the Security Council, France endorsed numerous resolutions condemning Saddam Hussein. Equally important was Mitterrand's positive response to Washington's request for military participation. The French government concluded that nonparticipation would jeopardize France's claim to be an active player in the region and exclude it from any role in the postwar peace settlement. On August 6, Mitterrand dispatched three ships to the Gulf to join two already stationed there, and, August 10 announced that the aircraft carrier *Clemenceau,* with an action force of some 2,000 men and forty helicopters, was steaming to the Gulf. However, it was not until Iraqi soldiers entered and sacked the French embassy in Iraq on September 14 that Mitterrand sent significant ground forces to Saudi Arabia. "Opération Daguet" consisted of some 4,000 men, tanks, helicopters, and jet fighters.[16]

Despite this support for the United States, France was, in the Gaullist tradition, determined to maintain its independence. The French expended considerable effort to find a diplomatic, face-saving solution to help their former ally, Iraq, extricate itself from its predicament.[17] On the military front, the French government stressed that French troops were under "operational control," meaning they were only "lent" to General Schwarzkopf for a certain time and a predetermined space but the mission would be executed under French command.[18] This fine distinction, however, could not hide the substantial Franco-U.S. military coordination.

At the heart of France's approach was an attempt to manipulate the question of linkage, which Saddam had suggested in early August (Iraq would withdraw from Kuwait if Israel would withdraw from the Occupied Territories of the West Bank and the Gaza). In a move that surprised the United States, Mitterrand, in a speech to the UN General Assembly on September 24, proposed a four-stage peace settlement, the first being an Iraqi declaration of intent to withdraw from Kuwait after which "everything becomes possible."[19] The initiative was accompanied by others, including a meeting between Arafat and Roland Dumas in October, a joint Franco-Soviet declaration on the Middle East, and outspoken support for an international peace conference to solve the other problems in the region, particularly the Israeli-Palestinian conflict. All French efforts to manipulate the timing of the international conference failed because of U.S. hostility to what it perceived as linkage and Iraqi indifference. In one final effort, on January 14, Mitterrand proposed a draft resolution in the United Nations that was divided into two clear sections to resolve the debate over linkage. In the first part, France called for Iraq to announce its withdrawal from Kuwait after which time the secretary general of the UN would send international observers to control and verify the withdrawal. As a consequential action, the UN Security Council would then "make an active effort to resolve the other problems of the region and, in particular, the Arab-Israeli conflict and the Palestinian problem through the convening, at an appropriate time, of a properly structured international conference."[20] This infuriated the British; the day before, Prime Minister John Major had met with President Mitterrand, but no mention of the initiative had been made.[21] In any case, Iraq did not respond to the proposal.

Great Britain took a much harsher stand toward Iraq and extended strong diplomatic and military support to the United States right from the start. Prime Minister Margaret Thatcher was quick to criticize the EC response as inadequate and emphasized the importance of the Atlantic Alliance and NATO as opposed to WEU. No doubt, Thatcher was concerned to shore up the "special relationship," which had been showing signs of weakening. It seems likely that the historical and economic ties between Great Britain and Kuwait also played a role in the British assessment. There are extensive financial ties between Great Britain and her former colony, and the powerful Kuwait Investment Office, which controls and invests large sums, has its seat in London. Finally, the British government's position was not confronted with any important internal opposition. Public opinion supported the hard-line stance and the Labour party, led by Neil Kinnock, endorsed Thatcher's policies.

Margaret Thatcher's resignation did not change British policy. On December 21, John Major, in a visit to Washington, officially offered President Bush his full support for the use of force against Saddam Hussein if Iraq did not withdraw from Kuwait by January 15, 1991. By the time the war broke out, the British had the second largest force in the Gulf region, operating under the command of General Schwarzkopf. The British also continued to support the U.S. position in the United Nations and consistently opposed French initiatives within the EPC that might introduce the concept of "linkage" or interfere with U.S. plans. Thus, in the final analysis, the British government believed that its national interests could best be protected by aligning itself with the United States at the expense of EC solidarity.

For Germany, the Gulf crisis could not have occurred at a more inauspicious time. In the midst of reunifying East and West Germany, Helmut Kohl's government was preoccupied by internal economic and political problems. Equally important in the equation were Articles 24, 26, and 87a of Germany's Basic Law, which address German security. They allow Germany to enter into a "system of mutual collective security" but also state that German armed forces may only be used for "defense purposes." At first, Kohl appeared willing to send forces within a WEU framework, but he immediately encountered opposition from the SPD and the FDP, who argued that the Basic Law prohibited German forces from being deployed outside of the NATO area. Although Kohl had promised to amend the constitution, military action was clearly unpopular with the German people.

Under strong pressure from a growing peace movement and internal opposition from Foreign Minister Hans-Dietrich Genscher and the Social Democrats, Kohl announced on August 20 that German participation would consist solely of monetary aid and logistical support. Eventually this included the full use of German naval and air bases and billions of dollars in pledged support for Arab front-line countries, Great Britain, and the United States. Although Kohl strongly supported the United States, it was clear that he did not consider the Gulf War a first priority. Instead, the absolute priorities remained the achievement of the unification of East and West Germany and the establishment of good relations with Eastern Europe and particularly the

Soviet Union. However, Germany's low profile strained relations with the United States. It was only under strong pressure from the United States that Kohl agreed in January 1991 to send eighteen Alphajets and 300 troops to Turkey, a fellow NATO member. In the final analysis, Germany's foreign policy further undermined the EPC's efforts either to speak with a "single voice" or to act in unison.

In the wake of the Gulf War, a great deal of discussion ensued over the performance of the European Community. Although there was intense criticism over the lack of European solidarity, several governments and Jacques Delors argued that the disarray among EC members could be ameliorated by further steps toward political and economic union. Negotiations in the Intergovernmental Conference on political union over a common foreign and security policy led to Title V of the Maastricht Treaty, which appeared to strengthen the EC's commitment to cohesion in foreign policy. However, the crisis in Yugoslavia has raised serious doubts over its applicability.

The Crisis in Yugoslavia

Initially, there seemed to be a general consensus within the EC over the mounting crisis in Yugoslavia. The EC had three major objectives: a united Yugoslavia, a political dialogue between all parties to implement needed democratic reforms, and a ban on the use of force. To achieve these objectives, the EC sought to wield economic and financial instruments. In May 1991, the EC threatened to suspend both the second financial protocol with Yugoslavia and negotiations over an association agreement with Yugoslavia unless the fighting ceased and independence movements in Croatia and Slovenia were halted. British Prime Minister John Major announced that "the first prize is to keep the federation together," a sentiment echoed by French Prime Minister Edith Cresson, who proclaimed that "Yugoslavia cannot be part of Europe unless she remains united."[22] When Croatia and Slovenia refused to bow to international pressure and declared their independence, the EC responded more or less in unison. The Twelve agreed at their meeting in Luxembourg on June 23 that they would not recognize Slovenia or Croatia if they unilaterally seceded from Yugoslavia.

The French and Spanish rejected secession. They feared that secession might provide a precedent for movements in their own countries (Basque, Catalonia, Corsica), and France was concerned with maintaining stability in a volatile region on the EC's borders. A centrally controlled Yugoslavia presented a much smaller threat of civil war than did numerous small, economically and politically undeveloped countries. France also worried that an independent Slovenia and Croatia would reinforce a German zone of influence in Central Europe. Finally, the French and others feared that support for secession would have negative implications for the Soviet Union.[23]

When heavy fighting broke out in Slovenia at the end of June, the EC responded quickly by sending a diplomatic mission to mediate between the parties. The EC claimed success when the warring sides agreed to a cease-fire and a three-month suspension of the declarations of independence of Croatia and Slovenia. Jacques Poos, the EC president, announced: "We have completed our mission. . . . If the Yugoslavs want to enter the Europe of the 20th century, they have to follow our advice. This is the hour of the Europe, not the hour of the Americans."[24] This proclamation of success, however, was quickly undermined as the cease-fire was disregarded. After two more diplomatic missions, an EC decision to place an embargo on armaments and military equipment to all of Yugoslavia, and the suspension of the second and third financial protocols with Yugoslavia, the Brioni Declaration was signed on July 7 by all the Yugoslav participants. They reaffirmed their commitment to the EC's June 30 proposals and agreed that a fifty-member European observer mission, requested by the CSCE, would be sent to monitor the cease-fire in Slovenia, and possibly Croatia, also in accordance with the "June 25th" declarations of independence of Croatia and Slovenia. However, despite the observer force, economic sanctions, and diplomatic efforts, the EC was unable to devise a solution acceptable to all sides. The Brioni Accords, which were supposed to be the starting point for negotiations, turned out to be little more than a delaying tactic used by the Yugoslav factions to consolidate their positions. The result was a deepening of the crisis and the slow breakdown of European consensus on the Yugoslav issue.

An EC Peace Conference and the
Question of a WEU Peacekeeping Force

With the failure of the Brioni Accords, divergences began to appear among the EC members. All agreed that the best solution was a federal Yugoslavia, provided that it did not require force. The opposition to the two breakaway republics remained firm, but there was increasing support for independence for Slovenia and Croatia after appropriate negotiations.[25] The agreement over nonrecognition was accompanied by a German proposal, endorsed by the EC, to organize a conference, and a French proposal, also endorsed, to create an arbitration commission. The convening of the conference was not without controversy. Italy, France, and Germany wanted to convene the conference as quickly as possible, whereas the British and the Dutch wanted to delay it until a ceasefire had been fully implemented. The Franco-German position was accepted under strong pressure from Germany.[26] The conference opened on September 7 at the Hague under the direction of Lord Carrington.

Despite agreement on convening the peace conference, EC solidarity collapsed over the issue of military intervention. In early August, France, supported by Italy, called for the convening of the WEU to consider sending a military force to intervene in Yugoslavia. The Germans favored the idea but would not send troops due to constitutional problems. The British (fearing another Northern Ireland imbroglio) opposed the plan, as did Spain and Greece. Given the internal disagreements, it came as no surprise that the WEU meeting held on August 7 ended with nothing more than an agreement to "continue its reflection."

On September 19, the Twelve met in the Hague and again discussed the possibilities for sending a European force to Yugoslavia. The Dutch had previously proposed sending in a European peacekeeping force under the WEU banner, while the French and Germans supported a UN Security Council mandate to send in a European force. John Major was unenthusiastic. He argued that it was irresponsible to send in a European peacekeeping force without a widely accepted ceasefire. British officials carefully laid out the dangers of getting involved in a drawn-out guerrilla war and clearly stated that they were not committed to contributing to a peacekeeping force. The British received support from the Spanish and the Greeks, while the French, Dutch, Belgians, and Italians backed some form of intervention. The continued fighting in Yugoslavia, however, rendered the discussion moot as none of the EC members were willing to send in peacekeeping forces without both Serbian agreement and an effective ceasefire. It took many months and numerous resolutions by the United Nations before the WEU could agree to act. On July 10, 1992, the WEU, strongly supported by the French, was able to agree to send a half-dozen ships and a number of helicopters to the Adriatic to monitor the UN embargo against Serbia and Montenegro.

Germany and the Struggle over Recognition

By the end of September two points were clear: the EC peace process was ineffective (as demonstrated by thirteen failed cease-fires), and a federal Yugoslavia was no longer viable. As Mitterrand stated: "Yugoslavia no longer exists in its original form. . . . We are obliged to accept that before our eyes, a partition has been achieved from the expressed desires of two republics."[27] However, France continued to oppose recognition of Slovenia and Croatia until the fighting ceased, insisting that it would lead to greater violence that would spill over into other republics. Mitterrand argued that independence must be decided in an international context and after problems such as borders, refugees, and human rights were resolved.

Germany, however, adopted a very different position. From the beginning, Germany had sided with Slovenia and Croatia for historical and economic reasons. Equally important was the priority given by the Germans to self-determination; the unification of East and West Germany had been based on this principle. Despite these factors, the German government initially acquiesced to the French and British position on nonrecognition. Helmut Kohl was anxious to preserve European unity before the Maastricht summit.

However, as it became clear that the EC was powerless to stop the fighting, the German government encountered increasing domestic pressure to do something about Yugoslavia. All of the major German political parties supported the breakaway republics, and the media presented a one-sided picture of Serbian aggression and atrocities against freedom-seeking Croats. The Catholic bishops in Germany also spoke out strongly in support of the Catholics in Slovenia and Croatia. Finally, the some 700,000 Yugoslav migrant workers in Germany, an estimated two-thirds from Croatia, constituted an important pressure group.

Immediately following the Maastricht summit, Hans-Dietrich Genscher declared that Germany would recognize Slovenia and Croatia with or without EC support. Germany was supported by Denmark and Belgium but faced stiff opposition from all the other EC members as well as from George Bush, Cyrus Vance (the UN envoy to Yugoslavia), UN Secretary General Perez de Cuellar, and Lord Carrington. When Germany refused to bend, the EC sought a compromise formula that would maintain the fiction of European unity. On December 17, the EC announced that any Yugoslav republic that applied for recognition by December 23 and fulfilled certain conditions would be recognized by the EC on January 15. Germany, however, went ahead and recognized Slovenia and Croatia on December 23 but agreed not to open official diplomatic relations until January 15. On January 15, despite a report from the arbitration committee led by Robert Badinter that Croatia did not meet the conditions for recognition, the EC recognized both Slovenia and Croatia. The Badinter group also stated that Macedonia had met the requirements for recognition, but Greece strongly rejected such a move by the EC.

Although both Britain and France strongly disagreed with the Germans over recognition, they agreed to go along for several reasons. First, after having just agreed to the Maastricht Treaty in early December, they were concerned with demonstrating the viability of an economic and political union. The French preferred to accept the EC compromise rather than be accused of breaking rank and destroying EC unity. British Prime Minister John Major was reported to have already agreed to support the German position on recognition in exchange for German support at the Maastricht summit.[28] Second, Cyrus Vance had negotiated a ceasefire on January 3, and it appeared that UN peacekeeping forces might be able to take up positions in Croatia. Thus the British and French argument that recognition would further increase the violence appeared to be invalid. Finally, EC members were furious with Serbia after the Yugoslav Air Force shot down a peacekeeping helicopter on January 8, 1992, killing five members of the EC monitoring mission.

Germany's insistence on early recognition had two important implications. First, Germany was not only willing to play a more assertive role in foreign policy but would openly oppose American and European policies when it perceived its interests to be at stake. These same interests, however, led Germany subsequently to retreat from its high-profile diplomacy. Throughout most of 1992, Germany remained in the background, concentrating on domestic problems and the rebuilding of the former East Germany. Second, it demonstrated the inherent limitations of EPC and the priority EC members give to national interests over Community interests. Interestingly, EC unity collapsed over an issue, diplomatic recognition, that was well within the competence of EPC.

The United Nations, the Crisis in Bosnia-Hercegovina, and the French Initiative

Throughout most of 1991, the United Nations remained relatively uninvolved in the Yugoslav crisis as it was expected that the EC would take the lead in finding a solution to the civil war. However, by September France was interested in enlisting UN support; on September 25, the UN passed Resolution 713 at the request of France, Britain, and Belgium. The resolution imposed an embargo on all deliveries of arms and equipment to Yugoslavia, supported the efforts of the EC, and invited the secretary general of the UN to begin consultations with the government of Yugoslavia.[29] By November, after it was clear that the EC member states could not agree on sending a European peacekeeping force to Yugoslavia (Croatia), the Twelve called on the UN Security Council to take up the question of sending a UN force instead. On November 27, the UN approved the establishment of a UN peacekeeping force in Yugoslavia—but only after certain conditions were met, the most important being the existence of a stable cease-fire. However, the absence of this condition prevented the dispatch of a UN force. It was not until January 8, 1992, (the day after the Serbs shot down an EC helicopter, killing five observers) that the UN decided to send fifty military liaison officers to promote the maintenance of the latest cease-fire. UN Special Envoy Cyrus Vance negotiated a cease-fire and then called for 10,000 UN peacekeepers to take up positions in the combat areas in Croatia. On February 21, the UN Security Council adopted Resolution 743, which endorsed the secretary general's proposal to deploy a United Nations Protection Force to Croatia. The force included military, police, and civilian components totaling more than 13,000 personnel and was established for an initial period of twelve months. Over the next four months, some 14,000 UN troops were deployed in Croatia. As during the Gulf crisis, EC members disagreed over the question of military participation. Each country decided individually its level of participation, and coordination was through the UN rather than the EC. The French, for example, immediately agreed to send troops, while the British and Germans refused. EC disagreements over military participation and diplomatic actions were exacerbated further by the spillover of the fighting into Bosnia-Hercegovina.

By February 1992 the attention of the EC and the UN was shifting to

Bosnia-Hercegovina. Everyone realized that Bosnia, with its three ethnic communities (Muslims, 43.7 percent; Serbs, 31.7 percent; Croats, 17.3 percent) was in imminent danger of sliding into a civil war. After the republic voted in favor of independence, Lord Carrington convened a separate peace conference to discuss Bosnia's independence and draw up a political plan that would give equal representation to all three groups.[30] The plan, however, quickly became obsolete as fighting broke out in Bosnia in early April. Faced with the spread of the civil war, the EC once again attempted to present a united front.

On April 6 the EC agreed to recognize Bosnia as an independent republic. In general, the members believed that postponing recognition of Bosnia would serve no purpose because the republic was already showing signs of instability. The EC was also able to agree to further sanctions against Serbia in May in response to its continued ground attacks and the worsening plight of Sarajevo. Further EC action, however, remained problematic due to internal disagreements. It was not until James Baker accused the EC of doing nothing that it decided on May 23 to impose a trade embargo on Serbia and Montenegro.[31] The trade embargo, however, was very weak, reflecting divisions within the EC. Germany and Britain wanted to impose full-scale sanctions immediately, while France and Greece argued that it was important not to cut off all links with Belgrade. In addition, the French argued that unilateral EC sanctions would be ineffective and that they should be implemented instead through a UN resolution. The result was an embargo that excluded medicine, basic necessities, oil, and did not cut off air links with Serbia. A total embargo was only later agreed to under UN Security Council Resolution 757.

Further disagreements occurred over sending a UN peacekeeping force to Bosnia and recognizing Serbia and Macedonia. Greece actively campaigned for recognizing the newly proclaimed Yugoslavia consisting of Serbia and Montenegro. Britain, Germany, the Netherlands, and Italy vehemently opposed recognition, while France argued that the EC should offer to recognize the new Yugoslavia if it would, in turn, recognize the other four republics. The problems of Macedonia further divided the EC. The arbitration commission and the EC favored recognizing Macedonia but were unable to convince Greece to drop its opposition. Greece insisted that it would never recognize an independent state with the same name as its northernmost province. Although EC members agreed not to recognize Macedonia, the issue over how to respond to the growing crisis in the besieged city of Sarajevo was more divisive, with tragic consequences for that city's inhabitants.

By the beginning of June 1992, the situation in Sarajevo was becoming increasingly desperate. On June 8, the UN Security Council agreed to send 1,000 Blue Helmets to protect the airport if a cease-fire could be implemented. As usual, the decision to participate was made on an individual basis rather than jointly through the EC. The French agreed immediately to send troops while the British and the United States refused outright. The Germans argued that their constitution prohibited them from sending troops. The Italians were not accepted by the Serbs, the Greeks were not accepted by the Bosnians, and the Belgians were already overextended in Cambodia. At an EC meeting in Lisbon held on June 27, the Italians and the French argued in favor of the use of force if necessary to help Sarajevo. The British remained cautious, while the Germans agreed that something should be done but not by German troops. After a great deal of debate, the EC could only agree not to exclude support for the use of military means. France, however, was not satisfied with EC diplomacy, and Mitterrand decided to act on his own.

On June 28, in a move that surprised almost everyone, Mitterrand flew to Sarajevo. He hoped that his visit could break the diplomatic stalemate and open Sarajevo to humanitarian flights. It was all too clear that EC diplomacy was paralyzed and French diplomacy might have a greater chance for success. Moreover, a bold move would shore up his domestic support at home which had fallen to new lows. Mitterrand's trip was an immediate success. The Serbs agreed to turn the airport over to UN forces; 1,000 Canadian peacekeepers arrived on July 2 to secure the airport. The first relief plane to arrive at Sarajevo was French.

Although Mitterrand's initiative was not openly criticized by the British, London was definitely unhappy with what it considered to be a complete lack of support for European solidarity. Mitterrand had only consulted with Portuguese Prime Minister Mario Soares (Portugal held the EC presidency) and Helmut Kohl before his trip, arguing that informing a large number of people would have made the trip more dangerous. Mitterrand later explained that his initiative was a perfect example of subsidiarity: "The European Council had decided upon a policy to follow in Yugoslavia but inside that policy, each country maintains its right to initiatives as long as it is not a substitute for the Community."[32] In addition to leveling accusations of *cavalier seul,* the British were upset over the timing of the visit. Great Britain was scheduled to assume the presidency of the Council on July 1, and Mitterrand's visit had caught them unprepared. This relatively minor spat, however, was followed by additional disagreements over the convening of an international (versus European) conference to mediate the Bosnian civil war and military intervention.

The International Conference and
Indecision over Military Intervention

Franco-British relations deteriorated even further with Mitterrand's call for a larger international conference under UN auspices at the G-7 summit on July 5–6 in Munich. He argued that this type of conference would have two advantages. First, the presence of the Security Council, and particularly the five permanent members, would have greater weight than the EC peace conference presided over by Lord Carrington. Second, the UN format would allow for participation by concerned neighbors such as Austria and Hungary. John Major, along with the Danish and Belgian governments, opposed the French proposal. Despite Major's initial hostility to an international conference, growing accusations that Britain, the EC president, was dithering over Yugoslavia led him to reverse his position. Growing domestic pressure for armed intervention, spearheaded by former Prime Minister Thatcher, was an important factor in his decision. On July 25, Major announced that he would convene an international conference at the end of August. The conference would be chaired jointly by the EC and the UN, and the participants would include the UN, the CSCE, the EC, and the belligerents. The length of time, however, between the announcement of the conference and its convening encouraged the belligerents to seize as much territory on the ground as possible.

The London conference opened on August 26 and included twenty-two nations. The participants did adopt thirteen principles that were supposed to provide a framework for peace, but negotiations collapsed as the fighting continued. In early September, a round-the-clock negotiating team was set up in Geneva led by David Owen and Cyrus Vance, the chief negotiators for the EC and the UN, respectively. By November they were trying to prevent the dismemberment of Bosnia into separate states. The latest plan, which proposed a "regionalized" state with seven to ten highly autonomous geographic units, turned out to be unrealistic, considering that Serbs control 70 percent of the territory in Bosnia, and was dropped.

Throughout the Geneva negotiations, diplomatic efforts were undermined continually by the savage fighting on the ground and the rising death toll in Bosnia. It was this specter of starvation, terrified refugees, and innocent civilian deaths that pushed the Europeans to discuss once again the use of force within a UN framework. On August 13, the UN Security Council passed a resolution that called on the member states to use "all measures necessary" to deliver humanitarian assistance to Sarajevo and other beleaguered parts of Bosnia. It did not call for the use of force to stop the fighting or to rescue people from detention camps. The resolution also did not indicate which countries would provide the troops, reflecting the long-standing division among Europeans. Germany, along with the United States and Russia, categorically refused to send troops. Germany once again cited its constitutional restrictions, while the United States explained that it would not send troops into another Vietnam-like quagmire. Even the French, who already had sent the largest force to Yugoslavia, were cautious. On August 14, Roland Dumas stated that France would send 1,100 troops to help protect the humanitarian convoys. Interestingly, John Major, who had initially refused to send troops, announced on August 18, in an amazing about-face, that Britain would send 1,800 troops for the same purpose. Several reasons explain his decision. First, he wanted to demonstrate a degree of firmness before the international conference. Second, British public opinion and the press were demanding action to stop the Serbian "genocide" of the Muslim population in Bosnia; and third, with Great Britain holding the EC presidency, he did not want to allow the French to appear to take the lead. On September 14, the UN Security Council agreed to a major expansion of UN peacekeeping forces in Bosnia and endorsed a recommendation by Boutros-Ghali that the troops could use force if attacked.

In the last three months of 1992, the EC's role in the peace negotiations was further reduced as the United States began to take a more active interest in the region. The reports of ethnic cleansing, torture of prisoners, and rape camps pushed the United States to call for a "no-fly zone" over Bosnia. In October, UN Resolution 781 created such a zone but did not provide for enforcement because of British and French opposition. On November 17, the UN authorized a naval blockade on the Danube River and the Adriatic Coast. Throughout December, the United States increased its rhetoric against Serbia, called for the enforcement of the no-fly zone, and threatened intervention if Serbia attacked Kosovo. However, despite the apparent willingness of the United States to take further action, opposition by the British and French, the December elections in Serbia, the intervention into Somalia, and the transition from President Bush to President Clinton together militated against decisive action. By January 1993, it was clear that any international intervention in the former Yugoslavia would, in all likelihood, follow the example of the Gulf War. The EC was unable to agree over the use of force; once again military action remained within the purview of individual European governments and/or the United States.

Conclusion

In the past two years, the EC has been faced with two major crises, one in the Gulf and one closer to home in Yugoslavia, which provide an opportunity to analyze the state of European Political Cooperation (EPC). It is true the EC member states consider EPC to be a useful framework for consultation and debate on foreign policy issues. In fact, EPC is an increasingly important component of member states' national foreign policies, and they often use the EC framework as a starting point for foreign policy actions. During the Gulf War and the Yugoslav crisis, economic and diplomatic actions were coordinated through EPC, and the Europeans were able to agree to certain common responses, such as trade embargoes and diplomatic sanctions. However, Europe's fragile political cooperation remains dependent on interstate bargains between member governments to protect national interests. Cooperation and coordination within EPC remain viable only as long as they do not undermine national interests, in which case European solidarity disintegrates. Thus, there is little evidence that a common foreign policy where EC members are willing to yield their foreign policy prerogatives to the Community is emerging.

Throughout the two crises, the degree of coordination achieved by the EC depended on the type of action contemplated. The EC, over the years, has created the institutional framework to support European convergence over certain diplomatic and economic policies. As a result, the EC was able to agree to various embargoes against Iraq and the former republics of Yugoslavia. The EC was also extremely active in trying to negotiate a political solution in the former Yugoslavia through the Troika and later through an EC-sponsored conference. Nevertheless, these agreements often were the result of compromises and masked sharp disagreements among the members. At the same time, even in these areas, members were willing to ignore EC decisions. Germany's decision to recognize Slovenia and Croatia, with or without EC approval, represents only the most striking example of the continuing primacy of national interests. Further evidence of this reality was seen in the willingness of member states to undertake national foreign policy actions that conflicted with EC diplomacy. For example, France, in both crises, frequently ignored the EPC to undertake national foreign policy initiatives. Mitterrand's proposal to the UN on January 14, 1991, to solve the Gulf crisis and his surprise trip to Sarajevo demonstrated France's unwillingness to remain within the constraints of an EC foreign policy.

The biggest problem facing EC unity continues to be the lack of a security or military arm. Thus, during a crisis that requires a military response the EC has been incapable of responding in unison. Despite efforts to enlist the WEU to coordinate between EC members, common foreign and security policy with its own effective institutions appears as far away as ever. It was this military inability and certain EC members' preference for the UN that propelled the Yugoslav issue into the UN forum. Unfortunately, the lack of an effective leader, a role played by the United States in the Gulf War, has curtailed the UN's effectiveness.

Like the Gulf War, the Yugoslav crisis has served to rekindle the debate over a common security and defense policy and the role of EPC. Despite the latest provisions contained in the Maastricht Treaty, such as agreement over "joint actions," dramatic changes are unlikely to be introduced. Although the rules governing EPC may be revised to increase the number of meetings and to give the Commission a somewhat louder voice, it will continue to express the interests and objectives of its most powerful nation-states.

Notes

1. European Communities, *Treaty on European Union* (Luxembourg: Office for Official Publications of the European Communities, 1992), p. 123. The treaty also states: "The common foreign and security policy shall include all questions related to the security of the Union, including the eventual framing of a common defense policy, which

might in time lead to a common defence" (p. 126).

2. See, for example, A. Pijpers et al., eds., *European Political Cooperation in the 1980's: A Common Foreign Policy for Western Europe* (The Hague: Nartinus Nijhoff, 1988); Martin Holland, *The Future of European Political Cooperation: Essays on Theory and Practice* (New York: St. Martin's, 1991); Christopher Hill, ed., *National Foreign Policies and European Political Cooperation* (London: Allen and Unwin, 1983); P. Ifestos, *European Political Cooperation: Towards a Framework of Supranational Diplomacy* (Aldershot: Avebury, 1988); R. Ginsberg, *Foreign Policy Actions of the European Community: The Politics of Scale* (Boulder: Lynne Rienner, 1989).

3. *Le Monde,* August 7, 1990.

4. *Financial Times,* August 22, 1990.

5. The Western European Union (WEU) did meet in August and September, but its role was negligible. When the war began, EC members that sent troops made their own arrangements with the United States.

6. Interview with EC official in Brussels, July 11, 1991.

7. "A disunited war front," *The Middle East,* March 1991, p. 21.

8. Ibid.

9. See *Le Monde,* October 25, 1990. Both Roland Dumas and Michel Rocard denied any negotiations. Yasser Arafat, however, announced that he had been France's envoy in an interview with *L'Express,* but the whole affair remains unclear.

10. *Le Monde,* November 7, 1990.

11. *Le Monde,* December 20, 1990.

12. *Le Monde,* January 7, 1991.

13. *Le Monde Diplomatique,* February 1991.

14. *Le Monde,* January 15, 1991.

15. For an analysis of France and the Gulf War, see Pia Christina Wood, "François Mitterrand and the Persian Gulf War: The Search for Influence," *French Politics and Society* 11 no. 3 (Summer 1992).

16. *Le Monde,* September 18, 1990.

17. The economic and military links between France and Iraq are well documented. France was second after the Soviet Union in sale of weapons to Iraq and accounted for 20 percent of Iraq's arms. Iraq's debt to France stood at approximately 26 billion French francs in 1990. *Le Monde,* August 3 and 4, 1990.

18. *Le Monde,* January 19, 1991.

19. François Mitterrand, "The Rule of Law," *Vital Speeches of the Day* 57 no. 1 (October 15, 1990), pp. 4–8.

20. *The Washington Post,* January 15, 1991.

21. *Le Monde,* January 17, 1991.

22. *Le Monde,* May 25, 1991.

23. *Le Monde,* August 14, 1991.

24. *Financial Times,* July 1, 1991.

25. *Le Monde,* July 16, 1991.

26. *Financial Times,* September 4, 1991.

27. *Le Monde,* October 11, 1991.

28. *The Economist,* January 18, 1992, p. 49.

29. *Le Monde,* September 27, 1991.

30. Lord Carrington's plan called for the creation of a bicameral system. It called for a Chamber of Citizens elected proportionally and a Chamber of Constituent Units giving Muslims, Serbs, and Croats equal representation. *Financial Times,* March 10, 1992.

31. According to Baker, "There are 35,000 diabetics now who have no insulin. There are 6,000 women and babies who have no medicine, baby formula, or milk. Anyone who is looking for a reason not to act, or arguing somehow that action in the

face of this kind of nightmare is not warranted at this time . . . is on the wrong wavelength." *Financial Times*, May 26, 1992.

32. *Le Monde*, September 5, 1992.

15

The EC, the United States, and the Uruguay Round

Finn Laursen

The Uruguay Round of international trade negotiations remained a contentious issue in EC-United States relations during 1991 and 1992. As with previous General Agreement on Tariffs and Trade (GATT) negotiations, conflict focused on Europe's common agricultural policy (CAP). The United States and other exporters of agricultural products have sought to force a revision of the CAP since the GATT talks began in 1986. The member nations of the Community finally endorsed significant reforms in May 1992, but they were not enough to satisfy the United States, and they failed to produce a breakthrough in the GATT negotiations. By this time, negotiators in Europe and the United States were becoming increasingly constrained by forthcoming elections. Although U.S. President Bush hoped that a GATT breakthrough might enhance his prospects for re-election in November, 1992, the desire to win votes in crucial farm states made it difficult for him to compromise. In France, President François Mitterrand barely secured a majority yes vote in the Maastricht referendum of September 20, 1992; his widely unpopular Socialist party had to contest parliamentary elections in March 1993.

In October 1992 the United States threatened a trade war with Europe over a longstanding dispute involving Europe's subsidies to oilseed producers. U.S. Trade Representative Carla Hills assembled a list of $300 million of annual imports from the EC, including white wine, and announced a 200 percent tax on these goods, to be levied after the presidential election if no settlement could be reached. By mid-November the EC Commission had reached an agreement with the United States that was expected to pave the way for a resolution of the Uruguay Round by the spring of 1993. This optimistic scenario, however, depended on the unknown intentions of the incoming Clinton administration as well as the ability of the EC to secure France's acquiescence to an agreement that was hotly contested by the farm lobby and the parties of the right.

The Uruguay Round started in Punta del Este, Uruguay, in September 1986 and was originally scheduled to last for four years. By the time of the mid-term review in Montreal in December 1988 some agreements had been reached in eleven of the fifteen areas included in the negotiations. The four areas where no agreements could be reached in Montreal were agriculture, textiles, protection of intellectual property rights, and reform of the safeguards system. A text agreed to in April 1989 on these four issues allowed the negotiations to continue. The final negotiations were scheduled for Brussels in December 1990.

However, the Brussels ministerial session in 1990 failed to solve the remaining issues, including the crucial agricultural issue.[1] The question then was whether the Round could still be salvaged.

Salvaging the Negotiations in 1991

At the Brussels meeting, GATT's director general, Arthur Dunkel, was asked to pursue intensive consultations until the beginning of 1991. These consultations convinced him that "the consensus in favour of a successful conclusion of the Round" remained. Also, all participants were said to be "aware that this phase calls for political statesmanship."[2]

The EC faced intense pressure to offer additional concessions regarding agricultural products. In 1990, it had taken eight meetings of farm ministers to agree on the 30 percent reduction in internal supports over a ten-year period (1986 to 1995), but this offer was rejected by the United States, the Cairns Group of fourteen farm produce exporters, and other GATT contracting parties at the Brussels meeting. The United States and the Cairns Group demanded a 75 percent reduction in internal supports by the year 2000, plus a 90 percent cut in farm export subsidies.

The Commission now started to work on CAP reforms that would include at least the following three points:

1. A switch from the support system based on guaranteed prices to direct income support for smaller farmers
2. A more aggressive "set-aside" policy to take land out of production to reduce cereals production
3. Greater controls on supply, including cuts in already existing milk quotas[3]

However, when the first Commission proposals reached the Council of Agricultural Ministers at the beginning of February 1991, they were opposed by France, the UK, the Netherlands, and Denmark; no decision could be taken.[4]

On the U.S. side there was a technical problem. According to the "fast track" authority given the administration by Congress, a final agreement had to be submitted to Congress before March 1, 1991. According to this authorization, Congress would vote the deal as one package and not allow amendments, which could unravel it.[5]

As this March 1 deadline approached, it became clear that no break-through could be produced so quickly; the necessary CAP reform would take much longer. The Bush administration therefore decided to seek a two-year extension of the fast track authority.

To get the negotiations started again, Arthur Dunkel suggested a formula that required all members to make "specific binding commitments" to nego-tiate reductions in each of the following three areas: internal supports, market access, and export subsidies. This formula was accepted by the EC at a meeting on February 20, 1991. It allowed the negotiations to begin again, although it was now expected that it would take several months to tackle the fundamental issues.[6]

The Uruguay Round was formally put back on the track on February 26, 1991, by GATT's Trade Negotiations Committee (TNC). No new deadline was set, but the negotiations were to be concluded as soon as possible. The fifteen areas under negotiation were now regrouped into seven, viz. (1) agriculture, (2) textiles and clothing, (3) services, (4) rulemaking, (5) trade-related aspects of intellectual property rights (TRIPs), (6) institutions, includ-ing dispute settlement and final act, and (7) market access. The rulemaking category included a number of areas, in particular: subsidies and countervail-ing duties, antidumping, safeguards, preshipment inspection, rules of origin, technical barriers to trade, import licensing procedures, customs valuation, government procurement, and a number of specific GATT articles and trade-related investment measures (TRIMs).[7]

The Bush administration obtained the two-year extension of the "fast track" authority from Congress in May. The administration intended to use the new fast track authority for both the Uruguay Round and a free trade agreement (FTA) with Mexico, which, added to the 1988 United States-Can-ada Free Trade Agreement, would lead to the creation of a North American Free Trade Area (NAFTA).[8]

Calls for Speedy Completion of the Round

Thus by the summer of 1991 the Uruguay Round was officially back on the track, and CAP reform was at least on the agenda. The Commission's proposals included a 35 percent cut in cereals prices over three years, with income support paid on a sliding scale so that small farmers would be compensated in full for loss of earnings. Bigger farmers would have to accept some loss. The proposals also called for a 15 percent cut in beef prices and a 4 percent reduction in milk quotas.

At their London conference in July 1991, the G-7 called for a rapid conclusion of the international trade talks. President Bush warned the other leaders that unless the GATT Round ended that year, there was a danger that it might never be completed. The determination to finish the Uruguay Round before the end of the year was included in the declaration from the summit.[10]

Moving Closer

The second part of 1991 saw the parties gradually moving closer on some of the central issues, including agriculture. When Arthur Dunkel reported to the TNC on July 30, 1991, he said that in agriculture, textiles and clothing, market access and services, "the combination of the work done before and after Brussels puts participants in a position to move with determination in the phase of negotiations proper." In many of the rulemaking areas and in TRIPS, "matters are ripe for the final political trade-offs since most, if not all, of the preparatory work has already been done." In areas where common negotiating texts were not yet available, such as TRIMs and antidumping, "once the essential political decisions are taken . . . agreement will fall in place fairly quickly."[11]

In the farm area some progress was made. Negotiators were coming closer on which types of domestic support do not distort trade. Such support would be put into a "green box" of accepted compromises and allowed. Negotiators also made progress on how nontariff border restrictions, such as import quotas, variable import levies, and voluntary export restraints, could be converted into tariffs. However, negotiators were still unable to agree on a definition of an export subsidy.[12] In mid-September, Arthur Dunkel asked the chairmen of the seven negotiating groups to try to reach agreements by the end of October or beginning of November so that the Uruguay Round could be completed by the end of the year.[13]

A good piece of news in respect to CAP reform came from Bonn in October. Chancellor Kohl had told his cabinet that it would be "a catastrophe" if the Uruguay Round failed. This strengthened the position of the economics minister, Jürgen Möllemann, who declared that "there has to be a change on the EC's position in agriculture, including export subsidies." This shift in the German position isolated the French and Irish within the EC Council. They no longer had the blocking minority they had enjoyed in concert with the Federal Republic.[14]

In October it was reported from Geneva that the EC and the United States were at last "talking seriously" about how to cut farm subsidies. At the same time, progress was reported in some of the other areas being negotiated. In respect to market access, where the objective was to cut tariffs by a third, some bilateral deals had been struck. In the area of textiles and clothing, a text on the elimination of the Multi-Fiber Agreement (MFA) over ten years was almost ready. In respect to dispute settlement mechanisms, agreement was within reach on how to speed up the work of dispute panels, on automatic acceptance of rulings, on an appeals body, and on how to discipline countries that do not implement GATT rulings. There had also been progress on a new General Agreement on Trade in Services (GATS). Progress here included the vital clauses on the most-favored nation (MFN) principle, national treatment, and market access. However, the United States still opposed extending the MFN principle to shipping, and difficulties remained in some other areas, including antidumping and TRIPs.[15]

Hopes were now pinned on a top-level meeting between President Bush, Dutch Prime Minister (and then EC president) Ruud Lubbers, and Jacques Delors in the Hague on November 9, 1991. One of the issues was whether the United States would accept the proposed EC direct income payments as production neutral. It was reported that the EC then would offer a 30 percent cut in internal subsidies over five years (compared to the 30 percent over ten years offered a year earlier). Since price cuts would lead to reductions in export subsidies, the main difficulty remaining for the EC would be market access. The Commission was under strong pressure to maintain border protection, especially against cereals substitutes. Ray MacSharry, EC farm commissioner, and Edward Madigan, U.S. agriculture secretary, failed to resolve the issues completely at a meeting in Brussels on November 7.[16] Could Bush, Lubbers, and Delors then make the "hard choices"?

Indeed, news emerged from the Hague that President Bush was willing to make concessions. Prior to the meeting between Bush, Delors, and Lubbers, the U.S. negotiators had been suggesting a 50 percent cut in farm support over five years (compared to demands of 90 percent cuts in export subsidies and 75 percent cuts in domestic supports over ten years a year earlier). Bush is reported to have mentioned a 30 percent cut in export restitutions over five years, or 35 percent over six years. Both sides indicated that they were willing to show flexibility to conclude the negotiations by the end of the year. Both stressed the importance of solving trade disputes through the GATT instead of using unilateral action.[17]

"So Near and yet So Far"

The news from the Hague meeting was welcomed in Geneva. U.S. officials, however, pointed out that there was still no agreement on the base year from which to calculate reductions, and there was no agreement on which domestic supports could be included in the "green box." The EC demand for "rebalancing" was also a problem. The EC wanted to control imports of cereal substitutes, such as corn gluten feed, as a kind of quid pro quo for reducing cereal exports. According to EC calculations, the EC would take 17 million metric tons of grain off the world market. In exchange the EC wanted to make sure that the EC domestic market was not further eroded by cheap U.S. feedstock substitutes.[18]

In the negotiations that followed, it became clear that these three issues were not easy to solve; moreover, other issues emerged.[19] The United States wanted the cut in export subsidies to be backed by a limit on export volume; a quantitative restriction on cereals exports was not acceptable to the EC at the time. The United States also wanted a commitment to further cuts after the first period of five years; the EC was only prepared to accept a commitment to a review. Further, while the EC wanted their proposed income support to be in the "green box," they were not willing to give the same treatment to US deficiency payments. "So near and yet so far," wrote the *Financial Times* on November 22. A new impasse seemed to have been reached.[20]

EC officials suggested that the United States had had second thoughts: there was resistance in Congress to make "unwise concessions" to the EC.[21] However, one European official also mentioned casually that the French were being "difficult."[22] Further, a trade diplomat suggested that "agricultural bureaucracies" on both sides had been too rigid. A top-level solution appeared necessary.[23]

When various agencies in Washington analyzed the impasse, they confirmed the U.S. view that the positions taken by Guy Legras, EC agriculture director general, in Geneva were quite unacceptable. It was especially the Brussels offer in respect to export subsidies that Washington found inadequate. U.S. analysts had concluded that the Brussels offer would in reality only amount to a 19 or 20 percent cut.[24]

At this point Bush and Lubbers intervened again. By telephone they agreed to launch a new effort. It was decided that farm negotiators would not be present at the initial attempt to break the deadlock. The U.S. side sent Julius Katz, deputy U.S. trade representative, and Robert Zoellick, under secretary for economic affairs at the State Department. The EC side sent Pascal Lamy, chief aide to Jacques Delors, and Hugo Paemen, the EC's chief negotiator. However, no immediate results emerged from the first meeting of these senior officials in Brussels on December 3, 1991.[25]

During December 1991, the EC and the United States held a number of meetings to try to break the impasse. At a meeting between Edward Madigan, U.S. agriculture secretary, and Ray MacSharry, EC commissioner for agriculture, in Washington, the United States is reported to have suggested that two-thirds of the 35 percent cut in export subsidies should be effected on export volumes. As a quid pro quo, the United States would freeze annual exports of nongrain feedstuffs to the EC at the average of the last five years.[26] However, the meeting did not lead to a breakthrough. At the same time, the EC held its Maastricht summit on economic and political union, but ministers only dealt briefly with the GATT, reiterating the Community's "firm commitment to a substantial balanced and global package of results of the Uruguay Round by the end of the year."[27]

In Geneva, Arthur Dunkel let it be understood that he would put forward a "draft final act" on December 20 that would include draft agreements from the negotiating groups as well as proposals by Dunkel and the chairmen of the negotiating groups on how to solve the remaining issues. Governments would then meet on January 13, 1992, to decide whether or not to accept the package. At the same time it was reported that the United States-EC gap on export subsidies was rather small. The United States wanted the EC to limit subsidized wheat on the world market to 11 million tonnes. Brussels was said to have offered 13 million to 15 million metric tons.[28] Such a limit, however, was clearly not acceptable to the French.[29]

A final EC-United States attempt to solve the impasse before Dunkel published his "final act" was made on December 18 in Brussels, where MacSharry and Madigan met to try to bridge the gap. The meeting was also attended by Ruud Lubbers. Again, no breakthrough was accomplished.[30]

Arthur Dunkel's "Final Act"

At midnight on December 20, 1991, Arthur Dunkel's 436-page "final act" was made public.[31] Even before it was made public, however, the French government had rejected it. The government of Edith Cresson claimed two days before the text appeared that it supported the position of the United States and that it was contrary to the interests of France and Europe.[32]

The Dunkel draft included important texts on services and intellectual property rights that had been provisionally agreed by the negotiators; it also contained texts that had not been agreed, including agriculture and antidumping. Negotiators had also agreed to form a new Multilateral Trading Organization (MTO) which would include GATT and the new GATS. The MTO would run an integrated dispute settlement system that should lead to faster dispute decisions and more discipline with respect to implementation.[33] The new GATS would extend liberalized trade to banking, insurance, transport, tourism, construction, telecommunications, and accountancy at a time when trade in services was valued at around $800 billion a year and growing by 12 percent a year. Four annexes defined rules to be applied to financial services, telecommunications, air transport, and people crossing borders to provide services. A central aspect of the GATS was the application of the MFN rule to services. This means that concessions given to one country must be extended to all other contracting parties. Exemptions from MFN would have to be announced by a country from the beginning and reviewed after five years. They should not be sustained for more than ten years.[34]

Regarding antidumping, subsidies, and safeguards, the negotiators had agreed on texts on subsidies and safeguards at the last minute. Arthur Dunkel produced the proposed revision of GATT's antidumping code, which specified measures to counter alleged dumping, i.e., exporting at prices below those charged on the domestic market. (The code has been used increasingly by the EC and the United States against Japan, other Asian exporters, and many developing countries in recent years.) Dunkel proposed that antidumping should only be allowed within strict limits. The safeguards text foresaw the phasing out of voluntary export restraints (VERs) and orderly marketing arrangements (OMAs) within four years. The EC secured an exemption for Japanese cars, the import of which can be limited until the end of the decade. The text on subsidies defined the subsidies that are legal.[35]

The text on textiles foresaw the phasing out of the MFA over ten years starting January 1, 1993. The MFA, which has existed for about thirty years, consists of a series of bilateral quota arrangements, which in reality means that this sector is outside the GATT rules. Imports would be increased 16 percent in the first stage, 25 percent in the period 1996 to 1999, and 27 percent between 2000 and 2002. Products dropped from the quota system should include the four groups: tops and yarn, fabrics, made-up textile products, and clothing.[36]

On the issue of export subsidies, Arthur Dunkel proposed cuts of 36 percent in budget outlays and 24 percent in volume over a six-year period, using 1986–1990 as base period. Domestic supports, Dunkel proposed, should be reduced 20 percent by 1999. However, two of the EC's demands, rebalancing and the inclusion of direct income support in the "green box," were not included by Dunkel, nor did the "green box" include the US deficiency payments. All import barriers, said his report, should be converted into customs duties and then lowered on average by 36 percent over the six-year period.[37]

Once the Dunkel final act was available, the EC's Article 113 Committee began its technical examination of it, and the General Affairs Council had a first discussion about the draft on December 23. At this meeting, only France and Ireland were totally negative; while the other delegations all had problems with some of the details, they appeared ready to use the draft as a working basis for final negotiations. Representatives from the Commission stressed the need to study the draft carefully.[38]

The General Affairs Council concluded that a final assessment was premature. But the Council expressed its concern about the agricultural chapter:

> Insofar as the Dunkel paper calls into question the foundation of the Community's agricultural policy, the paper is not acceptable and therefore has to be modified. Since the Community has embarked upon a far-reaching reform process of its agriculture policy, the proposed text was in particular evaluated in this light.[39]

The general conclusion of the Council was that "the paper is not balanced in total." It therefore invited the Commission to negotiate further necessary improvements to it.

When EC ministers for external trade and agriculture met on January 10, 1992, to finalize the EC's position on the Dunkel final act, it was clear that there were still major problems for the EC, in particular the "green box" question, which was of central importance for the proposed CAP reform. After a seven-hour meeting the ministers agreed to consider the Dunkel text a "reference document for the final phase of the negotiations." However, the EC would seek "substantial improvements and essential modifications."[40]

The TNC meeting in Geneva on January 13, 1992, then adopted a four-track strategy to conclude the Uruguay Round quickly. These were negotiations in respect to market access and initial commitments in services, work to ensure the legal conformity and internal consistency of agreement, and "work at the level of the TNC with a view to examining whether and if it is possible to adjust the package in certain specific places."[41] The latter "track" allowed for further negotiations with respect to the agricultural section.

EC Vice-President Frans Andriessen asserted that there was now a "window of opportunity" until Easter to reach an agreement. By Easter, the U.S. presidential campaign "with its announced heavy stress on isolationism and protectionism, will thereafter probably close that window for the remainder of 1992."[42] Doubts about the Easter deadline, however, emerged soon. Four weeks after the January 13 TNC meeting, the EC had not yet come up with proposals for altering the Dunkel text nor begun serious negotiations with the United States. This was slowing down progress on country-by-country negotiations in lowering tariffs and negotiations on initial commitments to liberalize trade in services.[43]

At the beginning of March 1992, the EC ministers of trade and agriculture met again to try to define an EC stance with respect to the agricultural chapter of Dunkel's final act. The Council remained split. One group, including the UK, France, Denmark, the Netherlands and Belgium, wanted to renegotiate the proposed reduction in subsidized exports. The other member states emphasized the need to get compensation to farmers included in the "green box."[44]

Agence Europe reported that the Commission believed it had a mandate to offer the following concessions:

1. With respect to rebalancing: not to include soya beans, but rather to limit the request for border protection to substitute cereal products (notably corn gluten feed).
2. With respect to reduction of export subsidies: accept reduction both in budgetary and quantitative terms.
3. With respect to market access: guarantee minimum access to the common market for certain products such as cheese.

These "concessions" were accepted by Germany but partly contested by most member states.[45]

When the Commission did send lists or tables containing the EC's position on agriculture to the GATT, the French government declared that the Commission "only committed itself," and the Italian minister for trade asserted that the "Commission was exceeding its powers by far."[46]

At this point, Chancellor Kohl decided to try to broker an agreement between his best allies, France and the United States, both of which were experiencing great difficulties (because of domestic politics) in finding the necessary flexibility to reach an agreement. He flew to the United States to meet President Bush at Camp David on March 21. He was reported to have the backing of President Mitterrand, as well as Jacques Delors, John Major, and Ruud Lubbers, to offer a trade-off: the EC would accept quantity restrictions on EC agricultural exports in exchange for a freeze on future U.S. exports of cereals substitutes to the EC.[47] After the meeting Kohl talked about "progress," but admitted that no agreement had been reached. Nevertheless, both sides remained determined to reach an agreement in April.[48]

In Geneva, the negotiators were becoming pessimistic. All four "tracks" of negotiations were in trouble. Everybody seemed to be waiting for a solution to the EC-U.S. farm differences. The view was that it was now a question of political will to make the necessary compromises. Increasingly it looked as if the Easter deadline would not be met. This heightened the likelihood of the negotiations going into limbo until after the US elections in November.[49]

In Brussels, Frans Andriessen said that it would be possible to end the negotiations if the principles of globality as well as parallel progress in all sectors were respected. The EC was asked to produce less, export less, and import more in the agricultural sector. At the same time, the United States wanted to exclude maritime transport, air transport, telecommunications, and financial services from the services sector. This would annihilate liberalization in services.[50]

Various independent observers suggested that the contours of a compromise were starting to emerge. *The Economist,* for instance, wrote:

> EC officials have hinted they may be willing to drop rebalancing. American officials have said they may be willing to soften their demand on export subsidies, and to tolerate the EC's proposed income supports as long as they are closely watched and the EC promises eventually to reduce them.[51]

Hopes now turned toward the transatlantic summit in Washington between George Bush, Jacques Delors, and Portuguese Prime Minister Anibal Cavaco Silva (then EC president) on April 22, 1992. The meeting was one of the semiannual meetings laid down in the transatlantic declaration of November 1990.[52]

The Washington summit did not produce a breakthrough. "New ideas," the specifics of which were not disclosed, were discussed, and the parties agreed that "the negotiations should go on." Delors said afterward that he hoped it would be possible "to make enough concrete progress before the end of June."[53] According to the *Financial Times,* the "new ideas" included an EC offer to come closer to the 24 percent cut in the volume of the EC's subsidized farm exports being demanded.[54]

Thus, in the end, yet another new deadline was set. At a quadrilateral meeting in Japan, a Japanese representative said that the Uruguay Round had become too technical for politicians while remaining too political for technicians.[55]

CAP Reform

Irrespective of GATT, the EC had good reasons for reforming the CAP. As John Major told the National Farmers' Union in London in February 1992: "Farmers earn less and less, food is in surplus, trade is distorted, developing countries are damaged, the pressures on the environment increase and the costs grow out of all proportion to the benefits."[56]

At about this time, serious negotiations within the EC about CAP reform were finally starting. The Portuguese presidency had worked out a compromise "working paper" that sought to make the Commission's proposals more flexible without altering their basic shape or design.[57] Various revised proposals were to follow.

Cereal prices lay at the heart of CAP reform. The Commission proposed a 35 percent cut in cereals prices, bringing the subsidized price of ECU 155 per metric ton down to ECU 100 over three years. A fourth compromise proposal, by the Portuguese presidency in May 1992, included a reduction of 27 percent, bringing the price down to ECU 112. The Germans, whose agriculture is relatively inefficient, feared a radical cut, while the more efficient French actually wanted a deep cut to avoid quotas. The UK, the Netherlands, and Denmark also favored deeper price cuts. The proposed price cuts were to be offset by direct payments to farmers. These in turn would be contingent on larger farmers taking 15 percent of their land out of production.[58]

A fifth compromise proposal from the Portuguese presidency included a 29 percent price reduction for cereals, implying a price of ECU 110 per metric ton. This would make EC cereals competitive on the world market, eliminate cereals export subsidies, and, thus, end the dumping so much criticized by the United States, the Cairns Group, and others.[59]

A reform package, including the 29 percent reduction in cereals prices, was finally adopted on May 21, 1992, after four days and three nights of negotiations. Italy had a problem with milk quotas because of illicit excess production that the other member countries were not willing to validate retroactively. In the end, the Portuguese presidency applied the weighted-majority voting rules to get the package through. The package included various concessions to different member states. Since a 29 percent reduction in cereals prices would reduce the price of livestock, it made possible a 15 percent cut in beef prices and a 5 percent cut in butter prices. Sheep and beef were to be subject to quotas, like milk. The various cuts were expected to eliminate export subsidies almost entirely by 1996–1997. After the deal, engineered by MacSharry and the Portuguese presidency, MacSharry challenged the United States to match the cuts and collaborate to achieve a deal in the Uruguay Round. The United States should accept the EC compensation payments to farmers and soften their demands in respect to volume reduction of subsidized exports.[60] The regulations implementing the CAP reform were adopted unanimously at the end of June. In the end, Italy did secure an increased milk quota.[61]

The French Referendum and U.S. Presidential Elections

The CAP reform was greeted with outrage by farmers in France and Germany. Demonstrations broke out in several French towns. Raymond Lacombe, president of the French farmers' union, Fédération Nationale des Syndicats d'Exploitants Agricoles, said that "agricultural Europe would become an American colony." The German farmers' union, Deutscher Bauernverband (DBV), found the reform "both wrong and disastrous," but Helmut Kohl stressed that the deal had created the preconditions for a GATT deal.[62]

Many Europeans now felt it should be clear to the United States where the EC's bottom line was. Seeing in particular how French farmers received the most radical reform since the CAP had been adopted in 1962, the United States should understand that domestic politics within the EC did not allow much more flexibility on the EC side. Calls for a swift GATT deal were becoming common in Europe. The *Financial Times,* for instance, wrote:

> What is needed now is a swift agreement between the EC and the US, with the former abandoning the demand for "rebalancing" and the latter accepting the EC's compensation payments for a predetermined period of years.[63]

A top-level EC-U.S. meeting at the end of May, including Frans Andriessen and James Baker, made it clear, however, that the United States was not yet ready to accept Europe's offer. The United States reiterated its call for the EC to reduce subsidized exports by 24 percent in volume. There were rumors that the United States was ready to give the EC up to ten years to reach such a reduction, but that the EC could only accept a maximum 18 percent reduction. It was also reported that the United States was asking the EC to take more than 15 percent of land out of cereals production, which would mean reopening the CAP reform package.[64] At the same time, it also appeared that the United States was ready to start a shouting match with the EC about oilseed subsidies.[65]

As a matter of fact, on June 9 Washington published a $2 billion EC food exports "hit list," half of which might suffer punitive tariffs if the EC did not change its oilseed subsidy regime. This regime, which set EC prices at about twice world prices, has been designed to draw EC farmers away from cereals production. During the 1980–1990 period, it had more than tripled the area devoted to production of rapeseed, sunflower seed, and soybeans in the EC. At the same time, U.S. exports of soybeans fell 63 percent. In April 1992, a GATT panel found this EC regime in violation of an EC-U.S. agreement under which U.S. oilseeds enter the EC duty-free. In June, the EC offered compensation to U.S. farmers, who demanded access instead of compensation, hence the threat of retaliation from the United States, which was followed with an EC threat of counter-retaliation. Eventually, the United States reluctantly accepted the idea of negotiating compensation at a GATT Council meeting on June 19. This gave the parties sixty days to seek a settlement.[66]

Despite the oilseed row, there was some optimism in early June in Brussels. It was reported that Frans Andriessen was ready to offer a 20 percent volume reduction in subsidized exports, with 5 percent swings within sectors. It was also reported that the United States was ready to accept the EC's new direct payments to farmers as not distorting trade if the EC would reduce domestic subsidies by 20 percent.[67]

However, by mid-June Frans Andriessen told EC foreign ministers that he was pessimistic about reaching an agreement before the G-7 summit in Munich, July 6–8, 1992.[68] In Geneva, where there had been an effort to get tariff and services negotiations going again, the Uruguay Round was said to be "totally and utterly blocked," and EC negotiators wondered whether the European Council meeting in Lisbon at the end of June could get things moving again.[69] The Lisbon summit reaffirmed the Community's "commitment to a swift conclusion of the Uruguay Round," but no new EC concessions were offered.[70]

When the UK took over the EC presidency on July 1, 1992, John Major started pressing for a deal,[71] but observers felt the situation in the Community resulting from the no vote in the Danish referendum on the Maastricht Treaty on June 2, 1992, made a deal more difficult. In response to the Danish referendum, President Mitterrand had called a referendum in France. Given his falling popularity and the continued protests from farmers against the CAP reform, France could not accept a deal before the referendum, which was scheduled for September 20.[72] John Major kept up his pressure for a deal at the Munich summit, but Mitterrand insisted that he could not accept a deal before the French referendum on the Maastricht Treaty, so nothing happened at yet another G-7 meeting.[73] Afterward, there was speculation that the opportunity for a GATT deal might come between the French referendum on

September 20 and the US election on November 3.[74] *The Economist,* however, concluded that a deal before November 3 could be ruled out.[75]

MacSharry and Madigan held a meeting in Ireland in late July, where they discussed both the Uruguay Round and the oilseeds dispute. On the GATT, MacSharry noted that the main outstanding issue was export volume. In respect to the oilseeds dispute, the United States had turned down the most recent EC proposal for compensation.[76] When a second EC compensation offer was rejected in August, MacSharry went to Washington on August 11, trying to avoid a "trade war on soy beans."[77] For the moment, at least, discussions continued. On both sides of the Atlantic, there was strong opposition to retaliatory measures. The August 18 deadline for compensation negotiations (according to Article 28 of the GATT) passed without leading to an immediate escalation in the dispute.[78]

At the end of September, the United States asked a GATT panel to come up with binding arbitration on the EC oilseed regime within thirty days. This was rejected by the EC, which would only accept a working party to propose a nonbinding solution. Where the United States estimated the loss of oilseeds producers in ten countries to be about $2 billion, the EC put the figure at no more than $400 million. Could the high-level meeting between the United States and EC, now scheduled for October 11, avert a trade war and finally produce a GATT deal?[79]

The meeting on October 11 included Frans Andriessen, Ray MacSharry, Carla Hills, and Edward Madigan. Prior to the meeting, impetus was said to have come from President Bush. One theory was that Bush, who trailed Governor Bill Clinton in the presidential election campaign, wanted a GATT deal as a promise of world economic revival. Should a deal be reached, it could be endorsed by the Birmingham meeting of the European Council on October 16.[80]

No immediate breakthrough resulted from this latest high-level meeting. The following day it was reported that France had threatened to boycott the Birmingham summit if the EC made concessions to the United States on subsidized farm trade. Apart from problems with respect to tariff cuts and liberalization of services, two critical issues remained in the agricultural dossier:

1. The EC's refusal to accept a 24 percent cut in the volume of subsidized farm exports
2. The EC's insistence that direct income support to farmers should not be considered subsidies[81]

The deal to avoid a trade war, finally reached in November 1992, included the following main elements: With respect to internal support, the EC accepted a 20 percent reduction over six years; with respect to market access, the EC accepted a 36 percent reduction over six years, as well as the idea of a minimum access of at least 3 percent immediately to increase to at least 5 percent at the end of the period; finally, with respect to export subsidies, the EC accepted a 36 percent reduction in money terms over six years and a 21 percent reduction in terms of quantities. This deal, however, was struck between the Commission and the U.S. Trade Commission. Given its unpopularity among farmers in the EC (especially in France), it appeared that the Community might simply be buying time.[82]

Concluding Remarks

Two years beyond the original deadline of the Uruguay Round, there is still no agreement; one can wonder why. Most economists believe that every group of states stands to gain by the compromise deal that looks so close. *The Economist* wrote:

> The gains within reach are not a theoretical fantasy; they are a matter of cold, hard cash. In sum, the flawed package that the Uruguay Round is poised to deliver would immediately raise global income, according to one careful (and conservative) study, by $120 billion a year—roughly one-half percent of today's gross world product. America's share of that pot would be $35 billion a year. Japan's share would be $28 billion, about the same as the EC's.[83]

President Bush, however, did not find it possible to move forward. The Community had the same problem, mainly because of France's resistance to further concessions. France could not accept a FF 2 billion reduction in cereals exports, not even if it could win FF 5 billion in industrial goods exports and FF 2 billion in exports of services once the Uruguay Round was completed.[84]

The problems of the Uruguay Round stem from domestic politics. Politicians easily give in to pressures from special interests. For this reason, it becomes difficult to reach optimal cooperation in the area of international trade. If it takes leadership to strike a bargain at GATT, one may conclude that the world's most pressing economic shortage is its deficit in leadership.

Notes

1. For more background, see Finn Laursen, "The EC, GATT, and the Uruguay Round," in Leon Hurwitz and Christian Lequesne, eds., *The State of the European Community: Policies, Institutions & Debates in the Transition Years* (Boulder: Lynne Rienner, 1991), pp. 373–385.

2. Arthur Dunkel, "The challenge after Brussels," *GATT Focus Newsletter* no. 78 (January-February 1991), pp. 6–7.

3. David Gardner, "Brussels prepares for CAP overhaul," *Financial Times*, January 4, 1991.

4. *Agence Europe*, February 6, 1991; David Gardner, "EC ministers 'unanimous'

on the need for farm reform," *Financial Times,* February 6, 1991.

5. Nancy Dunne, "Hills warns on deadline for Gatt 'fast track' negotiating authority," *Financial Times,* January 9, 1991.

6. William Dullforce, "EC accepts formula for negotiating farm trade reforms," *Financial Times,* February 21, 1991.

7. "Uruguay Round back on track," *GATT Focus Newsletter* no. 79 (March 1991); "Uruguay Round structure streamlined," *GATT Focus Newsletter* no. 81 (May-June 1991).

8. Guy Gugliotta, "Hill Puts Trade Talks on 'Fast Track'," *The Washington Post,* May 25, 1991.

9. "New efforts to press forward with negotiations," *GATT Focus Newsletter* no. 82 (July 1991); and "EC farm reform," *The Economist,* July 6, 1991.

10. "Les négotiations de l'Uruguay Round seraient conclues avant la fin de l'année," *Le Monde,* July 18, 1991.

11. "Uruguay Round poised to enter decisive phase," *GATT Focus Newsletter* no. 83 (August 1991).

12. William Dullforce, "Gatt negotiators closer on cut in farm subsidies," *Financial Times,* August 8, 1991.

13. *GATT Focus Newsletter* no. 84 (September 1991).

14. Christopher Parkes, "Bonn agrees Gatt farm strategy," *Financial Times,* October 10, 1991; David Dodwell, "German move lifts Gatt talks," *Financial Times,* October 14, 1991; Peter Norman et al., "Hopes rise for breakthrough on Gatt," *Financial Times,* October 15, 1991; and "GATT reprieved?" *The Economist,* October 19, 1991.

15. William Dullforce, "Cautious optimism for trade talks breakthrough," *Financial Times,* October 25, 1991.

16. David Gardner, "EC, US seek to resolve deadlock on trade talks," *Financial Times,* November 7, 1991; David Gardner, "EC and US seek deal on farming subsidies," *Financial Times,* November 8, 1991; and William Dullforce, "Bush and Delors try to end farm trade impasse," *Financial Times,* November 9, 1991.

17. William Dullforce and David Gardner, "Bush makes concession to unblock trade talks," *Financial Times,* November 11, 1991.

18. William Dullforce, "Gatt welcomes US farm offer," *Financial Times,* November 12, 1991; and David Gardner, "Farm subsidy accord is tantalisingly near," *Financial Times,* November 13, 1991.

19. William Dullforce, "Back into the thicket of subsidies," *Financial Times,* November 20, 1991; and David Gardner, "Support for MacSharry in farm talks," *Financial Times,* November 20, 1991.

20. "Impasse on farm trade," *Financial Times,* November 1991.

21. William Dullforce and David Gardner, "US and EC in farm talks crisis," *Financial Times,* November 11, 1991.

22. Nancy Dunne, "US stays calm over stalled agriculture talks with EC," *Financial Times,* November 22, 1991.

23. "Gatt impasse 'needs top-level solution'," *Financial Times,* November 25, 1991.

24. William Dullforce, "US tells EC to soften farm subsidy stance," *Financial Times,* November 27, 1991.

25. *Agence Europe,* December 4, 1991.

26. William Dullforce and David Gardner, "Hopes of breaking farm impasse hang on US talks," *Financial Times,* December 6, 1991.

27. *Agence Europe,* December 12, 1991.

28. William Dullforce, "US and EC step up efforts to end farm subsidy row," *Financial Times,* December 12, 1991.

29. *Agence Europe,* December 14, 1991.

30. David Gardner, "EC and US make last attempt to agree farm subsidies cuts," *Financial Times,* December 18, 1991; *Agence Europe,* December 20, 1991.

31. GATT Secretariat, "Draft Final Act Embodying the Results of the Uruguay Round of Multilateral Trade Negotiations," Doc. MTN.TNC/W/FA, December 20, 1991.

32. *Agence Europe,* December 19, 1991; and William Dullforce, "Paris quick to oppose Gatt conclusions," *Financial Times,* December 19, 1991.

33. William Dullforce, "Uruguay Round 'final act' offers a stark choice," *Financial Times,* December 23, 1991.

34. William Dullforce, "Services pact may be seen as milestone," *Financial Times,* December 23, 1991.

35. William Dullforce, "Fresh rule book on dumping and subsidies," *Financial Times,* December 23, 1991.

36. William Dullforce, "Far East benefits from textiles deal," *Financial Times,* December 1991.

37. William Dullforce, "EC feels pressure on Dunkel farm draft," *Financial Times,* December 23, 1991.

38. *Agence Europe,* December 23–24, 1991.

39. *Agence Europe,* December 25, 1991.

40. David Gardner, "EC seeks improved deal on trade," *Financial Times,* January 13, 1992.

41. "TNC adopts four-track strategy to conclude the Round," *GATT Focus Newsletter* no. 87 (January/February 1992).

42. Robert Graham, "Uruguay Round has Easter deadline, says Andriessen," *Financial Times,* February 2, 1992.

43. Frances Williams, "Uruguay Round in trouble again over deadline," *Financial Times,* February 7, 1992.

44. David Gardner, "EC ministers renew efforts to define Gatt stance," *Financial Times,* March 3, 1992.

45. *Agence Europe,* March 4, 1992.

46. *Agence Europe,* March 6, 1992.

47. Quentin Peel and Nancy Dunne, "German proposal may save next round of Gatt," *Financial Times,* March 18, 1992; *Agence Europe,* March 19, 1992; and Quentin Peel, "Kohl aims to break Gatt impasse in Bush talks," *Financial Times,* March 21–22, 1992.

48. Quentin Peel, "Kohl sees clear signs of movement in farm talks," *Financial Times,* March 24, 1992.

49. Frances Williams, "Uruguay Round talks halted in their tracks," *Financial Times,* March 27, 1992.

50. *Agence Europe,* March 28, 1992.

51. "Free trade's fading champion," *The Economist,* April 11, 1992.

52. David Gardner, "Delors may intervene over trade talks," *Financial Times,* April 2, 1992; Fances Williams, "Gatt deal 'hinges on farm subsidies'," *Financial Times,* April 13, 1992; Frances Williams, "Officials see Gatt Round running out of steam," *Financial Times,* April 14, 1992; and *Agence Europe,* April 15, 1992.

53. *Agence Europe,* April 24, 1992.

54. David Dodwell, "Fresh impetus for farm trade compromise," *Financial Times,* April 27, 1992.

55. *Agence Europe,* April 27–28, 1992.

56. David Blackwell, "Agricultural situation 'not sustainable,' Major warns," *Financial Times,* February 12, 1992.

57. David Gardner, "Compromise plan offered on EC farm policy reform," *Financial Times,* February 11, 1992; *Agence Europe,* February 12, 1992.

58. David Gardner, "EC ministers begin last push towards farm reform," *Financial Times,* May 19, 1992.

59. *Agence Europe,* May 21, 1992; and David Gardner, "Basis of a deal on radical CAP reform in sight," *Financial Times,* May 21, 1992.

60. David Gardner, "EC agrees shake-up of farm policy," *Financial Times,* May 22, 1992.

61. *Agence Europe,* July 2, 1992.

62. William Dawkins et al., "French, German farmers denounce EC reforms," *Financial Times,* May 23–24, 1992.

63. "Time for a Gatt deal," *Financial Times,* May 26, 1992.

64. *Agence Europe,* May 30, 1992; and Nancy Dunne and David Buchan, "US offers EC more time over farm subsidies," *Financial Times,* May 30–31, 1992.

65. "GATT's Uruguay round: Sticky," *The Economist,* May 30, 1992.

66. Nancy Dunne, "US set to spill beans on its EC oilseeds 'retaliation'," *Financial Times,* May 27, 1992; David Gardner and Nancy Dunne, "EC anger at US release of exports hit-list," *Financial Times,* June 11, 1992; Frances Williams, "EC threatens to counter-retaliate in subsidy dispute," *Financial Times,* June 19, 1992; and Frances Williams, "EC seeks oilseed subsidy compensation talks," *Financial Times,* June 20–21, 1992.

67. David Gardner, "EC sees signs of hope in farm row," *Financial Times,* June 12, 1992.

68. *Agence Europe,* June 15–16, 1992.

69. David Dodwell and Frances Williams, "Lisbon summit 'crucial to Gatt'," *Financial Times,* June 23, 1992.

70. *Agence Europe,* June 28, 1992.

71. Peter Norman and David Dodwell, "Major sees hope of early deal on Gatt," *Financial Times,* July 6, 1992.

72. Peter Norman, "All set for a second-best summit," *Financial Times,* July 4–5, 1992.

73. Peter Norman et al., "UK tries to break trade talks logjam," *Financial Times,* July 7, 1992; Peter Norman and David Dodwell, "Major fails to revive trade talks," *Financial Times,* July 8, 1992; and Jurek Martin, "G7's annual gathering borders on the irrelevant," *Financial Times,* July 9, 1992.

74. Peter Norman, "Opportunity for Gatt deal seen in autumn," *Financial Times,* July 9, 1992.

75. "The Uruguay Round: Death by procrastination," *The Economist,* July 18, 1992.

76. Tim Coone and Nancy Dunne, "Farm trade deal eludes Madigan and MacSharry," *Financial Times,* July 30, 1992.

77. *Agence Europe,* August 8, 1992.

78. *Agence Europe,* August 19, 1992.

79. Frances Williams, "US seeks Gatt ruling in oilseeds row," *Financial Times,* September 24, 1992; "US-EC trade war fears grow," *Financial Times,* October 1, 1992; and Frances Williams, "Gatt faces crisis over oilseeds row," *Financial Times,* October 2, 1992.

80. Nancy Dunne, "End Uruguay Round soon, says Hills," *Financial Times,* October 6, 1992; and Lionel Barber, "Deadlock on Gatt may be broken soon," *Financial Times,* October 8, 1992.

81. Lionel Barber et al., "France threatens summit boycott over trade row," *Financial Times,* October 12, 1992.

82. David Gardner et al., "Trade war averted as EC and US reach deal," *Financial Times,* November 21–22, 1992.

83. "GATT will build the world," *The Economist,* June 27, 1992.

84. Lionel Barber, "Talks on how to mollify France," *Financial Times,* October 9, 1992.

16

European Defense Integration: National Interests, National Sensitivities

Timothy J. Birch & John H. Crotts

The transition from bipolarity has created enormous instability on the Eurasian landmass. The western response to interconnected political, economic, and ethnic problems has taken the form of economic aid, confidence-building measures, and assistance to emergent, potentially democratic polities. Frequently, the claim is made that Western Europe's security could best be achieved within the framework of an overarching security system, the Conference on Security and Cooperation in Europe (CSCE). Accordingly, the utility of military force has been questioned.

In a climate of uncertainty, it is far from clear that Western interests can be served through a "civilian" power approach to international politics. This problem is acute, since the future form and intentions of regimes to the south and east cannot be predicted. Volatility seems inevitable. What is not clear is whether a system of collective security (CS) can effectively manage dislocations. As a public good, the provision of CS requires states to forgo more compelling national interests. This degree of selflessness cannot be assumed. The quandary is this: "Collective security requires states to behave so virtuously as to make collective security redundant. The ultimate paradox is that collective security works only when it need not."[1] Not surprisingly, therefore, the EC Twelve have moved beyond cooperation in the civilian aspects of foreign and security policy towards the grittier business of constructing a system of collective defense under a revitalized Western European Union (WEU). Europe's feeble showing in the Gulf War served as a catalyst for movement in this direction. In the view of Jacques Delors, "Once it became obvious that the situation would have to be resolved by armed combat, the Community had neither the institutional machinery nor the military force which would have allowed it to act as a community."[2] The urgency of this matter has been compounded by the specter of U.S. withdrawal from the defense of Europe.

The steps taken at Maastricht were notable insofar as they addressed the institutional arrangements governing Europe's future defense. While the process remains intergovernmental in nature, the Union Treaty envisages the gradual development of a European Defense Identity (EDI) within WEU, which at present is functionally distinct from the Community's political machinery. However, this arrangement could prove temporary.

Two competing visions of EDI have been advanced. First, the British have argued that EDI should avoid duplication of NATO's defense function. From this perspective, WEU functions as a bridge to NATO, while serving as the forum through which a more efficient European defense capability can be developed within the Atlantic Alliance. A second view, associated with French and EC Commission ambitions, calls for a merger between WEU and the European Union. Prior to Maastricht, the French had argued that WEU should be accountable to the European Council.[3] Further, Delors has made it plain that he regards WEU as transitional in nature, a vehicle to overcome "national sensitivities" on the road to defense integration. In his view, WEU's Article 5 should be transferred to the Union. To date, a coalition led by Britain has blocked such a development.

While the Community model may prevail in the long term, since economic unity "cannot be insulated from eventual political and military unity,"[4] there are reasons to believe that short- to medium-term (five to ten years) outcomes will more closely approximate the British model. This is not due to British success in defining the terms of the debate, but rather reflects the structure of incentives specific to the defense area.

Our analysis consists of three principal elements. First, the EC member states enjoy neither the comfort of a clear U.S. defense commitment nor the clarity of a single, compelling threat. We offer a brief overview of the nature of new threats and evaluate the ways in which existing defense structures are reacting to environmental change.

The incentive to retain the transatlantic link constitutes the second element of the analysis. It is widely known that the WEU lacks the means to effect independent operations. This legacy of the Cold War can be overcome only at great cost. Western European nations have traditionally relied upon U.S. assistance in managing not only the Soviet threat, but also challenges to interests outside the area. In consequence, the capabilities required to respond to geographically diffuse crises are yet to be developed. Additionally, the military technology gap persists. The application of advanced technology to military systems serves as a force multiplier, a crucial requirement in light of force reductions. Further, the future competitive position of European arms manufacturers will depend upon either continued access to U.S. technology or a concerted European attempt to redress the imbalance, with defections from collaborative ventures likely.

Third, retention of political autonomy, however qualified in particular cases, remains valuable to those European actors who have become accustomed to privileged status in the wider international system and within the EC. Certain states' commitments to postcolonial appendages and the French and British nuclear deterrents will serve as sticking points to defense integration. Moreover, some actors, particularly Britain, are troubled by the message EDI will send to Washington and the possible effects this might have upon her nuclear status as well as Euroatlantic defense trade, and cooperation more generally. In short, some states will be vulnerable to the effects of lost sovereignty in this area and can be expected to resist not only a federal solution, but any measure that compromises current privileges.

By way of a conclusion, we follow up our presentation of sticking points on the path to EDI with a discussion of likely institutional outcomes over both the short and long term. With respect to the former, we suggest that given national sensitivities and the existence of consensual decisionmaking in military affairs, the process of defense integration will remain intergovernmental, with subsidiarity as a rather visible characteristic. Over the long haul, though, the betting is on the realization of a very European EDI. To this end, we consider areas in which movement may serve to warn of a shift toward the Community model of EDI.

Same Hardware, New Faces

During the Cold War, the "threat" was clearly defined. The collapse of Soviet power removed the animating assumption of Western strategic thought. In its stead, defense planners are confronted with a variety of risks that may in time mature into direct threats. Western Europe stands at the geographic center of a confetti of medium and minor powers, many of which are both highly unstable and equipped with significant military assets. This "arc of crisis" stretches from the Maghreb through the Middle East into the territories of the former Warsaw Treaty Organization (WTO).

In Eastern Europe and the former Soviet Union (FSU), three interrelated difficulties present themselves. An economic crisis, from the Oder to the Urals, has been compounded by a crisis of state authority, irredentism, and persistent ethnic strife.[5] These persist at the intrastate and interstate levels. For example, an overt conflict between Hungary and Romania cannot be ruled out. Regional stability is imperiled by the fact that the states of the FSU retain enormous military assets that could be used to offset economic weakness or to satisfy resurgent nationalism.[6] The residual threat posed by Russia alone cannot be viewed with equanimity. Approximately 80 percent of the FSU's military-industrial capacity and 90 percent of its defense institutes and design bureaus are located in Russia.[7] Although U.S. intelligence has estimated that Russian military procurement was cut by 80 percent in the first quarter of 1992, the sobering fact is that the sale of twenty to thirty MiG-29s could finance aerospace R&D for twelve months.[8] In the conventional field, some progress has been made, but the Tashkent Agreements of May 15, 1992, leave Russia and Ukraine with armed forces as large as or larger than those of any other European nation. Such power must eventually be balanced or contained within an alliance, particularly if Europe opts to become more reliant on natural resources from this region. In the nuclear field, uncertainties also remain. Although agreements have been reached concerning the future status of "heavy" ICBMs, verification of inventory reductions remains problematic. While the threat from this quarter is not immediate, confidence-building measures have done little to enhance Western Europe's physical security.

A different sort of challenge is posed by the states of the Maghreb and Middle East. The chief difficulties in the Maghreb area pertain to the intractable problem of growing population in the face of economic contraction. This inherently unstable dynamic is compounded by the appeal of Islamic fundamentalism, which in turn raises questions about the stability of regimes and attitudes toward the west. This situation is shared with the Middle Eastern states, which are marked by divergent sets of interests among numerous ethnic groups, religious sects, and political factions. While the dominant fissure continues to be the Arab-Israeli dispute, the potential for regional conflagration lies also with the ambitions of the major powers in the region. Existing rivalries are likely to be exacerbated by two destabilizing factors. First, confrontation over control of ever-scarcer resources (oil and water) is likely. Second, "new" tensions have resulted from the introduction of ex-Soviet, Central Asian republics into the regional system. These Islamic republics are resource rich, highly nationalistic states with unstable political and economic regimes. Developments in this region are of particular interest to Europe due to its proximity as well as Turkey's membership in NATO and associate membership in WEU.

With the above remarks in mind, the alarming rate of proliferation of weapons must be considered. In 1988 alone, the Middle East absorbed 38 percent of total global arms exports. From 1980 to 1990, the size of active armed forces in the Maghreb increased by 45 percent (60 percent including Libya). Over the same period, the armed forces of the EC Twelve shrank by 6 percent.[9] Of course, the Western allies could always expect qualitative superiority in equipment. This cannot be assured in the future. The absence of effective political supervision of defense firms in the FSU, with economic hardship (see above), has led to the proliferation of advanced Soviet systems. According to French, British, and U.S. military intelligence officials, this is beginning to change the balance of power in strategic areas of the world.[10] For example, Iran is seeking to purchase about two-dozen ex-Soviet Tu-22 "Backfire" bombers and is spending $2 billion a year to rearm.[11] More worrisome, however, is the diffusion of medium range ballistic missiles (MRBMs) throughout the region, coupled with ongoing indigenous nuclear programs and the growing availability of biological and chemical agents. Depending upon where systems such as the Chinese M-9/M-11 are deployed, they have the range to attack parts of southern Europe. This will complicate regional defense planning.

Whither NATO?

The demise of the WTO has removed the obvious counterpoise to NATO. Accordingly, NATO has undertaken a broad reconceptualization of its role in European security. In part, the new role is political: an attempt to manage instability through dialogue and security-enhancing measures, particularly in the east. Additionally, NATO's force structure has been adjusted. The New Strategic Concept delineated at the Rome summit in November 1991 envisages smaller, more flexible forces geared to rapid reaction, with main defense and augmentation forces maintained at lower levels of readiness. The question is, to what will the Ace Rapid Reaction Corps (ARRC) actually react? More pointedly, where will it act?

The threats delineated above are located beyond NATO's formal treaty area. This fact naturally calls into question NATO's long-term viability as a collective defense system, notwithstanding the North Atlantic Council's (NAC) offer to make forces available to the CSCE for peacekeeping operations. In the short term, however, there is ample reason to believe the distinction between operations in and out of the area will be blurred. Historically, NATO has performed a dual-track function. While providing for defense against WTO forces, NATO also served as a "shadow alliance," that is, a forum for informal allied cooperation out of area.[12] Cooperation among more capable allies, particularly Britain, France, and the United States, will likely continue, given convergent interests in the Mediterranean and the Gulf. While the United States retains an abiding interest in preventing the emergence of a dominant power on the Eurasian landmass, Europeans will wish to share the burden of crises and residual threats.[13] This was made explicit in Brussels as early as 1989, when NAC members specified a range of shared concerns that in the future would unite them even in the absence of the Soviet threat.

With these factors in mind, the restructuring of NATO assumes added significance. The most likely arena of overt conflict seems to be toward the south. Not surprisingly, therefore, AFSOUTH has attracted a growing share of NATO resources. Notably, this trend began some years before the collapse of communism. From 1985 to 1991, the southern region absorbed an average of more than 33 percent of infrastructure funds for the period.[14] Further, the Gulf War furnished NATO with an opportunity to make improvements to AFSOUTH command, control, communications, and intelligence (C^3I) facilities, particularly in now-pivotal Turkey. Additional improvements in force capability are expected from cascading, as this pertains to Conventional Forces in Europe Treaty implementation, while future modernization plans include upgrades in the areas of lift, NBC, GPS, and C^3Is.[15] And, while the future size of U.S. forces cannot be predicted, it would appear that those forces that will remain are to be fully self-contained and mobile. Naval reorganization is also being effected, with STANAVFORMED due to be fully operational by 1995. This reorganization is taking place in light of lessons gleaned from the Gulf deployment. NATO infrastructure sustained this effort, while NATO air and naval assets ensured safe passage for approximately 90 percent of the total deployment.[16]

While NATO's formal collective defense remit is unlikely to be extended, it would appear that its defense function will consist of rendering assistance to ad hoc military coalitions in out-of-area operations. NATO's growing orientation to the south was reflected in the first exercise of the ARRC, which was predicated on an attack from south to north. NATO's perceived future value, however, may not be determined by the fact that the organization provides a cost-effective base for power projection, but rather by the degree to which it is supplanted by WEU.

Whither WEU?

Recent developments suggest that WEU may be moving toward greater autonomy within a looser alliance. A redefinition of roles, one that places WEU within the geographic and political orbit of the EC, is in the making in spite of U.S. opposition.

WEU's virtues are twofold; for one, the organization is not formally constrained by the in-area/out-of-area distinction, while WEU can also serve the interests of those actors most susceptible to military threats from the south. The overwhelming disadvantage of WEU is its lack of independent operational capabilities. This has been demonstrated by the Nine's efforts to contribute to military operations in the Gulf.

In 1987, the WEU coordinated mine-hunting operations in the Gulf. The resulting gaps in sea coverage in the western Mediterranean and the Channel were offset by German vessels deployed under NATO auspices, yet the WEU operation was marred by several shortcomings. No provision was made for an integrated command and control structure, while rules of engagement were determined by each national contingent. Ultimately, Dutch and Belgian ships came under British control, while French and Italian ships cooperated only to the extent of exchanging tactical information.

WEU's ability to field forces was again tested in the Gulf War. By mid-September 1990, over thirty WEU combat vessels were on station in the Gulf and Mediterranean. Again, however, there was no integrated command and control system; rather, military guidelines were drawn up by an ad hoc group of representatives from foreign and defense ministries. It was not until January 16, 1991, that a WEU Naval Coordination Authority was established on a permanent basis. Even so, WEU remained dependent upon NATO intelligence and tactical information. Consultation was also inadequate: each member state retained full control over its own deployments, and missions were assigned by national governments, with forces operating independently.[17] Notably, the largest European deployment, Britain's Operation Granby, was underway prior to WEU's involvement. In light of these deficiencies, ministers have begun the process of developing WEU's operational capabilities. The Vianden meeting of June 1991 produced an agreement to establish a satellite data interpretation center, whose tasks include training European experts in photo interpretation. A subsequent meeting, in Bonn on June 14, 1992, took note of the "considerable progress" made in setting up the satellite center. A feasibility study for the main system has been awarded to a German-led consortium, while France has proposed that the EC should agree on a military satellite based on the Helios system, codeveloped by France, Spain, and Italy. Similar initiatives have also been discussed within the Independent Europe Program Group (IEPG), whose defense ministers in March of 1992 called for a more coherent relationship with the emerging WEU-sponsored European Armaments Agency.

With respect to developing command and control, WEU ministers have moved to establish a planning cell. Although British and French differences over this body's structure vis-à-vis SHAPE continue to impede progress (particularly over the issue of double-hatting discussed below), the Military Planning Group, based in Brussels and under an Italian general, became operational on October 1, 1992. Its functions include contingency planning, preparing recommendations for necessary C^3I arrangements, and maintaining lists of national- and NATO-designated units available to WEU. Further, Joint Chiefs of Staff meetings are becoming more frequent. Additionally, British Defense Minister Malcolm Rifkind has offered to make British headquarters available to the WEU when these are not required by NATO. Some consideration has also been given to creating a WEU Rapid Reaction Force (RRF). Although this debate is ongoing, two discernible tendencies are apparent. Britain and Italy, with Dutch support, have suggested that a WEU RRF could draw units from NATO's ARRC, with national contributions being available under a double-hatted command for out-of-area operations. WEU's secretary general, Willem van Eekelen, has ruled out this command arrangement, however. The second tendency emphasizes the candidacy of the Franco-German Corps, scheduled to be fully operational by October 1, 1995. Reportedly, Spain and Belgium have expressed interest in contributing to the force, as have the Italians if the Franco-German Corps can be linked to WEU.

In either case, however, the ability of the WEU to effect independent deployment is suspect. The virtue of the British position lies in its cost-effectiveness and in the implicit assumption that NATO infrastructure would quietly sustain any projection of force. By contrast, the German constitution disallows such out-of-area activities and French law forbids the use of conscripts overseas. In addition, the Franco-German Corps cannot be deployed out-of-area due to intelligence and lift deficiencies. With respect to this latter difficulty, the Vianden meeting charged the WEU's Defense Representatives Group with commissioning a study of Europe's strategic mobility needs. In spite of the urgency of this matter, the report has not materialized. Suggestions have also been made that WEU might develop a multinational transport force modeled after NATO's airborne early warning force and equipped with a military version of the A340.[18] Nevertheless, existing strategic difficulties will be compounded by tactical-level interoperability problems that will generate formidable logistical burdens.

The November 1992 WEU ministerial meeting was important, cementing the associate status of Iceland and Norway, in addition to Turkey. Observer status was conferred upon Denmark and Ireland, while Greece was set to become a full member. Clarification of the relationships between WEU and the Independent European Programme Group (IEPG), and between WEU and EUROGROUP, is also expected. A cooptation of IEPG competences would clear the way for the establishment of a more viable Standing Armaments Committee.[19] It is clear that the European pillar is forming. What is not clear is whether WEU will move beyond "transparency and complementarity."

The Costs of an Independent European Defense Identity (EDI)

If EDI is to "move beyond," it will be necessary to meet the requirements of European defense outside the institution that has provided them in the postwar period: NATO. That is, it will be obliged to reproduce NATO on a European scale. If the scale is limited to Europe, two difficulties warrant analysis. First, Europeans will be forced to replace what will be lost as a result of a partial or complete U.S. withdrawal. This means everything from stockpiles (for example, European members of NATO possess no industrial strategic stockpile of critical items and raw materials; hence, they have little or no industrial surge capacity), to capabilities, to a competent defense technology base.[20] As noted above, this state of affairs is a result of overreliance upon U.S. military power during the Cold War. This legacy colors the current debate over the WEU RRF, the expressed short-term goal of European defense planners. Second, strong incentives to "buy European" would be exacerbated by a U.S. withdrawal. Three benefits would attend the course of building a more independent European sourcing capability. Obviously, vulnerability to the effects of shifts in U.S. policy would be reduced. In addition, European defense production could be managed in the interest of keeping production lines active and ready to meet the challenge of different contingencies. An added advantage of this would be the retention of jobs and money within Europe.

Since challenges to Western European defense are no longer one-dimensional, Western forces in general are reorienting from linear defensive doctrines to an interventionist posture, a transition anticipated by U.S. planners for over a decade. Accordingly, force requirements now hinge upon flexibility and mobility, with growing emphasis upon intelligence, interoperability of systems, and compatibility of national doctrines within multinational forces.[21] A Rapid Reaction Force under WEU control could meet these requirements. If it is to do so, WEU will be forced to address two problem areas. While flexibility of forces has been met through reconfiguration of national armed forces and the development of the ARRC force pool (a primarily European unit upon which WEU could conceivably draw), WEU needs mobility and intelligence resources.

With respect to the first requirement, there are two key elements. Mobility encompasses both strategic and tactical dimensions. Intervention can only be accomplished through heavy air and sea lift. Regarding the tactical element, today's battlefield requires an ability to conduct a ground battle of both depth and rapid movement of vanguard elements, as well as precision employment of rotary-wing and fixed-wing aircraft at points of attack. This three-dimensional approach throws a heavy burden on support trains. Helicopters tailored to the logistical role are crucial to the success of such fluid operations.

According to *The Economist,* the cost of providing for an adequate air and sea lift capability (which would include 150-plus transport aircraft and twenty fast transport ships) could be anywhere from $20 billion to $40 billion.[22] Europe's need for a satisfactory airlift wing is acute, as combined national capabilities are not impressive. For example, France's airlift arm consists of eighty-four Transalls, while the UK possesses eighteen VC-10s currently being refitted for the tanker role (as are six of their nine Tristars; the remaining three will serve as transports), and sixty C-130H Hercules transports. By way of comparison, the United States maintains in service 115 C-5 Galaxies, 250 C-141Bs, and 518 C-130s (of various configurations), along with 651 tankers. The options available to Europe, moreover, are not particularly attractive. In a nutshell, the choice is between procurement of capable U.S. aircraft (with the attendant political implications) and the development of less capable European alternatives at higher cost (calculated on load capacity). Britain has expressed interest in the C-17, which costs roughly $200 million per copy but can lift a 78-ton load. A cheaper ($120–150 million per copy), European aircraft could be developed on the basis of the Airbus A340–300, which could lift fifty-three tons. However, this aircraft, unlike its U.S. counterparts, was not designed for the military transport role. Predictably, it could not withstand landings on rugged airstrips, has no provision for loading ramps, and has limited cargo bay height. A more desirable option exists on paper in the European Future Large Aircraft Group's "Future Large Aircraft," which would be designed from the ground up as a military lifter. The most reliable estimates on the cost of the project predict a unit cost of $94 million, which compares favorably to the cost of U.S. aircraft. The maximum payload, at 25 tons, does not, and a fifteen- to twenty-year design-to-delivery wait is normal for such programs.[23]

Sealift, so crucial to the deployment of heavy mechanized formations, represents another problematic area. Of 153 voyages required by the UK during the Gulf War, 144 were undertaken by merchant vessels, the majority foreign-flagged. Of course, the crucial factor allowing sealift to occur at all is adequate three-dimensional naval protection. In this regard, European navies have deteriorated to the point that they require alliance with the U.S. Navy to undertake operations.[24] With the exception of Britain, France, and to a lesser extent, Italy, European navies are deficient in air defense ships and attack submarines.

The most serious weakness, however, stems from a lack of fleet carriers. The British Invincible class was designed for NATO antisubmarine warfare (ASW) service; the two operational vessels of this class, therefore, carry a combined total of only sixteen Sea Harriers. The Italian *Garibaldi* carrier is in process of receiving its Harriers, but again the number carried is not large. The French currently possess two aging Clemenceau class ships, each typically outfitted with sixteen Super Etendards, although future plans do include the acquisition of a 35,000-ton nuclear carrier vessel. Thus, the total number of European carrier-borne jet aircraft is the rough equivalent to the number carried by a single U.S. platform.

At the tactical level, such items as helicopters for transport, surveillance, and attack would be necessary. These are expensive additions and will be more so if developed and sourced from Europe. The first prototype Eurotiger is now airborne. This machine was originally designed as an antitank platform to counter Soviet armor. The estimated unit cost is double that of the "off-the-shelf" U.S. AH-64, widely considered the more capable system. Further, Eurotiger was not expected to be operational until 1998. This may be set back due to the fact that it must now be adapted for the combat support role dictated by the changed threat environment. Another major European helicopter project, the NH-90, is experiencing difficulties. Eurocopter, Agusta, and Fokker have been saved from a potentially disastrous loss by a French order for twenty. In the absence of this timely order, there were concerns that Germany would have been forced to look elsewhere, most probably to the Sikorsky Seahawk. The NH-90 program, which has now been running for twelve years and is two years behind schedule, is expected to deliver the first prototype in 1995.[25]

In conjunction with the need for increased mobility, an improved intelligence capability is required. This is as true for Europe as a whole as it is for a WEU RRF if Europe is to provide for its own defense. However, intelligence cannot be considered in isolation, as it is largely a function of technology. The technology base provides not only the systems that gather and process intelligence data but also serve as force multipliers. Further, defense technology, especially in the aerospace and electronics sectors, is by most measures increasingly "dual-use." Applied to nonmilitary products, this advanced, "value-added" technology is a primary determinant of power in contemporary international relations.

The notion of U.S. superiority in defense technology is unassailable. Because it has been U.S. policy to participate in research and development with its NATO allies, this resource has been accessible to European NATO members. A number of avenues for bilateral and multilateral exchange and cooperation have been established through various NATO-affiliated groups. The conference of national armaments directors, with its NATO army, air force and naval armaments groups, TriService group on communications and electronic equipment, and NATO defense research group, are notable in this regard, as is the advisory group for aerospace research and development. U.S. organizations involved in major, ongoing NATO cooperative projects include all three services, no fewer than five agencies, and the Ada Joint Program Office. The list of systems that are the product of U.S. collaboration with its NATO allies is long indeed. Unfortunately for EDI, the relationship is more valuable to Europe than to the United States.

In 1989, most estimates suggested that Europe suffered from a five-year lag behind the US and Japan in applying new technologies.[26] A U.S. Department of Defense (DoD) summary of critical technological capabilities relative to U.S. levels in 1991 indicated that the United States' NATO allies were generally on a par with the United States in seven of twenty areas.[27] The most recent DoD technology summary suggests that the allies remain behind in many crucial technological categories, including communications networking and electronic devices. The electronic devices category includes such items as radar, electronic warfare, platform/weapon control, computation, imaging, and communication (including satellite).[28] These are among the technologies that figure prominently in intelligence systems.

What technologies should be on Europe's shopping list? Given the threat assessment above, the Gulf War was an ideal showcase for U.S. technologies well suited to probable European requirements. These included projectiles with sensors, stealth, satellites for communications and surveillance, GPS, MLRS, C^3I, and JSTARS. One additional capability must be mentioned: U.S.-developed antimissile technology. In this connection, it is interesting to note the change in the French government's attitude toward U.S. SDI developments. Apparently, criticism has given way to interest. Further, France is expected to sign a broad space technology exchange agreement with the United States.[29] The costs of loss of access to the above technologies should be viewed as potential costs for Europe in the event of a disruption of the Atlantic link.

Thus far, disincentives for precipitous breakup of the Atlantic relationship have stopped short of an accounting for the costs of a completely independent EDI. The estimates of what it would cost Europe to "provide even the essentials of its private defense," including a nuclear component, run from 4 percent to 7 percent of annual GNP.[30] At present, the French Military Program Law has set France's defense budget at 3.1 percent of GNP.[31] In any event, defense budgets everywhere are shrinking. The German defense budget is down for fiscal 1993 by 2.5 percent, and projected allocations decrease by 3.0 percent per year through fiscal 1995.[32] For the period 1990/91 to 1994/95, the UK will spend 5.5 percent less, which in GNP terms is a drop from 3.9 percent to 3.5 percent.[33] If Europeans did not meet their spending targets in the face of a known threat during the Cold War, how could it be assumed that they would not opt for defection during a period of largely economic competition? Even in the case of the relatively "small" European fighter aircraft (EFA) project, defection was chosen by the German contingent. At the time of writing, it appears that the Germans have also been successful in persuading all parties with the exception of the UK to abandon EFA for U.S. alternatives.

National Interests: Whose Will Prevail?

In addition to the primarily economic costs outlined, movement toward an independent EDI will rest on another apparently scarce resource, political will. The poverty of the European response to the Yugoslav crisis is a case in point. The EC's attempt to broker a ceasefire was marred by independent action on the part of Germany. Furthermore, a French initiative to convene a 30,000-person intervention force under WEU command did not receive general support.[34] The French, subsequently, pursued a different course by persuading the Italians, Spanish, and Portuguese to join them in a WEU naval patrol in the Adriatic. Overlapping with a similar NATO effort, the French-led deployment did succeed in attracting half-hearted British and German contributions. However, the patrol could not examine suspect merchant ships, or even turn them back. To the extent that any kind of precedent has been set, it would appear to be this: "European" interests have been, and for the foreseeable future will remain, insufficiently compelling for certain governments to compromise narrowly defined national interests.

Any independent European defense identity must rest on the contributions of Britain, France, and Germany. These states' willingness to support movement in this direction naturally implies erosion of national autonomy. It is difficult, for example, to believe that these powers, which between them account for 80 percent of Community defense trade, would look forward to EC direction of firms that to date have been tightly aligned with national defense procurement strategies and defense industrial policies. France's most recent budget places disproportionate emphasis on procurement of French-built systems. In the UK case, through the 1980s, 75 percent of the equipment budget was spent domestically.[35]

Certain privileged member states may find the Community's embrace stifling. Britain and France, in particular, retain interests that are located beyond the geographic confines of Western Europe. If challenged, these might require an ability to respond independently of Community authorization. Such has been the case with British interventions in the Falklands. Further, Britain maintains overseas military commitments in places as remote as Belize, Samoa, Brunei, and Hong Kong.

Similarly, French interests are widely engaged, most particularly in francophone Africa, from which France, along with Belgium, Holland, and Portugal, source raw materials. The level of this interest is compelling, having led France to numerous military interventions in Zaire, the latest in January 1993. Deployment was effected by the USAF, as had been true with previous French operations in Chad and elsewhere.

German interests lie as much toward the east as toward the west, and their investments reflect such interest. In addition, the costs of reunification are likely to distract Germany from the European project. This has implications for EDI. First, Germany will be inclined to perpetuate NATO as long as there exists a risk of instability in its backyard.[36] German leadership of the air component of the ARRC is testimony to this. Second, the increased self-absorption of Germany casts French policy in a new light. It is widely held that the European project has been carried forward on the Franco-German axle, sometimes to the exclusion of British interests. For example, the British were not invited to the Franco-German defense planning meeting in April, 1992. Behind this activity, however, lies pronounced French anxiety over a resurgent Germany. French diplomatic initiatives have been interpreted as an attempt to build structures to contain German power, a goal that also served, historically, to anchor the U.S. presence in Europe.[37] For France, containment of Germany, rather than Community empowerment, seems to be the ultimate objective.

Finally, an independent EDI must possess a nuclear deterrent. The two nuclear powers are not likely to forfeit willingly expensive symbols of national prestige. Although France's 1992–1994 military program law reduces the share of the defense budget devoted to nuclear systems from 30 percent to about 20 percent, this remains an enormous commitment. Savings were achieved by stretching procurement schedules for future SSBNs and by the cancellation of the S45 ICBM and further orders for Hades. Interestingly, France has proposed that those Hades systems which remain could be given to WEU so that this organization might deter threats from MRBMs to forces deployed on missions out of area. Beyond coughing up this system, for which France clearly has no use, MRBM threats to French territory call for a credible, and therefore solely French, command arrangement.

For the British, any non-NATO defense option is unpalatable. This is a consequence of the UK's special relationship with the United States which, while affording some benefits, now acts as a potent constraint on Britain's ability to field the European option. What might be at stake is Britain's status as a strategic nuclear power. It is well known that British attempts to develop nuclear delivery systems have been unsuccessful. Hence, Britain has been obliged to source such systems from the United States. The Trident D5, procured at great cost, also carries with it a political burden. Refit work, first for Polaris and now for Trident, is conducted in the United States. British warheads are tested in the United States, while the missiles themselves will be sourced from the U.S. pool, with periodic exchanges every seven to eight years. Furthermore, to maintain the system and to ensure access to technological upgrades, Britain will remain dependent on U.S. goodwill.[38] In this sense, Britain is vulnerable to irredeemable transition costs that might result from a European defense merger. Nevertheless, Britain is proceeding with the construction of a further three Vanguard class SSBN hulls, which compounds unease over French notions of EDI. A possible solution may lie in Anglo-French collaboration, as appears to be the case in the field of air-launched cruise missiles. To date, there has been little progress with heavier systems.

Conclusion

Realization of an independent European defense identity in the short to medium term can be achieved only if states are willing to pay both political and economic costs. Not an easy option for any EC member, this is particularly unattractive for the UK. At the time of writing, the questionable status of the Maastricht Treaty adds further complications. We have left aside the issue of widening, currently on the EC's agenda, but the obvious point should be made that a defense commitment may only be possible if it is based upon a solid membership core. Consequently, we would expect EDI, and more broadly, the Common Foreign and Security Policy, to remain intergovernmental with respect to both process and outcome. Thus, WEU would remain compatible with, and probably dependent upon, NATO. With respect to the Community's overall institutional profile, we would expect various levels of depth in member states' commitments, with intergovernmental mechanisms prevalent in the areas of greatest national sensitivity, and opt-outs offered to those states whose interests cannot be reconciled with those of the wider Community.

Recall the spectrum of possible EDI models. The above scenario describes the perpetuation of the status quo, yet an EC-centered model, which is synonymous with the ambitions of political union, cannot be discounted over the long haul. Prediction of its precise institutional profile is beyond the pretensions of this paper. However, it is our view that Europeans will ultimately become responsible for their own defense, which may or may not involve the United States and NATO. To this end, the following are presented as indicators of movement toward a unionist vision of EDI.

Although relevant institutional frameworks can be erected quickly, these must rest on an independent defense base, the establishment of which will require significant lead time. First, procurement of high-priced equipment identified above and commitment to funding for big-budget systems-development projects would signal a measure of political willingness to construct EDI. Airbus is a precedent that demonstrates European will to tolerate absolute losses in the interest of improving relative position. Second, the European defense market has been witness to concentration of industry on a massive scale, particularly in the aerospace and electronics sectors, which together account for the great majority of production. This consolidation has taken place largely within national borders such that it appears as if national champion strategies are still being employed. However, the level of bilateral and multilateral cooperation in the developmental stage in conjunction with "tag-teaming" on bids and contracts is worthy of observation. A solid indicator would be the status of Article 223 of the Rome Treaty.[39] If it is amended, this will clear the way for sector-specific merger and acquisition activity *sans frontières*. Third, in connection with the technology base, funding levels and movement toward consolidation in the research and development/engineering sector may be worthy of attention. In the case of all movement indicators presented thus far, the financial and political burdens will be borne by national actors. However, the EC Commission may also find itself able to exercise political leadership in, for example, EUCLID, EUROGROUP, IEPG, and EDIG as it has been able to do in ESPRIT.

The indicators presented above do not represent an exhaustive treatment of this issue. In truth, at least one item has been left out. EDI may not, after all, be a European decision to make, but rather may be forced by a reorientation of U.S. policy. Complete U.S. disengagement from the defense of Europe could have catalytic effects upon the current debate.

Notes

The authors wish to express their gratitude to the following persons: Dr. David M. Wood, Dr. Birol A. Yesilada, and John Bellais of the University of Missouri-Columbia. In addition, thanks to the editors of this volume and to Carl Lauer at McDonnell Douglas Library, St. Louis, Missouri.

1. Josef Joffe, "Collective Security and the Future of Europe: Failed Dreams and Dead Ends," in *Survival* 34 no. 2 (Spring 1992), p. 44.

2. Jacques Delors, "European Integration and Security," *Survival* 33 no. 2 (March/April 1991), p. 102.

3. Oxford Research Group, "Defence and Security in the New Europe: Who Will Decide?" *Current Decisions Report* no. 7 (November 1991), p. 9.

4. Zbigniew Brzezinzki, "The Consequences of the End of the Cold War for International Security," *Survival* 34 no. 2 (Summer 1992), p. 9.

5. P. Zelikow, "The New Concert of Europe," *Survival* 34 no. 2 (Summer 1992), pp. 12–30.

6. Ibid., p. 16.

7. B. A. Bicksler and J. L. Lacy, "After the Fall: Russian Perspectives on Security Policy and Arms Control," IDA Document D1141 (Alexandria, Virginia: Institute for Defense Analyses, March 1992), p. 19.

8. Ibid., p. 23.

9. Mark Stenhouse, "NATO's Southern Region: The New Front Line?" in *Jane's NATO Handbook 1991–1992*, (London: Jane's), pp. 59–63.

10. "Russian Aircraft Marketing Threatens Power Balance," *Aviation Week and Space Technology*, September 14, 1992, p. 22.

11. "European ABM Defense Plans Anticipate Middle East Threat," *Aviation Week and Space Technology*, August 10, 1992, p.22; George Melloan, "Can't Anyone Here Play This Persian Gulf Game?" *The Wall Street Journal*, October 19, 1992, p. A17.

12. Margaret Sherwood, *Allies in Crisis: Meeting Global Challenges to Western Security* (New Haven: Yale University Press, 1990).

13. Keith Dunn, *In Defense of NATO* (Boulder: Westview Press, 1990).

14.. Stenhouse, op. cit., p. 59.

15. Jonathan T. Howe, (Admiral, USN), "Southern Guard," in *Jane's NATO Handbook 1991–1992*, op. cit., pp. 193–196.

16. Ibid., p. 196.

17. Willem van Eekelen, "Western European Union," in *Jane's NATO Handbook 1991–1992*, op. cit., pp. 159–162.

18. Nicholas Fiorenza, "No Near-Term Cure in Sight for Europe's Strategic Airlift Woes," *Armed Forces Journal International*, July 1992, p. 21.

19. WEU Sources, Paris, October 10, 1992; WEU Sources, London, October 15, 1992.

20. I. S. Baxter (Major-General) "Sustainability: A Concept Which May Come of Age," *Military Strategy in a Changing Europe*, B. Holden-Reid and M. Dewar, eds. (London: Brassey's, 1991), p. 230.

21. *Statement on the Defence Estimates*, London, HMSO, July 1992, pp. 89; "Arms and Equipment for a European Rapid Reaction Force," *Military Technology* 16 no. 3 (1992), p. 16.

22. "Survey: Defence in the 21st Century," *The Economist*, September 5, 1992, p. 10.

23. Nicholas Fiorenza, op. cit., April 1992, p. 21 and op. cit., July 1992, p. 21; *Military Technology*, March 1992, pp. 23–26. *The Military Balance, 1991–92* (London: Brassey's, 1992), pp. 24–25; *Statement on the Defence Estimates*, op. cit., pp. 30, 66–67.

24. Bruce George, "Introduction," in *Jane's NATO Handbook 1991–1992*, op. cit., p. 31.

25. "France's NH-90 Buy Saves Helicopter for Production," *Aviation Week and Space Technology*, September 14, 1992, p. 93.

26. Christopher Coker, ed., *Drifting Apart? The Superpowers and their European Allies* (London: Brassey's, 1989), p. 106.

27. U.S., Department of Defense, "The Comeback Capability" *Defense '91*, May-June 1991, p.25.

28. U.S., Department of Defense, Director of Defense Research and Engineering, *DoD Key Technologies Plan* (July, 1992).

29. "European ABM Defense Plans Anticipate Middle East Threat," *Aviation Week and Space Technology*, August 10, 1992, pp. 22–23.

30. "Survey: Defence in the 21st Century" in *The Economist*, September 5, 1992, p. 20.

31. "The French 1992–94 Military Programme Law," *Military Technology* (September 1992), pp. 42–43.

32. *Wehrdienst*, August 31, p. 2.

33. *Statement on the Defence Estimates*, op. cit., pp. 46–48.

34. John Zametica, "The Yugoslav Conflict," *Adelphi Papers,* no. 270, Institute for International Strategic Studies (London: Brassey's, 1992), p. 66.

35. Keith Hartley and Nicholas Hooper, "Costs and Benefits to the United Kingdom of the US Military Presence," in *Europe After an American Withdrawal,* J.M.O. Sharp, ed. (Oxford: Oxford University Press, 1990), p. 142.

36. Elizabeth Pond, "Germany in the New Europe," in *Foreign Affairs,* Spring 1992.

37. Oxford Research Group, op. cit., p. 9. See also W. Hanreider, "The Federal Republic, the US, and the New Europe: A Historical Perspective," in *Europe and the Superpowers,* Robert Jordan, ed. (New York: St. Martin's, 1991), pp. 66–87.

38. John Bayliss, *British Defense Policy* (New York: St. Martin's, 1989), pp. 70, 89.

39. Article 223 of the Rome Treaty covers the protection of member states' essential security interests "connected with the production of or trade in arms, munitions and war material."

PART 4

THE SINGLE MARKET

17

Merger Control in the EC: Federalism with a European Flavor

Daniel G. Partan

The 1992 program for the completion of the internal market has stimulated waves of mergers as firms seek to position themselves for effective participation within the Community and in world markets. This development has reinforced the Commission's view that centralized merger control is essential for success in completing the internal market:

> Although many such mergers have not posed any problems from the competition point of view, it must be ensured that they do not in the long run jeopardize the competition process, which lies at the heart of the common market and is essential in securing all the benefits linked with the single market. . . . [N]ational rules are inadequate as a means of controlling Community-scale mergers, mainly because such rules are restricted to the respective territories of the Member States concerned. Clearly, Community law must be applied in controlling and examining large-scale mergers, where the reference market is increasingly the Community as a whole or a large part of it.[1]

From the outset the achievement of the common market was recognized to require centralized control of competition policy. In this respect the Treaty of Rome establishes the European Community as a federal system: power over competition policy is divided between the Community and member states, Community law displaces inconsistent national law, and judicial control is exercised by the EC Court of Justice. Articles 85 and 86 and their implementing legislation establish the framework for Community competition policy, but the rules and authority contained in those articles have not been sufficient for effective control of mergers.

Article 86, which prohibits "abuse" of a "dominant position," was held in the *Continental Can* case to apply to mergers that strengthen an existing dominant position within a Community market,[2] but with its focus on "abuse," that article would not reach mergers that are merely intended to create a dominant position.[3] Article 85, which prohibits agreements and concerted practices that distort or restrict competition within the common market, was early regarded by the Commission as not applicable to agreements, such as mergers, "whose purpose is the acquisition of total or partial ownership of enterprises."[4] Nevertheless, in 1988 the European Court held in the celebrated *Philip Morris* litigation that Article 85 does apply to "the acquisition by one company of an equity interest in a competitor" where the effect is to restrict or distort competition.[5] The Court's decision opens the possibility of using Article 85 to reach mergers that involve the acquisition of a controlling interest in a competitor where that controlling interest results from an agreement between undertakings. Even so, Article 85 may not be broad enough to reach all merger activity that affects competition between member states in the European Community.[6]

Against this backdrop, the 1989 EC Merger Control Regulation[7] seems intended both to remedy the limitations of Articles 85 and 86 and to replace those articles as the Community vehicle for merger control. The Merger Regulation rests on the theory that Articles 85 and 86 are not sufficient to control mergers that distort competition.[8] Accordingly, the Regulation cites as its legal basis both Rome Treaty Article 87, which authorizes legislation to implement Articles 85 and 86, and Article 235, which authorizes legislation to fill gaps in the Treaty. By invoking Article 235, the Regulation intended that the Community will assume "additional powers of action necessary for the attainment of [Community] objectives."[9] Together with the enhancement of Community merger control powers, the Regulation sought to monopolize the review of the most significant mergers. The Regulation provides that it shall be "the only instrument applicable" to mergers that have the "Community dimension" that is required to bring them within the scope of the Merger Regulation.[10] The Commission is intended to exercise exclusive jurisdiction to regulate mergers that have a Community dimension; mergers that lack a Community dimension are to remain within national jurisdiction, free of Community control. Unfortunately, the actual division of jurisdiction could not be so clear and straightforward. Instead, the Merger Regulation divides jurisdiction to regulate mergers in a fashion that interweaves national and Community control over mergers on both sides of the Community dimension thresholds. This chapter examines the jurisdictional fabric of the Merger Regulation and explores the implications of the merger control regime for future harmonization of national and Community competition law.

The Regulation's Division of Jurisdiction to Review Mergers

The basic rule prescribed in the Merger Regulation is that a merger that "creates or strengthens a dominant position" and thereby impedes competition "shall be declared incompatible with the common market."[11] This rule is to be applied by the Commission to mergers that have a "Community dimension" defined in terms of turnover thresholds. Mergers that exceed the thresholds in principle fall within the Commission's jurisdiction, whereas those that are below the thresholds lack a "Community dimension" and fall within national jurisdiction.[12]

"Community dimension," as defined in the Merger Regulation, is measured by a three-part test: (1) the "combined aggregate worldwide turnover of all the undertakings concerned" must exceed ECU 5 billion; (2) each of at least two undertakings must have an "aggregate Community-wide turnover" that exceeds ECU 250 million; and (3) at least one of the undertakings must achieve more than one third of its aggregate, Community-wide turnover outside of a single EC member state.[13] Detailed rules address the calculation of turnover.[14] The Commission would have preferred lower thresholds (of ECU 2 billion and 100 million, respectively);[15] these or some other lower thresholds will be proposed when the Regulation is reviewed by the Council in 1993.[16]

The jurisdiction provisions of the Merger Regulation are designed to achieve the "one-stop shopping" that was a major policy objective of the Merger Regulation.[17] The basic idea is that enterprises should be able to know whether a proposed merger is subject to Community or to national control, and they should not be required to submit their proposal to both Community and national authorities. Regrettably, the matter has proved much more complex. The jurisdictional division accomplished by the Merger Regulation's thresholds for "Community dimension" fails to leave either to the Commission or to the member states unfettered control over mergers that fall on their respective sides of the "Community dimension" line.

On the surface, the Merger Regulation's provisions appear simple and straightforward. The Regulation states that it applies to all mergers with a Community dimension.[18] Subject to judicial review in the EC Court of Justice, the Commission is given "sole jurisdiction to take the decisions provided for in [the Merger] Regulation."[19] The Regulation further provides that "no Member State shall apply its national legislation on competition to any concentration [i.e., merger] that has a Community dimension."[20]

Confusingly, however, the Regulation defines mergers without reference to Community dimension,[21] and it also provides that "this Regulation alone shall apply" to mergers "as defined" in the Regulation, which includes both below-threshold mergers and mergers with a Community dimension.[22] Thus, although the scope of the control exercised by the Regulation is specified in terms of mergers with a Community dimension,[23] the exclusive application rule just quoted applies to all mergers without regard to the thresholds for Community dimension. What should be the meaning of the exclusive application provision? Does it mean to preclude only the application of Community law other than the Merger Regulation? Or does it mean also to preclude the application of national law, that is, to preclude both national law and other Community law?

As applied to mergers above the Community dimension thresholds, the exclusive application provision must be read together with the Merger Regulation's specific preclusion of the application of national competition law. Since rules of national law are specifically excluded in respect of mergers with a Community dimension,[24] the stipulation that "this Regulation alone shall apply" must have been intended to preclude application of other rules of Community law. The conclusion that the exclusion applies only to other Community law is borne out by the further stipulation that certain named competition policy regulations "shall not apply to concentrations [i.e., mergers] as defined in [the Merger Regulation]."[25]

As applied to below-threshold mergers, the exclusive application provision is ambiguous: read by itself, the quoted language could mean to exclude the application of national law as well as of Community law, but in context the provision seems directed only at other Community law. As noted above, the term "this Regulation alone" could not have meant to exclude both Community law and national law across the board, since a separate provision of the Regulation had already excluded national law from application to Community dimension mergers.[26] Although nothing is said about national law applicable to below-threshold mergers, the intent could not have been to exclude both Community and national law since that would leave below-threshold mergers unregulated.[27] Hence, the Merger Regulation, which does not itself regulate below-threshold mergers, operates to exclude the application of other Community law to below-threshold mergers but permits their regulation by national law. The effect of the Merger Regulation's attempt to exempt below-threshold mergers from the application of Community competition law is addressed in the sections that follow.

Even when read along the lines just indicated, the apparent simplicity of the Regulation's jurisdictional division is further marred by two additional provisions: the so-called German Clause and Dutch Clause. Reportedly, Germany would not accept the Merger Regulation without some mechanism for taking jurisdiction of mergers both above and below the Community dimension thresholds when such mergers could have a significant impact on competition in German markets. The "German Clause" authorizes the Commission to refer a merger to a member state where the merger is above Community interest thresholds but "threatens to create or to strengthen a dominant position" and thereby impede competition in a "distinct market" within that member state.[28] Commission action is discretionary, but there is provision for judicial review; the referral results in the application of national competition law. The Commission made its first use of the referral authority in February 1992 when it allowed the United Kingdom to review the effect on competition in certain products of a proposed concentrative joint venture in the construction materials industry. The Commission had approved the joint venture for concrete blocks and other structural concrete and masonry products but referred to the UK plans to produce bricks and clay tiles for the British market. In the Commission's view, the joint venture would have only a negligible effect on the wider EC market for bricks and clay tiles but would control a very high percentage of available production capacity in the United Kingdom.[29]

The "Dutch Clause" authorizes the referral of a merger in the opposite direction, that is, referral from a member state to the Commission. Under this provision a merger that lacks a Community dimension may be referred by a member state to the Commission where the merger creates or strengthens a dominant position and thereby significantly impedes competition within that member state.[30] At this writing no state has sought to refer a merger to the Commission under the "Dutch Clause."

Commission Review of Community Dimension Mergers

With the exceptions just noted, "one-stop shopping" applies to Community dimension mergers, but only in respect of competition policy. A merger above the Community dimension thresholds that is not referred to a member state pursuant to the "German Clause" is to be reviewed for its impact on competition exclusively by the Commission. The Commission's review is undertaken pursuant to the Merger Regulation, which serves as implementing legislation for Articles 85 and 86 in respect of mergers that have a Community dimension; the application of other Community legislation is excluded.[31]

Notwithstanding the otherwise exclusive application of the Merger Regulation, member states are authorized to review Community dimension mergers to "protect legitimate interests other than those taken into consideration" by the Merger Regulation.[32] This means that alongside Community review there may be national review of Community dimension mergers, but such national review must rest on grounds other than the potential impact of the merger on competition. Three "legitimate [national] interests" are specifically mentioned in the Merger Regulation: "public security, plurality of the media, and prudential rules."[33] The Regulation authorizes the Commission to recognize additional member state interests as "legitimate" provided such interests are "compatible" with Community law. Examples potentially include broad national interests in industrial and social policy, but the limiting factor will be the Commission's exclusive jurisdiction over Community competition policy under the Merger Regulation. Should a government wish to stimulate mergers for reasons of industrial policy, that is, to improve the international competitiveness of its industry, it will be difficult to frame such a policy without trespassing upon the Commission's reserved domain.

Although member state authority to protect its "legitimate interests" may prove complex in application, the intended division of jurisdiction is clear: to protect "legitimate [national] interests" recognized in the Regulation or by the Commission, the member state may undertake its own "national interest" review that will proceed separately from the competition policy review undertaken by the Commission. In the end, the member state may act only to further restrict or prohibit a merger that is approved by the Commission; the member state may not apply its national competition policy and in any event may not approve a merger that is disapproved by the Commission.[34]

Commission Review of Mergers that Lack a Community Dimension

The structure of the Merger Regulation implies that mergers below the Community dimension thresholds should be subject only to national review.[35] However, even though national authorities are free to apply national competition policies to mergers that fall below the Community dimension thresholds, nothing in national law can exclude Community law. Hence the competition rules of Articles 85 and 86 of the Treaty of Rome, which constitute basic Community law, should continue to govern below-threshold mergers just as they govern other economic activity within the Community.[36] It follows that the Community law embodied in Articles 85 and 86 should be applied to below-threshold mergers both by national authorities and by Community institutions.

Notwithstanding the logic of the above analysis, the Merger Regulation seems intended to confine below-threshold mergers to national review. As noted above, the Regulation does two things. First, it stipulates that it "alone" applies to mergers as defined in the Regulation.[37] This should mean that the Merger Regulation is the only Community legislation that applies both to above- and to below-threshold mergers. Second, the Regulation in addition specifically revokes for all mergers the existing regulations that implement the competition rules of Rome Treaty Articles 85 and 86.[38] Among the legislation that the Regulation withdraws is Council Regulation 17, the basic Council Regulation implementing Articles 85 and 86 of the EEC Treaty; this regulation is explicitly made inapplicable to all mergers as defined in the Merger Regulation. Hence, Regulation 17 is withdrawn both by the exclusive application provision and by the specific revocation provision.

Why this redundancy? Is the exclusive application provision intended to withdraw more than the specific implementing legislation? The question has two parts. First, would it be possible for the Merger Regulation to insulate mergers from the operation of Rome Treaty Articles 85 and 86? Second, even if the Merger Regulation cannot modify or revoke Rome Treaty rules, it does withdraw the regulations under which the Commission has applied those rules to mergers. Does the Commission retain the authority and the duty to apply Articles 85 and 86 to below-threshold mergers even though the relevant implementing legislation has been withdrawn?

As noted above, the Merger Regulation invokes both Rome Treaty Article 87 as legislation that implements the competition rules of Articles 85 and 86, and Treaty Article 235 as legislation that adds to the powers of the Commission in order to accomplish the goals of the Treaty.[39] Article 87 contemplates that implementing legislation will "define . . . the scope" of Articles 85 and 86. Therefore, it is the implementing legislation that governs Commission regulation of mergers, and not the terms of Articles 85 and 86. This would be true for Community dimension mergers, which are now governed exclusively by the Merger Regulation, but not for below-threshold mergers, which are not regulated under the Merger Regulation. Legislation is adopted under Article 87 to give concrete meaning and effect to Articles 85 and 86. In this sense the implementing legislation will replace Articles 85 and 86 as regulatory vehicles, but the implementation authority of Article 87 does not authorize total abdication of the Commission's role in implementing Articles 85 and 86.

Article 235 authorizes legislation that adds to the Commission's powers when necessary to attain the objectives of the Treaty. The gap-filling legislation contemplated in Article 235 does not amend the Treaty. Treaty amendments are governed by Article 236; they are adopted by a different procedure and require ratification by all member states. In some circumstances it may be difficult to distinguish Article 235 legislation from Article 236 Treaty amendments, but it is clear that Article 235 contemplates the enhancement, not the restriction, of the Commission's powers. Therefore, it would not seem possible to use Article 235 to reduce rather than to expand the Commission's powers. The conclusion must be that legislation adopted pursuant to Article 235 cannot rewrite the Treaty to exclude the application of Articles 85 and 86 to below-threshold mergers.

Turning to the regulatory role of the Commission, Rome Treaty Article 89 authorizes the Commission to "investigate cases of suspected infringement" of the principles laid down in Articles 85 and 86 and to take action by way of a "reasoned decision."[40] Article 89 was included to allow the Commission to act to give effect to Articles 85 and 86 in the period prior to the adoption of the implementing legislation provided for in Article 87. Does the withdrawal of that implementing legislation revive the Commission's Article 89 powers? The Commission seems to think that it does. On the adoption of the Merger Regulation the Commission stated that "it does not normally intend to apply Articles 85 and 86" to mergers "other than by means of" the Merger Regulation.[41] However, the Commission also expressed the view that its Article 89 powers continue in force and indicated that it may choose to utilize Article 89 powers in respect of mergers that lack a Community dimension. The Commission added that it would do so only where the merger exceeds its recommended thresholds of ECU 2 billion worldwide turnover and ECU 100 million Community-wide turnover.[42] The Commission considered that mergers below those levels do not warrant Community control because such mergers "would not normally significantly affect trade between Member States."[43]

The Commission's judgment about the trade impact of mergers that fall below turnover thresholds of ECU 2 billion worldwide and ECU 100 million within the Community implies that such mergers would not be subject to Articles 85 and 86. At the same time, the Commission's judgment also implies that mergers above these Commission-recommended thresholds would normally have a significant effect on trade between member states. Hence, such middle-range mergers should be subject to Commission regulation under Articles 85 and 86 even though they lack the "Community dimension" required for application of the Merger Regulation.

Although the Commission has not done so in two years of practice under the Merger Regulation, my conclusion is that the Commission must continue to review below-threshold mergers against the competition policy rules contained in Articles 85 and 86. In so doing, the Commission will be entitled to the considerable range of discretion that it enjoys in its enforcement actions, but its failure to act may be subjected to judicial review in the European Court of Justice.[44]

The Direct Effect of Articles 85 and 86 on National Law

National regulation of mergers can involve both national and Community law. As developed above, however, owing to the exclusive jurisdiction provision of the Merger Regulation, Community dimension mergers will no longer be subject to national law. The Merger Regulation implements and replaces Treaty Articles 85 and 86 for Community dimension mergers. Hence, unless the Commission refers a merger to a member state, Community dimension mergers will be regulated solely by the Commission acting pursuant to the provisions of the Merger Regulation.

Below-threshold mergers are not regulated by the Merger Regulation and will continue to be subject to national regulation under national law. In addition, where they affect trade between member states, I have argued that below-threshold mergers will remain subject to Commission regulation pursuant to Treaty Articles 85 and 86. The question remains whether, in the light of the Merger Regulation, Articles 85 and 86 will continue to have direct effect in national law. If so, those articles can be invoked in national courts in respect of below-threshold mergers either as the basis for a cause of action or as a defense to an action for enforcement of a prohibited agreement. In both instances, reference to the European Court of Justice will be available to obtain preliminary rulings on the interpretation of the Treaty articles.[45]

For the same reasons that the Merger Regulation cannot insulate below-threshold mergers from Commission review under Articles 85 and 86, the

Regulation will not disturb what would otherwise be the direct effect of those articles. Had the Regulation implemented Articles 85 and 86 with respect to below-threshold mergers, it would take the place of those articles and foreclose their direct effect in national law. Since the Merger Regulation applies to below-threshold mergers only by way of insulating them from existing Community legislation that implements Articles 85 and 86, the impact of the Merger Regulation on the direct effect of those articles is limited to whatever consequences the withdrawal of implementing legislation might have for the direct effect of Rome Treaty articles.

Council Regulation 17, implementing Articles 85 and 86, provides that anticompetitive agreements that are contrary to Article 85, para. 1, and the abuse of a dominant position that is forbidden by Article 86, "shall be prohibited, no prior decision [by the Commission] to that effect being required."[46] The effect of this provision is to render Articles 85, para. 1, and 86 directly effective in national courts.[47] Since Regulation 17 has been withdrawn by the Merger Regulation, what will be the impact of this change on the direct effect of Articles 85 and 86 with regard to below-threshold mergers?

In general, a Rome Treaty provision will have direct effect in national law when the provision is clear and precise, when it is unconditional, and when it allows no scope for, or margin of, discretion in its implementation.[48] When considering the direct effect of the competition articles after adoption of the Merger Regulation, a distinction must be drawn between Article 85 and Article 86. Article 85 is a complex provision. In outline the article has three elements: In para. 1 the article prohibits "as incompatible with the common market" certain anticompetitive agreements and concerted practices which may affect intra-Community trade; in para. 2 the article declares that agreements that are "prohibited pursuant to this Article shall be automatically void"; and in para. 3 the article provides that the prohibitions of para. 1 may be "declared inapplicable" where the agreement or practice is found to improve the production or distribution of goods without eliminating competition. Council Regulation 17 governs the grant of exemptions pursuant to Article 85, para. 3.

The EC Court of Justice has held that Article 85 must be read as a whole; hence, were it not for its implementation by Regulation 17, the prohibition of agreements pursuant to para. 1 would be dependent upon the absence of an exemption under para. 3, and only prohibited agreements would be void under para. 2. In other words, the prohibition of Article 85, para. 1, will not have the effect of voiding agreements under para. 2 unless there has been implementing legislation that regulates the question of an exemption under para. 3.[49] Where there is no implementing legislation, the availability of an exemption under Article 85, para. 3, would allow for a measure of discretion in the implementation of Article 85, para. 1, a result that would be inconsistent with the doctrine of direct effect. The EC Court of Justice so held in a case concerning the effect in national law of Article 85 prior to the adoption of Regulation 17. The Court said that unless enforced by the Commission under Article 89, the nullity provision of Article 85, para. 2, applies only "in respect of agreements and decisions which the authorities of the Member States, on the basis of Article 88,[50] have expressly held to fall under Article 85(1), and not to qualify for exemption under Article 85(3)."[51] This ruling means that unless the member state has established a specialized tribunal competent to enforce competition law,[52] a firm affected by a below-threshold merger cannot invoke Article 85 to void that merger unless such a decision has already been taken by the competent national authority. In such a case there would be no need to rely upon Community law, as the national action would be fully effective to accomplish the desired result. National courts, therefore, are normally not competent to apply the provisions of Article 85, para. 1 to below-threshold mergers in the absence of implementing legislation that removes the discretionary element from Article 85, para. 3.

The direct effect of Article 86 stands on a different footing. This is because Article 86 prohibits abuse of a "dominant position within the common market" as specified in the article without further qualification and without vesting in the member states or in the Commission authority to declare the provisions of the article inapplicable in any given context. Article 86 fits exactly the European Court's classical conception of Rome Treaty provisions that have direct effect in national law. The article provides a clear and unconditional prohibition of defined conduct, and the operation of the article does not depend upon discretionary action taken by national authorities or by the Commission.[53] Persons affected by a merger that lacks a Community dimension may therefore invoke Article 86 in litigation before national courts, and the matter may be referred to the EC Court of Justice for a preliminary ruling when there is need for interpretation of Article 86.

The Law Applicable to Below-Threshold Mergers

Since the Merger Regulation cannot exclude the application of Treaty Articles 85 and 86 to mergers that lack a Community dimension, we have seen that national courts will apply Article 86 and that the Commission may be required to apply both Articles 85 and 86 to review at least mergers that satisfy the Commission's recommended ECU 2 billion worldwide and ECU 100 million Community turnover thresholds. It is therefore relevant to ask whether the Treaty law applied to below-threshold mergers might be expected to differ from the Merger Regulation rules applied to Community dimension mergers.

The Merger Regulation distinctly moves Community law into areas not yet recognized as falling under Articles 85 and 86. The seminal *Continental Can* case[54] applied the Article 86 abuse of a dominant position rule to a merger that strengthened an existing dominant position through the acquisition of a competitor. The *Philip Morris* case[55] found Article 85 applicable to the acquisition of a minority interest in a competitor where such an acquisition might restrict or distort competition. Neither the Commission nor the European Court has yet applied Articles 85 and 86 to a merger through which the merged firm, for example, a concentrative joint venture, has acquired but not abused a dominant position, yet this is precisely the behavior that can be reached under the Merger Regulation. Indeed, in the one case in which the Commission blocked a proposed merger in the first two years of practice under the Merger Regulation, the Commission did so because it concluded that the resulting entity would acquire a dominant position incompatible with the common market.[56]

Furthermore, the definition of dominant position might prove to be more expansive under the Merger Regulation than it has been in Commission and Court practice under Article 86. Whereas the Regulation implies that a market share of more than 25 percent might amount to a dominant position,[57] Article 86 cases seem to have so far used a benchmark of 40 percent.[58] In its assessment of dominance, the Commission has followed the definition of a dominant position used by the European Court under Article 86:

> [A dominant position is] a position of economic strength enjoyed by an undertaking which enables it to hinder the maintenance of effective competition on the relevant market by allowing it to behave to an appreciable extent independently of competitors and ultimately of consumers.[59]

The Commission takes into account factors other than market share, including, for example, "not only the exclusion of actual competition but also the elimination of realistic potential competition," which gives the merged entity "an appreciable freedom of action uncontrolled by actual or potential competition."[60] Thus, even a very high market share will not necessarily establish dominance incompatible with the common market; a high market share "may be countered by other factors, such as the presence of sufficiently strong and active competitors on the market, the buying power of customers or the high probability of strong market entry."[61]

Oligopolistic dominance is another area in which the Commission's Merger Regulation practice may diverge from the law applied under Article 86. Neither the Merger Regulation nor Article 86 refers explicitly to situations of joint dominance, that is, where the market is dominated by a small number of firms. The Commission had generally handled such cases under Article 85, where the question was the existence of anticompetitive agreements rather than market dominance. In an early Merger Regulation case, the Commission explicitly left open the question of whether the Regulation applies to oligopolistic dominance. The merger involved would give three suppliers control of over 50 percent of the German market for power cables, but the Commission found that "the strong bargaining power of German public purchasers and the imminent change in procurement procedures . . . reduced the possibility of conscious parallelism on the part of the suppliers and prevented the creation or strengthening of an oligopolistic dominance."[62] More recently, in the case of Nestlé's acquisition of Perrier, the Commission objected that the deal would give Nestlé and the French BSN group a duopoly of the French mineral water market. Accordingly, the Commission required Nestlé to sell some Perrier brands.[63] The Nestlé case demonstrates that the Commission is now prepared to view oligopolistic dominance as covered by the Merger Regulation.[64] Thus, under the Merger Regulation, mergers that have a Community dimension may, in effect, be subjected to legal standards (different from the Treaty standard) that will remain applicable to mergers lacking a Community dimension.

Although it may appear anomalous to apply one standard to mergers reviewed under Articles 85 and 86 and a different standard to mergers reviewed under the Merger Regulation, this is fully understandable from the legal point of view. The two measures address the same issues but stem from different legal authority. The Merger Regulation is supported by Treaty Article 235, which authorizes the Council, "acting unanimously on a proposal from the Commission and after consulting the Assembly," to take "appropriate measures" to attain an objective of the Community where the Treaty "has not provided the necessary powers." This "gap filler" was invoked in the Merger Regulation precisely because, as they had been developed and applied, Articles 85 and 86 were inadequate to the task of merger control.

In legal theory, then, it is not startling to observe that mergers vetted under the Merger Regulation will be treated differently from mergers vetted under Articles 85 and 86. What is of more interest will be to observe whether in the dynamics of their application the two parallel legal procedures will be drawn closer together so that in the end what are now different standards will become essentially a unitary merger control standard.

One might easily expect such a development where the same institution undertakes to review both above- and below-threshold mergers. We have seen that this may be true where the Commission undertakes to review a merger that lacks a Community dimension by Merger Regulation standards but satisfies the Commission's threshold turnover figures of ECU 2 billion worldwide and ECU 100 million within the Community.[65] Commission review of mergers that fall between the two sets of threshold figures will apply Articles 85 and 86, but the Commission views that process as an interim measure pending Council acceptance of the Commission's recommendation for reducing the thresholds of the Merger Regulation. Since it views below-threshold merger review as an interim measure, the Commission is not likely to make vigorous use of it; indeed, the Commission has not yet undertaken such a review. There is thus little prospect that the Commission will move forcefully in the direction of eliminating the disparities between the Merger Regulation and Articles 85 and 86.

The EC Court of Justice may be the instrumentality for unification of Community merger control law. Two developments can be foreseen. First, Commission decisions under the Merger Regulation will sometimes be subjected to judicial review. Ample provision is made for recourse to the European Court, and the matters involved are of such importance that the option to litigate will not lightly be set aside. Two factors diminish the likelihood of judicial review. One is the time required, which will often exceed what might be possible in the context of a proposed merger. The other is the apparent willingness of the Commission to clear mergers subject to only minor conditions. Of some 120 proposed mergers notified to the Commission in the two years since the entry into force of the Merger Regulation, only one merger has been blocked, and very few have been modified by conditions required for clearance by the Commission.[66]

Whether or not the Commission's decisions are challenged in the European Court, rulings made by the Commission under the Merger Regulation will be invoked by the Commission when it applies Articles 85 and 86 to below-threshold mergers and in the European Court when it reviews the Commission's actions. That jurisprudence will also be invoked in national court review of claims of abuse of a dominant position contrary to Article 86. National court litigation will provide opportunity for preliminary rulings under Treaty Article 177, in which the European Court will be asked to interpret Article 86. In such cases, it would not be surprising for the European Court to find within Article 86 many of the theories that the Commission or the Court will have developed in their interpretation of the Merger Regulation. This cross-fertilization process will also operate in the reverse direction: theories developed by the Commission and the Court in their application of Articles 85 and 86 will be applied by the Commission to the Merger Regulation and by the Court when it reviews Commission action. In this way the European Court will be able to bring the two lines of decision closer together.

Conclusion

The interplay between the Merger Regulation and Articles 85 and 86 yields the result that Community law will apply to below-threshold mergers in two patterns: (1) The Commission will apply competition law developed under Articles 85 and 86 subject to judicial review in the European Court of Justice, and/or (2) national authorities and national courts will apply both national law and Community competition law developed under Article 86.

It is important to note that Commission review under the Merger Regulation has been confined to considerations of competition policy. The Commission has resisted efforts to broaden merger review to take account of industrial policy, that is, the need to restructure European industry to enhance competitiveness in world markets. This issue came to a head in the

Commission's 1991 decision to block the acquisition of Boeing's de Haviland commuter aircraft division by French and Italian aircraft manufacturing companies. Despite arguments that the joint venture would strengthen the European aerospace industry against world competition, the Commission denied clearance on the ground that the joint venture would acquire a dominant position incompatible with the common market.[67] In the Commission's view, "companies cannot be allowed to eliminate effective competition" since competition is "the most effective . . . way in which large companies can be forced to keep costs low, to react to the market, to innovate and to offer their customers a good deal."[68]

As we have seen, below-threshold mergers are not subject to the Merger Regulation, but this does not exclude their review by the Commission and by the European Court. At the same time, these Community institutions will be responsible for applying the Merger Regulation to mergers with a Community dimension. Although it is too early to find concrete examples of this dynamic, there is the opportunity, and one might think the probability, that interpretations of Articles 85 and 86 developed through Commission and Court review will bring Community competition law closer to the Merger Regulation.

The end result may be that the regime provided in the Merger Regulation will become general Community law under Articles 85 and 86 and will take precedence over national law for below-threshold mergers as well as for mergers that have a Community dimension. Merger review by the Commission and by the European Court may unify Community competition law with the Merger Regulation. Through the doctrine of the supremacy of Community law, merger review may also subordinate national law to Community law for below-threshold mergers. Movement in this direction would represent a return to the federalism that seemed inherent in the competition articles of the Treaty of Rome. It would help to restore the balance that was disturbed by the excessively narrow scope of exclusive Community control under the Merger Regulation. Unification of Community merger control law would also serve the broader interests of federalism by establishing uniform central control over all mergers that have a substantial effect on competition in trade between EC member states.

Notes

1. EC Commission, "Nineteenth Report on Competition Policy" [for 1989], pp. 33–34 (1990). There was also concern that overzealous national regulators might delay or otherwise impede efficient restructuring of European industry.

2. *Europemballage Corp. & Continental Can Co. Inc. v. Commission,* Case 6/72, 1973 ECR 215, [1973] 1 CMLR 199.

3. Downes & Ellison observe that "the Treaty of Rome does not seek to control corporate size, or its creation or acquisition, only its abuse." *The Legal Control of Mergers in the European Communities* (London: Blackstone Press, 1991), p. 7; (hereinafter Downes & Ellison).

4. EC Commission, "Memorandum on the problem of concentration in the common market," Competition Series, no. 3, para. 58 (1966). The Commission thought that Art. 85 might be interpreted to cover merger agreements between undertakings but that it could not reach takeovers that had the same economic effect as agreed mergers.

5. *[Philip Morris] British American Tobacco Co. & RJ Reynolds v. Commission,* Cases 142 & 156/84, 1987 ECR 4487; [1988] 4 CMLR 24.

6. Downes & Ellison, pp. 24–25, note "conceptual difficulties" in applying Art. 85 to the acquisition of shares from individuals rather than by agreement between undertakings.

7. Council Regulation (EEC) No. 4064/89 of Dec. 21, 1989 on the control of concentrations between undertakings, OJ 1989 L395/1, corrected text at OJ 1990 L257/13 (hereinafter Merger Regulation). The Merger Regulation took effect on September 21, 1990. The Regulation uses the term "concentrations," defined in a way that is both broader and narrower than national law concepts of merger. See Merger Regulation, Art. 3, and the extended discussion in Downes & Ellison, pp. 34–54. The Merger Regulation includes certain takeovers and "concentrative" (as opposed to "cooperative") joint ventures. See Downes & Ellison, pp. 133–61. Unless otherwise specified, I use the term "merger" to refer to concentrations as defined in Merger Regulation Art. 3.

8. Merger Regulation, preambular recital 6.

9. Merger Regulation, preambular recital 8. Article 235 authorizes legislation to add to the Commission's powers in situations in which the Rome Treaty "has not provided the necessary powers" to attain Community objectives. Amendments to the Rome Treaty follow a different route and must be ratified by all member states. See Art. 236.

10. Merger Regulation, preambular recital 7 and Art. 22, para. 1. The "Community dimension" is defined in Art. 1, para. 2.

11. Merger Regulation, Art. 2, para. 3. The Regulation thus reaches beyond the "abuse" of a dominant position addressed in Rome Treaty Art. 86.

12. Sir Leon Brittan, the Commission member in charge of competition policy, defined the Regulation's "fundamental policy objective" as "a simple, predictable and clear Community merger control system with the Commission responsible for cases above the thresholds and the Member States below." Brittan, *Competition Policy and Merger Control in the Single European Market* (Cambridge: Grotius Pub., 1991), p. 43; (hereinafter Brittan).

13. Merger Regulation, Art. 1, para. 2.

14. Merger Regulation, Art. 5; see, e.g., Cook & Kerse, *EEC Merger Control Regulation 4064/89* (London: Sweet & Maxwell, 1991), pp. 39–61; (hereinafter Cook & Kerse).

15. EC Commission, Statements entered in the Minutes of the Council, Statement ad Art. 1, [1990] 4 CMLR 314. The Commission's Statements are reproduced in Cook & Kerse, Appendix 7, p. 226.

16. Merger Regulation, Art. 1, para. 3, states that the thresholds will be reviewed within four years of the adoption of the Regulation, that is, by the end of 1993.

17. Brittan, pp. 27–32.

18. Merger Regulation, Art. 1, para. 1.

19. Merger Regulation, Art. 21, para. 1.

20. Merger Regulation, Art. 21, para. 2.

21. Merger Regulation, Art. 3.

22. Merger Regulation, Art. 22, para. 1.

23. Merger Regulation, Art. 1, para. 1. This scope is stated to be "without prejudice to Article 22," which contains the exclusive application rule.

24. Merger Regulation, Art. 21, para. 2, quoted in the text at n. 20 *supra.*

25. Merger Regulation, Art. 22, para. 2. Four regulations are specifically excluded,

including Regulation No. 17 Implementing Articles 85 and 86 of the Treaty of Rome, OJ Sp. Ed. 1959–62, p. 87.

26. Merger Regulation, Art. 21, para. 2.

27. *Accord* Downes & Ellison, pp. 62–63.

28. Merger Regulation, Art. 9, paras. 2–3.

29. *Tarmac/Steetley,* Case IV/M.0168, 12 Feb. 1992. Germany has sought referral of two proposed mergers under this rule, but in both cases the Commission denied referral and approved the merger. See EC Commission, XXIst Report on Competition Policy, 1991, Annex III.A.7, pp. 351, 371 (1992). In contrast to the Tarmac and Steetley construction materials case, the two German mergers involved auto batteries (*Varta/Bosch,* Case IV/M.0012, 31 July 1991) and telecommunication and power cables (*Alcatel/AEG Kabel,* Case IV/M.0165, 18 Dec. 1991), where the relevant markets were not purely national.

30. Merger Regulation, Art. 22, para. 3. Such a merger must affect trade between member states. At this writing no state has sought to refer a merger to the Commission under this clause.

31. Since the Merger Regulation implements Treaty Arts. 85 and 86, it should replace those articles in their application to Community dimension mergers. *See* Art. 87, para. 2(c), which provides that implementing legislation shall "define . . . the scope of the provisions of Arts. 85 and 86."

32. Merger Regulation, Art. 21, para. 3.

33. Ibid. *See* Downes & Ellison, pp. 65–67; and Bright, "The European Merger Control Regulation: Do Member States still have an Independent Role in Merger Control?" Part II, [1991] 5 ECLR 184–91.

34. *See* Interpretative Statement by the Commission re Art. 21, para. 3, n. 15 *supra.*

35. The Merger Regulation defines "concentration" in Art. 3 independently of "Community dimension," which is defined in Art. 1, para. 2. Art. 21, para. 2, prohibits the application of national competition legislation to any "concentration that has a Community dimension." Nothing is said about the application of national legislation to below-threshold mergers.

36. Art. 87, para. 2(c), quoted in n. 31 *supra,* authorizes implementing legislation that defines the scope of Arts. 85 and 86 in relation to mergers, but that provision would not authorize the total exemption of below-threshold mergers from the operation of those articles.

37. Merger Regulation, Art. 22, para. 1. Some commentators assume that this provision preempts use of Arts. 85 and 86 for control of Community dimension mergers. *See, e.g.,* Collins, "The Coming of Age of EC Competition Policy," 17 Yale Journal of International Law 249, 281 (1992).

38. Merger Regulation, Art. 22, para. 2. The implementing legislation gives the Commission authority to investigate and to impose fines for breaches of Arts. 85 and 86.

39. *See* text at n. 9 *supra.*

40. Art. 89 contemplates that the Commission will "authorize Member States to take the measures . . . needed to remedy the situation." Precisely how this would work in the case of a merger contrary to the principles of Arts. 85 and 86 remains to be seen. In contrast, implementing legislation adopted pursuant to Art. 87 could give the Commission independent investigatory and sanctioning authority. *See* Council Regulation 17, n. 25 *supra.*

41. Interpretative Statement by the Commission ad Art. 22, n. 15 *supra.*

42. *See* text at n. 15 *supra.*

43. Interpretative Statement by the Commission ad Art. 22, n. 15 *supra.*

44. Treaty Art. 175 authorizes Community institutions, member states, and natural or legal persons to challenge the Commission's failure to act where it has a duty to act

under the Treaty. Downes & Ellison, pp. 129–30, suggest that third parties may be able to invoke this provision to require the Commission to apply Arts. 85 and 86 to below-threshold mergers.

45. Treaty Art. 177 provides for reference from national courts to the European Court for preliminary rulings concerning questions of Treaty interpretation.

46. Council Regulation 17, Art. 1, OJ Sp. Ed. 1959–62, p. 87.

47. *See, e.g, Belgische Radio en Televisie v. SABAM & Fonior,* Case 127/73R, 1974 ECR 51; [1974] 2 CMLR 238. The Court said at para. 16 that Art. 85, para. 1, and Art. 86 "create direct rights in respect of the individuals concerned which the national courts must safeguard."

48. *See* Kapteyn and Verloren van Themaat, *Introduction to the Law of the European Communities* (Deventer: Kluwer, 2d ed. by Gormley, 1989), pp. 333–38.

49. Ibid., pp. 516–17.

50. Treaty Art. 88 provides that until implementing legislation is adopted under Art. 87, "authorities in Member States shall rule on the admissibility of agreements" in accordance with national law and with Art. 85, para. 3.

51. *Kledingverkoopbedrijf de Geus en Uitdenbogerd v. Robert Bosch GmbH,* Case 13/61, 1962 ECR 45, 52.

52. The Court has suggested that Art. 88's reference to "authorities in Member States" might include specialized courts entrusted with the task of applying competition legislation. *[Nouvelles Frontières] Ministère Public v. Asjes & Others,* Cases 209-13/84, 1986 ECR 1425; [1986] 3 CMLR 173. This suggestion opens the possibility that Art. 85, para. 1, will have direct effect in specialized national courts that are authorized to enforce national competition legislation.

53. *Ahmed Saeed Flugreisen v. Zentrale Zur Bekampfung Unlauteren,* Case 66/86, [1990] 4 CMLR 102.

54. *See* text n. 2 *supra.*

55. *See* text n. 5 *supra.*

56. *Aérospatiale-Alenia/de Haviland,* Case IV/M.0053, 2 Oct. 1991.

57. Merger Regulation, preambular recital 15 states that "without prejudice to Articles 85 and 86," a market share that does not exceed 25 percent "may be presumed to be compatible with the common market."

58. See, e.g., *Hoffman-La Roche v. Commission,* Case 85/76, 1979 ECR 461; [1979] 3 CMLR 211. The Court considered that market share of 40 percent to 65 percent provided strong evidence of dominance but required confirmation by other evidence.

59. *United Brands v. Commission,* Case 27/76, 1978 ECR 207; [1978] 1 CMLR 429 and [1978] 3 CMLR 83.

60. EC Commission, XXIst Report on Competition Policy, 1991, Annex III.7, pp. 333, 362 (1992). See, e.g. *Aérospatiale-Alenia/de Haviland,* Case IV/M.0053, 2 Oct., 1991; OJ 1991 L334/42. In *de Haviland* the resulting entity would have had about 65 percent of the EC market and about 50 percent of the world market for turboprop commuter aircraft.

61. Ibid., XXIst Report p. 363. An example is *Alcatel/Telettra,* Case IV/M.0042, 12 April 1991, where the Commission cleared an acquisition that would give the merged entity 82 percent of the Spanish market for telecommunications transmission and microwave systems. The Commission found that the monopoly purchaser, the Spanish government agency Telefonica, could readily switch to other firms that were ready and able to supply similar equipment.

62. *Alcatel/AEG Kabel,* Case IV/M.0165, 18 Dec. 1991; id., XXIst Report p. 362. Germany had asked the Commission to refer the case to the Bundeskartelamt for examination under German law, which contains a presumption of oligopolistic dominance where three companies have a combined market share exceeding 50 percent. This request was denied. See n. 29 *supra.*

63. Nevertheless the Commission cleared the Perrier acquisition on terms that would leave Nestlé and BSN with two-thirds of the French mineral water market. *Financial Times,* July 23, 1992 and July 27, 1992.

64. The Court of First Instance recently vacated a Commission effort to apply Art. 86 to a situation of joint dominance, but the Court did not exclude the application of Art. 86 in all cases of oligopolistic dominance. *Italian Flat Glass,* Cases T-68, 77 & 78/89, March 10, 1992.

65. The Commission may also review a below-threshold merger when the merger is referred by a member state under the "Dutch Clause." See text n. 30 *supra.* Should the Commission review such a merger, however, the Commission will apply the Merger Regulation; hence, such a review will not develop the jurisprudence of Arts. 85 and 86.

66. *See De Haviland,* n. 56 *supra,* and *Nestlé,* text at n. 63 *supra.* See also *Financial Times,* September 28, 1992.

67. *See* nn. 56 & 60 *supra.* The Commission adopted the *de Haviland* decision by a margin of one vote.

68. Commission, XXIst Report on Competition Policy, 1991, point 45, p. 42 (1992).

18

The EC: Capitalist
or *Dirigiste* Regime?

Walter Goldstein

There was a striking omission from the 250 pages of turgid legal prose that spelled out the European treaty of union that was signed in Maastricht. There was no definitive statement about the industrial policy that the EC would use in modelling its development. There was an implied commitment to a free market economy within the common tariff area, but there was also a widespread acceptance of *dirigisme* and intervention by state agencies and nationalized monopolies.

The clash between a laissez faire and an interventionist ideology had started in the earliest years of the EC. The 1958 Treaty of Rome and the 1987 Single European Act had assumed that "distorting" subsidies would be minimized and state monopolies investigated, and that the free trade principles of the General Agreement on Tariffs and Trade (GATT) treaty would be honored. However, not much was done to deregulate the sprawling EC public sector, privatize state-sanctioned cartels, or trim the vast subsidies they received.

The original six countries struggled to create an integrated EC Twelve and to unify their disparate interests, but they did not unify their market ideologies. If the seven EFTA nations join the European Economic Area (the EEA Nineteen) in the 1990s, this values gap could become critical. One-third or one-half of the EEA cannot play by market rules that the rest reject. Arguments raged for thirty years about costly EC farm subsidies and prices. They could spread next to services and labor-intensive manufacturing if the clash is not resolved.[1]

The issues at stake are threatening. State-managed operations and nationalized monopolies account for 20 percent or more of GDP and employment in several EC nations. If all EC import duties, nontariff barriers, public sector funding, and government procurement were added together, the EC could come to resemble the Fortress Europe that trade rivals caricature.

Moreover, if the downturn in world trade persists, the arguments over protectionism and industrial subsidies will escalate. The stronger EC economies might then reject public bailouts for failing industries and cost-ineffective farming, but the weak could clamor for public transfer payments to maintain high employment levels and balance their accounts.

Two qualifications need to be added. First, Japan and the United States practice many of the same tricks of trade distortion; they are in no way exemplars of pure competition. Second, the EC Twelve (or the EEA Nineteen) differ greatly in their tolerance for state intervention; Britain and Holland argue for a Thatcherite model of capitalism while a resort to *dirigisme* helps keep the French, Italian, and Spanish economies afloat.[2]

The Single European Act was supposed to demolish all internal barriers and legal obstacles. However, most EC countries invest public funds in their aerospace, computer, and electronics enterprises; even if they go bankrupt they are retained as the national "champion" in world markets. In contrast, conservative regimes sell off their ailing firms to foreign interests or let them sink without trace.

The consequences of this ideological clash within the EC have been obscured since the Maastricht Treaty was signed. Most protest concentrated on the constitutional innovations proposed by the Treaty; disputes over industrial policy lost saliency. There were more important issues to argue—from the "widening" of the EC's membership to the "deepening" of its political and parliamentary controls.

Rancor increased as arguments about ratifying the Treaty heated up in Denmark, France, Britain, and Germany. Opposition factions denounced the Economic and Monetary Union (EMU) that was to integrate the European economy. The European Political Union (EPU) was also attacked. It was argued that the EC Twelve were not yet ready to harmonize their foreign policies or replace NATO with a "European Defense Identity." Both the EC Social Charter and the Schengen plan (to eliminate EC passport and frontier controls) were pushed aside, largely because unemployment and illegal immigration soared as the recession bit deeper.[3]

Protests sharpened as the Commission revealed plans to regulate health, education, transportation, and environment policy and to harmonize product and safety standards. Too much power was moving from national governments to the centralized agencies in Brussels, it was claimed. Hopes to revive GDP growth by deregulating the EC business milieux began to fade.

To head off criticism, EC President Delors invoked a novel principle, "subsidiarity." He pledged that Brussels would take as little power as possible so that national diversity and local self-government would be preserved. His promises were not well received. Most of the EC states were staggering under debt, high unemployment, and draconian cuts in public outlays. They feared that they would soon be powerless to reflate their flagging economies or buy social peace.[4]

Economic Integration and Political Discord

The most vehement complaints were voiced when the exchange rate mechanism (ERM) imploded in September 1992. It was assumed that the fixed parity grid of currency values in the ERM would fulfill two objectives. First, it would tie all twelve currencies to the strongest, the deutschemark, through the ERM. This would enforce a "convergence" of exchange rates and curb any slippage into deficit financing or inflationary expansion by the weaker EC states. Second, it would strengthen the will of governments to stave off a currency devaluation by outlawing inflation and bonding the money supply to the deutschemark. By fixing parity zones, the ERM would regulate GDP growth and cement the second-stage foundation for the EMU.

The plan went haywire as the currency markets collapsed in two days of speculation and panic. Britain and Italy could not stand the shorting of $1 trillion a day against the fixed parities of the ERM. Speculators kept borrowing marks and shorting the pound and the lira; interest rates were driven to absurd heights (reaching 500 percent for overnight funds in Sweden), and countries forfeited vast currency reserves to stanch the panic. The forced convergence of EC monetary policies failed and the ERM crumbled. The currency markets had triumphed over the EC's political will. Britain and Italy were forced to devalue by 10 percent and to drop out of the ERM. Eventually, they might have to quit the EMU, too.

The panic left the EMU design and the Maastricht plan suspended in doubt. If the dropouts came to enjoy cost advantages of 10 percent or more within the EC bloc, they would soon undermine the single market structure, but if they are cut out of the EMU and the single market, the EC would be sorely damaged. It might be able to proceed as a two-speed or as a "variable geometry" operation, but it would no longer be an integrated union of the EC Twelve or the EEA Nineteen. Moreover, the creation of an EC Central Bank and a single currency unit, the ECU, would be badly set back. The EC would no longer be able to challenge the global power of the yen or the dollar with an ECU if it was limited in financial clout.

There was a further distraction that turned attention away from the EC's unresolved dilemma. The EC had planned to construct a single market of 325 million people that could rival the United States and Japan in size and wealth. If all the EC Twelve and EFTA joined the EEA they would command an aggregate GDP of $6 trillion and 46 percent of world trade. Moreover, if the dollar kept on losing value, the ECU would become the leading reserve and transaction currency; and the EC would be able to dictate its terms of trade to rival blocs in North America or the Pacific rim. As a unified bloc, the EC would rewrite first its own constitution and history, and then the rest of the world's.[5]

This ambitious design was gravely set back in 1991. The downturn of business affected all three blocs simultaneously, and the EC group lost some of its buoyancy. Europe recorded a sharp trade deficit with the United States and Japan and an even sharper deficit in high-technology commerce. Germany no longer served as the locomotive of European growth, and its rigid monetarist doctrines infuriated its neighbors. Just at the time that they needed to reflate their money supply and devalue their currency, the Bundesbank hiked interest rates.

Driven by the Germans' historic fear of inflation, the Bundesbank acted not as the EC bank of last resort but as Germany's first weapon of defense. Most of the EC states were furious. If that was a harbinger of the monetary discipline Germany would eventually impose through the EMU—after it had become a fully fledged union in 1999—they wanted to rewrite the rules. Many of the "Club Med" and the weaker economies needed to pump red ink to keep their people employed. They were not prepared to forfeit their economic sovereignty so that Germany could run the EC with conservative dogma.[6]

It was in this light that the debate over industrial policy lost some of its drama. There had often been clashes between the EC commissioners responsible for competition and for industrial development. One wanted to curb the restraint of trade perpetrated by statist monopolies and nationalized industries; the other sought to promote the interventionist agenda of socialist planners and *dirigiste* bureaucracies. The first dared to censure governments for shutting out foreign imports or subsidizing local firms; the second approved a set of mergers and acquisitions that spread across Europe.[7]

The clashes died down as the recession continued and the debate over the EMU and the Maastricht Treaty warmed up. There was simply no point to pit the advocates of free market and interventionist beliefs against each other when the basic structure and the prosperity of the EC stood in peril. Severe budget deficits had accumulated, and unemployment had stalled at 10 percent or higher in most EC countries. Plans to liberalize the internal market were discarded at a time when higher subsidies were needed to keep banks and jobs open.

EC Hopes for Economic Growth

The turn from Europhoria to a mood of pessimism was decisive. A comprehensive white paper had been issued by the EC in the balmy era of the 1980s on future prospects for economic growth. Named for its leading author, the Cecchini Report assembled a macro- and microeconomic analysis of the EC economies and their industrial sectors. It cheerfully found that the EC could hike GNP by 6.5 percent if frontier and custom controls were removed and economies of scale were realized.[8]

The report followed two lines of analysis. First, it suggested that supply-side gains could be won by lowering internal barriers, stimulating output, and cutting production costs. These could add up to 2.4 percent to GNP. Second, by merging EC companies, curbing monopoly practices, raising competitive standards, and thus cutting prices, GNP could be boosted by another 3.7 percent. A further spurt in output could add 2 million new jobs, hike GNP 4.8 percent, and improve the operating efficiency of many industries. If all these gains were secured, the lag in performance between the EC and Japan or the United States could at last be remedied and GNP could leap forward. Two hundred fifty staff helped write the report and their optimism proved to be contagious.[9]

The surge of optimism was based on three assumptions. If market opening initiatives prompted a higher level of competition, prices would fall and demand would soar. More to the point, if public procurement could be privatized and capital investment funding increased, an increment in export revenues and industrial growth could add 11.5 percent to GNP.[10] It was in this heady mood that the Maastricht Treaty was written, but it all caved in when the 1991 recession dragged painfully on.

The EC's expectations were undermined by plunging business trends. First, the trillion yen boom in Japan's stock and property markets crashed, abruptly closing an era of cheap interest rates and capital exports. Second, Germany hiked its taxes, public sector debt, and interest rates, stalling growth and employment right across Europe. Third, the recession in the United States and the rest of the world cut deeply into the operating profits of the EC's export and financial companies.

The rise in European interest rates and the retrenchment in U.S. and Japanese markets brought to an end the EC boom of the late 1980s. As the debates over the Maastricht Treaty gained in rancor, the drive for political unity waned. Basic questions about EC strategy were raised once again. Would the EC bloc really gain by integrating its industrial structures, lowering its internal barriers, and opening its markets to outside rivals? Or would it benefit more by preserving its nationalist controls and protectionist policies? Unlike the free traders, the *dirigistes* urged that the EC's embryo market needed the fullest possible protection.[11]

The argument was posed with Gallic logic. Sixty percent of EC trade flows through internal or protected markets; the other 40 percent meets fierce competition in North America and the Pacific rim. In most industries, and especially in farming, the EC is a high-cost producer. It could not realize scale economies or integrate its state subsidized sectors if it had to play by GATT rules or honor the shibboleths of laissez faire, but the opposition held that if the EC waged trade warfare with rival blocs, it would waste valuable resources on noncompetitive industries. It would surely gain more by trading in an open world than in a closed regional market. The case was cogently made against subsidizing coal, grain exports, the Airbus, and forbidding EC automobile imports, but it fell on deaf ears.

Sectors and Structures in the EC Economy

A protectionist bias can be found in practically all of the EC economies. Automobiles, engineering, electronics, and computer companies have been distinguished by their near total reliance on home country markets, subsidies, or state assistance. Only a few EC firms claim to be world companies. Most of their R&D, marketing, employment, and production is limited to their national base. Unlike the multinational corporations (MNCs) built in large numbers by the United States and by Japan, EC enterprises have largely stayed at home. Few have built assembly plants or placed their costly foreign direct investment (FDI) in neighboring states—let alone overseas—but most have also given up hopes of world class leadership.[12]

EC governments have resorted in a number of cases to protectionist measures to seal off the home market. Some shut out foreign MNCs, such as the "transplants" that Honda and Toyota aimed to build, or they restricted MNCs' deployment in sectors ruled off limits to foreign competition. The most conspicuous examples emerged in the award of public sector procurement. Contracts worth billions of dollars, amounting to nearly 15 percent of GDP in some countries, were reserved for nationally owned enterprises. Foreign competition was firmly excluded, yet after years of struggle the EC simply had to welcome such powerful MNCs as Hitachi, Mitsubishi, AT&T, and IBM. It could no longer survive effectively without them.[13]

The campaign against incoming MNCs and cheap imports from Asia continued through the 1970s and 1980s, and a last-ditch defense was raised at the Uruguay Round of GATT talks to maintain the EC's farm export subsidies. Even though the EC had pledged to liberalize its trade barriers and economic restraints, it refused to throw open its prized markets or to correct the course of protectionism that ran strongly through the federal institutions in Brussels. A committee appointed by GATT reviewed the EC's arsenal of antidumping and export subsidy measures; it concluded that the EC had become a protectionist haven.[14] It was ironic that the French premier, Edith Cresson, had scorned Japan for instigation of trade warfare.

In its prosperous years, the EC had attempted to force a breakthrough in industrial technology by launching a set of ambitious and costly programs. Transnational ventures were funded to promote EC companies entering high-tech industries. Over $100 billion in state funds were allocated among the twelve nations for projects that were too expensive for any one nation or industrial conglomerate to finance. The aim was to bring together the R&D efforts of state-run enterprises, to provide loans below market rates, to guarantee their capital reserves, and possibly to shut out foreign competition—as in the case of computers, automobiles, and electronics.[15]

The centerpiece of the collaborative effort was the Eureka program. It was supposed to provide 300 awards for semiconductor and microchip research, but it was not clear if the program brought any innovative technology into profitmaking production. A similar doubt arose over the $5 billion that went to a Joint European Submicron Silicon Initiative, JESSI, for semiconductors; this was ten times the sum that the United States put into Sematech. Another $5 billion was earmarked for 450 ESPRIT programs in microelectronics and information technology and $1.6 billion for the JET, BRITE, RACE, and COMETT projects in telecommunications, aerospace, and data processing. Controversy swirled over $20 billion paid for the Airbus Industrie consortium; $5 billion for the thirteen nations grouped in the European Space Agency to loft twenty-eight weather or telecommunication satellites; and $30 billion to four NATO nations to build a new fighter aircraft.[16]

Tough questions must be asked about these high-cost uses of public funds: Are they too thinly spread to be effective? Will the deficit in advanced technology persist if the EC insists on funding its R&D from nonmarket sources? Will high-tech companies repeat their previous pattern of failures if they depend on government handouts and import protection? No one in the EC today hastens to find convincing answers.

The Limits of Intervention

The EC today faces a dilemma of political and technological significance. Between 1977 and 1986 the output of all high-tech industries had grown by 15 percent in Japan and 10 percent in the United States, but in the EC growth was only 6.8 percent. High-tech firms had added 22 percent to GDP in the EC, but 29 percent in the United States and Japan. This was the high-tech deficit that had to be rectified, but how could it be best accomplished? The advocates of planning called for more intervention and financing by state agencies, while the free market camp called for closer cooperation with foreign MNCs and a relaxing of regulatory controls.[17]

Analysis at the company level shows that EC firms had lost a fortune despite (or because of ?) state funding. France put more than $1 billion each into CSF-Thomson and Machines Bull to reclaim the markets they had lost in consumer electronics and computer manufacturing. Both had to write off huge losses, even though duties had been raised to impede Japanese imports competing in their TV, VCR, and computer markets. Siemens in Germany bought out Nixdorf computers, and Thomson bought the RCA electronics giant from General Electric, yet both lost billions by trying to exploit new technologies for high-definition television or microchips.[18] After such losses, should they have been downsized, it was asked, and not bailed out?

Oddly, most of the EC leaders urged the remedy of privatizing industry and relying on stock market funding in the Third World and Eastern Europe, but they refused to sell off their own state-run and high-tech firms or to open their own frontiers. In theory, the EC outlawed tied contracts for public procurements or preferential treatment for state-owned monopoly firms, but in practice, 3 percent of GNP went to the cheap credit loans and grants that kept state run companies afloat. Valuable military or PTT procurements were reserved for the benefit of "national champions." More than 20 percent of their overblown costs could be cut if these subsidies were removed.

The average rate of government payments to industry dwarfs the sums paid in the United States or Japan. Payments range from 2 percent of GNP in Britain or Germany to 5 percent in Belgium and Ireland. Measured against manufacturing output, the EC average was 8.6 percent, but the rate in Ireland and Italy went to 15 or 17 percent. Payments to the nationalized PTT or airlines were excessive: Alitalia and Air France demanded $400 million each; Germany refused to follow Britain by selling off Lufthansa and Deutsche Telefon.[19]

In fact, if the Uruguay Round of GATT ever led to a cut in import tariffs, EC governments would have to increase the soft loans, cash grants, tax waivers, or equity payments they made to "national champion" firms. A third of all manufacturing and banking in France and Italy is run by state concerns, and public sectors employ millions of people. Three state conglomerates in Italy (ENI, EFIM, and IRI) and one in Spain (INI) control nearly 500 affiliates each. They account for a major fraction of GNP, capital spending, and skilled employment. Their holdings include the leading firms in electronics, coal, oil, engineering, automobiles, computer manufacturing, banking, insurance, and financial services.

Reliance on Public Funding

The most prominent case of public funding is that of the four nationalized EC firms in aerospace that built Airbus. It drew $20 billion in tax funds for its R&D, and it wrote favorable contracts with many nationalized airlines. As it grew to become the second largest aircraft builder in the world, it was paid $2.5 million by French and German authorities for each of the ninety-five planes it sold in 1990. This violated the GATT subsidy code, but it allowed Airbus to secure 30 percent of world sales. It also prolonged a bitter dispute with the United States over the conduct of international commerce.[20]

The preference for government over market financing is shared widely in Europe. Though the EC has asked many state-owned firms, such as Renault and British Aerospace, to give back their cheap credits and grants, total subsidies have remained at ECU 85 billion a year since 1986. Much of it went to state-owned conglomerates that have borne years of heavy losses.

For example, ENI and INI own the biggest steel, shipbuilding, coal, airline, and telephone monopolies in Italy and Spain. Few of them have made any profit for years. Most are interlocked with national invalids like Alitalia, Montedison, and other strategic bankrupts. Stupendous losses are run up by the EC's computer, chemical, aerospace, and electronics enterprises. If they were sold off, the flow of subsidies could be stemmed, privatization could be boosted, and massive revenues could be saved. Instead they are revered as sacred cows.

Apart from channeling state funds to national champions, the EC has indulged heavily in protective mergers. The aim was to provide tax or equity benefits to keep companies alive and to block entry to foreign rivals. Cross-border deals between Volvo and Renault, between the General Electric companies of France and Britain, or between Plessey and Siemens, have been encouraged.[21] The Commission is supposed to outlaw restraints of trade, but it rarely moves against the statist monopolies that dominate high-tech and export sectors. It did veto a French-Italian bid to take over a Canadian aircraft company, de Haviland, but it allowed many other mergers to go through.

Public funding for the ESPRIT or Eureka projects in microelectronics, high energy physics, or high-definition television has become vital to their survival. Joint ventures have been sanctioned in the public sector between some of the largest firms, such as C. S. F. Thomson and the French nuclear agency. In many cases the aim was to obstruct Japan's penetration of the EC market, in others to secure economies of scale for European companies striving for price and market leadership.[22]

If penetration by foreign MNCs succeeds, the EC's only feasible choices will be to cross-license production with U.S. or Japanese firms or to share patents and costs among "national champions." For example, mergers have been pursued by Bosch in Germany, the Italian-French twin companies of SGS and Thomson, ICI in the UK, and Philips in the Netherlands, but the receipt of public payments, and the pursuit of joint ventures between state monopolies and subsidized enterprises, did not bring about a rise in market share or of profit margins. In too many cases it led to a stifling of import competition.

The Impact of Multinational Corporations

The JESSI and Eureka projects were designed to pool research funds and catch up with foreign competition, but the strategy has not worked well. The EC share of world microchip production fell from 16 percent in 1978 to 9 percent in 1990; its trade deficit in electronics is $30 billion. Unless the EC cooperates with IBM Europe or Fujitsu (which now owns 80 percent of ICL, Britain's last large computer firm), it will not be a vigorous player in the market. IBM Europe spends more on R&D than all the EC firms together, and it takes a larger market share. One chip maker, Philips, lost $2.5 billion on a turnover of $27 billion; it now has licensed its one-megabyte SRAM (static random access memories) in Japan as its previous investment in R&D went to waste.[23]

The pace of technology moves so rapidly that the EC's high-tech firms can no longer survive by shutting out foreign rivals—or by relying on government loans and joint ventures. After Japanese MNCs won a major share of Europe's microchip market, EC firms had to buy expensive R&D from MNCs like IBM and DEC or formally enter production pacts with them. Since 1991 the largest EC computer firms have laid off 100,000 skilled workers and their profits were wiped out.[24]

The first EC ploy was to block MNC exports with quotas, antidumping, and domestic content restrictions. The EC companies, however, still failed to prosper, so the next step was to solicit equity or procurement payments from EC states. In some sectors a requirement was set that 40 percent of the MNCs' value-added output must come from local sources. In the case of Japanese cars assembled in Spain and the UK it was 80 percent. These restraints of trade won additional time to modernize or extend production runs, but they did nothing to cut costs, improve product designs, or extend market share. In the end they were fruitless. The recession cut into their marketing prospects and exhausted their financial reserves.

Of course, no change in rules or tax laws by the EC could ever force a foreign MNC to move jobs or plants into Europe. In fact, many of the MNCs kept their high value-added work at home and opened only screwdriver assembly plants in the high-wage economies of Europe. But as talk turned to real fears that a Fortress Europe would be built, Nissan cars, Ricoh photocopying machines, and U.S. telecommunications subsidiaries rushed to build plants within the EC tariff net.[25]

As a result, overseas rivals aggressively muscled into Europe's domestic markets, and EC exports in the high-tech sectors began to decline. It quickly became evident that Europe's inadequate investments and R&D funding could not be supplemented by adding further tariffs and trade controls.

The impact of foreign MNCs in Europe cannot be underestimated. For the United States alone it is estimated that the affiliate companies of U.S. MNCs, such as IBM Germany or Ford and Exxon in Britain, report an annual turnover that is nearly ten times greater than the value (roughly $75 billion) of U.S. exports to the EC. It is not surprising that the EC records a trade imbalance as well as a high-tech deficit with rival industrial blocs. It has failed to outsmart the foreign MNCs that have sunk deep roots into their own domestic economy or to keep pace with the cheap products coming from Southeast Asia.

Most foreign MNCs are concentrated in highly capitalized sectors. Some import and assemble components or produce only for the local market; others have established offshore affiliates to specialize in third-country export trade. It is significant, too, that European MNCs have tried to catch up with the internationalizing of production by moving affiliate operations into the United States. Air Liquide, British Petroleum, BASF, and Philips put massive amounts of FDI into the United States. Today they rely on overseas revenues to support the parent firm. The pattern was first set by U.S. and Japanese multinationals, and the EC firms were slow but steady copiers. The global worth of MNC capital and production is now immense.[26]

It is clear that overseas capital and revenue flows are so valuable to the EC that protectionist payments or discriminatory tariffs could play havoc with its best industries. Europe needs IBM and Fujitsu plants on site nearly as much as it needs the offshore earnings brought home by French banks, German chemical companies, and Britain's varied MNCs. If the bargaining over farm price supports during the Uruguay negotiations between the United States and the EC had collapsed in 1992, the transatlantic trade in manufacturing exports and services could have been gravely injured. Pressure was put on the EC to compromise on $300 billion worth of agricultural trade so that $4 trillion worth of global commerce in goods and services would not be imperiled by trade warfare.

It is remarkable that more than half of the MNCs' funding in the EC goes to Britain. The explanation is simple. It is not that labor rates or factor costs were favorable in Britain—which had been noted for its frequent strikes and erratic fiscal policy. It was that the UK imposed far fewer constraints on incoming capital and competition. World class firms in manufacturing and service sectors found it easier to operate in the UK than elsewhere, and their contribution to Britain's balance of payments and industrial productivity surpassed the benefits brought from North Sea oil drilling.[27] If this trend continues, the EC Twelve might discourage the spread of MNC activity, while Britain will gain disproportionately from the opening up of a larger EC market.

In principle, the Treaty of Rome outlaws state aid and intervention no matter if it comes in debt write-offs, low interest loans, or direct grants. In theory, the EC holds to a policy of competition and rejects the axioms of a mixed economy, but if it ever applied a consistent policy of deregulation and privatization, national governments would have to outlaw grants to state-owned companies and eliminate all barriers to foreign trade and capital. No EC state would consent to such sweeping changes.

It is estimated that public subsidies per worker (in 1981–1986) came to $6,000 in Italy, $1,200 in France, $940 in West Germany, and $750 in the UK. Since state-run firms account for 15 percent of all employment in France and 10 percent or more in West Germany and Italy, these per capita inputs are indispensable to Europe's prosperity. They cannot possibly be touched until the EC recovers from its prolonged recession.[28] If the payments were reduced—or eliminated—a major part of the EC workforce would find itself as stranded as the skilled but workless millions in Eastern Europe.

Longer term prospects are equally daunting. If the EMU ever moved to the point of curbing deficit financing and expansionary spending, EC governments would have to curtail most of their job protection and commercial subsidies. It is doubtful that any of the twelve parliaments are prepared to entertain such revolutionary and disturbing prospects. Most have dug in to fight the rapidly industrializing states of Asia. Most share a common belief with the EC Commission. They do not look on free trade or open markets as beneficial weapons. Their prime concern is to defend a workforce threatened by the adverse operation of the laws of comparative advantage.

Obstacles to European Union

The gathering force of global competition raises anxiety across Europe. Industrial productivity and capital investment have been relatively stagnant across the EC, but they increased smartly elsewhere. The newly industrializing countries (the NICs as the UN calls them) have recorded GDP growth of 5 percent a year, with higher rates in China and Mexico. They are bursting with vigor to take over the best global markets.

Most EC states have limped along at 2 percent; Britain and Germany actually went to zero. To make matters worse, most EC members have suffered an inflation of wage and credit costs and a downtrend in labor productivity. In the meantime, trade across the Pacific has expanded rapidly, and MNCs coming from Japan or Southeast Asia have slashed prices for electronics, automobiles, and consumer durables.

Japan has built up a new industrial challenge by merging its MNC production lines with start-up plants in NICs, such as Taiwan, South Korea, and Thailand. It is likely that U.S. or other MNCs will copy their lead in the NAFTA trading bloc. If that occurs, the struggle for comparative advantage will leave the EC group in a vulnerable position. It relies far too heavily on managed trade and state-rigged industry to compete with global MNCs and their NIC partners.[29]

Sixty percent of the EC's high value-added trade is intrabloc and subject to some form of intervention. This reflects a debilitating weakness rather than bloc solidarity. The market share taken by EC exports or MNC enterprises in the NAFTA or Pacific rim bloc is not impressive, and EC prospects for improving its position in the 1990s are not bright. Europe competes poorly in cheap goods or primary commodities, and its exports of high-tech goods and services are overpriced.

There is another weakness that the EC has failed to repair through joint action. Too many industrial sectors have lagged in extending industrial plant, workers' training, R&D labs, and productivity ratios. This is most visible in the automobile industry, where U.S. and Japanese factories produce twice as many cars with half of the EC's personnel.

A few of the EC's largest auto companies tried to stifle Japanese competition by limiting imports to 11 percent of the EC market—but France and Italy allow imports up to only 2 percent. Rather than gearing up to fight for larger market shares, EC car companies have relied on the closure of domestic markets to attain economies of scale. Volkswagen, Peugeot, and Fiat built few overseas operations and depended on protected markets at home. The UK reversed the course. It scrapped its profitless British cars and manufactured Japanese cars in its disused facilities. They are now Japanese-owned and run "transplant" operations, and their profit margins rose to a historic high.[30]

A useful comparison can be made with the United States, where Japanese exports and "transplants" took 30 percent of an open market. They challenged Ford and GM to match them (1) in quality control, (2) in pricing and marketing strategy, and (3) in extending their MNC plant overseas. As a result, Ford and GM were forced to modernize aging plants in the United States and to extend their valuable offshore production. If Japan had been allowed to take 35 percent of all EC markets (as it did in Denmark and Ireland), it might have pushed EC auto firms to compete more vigorously at home and to build MNC plants overseas.

A similar lesson should have been learned in the steel, electronics, engineering, insurance, banking, airlines, and service industries. As European firms came to rely on import protection, public funding, or forced mergers, many of them lost their export markets and their cutting edge. It appears that a shift of power to the Brussels agencies will not help repair the lag in Europe's industrial performance.

It is clear today that most EC firms cannot measure up against competitors with low costs and cheap currencies. High-tech and mobile MNCs work with rapidly changing inputs of capital, R&D, skilled labor, and firm-specific technology. Too many of Europe's leading firms have lagged in this race. The protective milieu of the EC has not encouraged EC-owned enterprises to modernize or internationalize production. On one side the EC has favored a mixed economy and rejected the deregulation axioms of the Reagan and Thatcher regimes, but on the other it refused to build a collective industrial policy—of the order vigorously pursued by MITI in Japan.[31]

Can the EC Create an Industrial Policy?

The argument of this chapter is that the 1992 design for a single market was built on a false premise. The logic of integrating Europe's internal markets and imposing a common external tariff was wrongly formulated. Even if it eventually becomes a unified entity, few EC industries will realize the economies of scale or the market power achieved by giant MNCs and the fast-growth economies with which it must compete.

Given its current political stasis, the EC is probably stuck with its dependence on state funding, tariff protection, and limitations of cheap imports. Though foreign trade amounts to 20 percent of its GNP, it is not likely to transform its political solidarity into economic strength. It is more likely to turn from trade creation to the tactics of trade distortion. The EC is geared for a defensive posture. It is not ready to face the chilling competition prompted by free trade or to compose an industrial policy that is sensitive to market signals.

There are three scenarios of development that might unfold during the 1990s.[32] The first is pragmatic: the EPU and the EMU will be constantly delayed, but the EC will survive as a simple trading club or internal customs zone. It might add the seven EFTA states to compose an EEA Nineteen and try to expand GNP growth once the recession ends—if all members agree.

The second choice goes further: the EC will admit the seven EFTA nations but keep out the six Mediterranean and Eastern European nations clamoring for admission. It will convert the EMU into a two-speed mechanism to harmonize the stronger economies within a common (and not a single) currency while excluding inflation-prone and weaker countries like Britain, Italy, Spain, and the "Club Med" states. As a union of only five or six countries, it will enjoy little economic clout.

The third choice is idealistic and impractical: that the federal structures of a single market will unite national sovereignties and the rival economic aspirations of Europe into a tight supra-state. The start of the single market in January 1993 was supposed to herald the next stage in the evolution of a United States of Europe. But it is not likely to create the common industrial policy or the single economic structure that such a federal regime requires. The Maastricht plans to concentrate political and economic authority within a centralized EPU and EMU were obviously stillborn.

At this time only the first choice looks feasible. Internal barriers to the movement of people, goods, and funds have been partially dismantled, but an arsenal of protective defenses has been left in place. A report by GATT rebuked the EC in 1991 for laying foundations for a Fortress Europe. It decried the EC's use of restrictive rules, nontariff barriers, and bilateral limits to free trade—especially in textiles, agriculture, and automobiles. GATT thus urged the EC to lower its wall of NTBs and honor the principles of free trade.[33]

It is not likely that the EC will discard its neomercantile and regulatory bias. Despite grave setbacks to the Maastricht timetable, a majority in the Commission aims to promote industrial policies and company mergers across EC frontiers. Even if the EC can no longer write a constitutional compact, it still hopes to boost Europe's prosperity. What will happen to these grandiose plans if the EC comes apart or its economy contracts? Such questions defy sure answers.

There is a serious error in the EC's planning. Time is running out. Japan, North America, and a considerable number of MNCs are gearing up for fast change and rapid growth in the 1990s. Europe is not. If it relies on trade deflection rather than industrial competition to boost GDP, it will make a mistake. The fast-lane performance of high-tech and capital-intensive firms depends on export prowess. It is only in world markets that global economies of scale can be attained. Trade distortion, rather than trade creation, will not do.

Industrial policy can help merge state monopolies or shelter EC national champion firms behind NTB defenses, but if it provokes trade wars, all parties can suffer badly. It is for this reason that the EC will likely resign itself to an imperfect and unfinished design. Conditions are not favorable for the completion of the Single Market Act in 1993, nor does the EC enjoy the profit margins or trade surplus needed to restructure its ailing industries and twelve disparate economies.

So the EC market and its industrial base are likely to remain half built for years to come. The EC might raise GDP growth but it will be in no position to launch the comprehensive industrial policy that *dirigiste* planners had eagerly envisaged. The EC cannot realistically create a MITI-like agency for central planning, nor can it brusquely deregulate its twelve state-protected markets. Scholars who now propose theories of "neofunctional integration" will have to wait for many more years until the EC moves to adopt the clear-cut mode of industrial policy that they so blandly predicted.

Notes

1. A recent comment of *The Economist* (November 14, 1992) is worth citing at length:

> The Community's 1992 programme started from a belief in competition as a spur to efficiency . . . by aiming to merge markets through deregulation. . . . The deregulatory push of the single-market experiment is increasingly seen as a threat. Europe's rightist xenophobes and leftist interventionists are making common cause.

2. The weaker EC economies depend to an alarming extent on public spending and deficit financing. Greece, Italy, and Belgium lead the club, with deficits amounting to 10 percent or more of GDP. Their public debt totals over 100 percent of GDP. See the tabulated data in *The Economist,* August 8, 1992.

3. The impact of the 1991–92 recession on the EC'92 program of unification is examined by the author in detail in "EC Stalling," *Foreign Policy* no. 85 (Winter 1991–1992).

4. The plight of the EMU, EPU, Social Charter, and other components of the Maastricht Treaty, and the subsidiarity proposal advanced by M. Delors, are analyzed in my review of the EC ratification process, "Europe After Maastricht," *Foreign Affairs* 71 no. 5 (Winter 1992–93).

5. The sources of these economic data (and others to follow) appear in my chapter in a recent book, edited by Robert J. Jackson, *Europe in Transition* (New York: Praeger, 1992).

6. The most thorough analysis of EC economic issues appears in two opinionated conservative journals, the *Financial Times* and *The Economist.* For example, the latter argues (November 28, 1992) that the Maastricht Treaty and the EMU be kept as the defects of any alternative would be greater.

7. A businessperson's guide to the rulings of EC Commissioners on Competition and Industrial Policy is provided in James W. Dudley, *1992: Understanding the New*

European Market (Dearborn: Financial Publishing, 1990).

8. After a searching debate, the EC Commission published the report: Paolo Cecchini et al., *The European Challenge* (Aldershot: Wildwood House, for the EC, 1988).

9. For a useful analysis of Cecchini's findings, and of the influx of MNCs into the EC, see Norman S.Fielke, "Europe in 1992," *New England Economic Review* May-June, 1989.

10. A noted economist, Richard Baldwin, optimistically doubles the growth estimate advanced by Cecchini, in "The Growth Effects of 1992," *Economic Policy* no. 9 (October 1990).

11. Theoretical disputes over trade protection have directly influenced the deliberation of policy. For two powerful contributions to recent debates see Jagdish Bhagwati, *Protectionism* (Cambridge, Mass.: M.I.T. Press, 1988); and Paul R.Krugman, *Rethinking International Trade* (Cambridge, Mass.: M.I.T. Press, 1989).

12. For a critical guide to the impact of MNCs and their use of FDI deployments see Jeffrey J. Schott, "Trading Blocs and the World Trading System," *World Economy* 14 no. 1 (1991); and Phedon Nicolaides, "Investment Policies in an Integrated World Economy," *World Economy* 14 no. 2 (1991).

13. A probing analysis of the impact of Japanese investment and MNCs appears in the essays edited by B. Burgenmeier and J. L. Munichelli, *Multinationals and Europe, 1992* (London: Routledge, 1991).

14. On the GATT report see "European Countries Blasted for Restrictive Rules," *Wall Street Journal,* April 17, 1991.

15. Surveys of high-tech and export industries appear in two useful collections: *The Dynamics of European Integration,* William Wallace, ed. (London: Pinter, 1991); and Gary C. Hufbauer, ed., *Europe 1992* (Washington: Brookings, 1990).

16. See The EC Commission's "Assessment of the Economic Effects of Completing the Internal Market," published as *The Economics of 1992* (London: Oxford, 1988).

17. Comparative achievements of Japan, Europe, and the United States in developing high-tech firms and strategic industries are carefully evaluated by Lester Thurow, *Head to Head* (New York: Morrow, 1992).

18. Adjustment to the exigencies of technological change is difficult to gauge. The mechanism and consequences of the adjustment process are expertly reviewed in essays collected by Karel Cool et al., *European Industrial Re-structuring in the 1990s* (New York: N.Y.U. Press, 1991).

19. Changing relations between the state and private sector operations are thoroughly examined in Loukas Tsoukalis, *The New European Economy* (New York: Oxford, 1991).

20. The bitter controversy over Airbus financing is noted in Rene Schwok, *U.S.-EC Relations in the Post-Cold War Era* (Boulder: Westview, 1991).

21. A wealth of material on horizontal agreements in high-tech industries and the state aid approved by the EC appears in the Commission's *Eighteenth Report on Competition Policy* (Brussels: EC, 1989).

22. Securing economies of scale and a greater market share through competition and joint venture production will be vital to international trade. A breakdown by industrial sectors appears in the essays edited by Alan Webster and John Dunning, *Structural Change in the World Economy* (London: Routledge, 1990).

23. The technology dynamics of EC industrial competition is assessed in Gerald R. Faulhaber and Gaultiero Tamburini, *European Economic Integration: The Role of Technology* (Boston: Kluwer, 1991).

24. See the editors' analysis of EC-Japanese competition in *Single Market Europe,* Spyros G. Makridakis and Michelle Bainbridge, eds. (San Francisco: Jossey-Bass, 1991).

25. The gathering rush of Japanese MNCs into Europe is noted in T. Ozawa, "Japanese MNCs and 1992," Burgenmeier and Munichelli, op. cit.

26. Excellent compilations of trade data are given by David Cameron, "The 1992 Initiative," in *Euro-Politics,* Alberta Sbragia, ed., (Washington DC: Brookings, 1992).

27. Though a little dated, see the assessment of comparative advantage in *The European Internal Market,* André Sapir and Alexis Jacquemin, eds., (New York: Oxford, 1990).

28. The economic costs of EC labor subsidies are noted in Stephen Padgett and William Paterson, *Social Democracy in Postwar Europe* (London: Longman, 1991).

29. Contrast the optimistic essays in *The Dynamics of European Unity,* Roy Price, ed. (London: Croom Helm, 1987) and the stark economic calculus of Joseph Grieco, *Cooperation among Nations* (Ithaca: Cornell, 1990).

30. The consequences of moving production to offshore export platforms are noted in Maurice Basle's essay on Britain in *Europeans on Europe,* Mairi Maclean and Jolyon Howorth, eds. (London: Macmillan, 1992).

31. On the question, Why can the EC not build a planning agency like MITI?, see the essay on neofunctionalist theory by Robert Keohane and Stanley Hoffmann in William Wallace, op. cit.

32. I developed the three secenarios at greater length in my analysis in *Foreign Policy,* op. cit.

33. See *Wall Street Journal,* op. cit., and the editor's conclusions in *European Competition Policy,* Peter Montagnon, ed. (London: The Royal Institute of International Affairs, 1990).

19

Europe Calling Europe: Creating an Integrated Telecommunications Network

Wilson P. Dizard

When Jacques Delors and his associates planned the Single Europe Act in the mid-1980s, there was a curious omission in their strategy for speeding up European economic integration. It involved the critical role telecommunications and information resources would play in assuring that full integration took place.

The Single European Act did not mention the subject. The omission was not for lack of understanding of the need to strengthen European communications facilities. Over the years, telecommunications has been one of the most sensitive and contentious of Community issues.[1] At the 1980 Dublin summit, the European Commission addressed the Community's strategy for matching U.S. and Japanese high-tech competition, particularly in telecommunications goods and services. The EC Twelve collectively have had a large trade deficit with the United States and Japan in this sector, with few prospects for catching up. At the time of the Dublin meeting, EC countries accounted for only 15 percent of global trade in communications goods and services. The Commission proposed doubling these capabilities by 1990, a goal that was only partially achieved. The need to strengthen EC resources in this sector has been stated in clear terms by a French industry minister, Alain Madelin:

> Europe has no choice but to become a third pole of equivalent weight to the U.S. and Japan. Or else, poor in raw materials, politically divided, technologically dependent, it will in fact become nothing more than a subcontractor for the other two.[2]

Telecommunications was played down in the Single Europe Act primarily for political reasons. Almost all EC governments resisted the idea of restructuring their Post-Telephone-Telegraph (PTT) operations to meet regional needs. In particular, the prospect of competing with private firms in telecommunications services was unwelcome. The PTTs were political sacred cows—state monopolies, major employers of unionized civil servants, and big contributors to national treasuries. By the mid-1980s, only the United Kingdom had moved toward open competition. British Telecom, the national monopoly, was privatized, and at the same time, limited competition in telecommunications services was introduced. Other countries, notably France, were spending large sums to improve their domestic facilities within the framework of government ownership.

The Imperatives for Change

Despite these improvements, EC telecommunications facilities in the mid-1980s were clearly inadequate to support the level of regional economic integration proposed in the Single European Act. The Community has lagged well behind North America in its telecommunications practices. Although the two regions have roughly the same population, North Americans use their telephone systems three times as much as Europeans.[3] Moreover, the overall reliability of public telecommunications services within Europe has been considerably lower, particularly for business users. In a 1990 survey, the European Association of Information Services (EUSDIC) found that almost 25 percent of its members' international calls on public data networks were not completed.[4]

The EUSDIC survey and other indications of the region's communications inadequacies sparked a major effort by the EC's Brussels bureaucracy to force changes in this sector. This effort was strongly supported by European industry, which was frustrated by problems of doing regional business through facilities dominated by twelve separate and often uncoordinated telecommunications systems. The result has been significant progress, given the political and economic obstacles involved, toward an integrated regional communications system.

In this chapter we will look at three aspects of this change:

- A summary of EC actions to strengthen the region's telecommunications resources since the beginning of the EC-92 process
- The parallel growth of a stronger regional telecommunications private sector, including link-ups with U.S. firms
- The future prospects for EC communications development

Despite some early hesitations about reforming EC telecommunications, Community actions have been an important element in strengthening this sector. A U.S. event was an indirect but powerful factor in bringing this about. In 1982, the U.S. Department of Justice issued a consent decree that laid out conditions for breaking up AT&T, the U.S. version of a PTT. Among its other effects, the department's decision has revised the notion that telecommunications is a natural monopoly requiring centralized management. The AT&T breakup has spawned thousands of new competitive enterprises, resulting in an expanded range of advanced services.

The lesson was not lost on Brussels planners. The ending of AT&T's quasi-monopoly had a strong impact on the Commission's plans for reforming EC telecommunications. Its proposals were outlined in a Green Paper issued in 1987. The sensitivity of member governments to change was reflected in the fact that the Green Paper had no legal force. As approved by the EC Council, it contained a commitment in principle to change rather than detailing specific actions. Nevertheless, the Green Paper was unequivocal in emphasizing the importance of telecommunications to the EC-92 program's success:

> The strengthening of European telecommunications has become one of the major conditions for promoting a harmonious development of economic activities and a competitive market throughout the Community and for achieving the completion of the Community-wide market for goods and services by 1992.[5]

The Green Paper focused on two major goals: achieving an efficient regional network structure to support other EC economic programs, and strengthening the private telecommunications sector to compete regionally and in global markets. The two goals were complementary. The European telecommunications equipment sector has been historically divided into twelve separate industries, each primarily serving a national market and each usually protected by its government from outside competition. This pattern did not fit the EC's need for integrated regional communications or for greater competition in world markets.

Restructuring the PTTs

Reorganizing the PTTs in member states was the most difficult political issue facing officials in Directorate General XIII (DG-13), the EC office charged with implementing the Green Paper. Basically, this required modifying PTT monopolies in ways that would open the regional market to more competition and more services. To achieve this, the Green Paper included a critical compromise. Politically, no EC member states could agree to full deregulation of their PTTs. The Green Paper compromise was to allow the PTTs to keep full control over the largest share of their operations—ordinary voice telephone service. The rest would be open, for the first time, to competition between the PTTs and private firms. This meant, however, that over 95 percent of European public telecommunications services were out of bounds for EC competition reform.

Despite this limitation, the small percentage of public telecommunications services targeted for change was a significant element in the Brussels reform plans. (These services are generally described as value-added services, as distinct from basic voice telephony.) Collectively, they represent the sector's fastest-growing area. A 1991 survey by Britain's National Economic Research Association puts the potential value-added services market in the EC region at $15 billion annually by the end of the decade.[6] It includes new or improved services such as high-tech data networking, electronic mail, specialized satellite networks, electronic funds transfer, regional conference calling, and multimedia communications. These are, moreover, the advanced services most needed by European industry, and which had been either nonexistent or woefully inadequate in most EC countries, thanks to the PTTs' penchant for preferring the simple technologies and assured revenues of ordinary telephone service.

Brussels's strategy for restructuring EC telecommunications concentrated on forcing changes in the PTTs that would strengthen their ability to compete against new private-sector services. This required reorganization of the PTTs in ways that put them on a more cost-efficient basis. An important part of this change was separating the PTTs' telecommunications operations from their money-losing postal services. (As a result, PTTs are now known in EC-speak as telecommunications administrations.) In addition to spinning off postal services, the new telecommunications administrations were required to reorganize in ways that would ensure a clear separation of regulatory and operational functions. As the 1987 Green Paper pointed out:

> In a more competitive environment, the Telecommunications Administrations cannot continue to be both regulator and market participant, i.e. referee and player. . . . (They) should be market participants in the competitive sectors, in an improved competitive environment, in order to insure full service to the whole spectrum of users and industry.[7]

The second part of DG-13's strategy was to assure that new private-sector entrants into the formerly monopolistic telecom services field would have a fair chance to compete against still-powerful public telecommunications authorities. This was done by setting criteria to assure nondiscriminatory access by private firms to the government-controlled networks they needed to provide value-added services. It was a critical point, given the telecommunication authorities' inclination to make life difficult for any competitors.

Establishing the ground rules for this requirement (known as the Open Network Provision) involved some of the fiercest controversy in implementing the Green Paper's recommendations. The open network "framework directive," approved in June 1990, set out the general terms and conditions for allowing private competitors fair and equal access to government-controlled networks. The directive did not, however, set a timetable for meeting this goal. The result was protracted wrangling as some EC governments sought to put off the inevitability of competition. The French and Spanish obtained a postponement until the end of 1992 for the inauguration of competition in data networking, the most lucrative of the services involved. The Greeks and Portuguese were given until 1996 to comply, under the general EC rubric of allowing the "southern" countries longer adaptation periods for complying with Commission directives. [8]

Setting Common Standards

Another barrier to a more efficient regional communications structure was the jumble of technical standards that limited interconnections between the twelve national systems. An early directive, in July 1986, set the stage for harmonizing the testing and certification of telecommunications terminal equipment, with the goal of guaranteeing the right to connect such equipment to public networks throughout the Community. In order to assure common technical standards, the EC has also sponsored a European Telecommunications Standards Institute.

The Commission's 1989 directive on telecommunications equipment was significant for another reason. It involved the Commission's power, under the competition provisions of the Treaty of Rome (Article 90), to prevent member governments from unilaterally restricting competition by conferring monopoly or other special rights. The directive, which was issued under Article 90 authority, was challenged in the European Court. The Court basically upheld the Commission's action, and in effect confirmed the Commission's competence to issue such directives without requiring approval of the European Parliament or the Council of Ministers. The decision was a landmark case in the overall balance-of-power struggle between the Commission and the Council. The Commission, less protective of national interests than the Council, was clearly strengthened by the Court's decision, allowing it greater scope to regulate telecommunications on a regional basis.

Meanwhile, the Commission took other steps to expand the capabilities of the regional telecommunications structure. Among its actions were decisions on harmonizing regional use of radio frequencies, mobile telephones, and digital cordless telecommunications. More recently, the Commission has moved to reconsider the remaining national monopolies on basic voice telephone and network infrastructure, a campaign sparked by Sir Leon Brittan, the EC's vice president for competition issues. A decision to open up voice telephony to competition will have a major effect on the pattern of future EC regional telecommunications.[9]

One of the most controversial of regional coordination issues involved satellite communications. Here the twelve member states were dealing with a technology that is primarily a regional resource not completely subject to national regulation. Their interim solution was to set up a regional cartel, Eutelsat, that operates satellites through which PTT organizations channel telecom services. Eutelsat has been a reasonably effective organization. It is not designed, however, to provide the wide choice of advanced services routinely available in the United States, where unregulated direct access to satellites, primarily for business communications, is a competitive, growing business.

European companies wanted a similar arrangement, one that would allow them to bypass Eutelsat and local telecommunications authorities. The issue is important to them. Not only does it open the prospect of more direct control over their corporate communications, but it also can free them from many of the high tariffs charged by most telecommunications administrations. They got substantially what they wanted in a decision that was the most dramatic step toward regional telecommunications integration in the entire EC-92 process. In a draft Green Paper on satellite policy, issued in November 1990, the EC Commission recommended major deregulation of member nation controls over satellite communications. Specifically, the draft proposed permitting private ownership of earth stations, with unrestricted access to satellites, subject to some regulatory procedures. Full commercial freedom for both public and private satellite service providers would also be allowed, including direct marketing of satellite capacity to potential customers.

The Commission's draft proposals were endorsed by EC telecommunications ministers in November 1991. The proposals, when implemented, will have particular importance for one of the fastest-growing satellite areas—channels for cellular telephones and other mobile communications uses. The EC satellite plan stipulates that once a mobile-satellite operator obtains a license in one EC country, the license will be valid in all other member states. There is still, however, residual opposition within EC governments to giving up controls over satellite traffic. The Brussels proposals will have to run the gauntlet of approval by national legislatures. Most observers believe that the proposals will be adopted with some changes but that it will be several years before they are finally put into effect. Meanwhile, European and U.S. satellite entrepreneurs are positioning themselves to take advantage of the liberalized satellite rules when they are finally approved.[10]

Strengthening the Private Sector

As noted earlier, the primary aim of EC telecommunications strategy has been to restructure member state policies and operations in ways that support an efficient regional network. The other part of the strategy is to strengthen the Community's private telecommunications goods and services sectors in ways that will make them more competitive. This calls for changes in the pattern that has divided the market among twelve separate industries. Most companies have operated largely in their own national markets, favored by protectionist policies, resulting in high costs, inefficient production, and less opportunity to sell their products regionally or in the wider world markets.

This situation is changing fast. The EC directives mandating an integrated European network open the prospect of a competitive, expanding regional market for the first time. The telecommunications industry has reacted by reorganizing itself in a spate of cross-border mergers, acquisitions, and working agreements. What was, only a few years ago, a collection of separate nationally based industries is now being reshuffled into fewer, and stronger, corporate alliances. These link-ups are primarily regional, but they also include U.S. firms looking for commercial footholds in the new European market.

This development is part of the larger global shift toward international corporate alliances, particularly in high-tech industries. As noted earlier, world markets in telecommunications and information are dominated by U.S. and Japanese companies, with the Europeans a poor third. In 1991, EC countries had an overall deficit of $35 billion in electronics trade with the rest of world, much of it involving communications-related products. The EC's interest in expanding telecommunications exports is strengthened by the fact that this sector may account for as much as $500 billion in global trade annually by the mid-1990s.

Overseas markets are important for European telecommunications firms, but their more immediate interests are closer to home. EC planners project overall sectoral growth to expand from 3 percent of the region's gross domestic product in 1989 to 7 percent by the year 2000. Dataquest, a U.S. research firm, is even more bullish, predicting an annual sectoral growth rate of 9 percent during the 1990s, double the rate of growth in the United States.[11]

These are the realities driving European industry to restructure itself for new markets. The other reality is the fact that U.S. and Japanese firms are moving aggressively into this market, either directly or through partnerships with regional companies. While European companies are breaking loose from their national moorings, U.S. and Japanese firms have had no difficulty in dealing with Europe as a single market.

In addition to curbing the PTT monopolies, Brussels has taken other steps to encourage private-sector competitiveness. The Commission has subsidized advanced electronics research on a regional basis, in cooperation with European industry. The equivalent of billions of dollars has been invested in two major programs—RACE and ESPRIT, both heavily weighted toward telecommunications research. Additionally, the Commission is working closely with the private sector to identify regional needs. One result is a 1992 initiative with the European Roundtable Industry Group, a consortium of major industries, to develop an EC-wide infrastructure plan, 25 percent of which would involve telecommunications needs.[12]

The shift to competition in the new regional telecommunications market has been difficult for many European firms. One example is Germany's Siemens, the largest of Europe's electronic conglomerates. The company, with $40 billion in annual sales, has historically focused its telecommunications activities on the German market, and particularly on the Bundespost, the former PTT. Despite Siemens's production and marketing expertise, the firm was earning net profits of under 3 percent in the early 1990s. Its turnaround strategy has involved a massive internal reorganization plus outside acquisitions and partnerships. The latter included the United States's Bendix Corporation; Plessey, a major British electronics firm; and Nixdorf, a German computer company.

While these moves have been generally helpful, Siemens still has problems in strengthening its regional presence. Its attempt to set up a regional electronics consortium, involving Philips, the Dutch electronics giant, and SGS-Thomson, a Franco-Italian semiconductor group, fell through in 1992.[13] A Siemens's alliance with IBM to develop advanced semiconductor chips was also ended in 1992, when the company decided it could not compete against Japanese domination of the global memory chip market. Earlier, Philips cut back its operations in this area. These decisions seriously hurt European prospects for a strong presence in the critical area of chip research and production.

Changing U.S.-EC Trade Patterns

One of the striking developments in EC private-sector telecommunications has been the "double invasion" of European firms into the U.S. market and the equally aggressive moves of U.S. companies into Europe. A U.S. presence in Europe is not new: IBM and ITT, among other firms, have been major players there for decades. This was not true of European firms contemplating operations in the United States. For all intents and purposes it was a closed market for them. The reason was that, for decades, AT&T dominated the telecommunications equipment market through its Western Electric manufacturing affiliate. All local Bell telephone companies—the largest customers for such equipment—were required to buy from or through Western Electric. This virtual monopoly was ended in the 1982 agreement breaking up AT&T. As a result, the U.S. equipment market—the largest on earth—became fully competitive.

This prospect was not lost on European manufacturers. In the past ten years, every major EC firm producing telecommunications equipment and services has moved into the U.S. market, many of them setting up manufacturing facilities for their products. The prime example is Siemens, with sixty manufacturing and assembly facilities employing 15,000 people who produced products worth over $4.5 billion annually in the early 1990s. A less well known firm, France's Alcatel Alsthom, has overtaken AT&T in recent years as the world's largest maker of telephone equipment. A state-owned company privatized in 1986, Alcatel is active in the U.S. market. An early acquisition was ITT Corporation's telecommunications business, which has acquired in return for giving ITT a minority stake in Alcatel's telecommunications division. In 1991, Alcatel bought Rockwell International's telephone transmission equipment business, making Alcatel the number two firm in this U.S. market.[14]

Other European firms have followed suit. Britain's Cable & Wireless is now the fifth largest U.S. telephone service supplier, the result of its acquisition of independent phone companies in recent years. British Telecom, the privatized UK company, has invested $1.5 billion in a 22 percent stake in McCaw Cellular Communications, the largest U.S. cellular-phone operator. Two other major European telecommunications services suppliers, France's Telecom and Germany's DBP Telekom, have also moved into the highly competitive U.S. telecom services market.[15]

These European moves have been matched by equally aggressive U.S. entry into EC markets in recent years. The earliest move was made in 1984 by AT&T, which formed a joint venture with Philips in hopes of assuring better access to the regional equipment market. It was a mismatch from the start, and Philips pulled out of the venture in 1990. AT&T has since revamped its European operations and is now a major player in both manufacturing and services. In the late 1980s, the company was chosen over European firms as a partner by Italy's state-owned equipment maker to help modernize the country's decrepit phone system. AT&T's two U.S. long-distance competitors, MCI and Sprint, have also expanded into the EC telecom services field.

The surprising U.S. entrants into the European market are the "Baby Bells," the seven regional telephone companies. This was a consequence of restrictions placed on their U.S. operations in the wake of the AT&T breakup in 1984, requiring them to focus primarily on local telephone operations. The restrictions did not generally apply to international ventures, with the result that the cash-rich regional companies have sought out overseas business ventures. Europe has been a prime target for Baby Bell investments. A striking example is their operations in Great Britain, where four of the companies (Nynex, U.S. West, Southwestern Bell, and Pacific Telesis) collectively dominate the small but growing cable television industry. On the continent, Pacific Telesis is a partner in a German cellular-phone network and has won licenses for cellular-phone and paging systems in Portugal. Bell South has a Dutch partner for a wireless data network.[16] US West and Telecommunications Inc. (TCI), which is the largest U.S. cable-TV company, have established a joint venture group to manage telephone and cable-TV investments in Britain, Norway, Sweden, and Hungary.

These and other U.S. investments have shaken many of the old-boys' club attitudes in the European communications sector. In particular, AT&T's

decision to operate data communications networks throughout the region has had a wake-up call effect on European service providers. Other U.S. firms also play an important role as information service providers in the Community. General Electric Information Services, IBM, and General Motors' Electronic Data Systems each have expanded into Europe-wide data networking in recent years. For both U.S. and European firms, the economic stakes involved in the new European telecommunications goods and services market are huge. According to CIT Research, a London consulting firm, the Western European market in this sector will top $240 billion annually by the year 2001, an increase of 40 percent in a decade.

U.S. firms have positioned themselves strongly to capture a significant share of this business. By and large, EC-92 telecommunications initiatives have facilitated their expansion into European markets, and the transition to a regional market is clearly in their interests. Moreover, the shake-up in the old-line European firms has provided greater opportunities for U.S. companies to develop investment, mergers, and other working relationships with their European counterparts.

Resisting the New Protectionism

Although EC policy has been generally receptive to a greater U.S. role in the European telecommunications sector, questions remain as to whether this will continue. The problem is not the much-exaggerated fear of a Fortress Europe. The North Atlantic economies are too intertwined to tolerate a return to the more blatant forms of protectionism. The problem is more subtle. In telecommunications, European industries have pressured the EC bureaucracy for relief in the form of subsidies and other help designed to meet foreign competition. In a 1991 report to the Commission, the French Syndicat des Industries de Télécommunications (SIT) cited the example of fax machine production: "Already all the fax machines sold in Europe use foreign technology and components, because there is no longer such technology which is strictly European." One proposal in the report called for EC help in providing financing terms equivalent to those enjoyed by non-European companies.[17]

European governments and industries will continue to pressure the EC for subsidies and other special advantages in dealing with foreign competition, particularly in telecommunications and other high-tech sectors. A more serious problem may be posed by efforts to limit U.S. investment in Europe. In 1992, the EC's competition commissioner, Sir Leon Brittan, suggested the need for the Community to address the problem of distinguishing between "good" strategic alliances and those which might be anticompetitive. He called for striking a correct balance between, on the one hand, giving a rapid response that firms require for their strategic alliances if they are to compete in a changing world market, and, on the other hand, identifying anti-competitive alliances that have no objective benefits and threaten competition.[18]

Setting the ground rules for identifying good and bad mergers could prove troublesome to U.S. companies seeking to expand into Europe. However, the 1989 Merger Regulations do not discriminate between EC and non-EC companies, requiring both to meet minimum thresholds for a priori notification of mergers to the Commission.

Although the public focus in U.S.-EC trade disputes has usually been on agricultural policies, telecommunications and information issues have been also major subjects for negotiation between the two trading partners. In recent years, telecommunications and information disputes have ranked high on the annual publications issued by the EC and the U.S. government, each listing the alleged trade-barrier sins of the other. The most publicized case has been the European Council's 1989 decision to require a majority of European-origuated programs on regional television stations "where practicable and by appropriate means"—a requirement aimed at reducing the amount of imported U.S. programming transmitted by the stations.[19]

Although both sides support more open trade in general, the U.S. position is affected by protectionist congressional legislation, notably the Trade Expansion Act of 1988, which mandated retaliatory action against countries that did not open their markets to U.S. telecommunications goods and services. In 1991, the White House Office of the U.S. Trade Representative cited continuing EC telecommunication restrictions as grounds for possible retaliation—the first major application of the 1988 legislation in this sector.

In summary, telecommunications has been a litmus test of the impact of the Europe 1992 process. The sector is politically sensitive, technologically complex, and economically critical to the Community's goal of a barrier-free regional market. The EC Commission has been generally successful in its telecommunications policies when it has acted pragmatically, adapting to achievable goals. An example, cited earlier, was its decision not to get involved in the sensitive subject of opening up national voice telephone services to regional competition. The Commission focused instead on liberalizing the market in advanced services, where its directives have had a strong impact on strengthening EC telecommunications resources.

Shaping a New Agenda

The process is by no means complete. By the end of the Europe 1992 cycle, Western European telecommunications were still inadequate to meet present and potential needs of a barrier-free trade area. The subject will be on the EC agenda for a long time to come. Four major challenges will have to be addressed if the Commission's goals in this area are to be met:

Carrying out Decisions Already Taken

As noted earlier, most EC countries have been slow to implement directives approved at the Brussels level. Government officials, particularly those who were involved in the old PTT organizations, still resist giving up the century-old practices and privileges of their communications monopolies. By the end of 1992, only a few of the telecommunications directives approved by the European Commission had been ratified by all twelve national legislatures, usually because of objections raised by government telecommunications agencies.

Despite these rearguard actions, most telecommunications directives will be substantially in place by the end of 1993. The pressures to implement them at the national level will be primarily economic, not political. As individual countries liberalize their communications systems, profitable new businesses will emerge, serving both national and regional needs. The urge not to get left out will be a powerful incentive for other governments to open up their telecommunications sector to more competition. The alternative was outlined by AT&T chairman Robert E. Allen in a 1992 talk to European executives:

> Customers have power, and they have options. They can shift their investments to countries where the telecommunications system provides competitive choices. Or, if they choose, the technology gives them the option of bypassing national networks.[20]

Setting up a Regulatory Framework for Administering Current and Future Telecommunications Directives

The EC directives process has been described as a competition between thirteen regulatory systems—twelve in the member states and the thirteenth in Brussels.[21] Now that most EC telecommunications directives are in place, the question of monitoring and regulating their application becomes critical. The Commission has moved carefully in this area. A July 1992 proposal by the Commission proposed setting up a Community Telecommunications Committee—a somewhat watered-down version of the tougher regulatory watchdog group advocated by some Eurocrats.

The Community Telecommunications Committee would be made up of national regulatory authorities. Its purpose is to help the Commission develop future Community-wide telecommunications arrangements, including the issuance of what would be called "Single Community Telecommunications

Licenses." Region-wide licensing would presumably end the present practice whereby member states unilaterally license telecommunications services if they can argue that it is necessary to meet special local circumstances.[22] Progress in implementing the Telecommunications Committee proposal was initially slow, although many industry observers see it as a useful step toward establishing Brussels's regional authority to override protectionist national practices.[23]

EC-watchers in Brussels point out that bureaucratic infighting within the Commission will be an important element in determining how its regulatory role in telecommunications will be shaped. The bureaucracies involved are DG-4, the directorate-general that deals with competition and antitrust policy, and DG-13, the telecommunications directorate-general. Both have a stake in how EC industrial policy in the communications sector is finally resolved.

Expanding EC Deregulation to Include Voice Telephone Services

As noted earlier, the telecommunications services deregulated under EC rules by the end of 1992 represent about 5 percent of all such services in the Community. For political reasons, the Commission backed off from even a partial deregulation of ordinary public voice telephone services—the other 95 percent are jealously guarded as a lucrative monopoly by eleven of the twelve telecommunications administrations. The exception is the United Kingdom, which has moved cautiously but steadily toward voice telephone competition.

This situation is changing. By 1992, the Commission indicated that it was prepared to take on the sticky issue of deregulating monopolies in voice telephone services as well as national network infrastructures. The initiative was led by Sir Leon Brittan, EC commissioner in charge of competition. He argued that deregulation was needed, among other reasons, to reduce the excessively high tariff charges Europeans paid for telephone calls—often four times greater for a three-minute long-distance call as the same call over the same distance in the United States.[24] Despite overwhelming evidence of the need to change for economic efficiency reasons, most EC member states have resisted attempts to introduce competition to their monopolistic voice-telephone services.

This opposition has been the primary factor in delaying Commission actions in this area. In October 1992, it issued a watered-down document on the subject, calling for a six-month "consultative period" for member states and other interested parties to provide their views on four options ranging from doing nothing to full liberalization of telephone services.[25]

Integrating EC Telecommunications with the Rest of Europe

Given the nature of telecommunications technology, the Community's infrastructure must be integrated with those in the rest of Europe. This will not be difficult in the EFTA countries, whose communications systems are, by and large, technically and operationally compatible with the EC's new regulations.

The former Communist countries of Central Europe are another matter. Without exception, their telecommunications systems were kept at Third World standards over the past forty years, with the added burden of being tied to Soviet technical and operational patterns. They all face daunting problems in upgrading these systems, including integrating them into the Western European network.

This will be a slow process. The best prospects lie in eastern Germany, where the Federal Republic is committed to a $30 billion, five-year effort to upgrade telecommunications.[26] In other parts of Central Europe, both the European Community and the European Bank for Reconstruction and Development have given high priority to telecommunications in their aid efforts. In 1991, PHARE, the EC's program for supporting Eastern European reconstruction, began initial funding of telecommunications projects in Poland and Bulgaria.

In summary, there is still some distance to go before attaining a Western European telecommunications resource capable of matching the region's political and economic needs. Nevertheless, the Europe 1992 initiatives have played a critical role by eliminating many of the political, economic, and technical barriers that have blocked regional integration in this sector. The EC directives have defined the basic regulatory ground rules for a regional telecom system. Getting these rules approved and enforced has proven more difficult. Century-old PTT monopolies are not easily changed. The economic imperative to develop an integrated regional network is the most powerful factor in generating and sustaining the EC telecom reforms. The countries that lag in strengthening their networks to meet national and regional needs will be increasingly disadvantaged as Europe's economic integration continues.

Notes

1. For a useful survey of the evolution of European Community telecommunications policies, see Michel Carpentier, Sylviane Farnoux-Toporkoff, and Christian Farric, *Telecommunications in Transition* (New York: John Wiley & Sons, 1992). See also Thomas J. Ramsey, "Europe Responds to the Challenge of the New Information Technologies: a Teleinformatics Strategy for the Nineties," *Cornell International Law Review* 14 (1981), pp. 237–285.

2. Quoted in *European Trends* no. 2, The Economist Intelligence Unit, 1989, p. 49.

3. Michel Carpentier, "The Single European Market and Telecommunications in a World Context," *Single Market Communications Review,* January 1991, p. 28.

4. "Data Networks Disappoint," *Communications Week International,* July 16, 1990, p. 1.

5. *On the Development of the Common Market for Telecommunications Services and Equipment,* Report COM 87(260), Commission of the European Communities, Brussels, 1987. For an analysis of the Green Paper, see Morris Crawford, "The Common Market for Telecommunications and Information Services," Center for Information Policy Research, Harvard University, Report P-90-6, July 1990.

6. "The Search for Equity Continues," *Communications Week International,* December 16, 1991, p. C-14.

7. *On the Development of the Common Market for Telecommunications Services and Equipment,* op. cit., p. 9.

8. The Open Network provisions are analyzed in William B. Garrison, "The European Telecommunications Directives: Provisions Requiring Regulatory Restructuring," *Communications Committee Monograph Series* 1990–1992. Section of International Law and Practice, American Bar Association, August 1990. See also: Robert M. Frieden, "Open Telecommunications Policies for Europe: Promises and Pitfalls," *Jurimetrics Journal,* Spring 1991, pp. 319–328.

9. Oliver Stehmann, "Liberalizing the Intra-EC Long- distance Market: Promoting Competition in Basic Telephone Services," *Telecommunications Policy,* April 1991, pp. 129–136.

10. For a survey of the opportunities and barriers involved in the EC satellite proposals, see Susan Bruno, ed., *The New European Satellite Smorgasbord,* Center for Strategic and International Studies (Washington: 1992).

11. Shawn Tully, "Europe Goes on a Telephone Binge," *Fortune,* August 28, 1989, p. 107.

12. "Euro-infrastructure Group Proposed," *Communications Week International,* May 11, 1992, p. 6.

13. "Plugging Into Each Other's Strengths," *Financial Times,* March 27, 1992, p. 23.

14. "A French Giant Stalks the U.S. Telephone Market," *New York Times,* November 25, 1991, p. D-1.

15. "Carriers Storm U.S.," *Communications Week International,* May 11, 1992, p. 9.

16. "Brr-Ring! America Calling," *Business Week,* June 1, 1992, p. 98.

17. "French Telecom Industry Warned Over Competition," *Financial Times,* June 18, 1991, p. 12.

18. Quoted in *Eurocom,* Bulletin of the Commission of the European Communities 4 no. 6 (June 1992), p. 3.

19. Anton Lensen, *Concentration in the Media Industry: The European Community and Mass Media Regulation* (Washington, D.C.: The Annenberg Washington Program in Communications Policy Studies of Northwestern University, 1992).

20. Quoted in "Dialing for European Phone Dollars," *Washington Post,* August 9, 1992, p. H-1.

21. Brian Hindley, "Trade in Services Within the European Community," in *Free Trade in the World Economy,* Herbert Griersch, ed., (Boulder: Westview Press, 1987), pp. 278–280.

22. The details are discussed in "Proposal for a Council Directive on . . . the establishment of a Single Community Telecommunications License and the setting up of a Community Telecommunications Committee (CTC)." Commission of the European Communities. COM(92) 254 final - Syn 438. Brussels, 15 July 1992.

23. "License Agency Proposed," *Communications Week International,* April 6, 1992, p. 4.

24. "Brittan Critical of Telephone Monopolies," *Financial Times,* February 2, 1992, p. 2.

25. "Vote Yes," *Communications Week International,* September 21, 1992, p. 50.

See also: "EC Targets Tariffs," *Communications Week International,* May 11, 1992, p. 1; Oliver Stehmann, "Liberalizing the Intra-EC Long-distance Market," *Telecommunications Policy,* April 1991, pp. 129–136; "The Wimps Win," *The Economist,* October 24, 1992, p. 83.

26. For a survey of the Federal Republic's activities, see *Germany in Transition: The Telecom Challenge,* International Communications Studies Program (Washington: Center for Strategic and International Studies, 1992).

20

EC Environmental Policy: Atypical Ambitions and Typical Problems?

Alberta Sbragia

Environmental policy now helps shape economic activity in most developed economies. It affects firms, governments, and individuals alike. Policies directed toward environmental protection increasingly influence business-government relations and relationships among governments as well as the operations of private and public firms, municipal governments, and households. In fact, attempts to control, remedy, or prevent environmental degradation affect economic activity in so many ways that environmental policy has become, if only implicitly, an important component of the political economy of advanced industrialized states.

Given the degree of penetration into everyday operations accompanying efforts to protect the environment, it is noteworthy that environmental policy may well be one of the European Community's most important success stories. Using the argument that "Western European man, as he moves freely from country to country within the framework of the Common Market, has a right to expect broadly similar environmental conditions at least as far as his own health is concerned,"[1] the Community moved into the newly emerging policy space opened up by concerns for environmental protection. In fact, it staked out an unusual degree of jurisdiction from the beginning of policy activity in this field. Brussels quickly claimed jurisdiction over issue areas within the member states that in a federal state would typically have been ceded to the center only grudgingly, if at all. Given that the first environmental measures were passed at a time when the Community had allegedly begun to slide into "Eurosclerosis" and that such measures did not rest upon a legal text explicitly granting the Community responsibility for environmental protection, the degree of authority that the Community claimed and the member states accepted is striking.

The role of the Community in this field is complicated by the fact that implementation and enforcement of EC directives lags behind, far behind in some cases, the legislative output. The Community has clearly had more impact on policy formulation and legislation than on policy implementation.

Nevertheless, if one assumes that institution-building will characterize this policy area as it has characterized the Community as a whole,[2] the staking out of "turf" in the formulation process is significant. There can be no implementation "problem" if the policy is not there to be implemented.[3]

Although we shall return to the dynamics of implementation, it is important to note at the outset that one of the reasons implementation is problematic is because of the very ambitiousness in jurisdictional terms of the Community's programs. The Community, for example, claimed jurisdiction in the area of municipal solid waste landfills at roughly the same time as did the federal government in the United States—a striking similarity given the significant power of Washington within the U.S. federal system in environmental policy.[4] Furthermore, the U.S. federal government does not publish "report cards" on the condition of state beaches as the Commission regularly does concerning the state of the member states' beaches. Since the post-1970 federal role in U.S. environmental policy is an unusually powerful one by U.S. standards, the degree of jurisdiction claimed by Brussels is significant given that the Community is not a federation. For any student of federal systems, the degree of penetration into the activities of the member states that Brussels claims in those areas of environmental protection in which it legislates is striking.[5]

The scope of Brussels's jurisdiction is particularly noteworthy because environmental protection was not even mentioned in the Treaty of Rome. The "common market" envisioned by the Treaty did not include an environmental dimension. Yet, in Ludwig Kramer's words,

> Community environment policy developed and flourished in the absence of explicit powers in the original EEC Treaty. . . . It says a great deal for the tactical and strategic skills of the Community administrations and the environment authorities in the Member States that the design and implementation of a Community environment policy was possible. A comparison of starting position and results between environment policy and other areas e.g., consumer policy, social policy, energy policy or transport policy, provides an eloquent illustration of this.[6]

By 1992, no discussion of the "single market" could ignore the environmental dimension of intra-EC trade.[7] The policy areas under the Community's competence included the whole field of environmental protection, encompassing those measures *not* linked to intra-Community trade and *not* necessarily involving transborder pollution. For example, in March 1991, the Council of Environment Ministers adopted a directive requiring all cities with populations over 15,000 to treat waste water with a secondary waste water treatment plant by the year 2000.[8]

By 1992, environmental protection, in fact, had become one of the most dynamic areas of legislative activity at the Community level. The Community regularly legislated in the field, and the policy area was widely viewed as firmly within the Community's area of responsibility. Although member states may have a stronger standard of environmental protection than the Community's standard in those areas not linked to the internal market, the overall dynamic within the policy sector has been one of significantly upgrading most of the member states' protection of the environment. While it is conceivable that the concept of "subsidiarity" might be applied in the future to this area and might dilute or weaken the Community's jurisdiction, at the time of writing Brussels is the center of environmental policymaking, which in turn is an integral feature of the Community. The Court of Auditors, writing in March 1992, began its report on the Community's environmental policy by noting that "over the years, the protection of the environment has gradually become an essential feature of Community activity."[9]

A Policy Overview

EC environmental law now covers all major areas. In the case of British environmental policy, for example, Nigel Haigh finds that "not many areas of policy have now been left entirely untouched by the EC even if the depth of EC involvement remains uneven."[10] David Vogel concludes that "by the mid-1980s, virtually all aspects of national environmental policy had been addressed, in one form or another, at the Community level."[11] Air and water pollution as well as, most recently, waste have received the most legislative attention, but the Community has also legislated in the areas of chemicals, wildlife, and noise.[12]

Community influence over environmental policy must be differentiated by issue area and, to a lesser extent, by country. (In general, Community policies have been a significant influence in all member states except Denmark.) In examining the British case, Haigh concludes that

> some fields, such as the control of hazardous chemical substances, have largely been defined by EC policy. Others, such as pollution of air and water, while profoundly affected by EC concepts, retain distinctively national characteristics. In contrast, town and country planning which plays such a central role in the protection of the environment in Britain has so far been much less influenced by the EC.[13]

The differentiation by issue area of "central" control is familiar to students of U.S. environmental policy.[14] In the Community's case, such differentiation means that political dynamics can vary significantly across issue areas within this policy arena.

Environmental considerations have become more important in the Community's external relations. The Community's relations with African,

Caribbean, and Pacific (ACP) countries, for example, reflect the cumulative impact of environmental activism. Lomé IV, signed in 1989, included new environmental provisions, including a ban on EC hazardous and radioactive waste exports.[15] The Community received a good deal of international notice when its proposals to the United Nations Conference on Environment and Development included a carbon energy tax as an instrument to limit carbon dioxide emissions (which contribute to the greenhouse effect).[16] Although the proposal was conditional on the United States and Japan also agreeing to impose such a tax, the Community's position indicated the growing acceptance within the Community of using economic instruments to achieve environmental protection goals.[17] Within the issue area of greenhouse policy itself, Michael Huber argues that "fiscal measures are at the center of the EC greenhouse policy and the entire political debate."[18]

Overall, the Community has been so active in the environmental area that in 1990 the Commission stated that "environment policy—developed in fits and starts over the last two decades—today commands a position at the very center of the European Community stage."[19] An important actor on that stage has not yet, however, materialized. In 1990, a European Environmental Agency was approved (EEC/1210/90) that, while not having the enforcement powers of the Environmental Protection Agency in the United States, would collect and disseminate comparable data on environmental conditions. At the time of writing, however, the agency has not yet been established, as the member states have been unable to agree as to where it should be located.[20]

Although the issue of the agency continues to fester, the Community took two steps in 1992 that may be of strategic importance for the development of the policy sector over the next decade. Both steps relate environmental policy more closely and more explicitly to economic questions and issues. Environmental policy is moving out of its "policy ghetto."

In March 1992, the Commission approved the fifth environmental action program, "Towards Sustainability," which stresses the integration of environmental concerns into other policy areas. Cross-sectoral integration is an issue which will receive more sustained attention in the future than it has heretofore. The Commission will focus future policy activity on economic sectors—industry, energy, transport, agriculture, and tourism—rather than on specific media such as air or water as it has done in the past.[21] Furthermore, the program emphasizes both the importance of economic or market-oriented policy incentives, such as tax incentives and the sharing of responsibility for environmental protection among a wide range of actors, including industry. The latter objective would be realized by the establishment of a general consultative forum that would provide advice on environmental issues and (perhaps most importantly) bring environmental and industry groups together in one setting. Mazey and Richardson conclude that if the forum is indeed established, "the two competing interests will have been incorporated rather directly into the policy process."[22]

Secondly, on November 4, 1992, the Commission, in a communication entitled "Industrial Competitiveness and Protection of the Environment," put forth the view that industries that operate in environmentally friendly ways develop comparative advantages that make them more competitive. The communication argued that

> environmental considerations themselves can improve the sources of or underlying requirements for competitiveness. In practice, environmental considerations can promote competitiveness in a number of ways: either through so-called "first mover" advantages at the time of the creation of substantial markets for environmental protection technologies . . . or through improvements to the organisation and management of the productive system, in particular as a result of the introduction of clean technologies.[23]

By conceptualizing environmental regulations as potentially strengthening international competitiveness, by arguing that environmental protection strengthens firms' competitiveness, the Commission challenged the notion of a trade-off between competitiveness and environmental protection. Such an argument has been made for some time by the Danes and the German environment minister, Klaus Topfer, who has defended his stringent environmental regulations as promoting the competitiveness and efficiency of German industry by forcing it to adopt new and more efficient technologies.

The argument that environmental regulations themselves can increase international competitiveness of firms through the introduction of new, more environmentally friendly production (rather than "end-of-pipe") technologies is potentially a far-reaching one. In fact, such a view, if widely accepted, would lead to a reconceptualization of environmental policy's role in a state's political economy. Environmental policy would be redefined as a central element of industrial policy.

Policy Evolution

The Community's first attempts in the area of environmental protection began in 1972. The heads of state and government, meeting in Paris in 1972 (several months after the 1972 United Nations Conference on the Human Environment, usually known as the Stockholm Conference), agreed with the Commission and the European Parliament that environmental policy should be developed at the Community level rather than through intergovernmental arrangements.[24] Although environmental policy is now often associated with the Single European Act, the latter actually represented only a step in the institution-building process that this sector had been undergoing since mid-1973 when the first environmental action program was adopted.

The movement by the Commission into the environmental arena before the passage of the SEA was significant. Between 1973 and 1987, roughly 100 directives (of which approximately twenty were important) were passed on environmental issues at the EC level. The primary focus of those directives was in the area of pollution rather than, for example, nature conservation.[25]

Although the stringency of such directives was not comparable to the stringency of U.S. environmental laws, the jurisdiction claimed by Brussels was striking. Given that the policy area was new, that the Treaty of Rome offered no explicit legal basis for action, and that the Commission claimed jurisdiction over environmental matters that were not necessarily related to trade or transborder pollution as well as those that were, the lack of controversy surrounding the principle that the Community should be active in this area, coupled with the amount of legislative activity that occurred, makes environmental policy distinctive.

The Commission's first proposal on environmental quality, adopted on June 16, 1975, concerned the quality of surface water from which drinking water was drawn. It symbolized the bold "staking of turf" that was to characterize Community environmental policy, especially when compared to many other policy areas. The scope of the directive was more far-reaching than national legislation and, strikingly, claimed jurisdiction over national water as well as that which crossed borders. In the Commission's words,

> at the time the directive was proposed, no provisions of the same scope and technicality existed in the national laws of the Member States. Belgium was the only country with legislation governing water quality, but this covered far fewer parameters than the draft directive and contained no provisions on water treatment like those in the directive. . . . Member States . . . were required to apply the directive without distinction both to national waters and to waters crossing their frontiers.[26]

On December 8, 1975, the Council of Ministers approved a directive dealing with the quality of bathing water. Again, "an examination of the legal position in the Member States revealed that no provisions of the same scope and the same degree of technicality as those contained in the draft directive already existed in the national legislations."[27] The member states were given ten years to bring their bathing water to the quality levels specified and also agreed to a certain frequency of sampling. It is because of this directive that tourists are now provided by the Commission with a "report card" on the environmental state of various beaches.

Although the framework directive (76/464) on controlling the discharge of dangerous substances into the aquatic environment had a conflictual legislative history, with the United Kingdom disagreeing with the other eight members, the United Kingdom did not argue that Brussels lacked the authority to legislate in this issue area. Rather, the argument centered around how standards should be set, an important issue for the content of policy but one that did not challenge the right of Brussels to set standards in the first place.[28] That pattern of conflict has also characterized other controversial directives.

In the period before the Single European Act, then, the Community was often bold in the stringency of standards it imposed when compared to its member states' standards (albeit not when compared to the stringency of U.S. standards), but it was always bold in the jurisdictional claims it asserted.

The Single European Act

The Single European Act, with its explicit discussion of environmental protection, is often viewed as the foundation of the Community's environmental policy. Yet the action programs and the directives that had marked the Community's efforts in the period 1973–1986 in fact laid the foundation for the SEA and for future policy activism. The Single European Act, for its part, gave the Commission a firm legal footing for future initiatives in this field, mandated the setting of high environmental standards in the construction of the environmental dimension of the single market (of particular concern to Denmark), explicitly allowed national governments to set higher environmental standards than those decided at the Community level if such standards would not act as nontariff barriers, and increased the European Parliament's role in the legislating of environmental policy (which was to be particularly important in the setting of auto emissions standards).

In the area of decisionmaking, the SEA changed the voting rules, thereby dividing environmental policy into two categories. Environmental measures linked to the creation of trade can be decided by qualified majority voting, while those measures linked to traditional environmental preservation goals require unanimity. Whether a draft directive should be proposed under the rules of qualified majority voting or of unanimity has been a source of controversy. In spite of the possibility for qualified majority voting, however, Hildebrand has found that such voting "was not used as frequently as one might have expected. Thus, at least until late 1991, much of the Community's environmental policy continued to be contingent on a unanimous decision by the Council."[29] Nonetheless, the Community has passed environmental legislation of increasing stringency in a wide range of issue areas.

In those areas linked to market integration, the balance between the construction of the market and the establishment of high environmental standards (which may act as nontariff barriers) presents a constant source of tension, with the European Court of Justice playing an important role. What is significant, however, is that the tension exists: the demands of the single market are not by any means taken as a given.[30]

Maastricht

The Treaty on European Union signed in Maastricht changes the Community role in environmental policymaking by emphasizing the issue of subsidiarity, including the precautionary principle,[31] strengthening the requirement that environmental concerns be integrated into other policy areas, and requiring that a high level of protection be incorporated in all environmental legislation (rather than simply in those areas linked to market integration). Perhaps its most important impact, however, will be on the process of decisionmaking. Under the SEA, those environmental measures agreed to by unanimity were referred to the Parliament for nonbinding consultation only. By contrast, those (fewer) measures decided by qualified majority voting increased the power of the Parliament by introducing the so-called "cooperation procedure."

Maastricht significantly extends the use of qualified majority voting (and the use of the cooperation procedure) for environmental measures and also introduces an extraordinarily complicated new procedure—that of "co-decision"—for some environmental legislation. Production standards, for example, will be subject to the new procedure as will pollution control standards. The "co-decision" procedure essentially allows the Parliament to veto proposals desired by the Council of Ministers.[32]

If Maastricht is ratified, there will be four different procedures that can be applied to legislation in the environmental arena, leading to a great deal of confusion. In the words of a recent study,

> the text of the new Article 130s agreed in Maastricht is not clear as to when each of these procedures should be followed, and arguments between the EC institutions over the appropriate procedure to be adopted in a particular case are bound to occur. It is likely that the Court of Justice will be called upon sooner or later to resolve these uncertainties.[33]

The Role of the Member States

This policy area is characterized by complex interactions between the Community and its member states, which diverge considerably from one another in their state of environmental awareness and administrative capacity for environmental protection. One cannot analyze the environmental policies of any member state by examining solely EC legislation *or* national legislation. In Nigel Haigh's words, "it is not possible . . . to understand the environmental policies of any of the Member States simply by examining EC legislation, and assuming that national legislation must be a reflection of it. EC legislation . . . has become inseparably intertwined with national policies and practices."[34]

Three member states—the Federal Republic, Denmark, and the Netherlands—have played key roles in shaping Community environmental policy by supporting stringent, far-reaching measures. In fact, much conventional wisdom holds that the national policies of those three "green" states are far more advanced than those of the Community. In the case of Germany and the

Netherlands, however, such has not always been the case. Von Weizsacker concludes that "without the EC many environmental regulations such as an ambitious directive on drinking water quality would not have been introduced even in Germany."[35] The same applies to the Netherlands. A recent study concluded: "Most EC environmental directives set standards exceeding those of the Dutch. In seventy-eight EC directives the standards were more specified or restricted than in the corresponding Dutch legislation of that time."[36]

The United Kingdom, until 1990, played a key role by delaying legislation and forcing compromises that were often interpreted by the "green three" as anti-environment. However, in 1990, the United Kingdom began to change its environmental stance in the Community and in national legislation came to be associated with such ideas as the integration of environmental policies into other areas and the use of "critical loads" criteria, both ideas favored by many environmentalists.[37] At the Edinburgh Summit of December 1992, however, the British, using subsidiarity as their rationale, tried to weaken EC environmental policy. The position was taken although the UK's ministry of the environment was opposed to such weakening, and it remains to be seen how the British position will evolve.

For the other member states, the Community's activism in this policy area undoubtedly had the impact of moving environmental issues up the political agenda faster than most national political elites would have done if left to their own devices. To generalize, environmentalists in all the member states except for Denmark, the Netherlands, and the Federal Republic of Germany view the Community as a progressive force in the field of environmental protection. In the case of Germany and the Netherlands, the Community has had more of an impact than is commonly recognized. Denmark is the outlier.[38]

Institutional Structure

As already mentioned, the Community's first action program was adopted in 1973. However, a directorate-general (DG-11) was not created until 1981. Although DG-11 is responsible for the "environment" item in the Community's budget, actual operational jurisdiction is spread out over a wide range of directorates-general. The Court of Auditors summed up this fragmentation well (a fragmentation, incidentally, found in nearly all national systems both inside and outside the Community):

> A number of departments have responsibility for specific aspects of environmental policy. DG XI (Environment, nuclear safety and civil protection) has a general responsibility in this field and handles the budget appropriations covered by the 'environment' headings. The Institute for the Environment

Table 20.1   Estimate of Community Expenditure on the Environment in 1991

	Period	Duration (years)	Total (in ECU millions)	Annual Average (in ECU millions)
Environment title of the budget plus support	1991	1	109.0	109.0
Environmental research:				
specific research program	June 1991– Dec. 1994	3.5	261.4	74.7
multinational JRC program	1992-1994	3	148.5	49.5
Structural Funds:				
Community support frameworks:			2,539.1	573.4
Objective 1	1989-1993	5	1,780.6	356.1
Objective 2	1989-1991	3	492.1	164.0
Objective 5b	1989-1993	5	266.4	53.3
ENVIREG	1991-1993	3	500.0	166.7
Objective 5a	1989-1993	5	39.0	7.8
Forests (articles B2-515 and B8-255 of the budget)	1991	1	20.0	20.0
ECSC operational budget	1991	1	30.0	30.0
			3,647.0	1,031.1

Source: Official Journal C245, September 23, 1992.

and the Institute for Remote Sensing Applications, both located at Ispra, are part of the Joint Research center. Within DG VI (Agriculture) and DG VII (Transport) there are specialized departments which deal with environmental and ecological questions. The terms of reference of DG III (Internal market and industrial matters) include the implementational aspects of several directives, such as combating noise pollution. DG V (Employment, Industrial Relations and Social Affairs) and the European Foundation for the Improvement of Living and Working Conditions in Dublin also have some responsibility in environment matters. Other aspects are the responsibility in particular of DGs XIV (Fisheries), XVI (Regional policy), XVII (Energy), XVIII (Loans and Investments) and the European Investment Bank.[39]

Expenditures in the environmental area are notoriously difficult to calculate, partially because so many activities can be classified as environment-related. The most authoritative recent calculation, drawn up by the Court of Auditors, came up with an annual expenditure of at least ECU 1 billion. The breakdown is given in Table 20.1.

Although the Court confirmed that environmental expenditures have indeed increased significantly, its report also confirmed what many suspected about the Community's environmental policy—that the problems now being faced were those of integration across sectors and of implementation. Legislative activity has been so intense that it by far outstrips that which is being done operationally after legislation is passed. Compliance with legislation has increasingly come to be viewed as a major problem. Cross-sectoral integration is becoming viewed as necessary, but an institutional response to the need has not yet crystallized.

It should be noted that both the implementation and the integration of environmental policy are exceptionally difficult, partially because of the intrinsic nature of this policy area and the degree to which it affects all actors in a given society. Although the United States was a pioneer in this area, it still faces serious problems of coordination and implementation.[40] Given that the central administrative capacity of the Community is much weaker than is that of the U.S. federal system, the problems outlined by the Court of Auditors are to be expected. How they are addressed—or whether they are addressed— will do much to shape the contours of the Community during the next twenty years or so.

The Commission's organizational structure—widely viewed as extremely fragmented and compartmentalized—is especially inhospitable to cross-sectoral integration. While the need for integrating environmental concerns in other policy areas is emphasized in the Fifth Action Program, it was originally raised in the Third Action Program on the Environment in 1983. Most subsequent legislation and thinking, however, has "ghettoized" issues linked to environmental protection.[41] A recent study conducted for the UK presidency (which, in the Council of Environment Ministers, emphasized the need for integration) concluded that attempts to integrate environmental concerns have met with only modest success, although some improvement can be noted in the past several years. There is little interest in such integration in many of the DGs, and the formal mechanisms needed to obtain such integration have not been developed.[42]

The lack of interest in environmental issues in many DGs—and, according to industry, the lack of interest in its perspective in DG-11—shapes the political dynamics surrounding issues with environmental implications. Environmentalists find it difficult to gain access to DGs other than DG-11, but even if that were to change, the fact that so many DGs' policies have environmental consequences makes the task of lobbying extremely arduous. (Greenhouse policy, for example, involved DG-1, DG-2, DG-3, DG-6, DG-7, DG-8, DG-9, DG-12, DG-17, and DG-21.)[43] Mazey and Richardson argue that the task of lobbying the Commission on environmental matters "demands vast resources if the 'environmental waterfront' . . . is to be covered properly."[44] Industry, for its part, defends its position by trying to rally Directorates General viewed as more sympathetic to industrial interests than is DG-11.

While cross-sectoral integration of environmental issues has recently become a problem worthy of note, the implementation (which in legal circles refers to the incorporation of directives into national law) and particularly the enforcement of environmental policy has been viewed with concern by the Commission and scholars for some time.[45] The problem has several facets, none of which can be discussed adequately here. Environmental policy is difficult to enforce even when strong administrative capacity and strong political will are both in evidence. Within the Community, the member states are responsible for ensuring compliance, and given the wide disparity in both administrative capacity and political will found in the Twelve, it is not surprising that compliance with the many directives agreed to in Brussels varies dramatically. The Court of Auditors, using on-site inspections, found many examples of noncompliance and concluded that "there is a significant gap between the set of rules in force and their actual application."[46]

Until now, the Commission has relied on interest groups to monitor the activities of national governments and bring noncompliance to its attention. Critics of such a strategy argue that the Commission has focused more extensively on those countries in which environmental groups are relatively strong and in which compliance is actually likely to be more widespread than in countries with weak environmental movements in which noncompliance may be widespread.

The Commission hopes to address some of the problems it faces in implementing environmental policy, according to the Fifth Environmental Action Program, by establishing a so-called Implementation Network. This institution is to bring together officials concerned with implementation from both the Community and the member states. Clearly, however, there will be an "implementation deficit" within the environmental policy sector for a long time to come, and the effectiveness with which it is addressed will determine whether environmental policy will in fact be considered a Community "success story."

Conclusion

The challenges to be faced by environmental policy in the next decade have emerged during the 1990–1992 period. The question of compliance will be viewed as of increasing importance since compliance in the face of others' noncompliance will be viewed as anticompetitive. Less familiar issues will also be debated. One will be the relationship between environmental regulations and the competitive advantages of industry, while another will concern those areas where cross-sectoral integration should be seriously attempted. Perhaps most concretely, the movement toward market-oriented policy instruments rather than legal regulation may well reshape much of the environmental policy landscape. Such instruments will introduce economic concepts (such as cost-benefit analysis) into a policy area where they have been conspicuous by their absence until very recently. While the past activities of the Community have been remarkable and surprising in many ways, the future policy debate is likely to be one in which the environmental and economic dimensions of human activity will be linked in ways unimagined twenty years ago.

Notes

I am grateful to Tom Allen and the University Center for Social and Urban Research at the University of Pittsburgh for research support and assistance.

1. Commission of the European Communities, *State of the Environment: First Report*, 1977, p. 13.

2. See, for example, Alberta M. Sbragia, "Asymmetrical Integration in the European Community: The Single European Act and Institutional Development," *The 1992 Project and the Future of Integration in Europe*, Dale L. Smith and James Lee Ray, eds. (Armonk, New York: M.E. Sharpe, 1993), pp. 92–109.

3. For an analysis that interprets the gap between policy formulation and implementation much more negatively, see Paul Hagland, "Environmental Policy," *The State of the European Community: Policies, Institutions and Debates in the Transition Years*, Leon Hurwitz and Christian Lequesne, eds. (Boulder: Lynne Rienner, 1991), pp. 259–272.

4. See, for example, United States General Accounting Office, *Non-Hazardous Waste: State Management of Municipal Landfills and Landfill Expansions*, GAO/RCED-89-165BR, June 1989; Linda Greenhouse, " Ruling on Peril of Municipal Waste is Overturned," *The New York Times*, November 17, 1992, p. A-11; "Europe: Early Draft of EEC Landfill Directive Would Have Major Impact on UK Practices," *Ends Report*, April 1990, Report 183, pp. 31–33; "Waste Management 85: Europe Sets a Test for the UK's Landfills," *Ends Report*, June 1990, Report 185, pp. 16–18; "Waste: Proposals for the Harmonisation of Landfill Standards," *European Report*, April 17, 1991, no. 1670, Internal Market Section, pp. 2–3.

5. For an analysis of how such penetration is cushioned, see Angela Liberatore, "Problems of transnational policymaking: Environmental policy in the European Community," *European Journal of Political Research* 19 (1991), pp. 281–305.

6. Ludwig Kramer, *EEC Treaty and Environmental Protection* (London: Sweet & Maxwell, 1990), pp. 23–24.

7. See, for example, "1992: The Environmental Dimension," *Task Force Report on the Environment and the Internal Market* (Bonn: Economica Verlag, 1990).

8. "Water Treatment: EEC Ministers Adopt Directive," *European Report*, March 19, 1991, no. 1662, Internal Market section, p. 7.

9. "Special Report no. 3/92 concerning the environment together with the Commission's Replies," *Official Journal of the European Communities*, Information and Notices, C245, September 23, 1992, 92/C 245/01, o.1.

10. Nigel Haigh, *Manual of Environmental Policy: the EC and Britain* (Essex: Longman, 1992), preface.

11. David Vogel, "Environmental Policy in the European Community," *International Environmental Politics and Policy: Some Recent Controversies and Developments*, Sheldon Kamieniecki, ed. (SUNY Press, forthcoming). Feeley and Gilhuly conclude that "the EC has enacted a substantial body of environmental law in areas such as air, water, waste, toxic substances, and noise pollution." Michael Scott Feeley and Peter M. Gilhuly, "Green Lawmaking: A Primer on the European Community's Environmental Legislative Process," *Vanderbilt Journal of Transnational Law* 24 no. 4, pp. 653–688.

For an excellent, succinct overview of the legislation in specific areas—such as water pollution, waste, air, chemicals, wildlife, etc.—see Nigel Haigh, "EEC: Policy and Implementation," *European Environmental Yearbook* (London: DocTer UK, Ltd for International Institute for Environmental Studies, 1990). For more detailed discussions of major directives in all issue areas up through the end of 1988, see Stanley

P. Johnson and Guy Corcelle, *The Environmental Policy of the European Communities* (London: Graham & Trotman, 1989). For a listing and brief description of all legislation by issue area through 1991, see Anne Van Goethem, *European Community Activities on Environmental Matters-1992* (Europe Information Service), pp. 25–79. For the most up-to-date listing of EC legislation, see Nigel Haigh, *Manual of Environmental Policy*.

12. The political dynamics surrounding legislation to limit car emissions have been particularly contentious and protracted. For two interesting studies of different phases of the negotiating process, see Ian Turner, *Environmental Policy in Europe: Uniformity or Diversity? A Case Study of the EEC Car Emissions Decisions*, CEED Discussion Paper no. 7 (London: The UK Centre for Economic and Environmental Development, and Henley: The Management College, March 1988); Charlotte Kim, *Cats and Mice: The Politics of Setting EC Car Emission Standards*, Working Document no. 64 (Brussels: Centre for European Policy Studies, May 1992); Sonja Boehmer-Christiansen and Helmut Weidner, *Catalyst versus Lean Burn: A Comparative Analysis of Environmental Policy in the Federal Republic of Germany and Great Britain with Reference to Exhaust Emission Policy for Passenger Cars 1970–1990* (Wissenschaftszentrum Berlin Für Sozialforschung [WZB]), FS II 92–304, 1992.

13. Nigel Haigh, *Manual of Environmental Policy*, preface.

14. See, for example, Harvey Lieber, "Federalism and Hazardous Waste Policy," *The Politics of Hazardous Waste Management*, James P. Lester and Ann O'M. Bowman, eds. (Durham, North Carolina: Duke University Press, 1983), pp. 60–72; Richard N. L. Andrews, "Environmental Policy-making in the United States," *Towards a Transatlantic Environmental Policy* (Washington, DC: The European Institute, January 1992), p. 108.

15. Commission of the European Communities, Directorate General for Information, Communication, Culture, *Environment in Development: European Community Policy and Action*, Europe Information, June 1992, pp. 7–9.

16. See, for example, Commission of the European Communities, Directorate General for Economic and Financial Affairs, "The Climate Challenge: Economic Aspects of the Community's Strategy for Limiting CO_2 Emissions," *European Economy*, no. 51 (May 1992); House of Lords, Select Committee on the European Communities, *Carbon/Energy Tax*, Session 1991–92, 8th Report (London: HMSO, 1992); Mark Pearson and Stephen Smith, *The European Carbon Tax: An Assessment of the European Commission's Proposals* (London: Institute for Fiscal Studies, December 1991).

17. See, for example, Michael Grubb and Chris Hope, "EC Climate Policy: Where there's a will . . ." *Energy Policy* 20 no. 11 (November 1992), pp. 1110–1114.

18. Michael Huber, "The EC Greenhouse Policies, 1988–1992," Working Paper, European Policy Unit, European University Institute, June 1992, p. 21. See also Markus Jachtenfuchs and Michael Huber, "Institutional Learning in the European Community: The Response to the Greenhouse Effect," *European Integration and Environmental Policy*, J.D. Liefferink, P.D. Lowe, and A.P.J. Mol, eds., (London: Belknap, forthcoming).

19. *Environmental Policy in the European Community*, Fourth Edition, European Documentation (Luxembourg: Office for Official Publications of the European Communities, 1990), p.5.

20. The financing of environmental projects has fared somewhat better. On December 12, 1991, the Council of Ministers established a financial instrument for the environment (LIFE). It will finance priority projects and was given an initial budget of ECU 400 million. Anne Van Goethem, *European Community Activities*, p. 4.

21. For an interesting reaction to the action program, see "Opinion on the Proposal for a Resolution of the Council of the European Communities on a Community Programme of Policy and Action in Relation to the Environment and Sustainable Development," Economic and Social Committee, COM(92) 23 final, July 1, 1992.

22. Sonia Mazey and Jeremy Richardson, "EC Policy-Making: An Emerging European Policy Style," *European Integration and Environmental Policy,* Duncan Liefferink and Philip Lowe, eds. (London: Belhaven Press, forthcoming, 1993).

23. *Industrial Competitiveness and Protection of the Environment,* Communication of the Commission to the Council and to the European Parliament, p. 1. See also "Industry/Environment: Promoting Competitive but Green Business Activities," *Europe Environment* no. 398 (November 17, 1992), Section I, pp. 1–2.

24. Hildebrand argues that "it is clearly in light of the fear of trade distortions that the Federal Republic of Germany and the Netherlands were among the strongest supporters of a concerted Community environmental policy." Philipp M. Hildebrand, "The European Community's Environmental Policy: 1957 to '1992': From Incidental Measures to an International Regime?" *Environmental Politics* (forthcoming).

25. *The European Community and the Environment,* Third Edition, European Documentation (Luxembourg: Office for Official Publications of the European Communities, 1987), p. 29.

26. Commission of the European Communities, *State of the Environment,* First Report, 1977, p. 21.

27. Ibid.

28. See, for example, D. Taylor, G. Diprose, and M. Duffy, "EC Environmental Policy and the Control of Water Pollution: The Implementation of Directive 76/464 in Perspective," *Journal of Common Market Studies* 24 no.3 (March 1986), pp. 224–246.

29. Philipp M. Hildebrand, "The European Community's Environmental Policy."

30. For an overview of the Single European Act and its impacts, see Ludwig Kramer, "The Single European Act and Environment Protection: Reflections on Several New Provisions in Community Law," *Common Market Law Review* 24 (1987), pp. 659–688; Philipp M. Hildebrand, "The European Community's Environmental Policy."

31. Jorgen Henningsen defines the precautionary principle as saying "that action should be taken in spite of some uncertainty about whether a chemical might be deadly, toxic or carcinogenic, or even in spite of some uncertainty about whether a certain temperature increase on the global climate will happen in 30 or 50 or 80 years." Jorgen Henningsen, "The Seven Principles of European Environmental Policies," *Towards a Transatlantic Environmental Policy: Conclusions from an International Round Table Seminar* (Washington: The European Institute, 1992), p. 26.

32. For a discussion of the impact of the Treaty on European Union on environmental policy, see Nigel Haigh, *Manual of Environmental Policy,* pp. 2.3–2.6; and Barbara Verhoeve, Graham Bennett, and David Wilkinson, *Maastricht and the Environment* (London: Institute for European Environmental Policy, 1992), pp. 26–30.

33. Ibid., p. 27.

34. Nigel Haigh, "EEC: Policy and Implementation," p. 62.

35. Ernst U. von Weizsacker, "Environmental Policy," *The Federal Republic of Germany and EC Membership Evaluated,* Carl-Christoph Schweitzer and Detef Karsten, eds. (New York: St. Martin's, 1990), p. 51.

36. Marco H.J.M van Maasacker and Maarten J. Arentsen, "Environmental Policy," *The Netherlands and EC Membership Evaluated,* Menno Wolters and Peter Coffey, eds. (New York: St. Martin's, 1990), p. 76.

37. Marc Levy, "The Greening of the United Kingdom: An Assessment of Competing Explanations," paper delivered at the annual meeting of the American Political Science Association, 1991.

38. After comparing 140 environmental directives with their Danish counterparts, Lise Lyck concluded that "any interpretation of EC standards as maximum standards will lower the Danish environmental level." Lise Lyck, "Environmental Policy," *Denmark and EC Membership Evaluated,* Lise Lyck, ed. (New York: St. Martin's Press, 1992), p. 143.

39. "Special Report No 3/92 concerning the environment together with the Commission's Replies," *Official Journal of the European Communities,* Information and Notices, C245, September 23, 1992, 92/C 245/01, 1.10.

40. See, for example, United States General Accounting Office, *Observations on Compliance and Enforcement in EPA's Drinking Water Program,* May 10, 1991, GAO/T-RCED-91-47; United States General Accounting Office, *Drinking Water: Compliance Problems Undermine EPA Program as New Challenges Emerge,* June 8, 1990, GAO/RCED-90-127.

41. Markus Jachtenfuchs and Michael Huber, *Institutional Learning,* argue that the traditional view of environmental policy "considers the economy and the environment as two separate spheres. Environmental problems . . . stand for themselves. They have to be solved by means of environmental policy (standard-setting), typically by 'end-of-pipe' technologies."

42. David Baldock et al., *The Integration of Environmental Protection Requirements into the Definition and Implementation of Other EC Policies* (London: Institute for European Environmental Policy, 1992), p. 18.

43. Michael Huber, "The EC Greenhouse Policies," p. 26.

44. Sonia Mazey and Jeremy Richardson, "Environmental Groups and the EC: Challenges and Opportunities," *Environmental Politics* 1 no. 4 (1992).

45. See, for example, C.M.S. Glim, *European Environmental Legislation: What Does It Really Mean? An Exploratory Study on the Implementation of Three EC Environmental Directives in the Memberstates* (Delft, Netherlands: Eburon, 1990); *Implementation and Enforcement of Environmental Legislation,* Select Committee on the European Communities, House of Lords, Session 1991–1992, 9th Report (London: HMSO, Volumes I & II); "Environmental Policy in the European Community: The Problem of Implementation in Comparative Perspective," *Towards a Transatlantic Environmental Policy: Conclusions from an International Round Table Seminar* (Washington: The European Institute, 1992); Ludwig Kramer, "EEC Treaty and Environmental Protection," pp. 4–7.

46. Court of Auditors, "Special Report No 3/92 Concerning the Environment Together with the Commission's Replies," *Official Journal of the European Communities,* 92/C 245/01, September 23, 1992, p. 5.2.

21

1992:
Who Wins? Who Loses?

Dale L. Smith & Jürgen Wanke

With the signing of the Single European Act in February 1986, the European Community set in motion a remarkable period of accomplishment and progress. After fifteen years in which the most common perception was one of stagnation and "Eurosclerosis," the EC was again on the move under the banner of "1992." Throughout the late 1980s, the Community moved steadily toward its goal, and that progress, combined with the new possibilities that resulted from the end of the Cold War, led both Community and national leaders to begin planning for the next step in the process of integration. Those plans culminated with the Maastricht Treaty on European Union in December 1991. Divisive debates resulting from the Treaty will likely slow the progress of future integration. However, differences of opinion on how and when to move to the next stage in the process of integration are separate from the issue of completing the internal market by 1992. That objective was accomplished, and the vast majority of the changes required for the single market were in place by January 1993.

Unlike the Maastricht Treaty, there is still widespread agreement that the single market will result in net benefits to the Community. Economic theory, as well as most empirical studies, furnish evidence that important, long-term benefits will be derived from the 1992 project. However, even if we agree that completion of the single market will produce net gains in Community welfare, there is no reason to believe that the costs and benefits will be borne equitably by all member states. The French debate over the Maastricht Treaty illustrates the increasing importance of distributional issues within the EC, and if the consequences of 1992 further aggravate existing asymmetries within the Community, then the conflict between the winners and losers will be a significant impediment to further integration. For these reasons it is important to go beyond the earlier focus on *net* benefits at the *Community* level and begin to examine the potential distribution of the costs and benefits among the member states.

Interestingly, however, the distribution of gains and losses *within* the

Community has not been a primary focus for those studying *European* integration. The economic liberalization and political reconciliation that accompanied the integration process in Europe was assumed to be good, and so early theories concentrated on explaining the causes of integration rather than its consequences.[1] Only in those issue areas and regions where the process has proved to be divisive have we found studies of the distributional consequences of integration. Within Europe these have clustered around two issues: Britain's membership and the Common Agricultural Policy (CAP).[2] However, when scholars in the 1960s and 1970s moved beyond Europe and began to examine regional integration attempts among developing countries, the question of who wins and who loses became a much more central concern. Gaps in the levels of economic development between countries in Third World integration efforts were often much larger than in Europe in the 1960s and early 1970s, and it has long been argued that integration between states at similar levels of development is likely to be much more successful than between states at very different levels.[3] Axline notes that Third World integration schemes based upon the European pattern of economic liberalization lead to "asymmetrical patterns of exchange and to polarization."[4] Not only does growth tend to cluster in the economically more advanced areas, but it also attracts economic resources from less developed areas within the community, resulting in poles of growth, as well as poles of stagnation.[5] This dynamic only serves to exacerbate already existing inequalities among the member states and increase the likelihood of conflict and disintegration within the community.

Earlier rounds of liberalization within the EC were among a core of relatively homogeneous states. For this reason, previous economic research virtually ignored the distribution of costs and benefits as it was assumed that the adjustment costs resulting from new stages in the integration process were relatively small due to the similarity of economic structures across the member states.[6] However, with the northern tier expansion in 1973 and especially the southern tier expansions of 1981 and 1986, in which Greece, Spain, and Portugal gained membership, the Community became considerably more heterogeneous. These were not the advanced industrial states of northern Europe, but rather states that still relied heavily on traditional, labor-intensive industries. Just as integration schemes in the Third World among states at different levels of development led to conflicts over the distribution of benefits, there could well be increased conflicts occurring over similar issues within the EC.

Our analysis of the effects of completing the single market on the member states examines the states' ability to take advantage of, and their vulnerability to, the types of changes the single market will introduce. Focusing on those industrial sectors that will be most affected by the completion of the internal market, we present analyses of (1) how these states have performed, relative to each other, in these "sensitive" sectors; (2) the extent to which each state is concentrated in expanding versus stagnant sectors; and (3) the degree to which they are likely to be affected—positively or negatively—by the single market changes. The final section summarizes the analyses.

The Crossnational Distribution of Costs and Benefits

As we noted earlier, attempts to determine the costs and benefits that will result from the 1992 program have usually focused on the Community as a whole. The EC Commission's own research project, which produced the Cecchini Report (1988), combines assessments of the costs of existing barriers with estimates of the benefits that will be derived from increases in market integration. Employing both microeconomic analyses of individual industrial sectors and macroeconomic simulations of the Community economy, the project predicts substantial increases in Community welfare. According to their simulations, the medium-term macroeconomic consequences of the completion of the single market will lead to a 4.5 percent increase in GDP; a reduction in consumer prices of 6.1 percent; and an absolute increase in employment by 1.8 million.[7] If governments exploit these improved economic conditions and change their policies in order to decrease their budgetary and balance of payments deficits, then the positive effects of 1992 will be substantially increased over the medium term. Under such circumstances, GDP could increase by 7 percent and 5 million new jobs could be created.[8]

From our perspective, the issue is not whether the Community as a whole will benefit; there is compelling evidence that it will. Rather, the issue is how the benefits, along with the costs, will be distributed across the member states. This is the key question, for it is these distributional issues that will help determine the effect of this step in the integration process on the ones that will follow. Even though we may not be able to determine with precision the extent of the benefits that will accrue to the Community following the completion of the single market, we can determine (on the positive side) which countries are in the best position to take advantage of these changes, and (on the negative side) which member states are most vulnerable to the sorts of changes that the single market will produce.

Our analysis of the costs and benefits of the completion of the internal market on industrial employment in the member states will proceed in four stages. The first step is to identify those economic sectors that are likely to be most sensitive to the sorts of changes entailed in the completion of the single market. They include markets that are heavily dependent on public procurement, as well as other sectors that have been traditionally protected by nontariff barriers, such as differing national standards. After identifying a set of forty "sensitive" sectors, the second step in our analysis evaluates the competitiveness of each sector relative to the same sector in the other member states. This provides an indicator of the performance of each member state in these sensitive sectors and helps in assessing which states are best situated to take advantage of the increased growth resulting from the completion of the single market. In the third step, we examine the degree to which each state is concentrated in the more desirable high-growth sectors, and in the final step, we focus on the extent to which a state's production in specific sectors conforms to its underlying comparative advantage.

Identification of the "Sensitive" Sectors

The analysis of the impact of the 1992 program on European industry requires, as a first step, the identification of those sectors that are most "sensitive" to the completion of the internal market. The removal of tariff barriers and earlier efforts at harmonization have already led to basically a barrier-free market in many industries, and these industrial sectors will be less affected by the 1992 program. However, significant barriers still exist in certain areas, and it is these sectors—those that will be most affected by the completion of the single market—that should be the focus of our analysis. For the identification of the sensitive sectors, we rely on a recent study by the EC Commission[9] that identifies forty industrial sectors (out of a possible 120) with one or more of the following characteristics: (i) moderate to high nontariff barriers; (ii) low levels of penetration; (iii) moderate to high discrepancy in the prices of identical products; and (iv) potential for economies of scale. A list of the forty sectors is provided in Table 21.1.

Crossnational Sectoral Comparisons: Performance

Having identified the industrial sectors to be studied, the next step is an analysis—in a sense, a snapshot—of the relative performance in each of these sectors across the member states. In our study, performance will be based on the intra-Community trade ratio, which is the ratio of intra-EC exports to intra-EC imports for a specific country and industrial sector. Country i's intra-EC trade ratio in sector k is defined as:

$$TradRat_{ik} = X_{ik} / M_{ik}$$
where
X_{ik} = exports in sector k by country i to the EC
M_{ik} = imports in sector k by country i from the EC.

This sector- and country-specific trade ratio is the best single indicator of how well a particular industrial sector in a particular country is performing *relative* to its competitors in other EC countries. For example, a trade ratio of 1.0 indicates that exports to other member states are equal to imports from those same states. A value well above 1.0 (exports exceed imports) is

Table 21.1 The 40 Industrial Sectors Most Affected by the 1992 Project

NACE Code	Sector Name	Sector Class	Factor Class
330	Office Machinery	1	1
344	Telecommunications Equipment	1	1
372	Medical & Surgical Equipment	1	1
257	Pharmaceutical Products	2	1
315	Boilers, Tanks & Containers	2	3
362	Railway Rolling Stock	2	3
425	Wine & Beverages Based Thereon	2	2
427	Brewing & Malting	2	2
428	Soft Drinks & Natural Spa Waters	2	2
341	Insulated Wires & Cables	3	5
342	Electrical Machinery	3	3
361	Shipbuilding	3	4
417	Spaghetti, Macaroni, Etc.	3	2
421	Cocoa, Chocolate & Candy	3	2
345	Electronic Equipment	4cns	1
346	Domestic Electric Appliances	4cns	1
351	Motor Vehicles	4cns	1
438	Carpets, Linoleum, Etc.	4cns	5
451	Footwear	4cns	4
453	Clothing	4cns	4
455	Other Textile Goods	4cns	4
491	Jewelery, Etc.	4cns	4
493	Photographic & Cine. Laboratories	4cns	1
494	Toys, Games & Sports Goods	4cns	4
321	Agricultural Machinery	4inv	5
322	Machine Tools	4inv	1
323	Textile Machinery, Sewing Machines	4inv	3
324	Machines For Food, Drink & Tobacco Indust.	4inv	5
325	Plant For Mines & Steel Industries	4inv	5
326	Transmission Equipment	4inv	1
327	Other Machinery	4inv	5
347	Electrical Lighting Equipment	4inv	3
364	Aerospace	4inv	1
247	Glass & Glassware	4int	1
248	Ceramic Goods	4int	1
251	Basic Industrial Chemicals	4int	1
256	Other Chemical Products	4int	1
431	Wool Industry	4int	5
432	Cotton Industry	4int	4
481	Manufacture Of Rubber Products	4int	1

Notes:
Sector Class:
1. High-tech, public-procurement related markets
2. Traditional, public-procurement and regulated markets (strong price dispersion)
3. Traditional, public-procurement and regulated markets (weak price dispersion)
4cns. Sector with moderate non-tariff barriers (consumer goods)
4inv. Sector with moderate non-tariff barriers (investment goods)
4int. Sector with moderate non-tariff barriers (intermediate goods)

Factor Class:
1. Sectors with high capital and R&D content
2. Sectors with a high capital but low R&D content
3. Sectors with high skilled labor content
4. Sectors with high labor content
5. Sectors with a low labor and capital content

indicative of a strong sector that is outperforming its competitors within the rest of the EC, while a ratio of less than 1.0 is evidence of a sector that is not performing well.[10]

We have used the following criteria to define strong, balanced, and weak sectors:

if $TradRat_{ik} < 0.9$ then sector k for country i is defined as weak;

if $0.9 \leq TradRat_{ik} \leq 1.1$ then sector k for country i is defined as balanced; and

if $TradRat_{ik} > 1.1$ then sector k for country i is defined as strong.[11]

Figure 21.1 contains the performance profiles of the member states. It shows the percent of industrial employment in each type of sector: strong, balanced, and weak. What is clear at a glance is that Germany has the highest proportion of its industrial employment in strong sectors (40.2 percent) while at the same time having the lowest percentage in weak sectors. Other countries that have a large proportion of their industrial employment in strong sectors include Belgium, the Netherlands, Italy, and Ireland.[12] France and Spain occupy a median position where employment in the balanced and weak sectors is larger than in the strong sectors. Finally, Greece, Denmark, Portugal, and the United Kingdom all have, on average, twice the employment in

Figure 21.1 National Performance Profiles in the Economic Sectors Most Affected by 1992

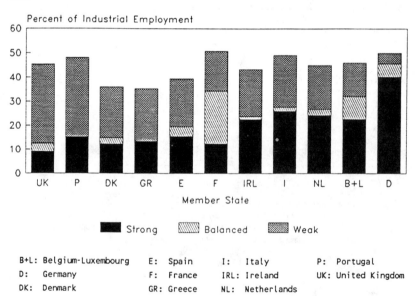

weak sectors as in strong sectors. The two poorest countries, Greece and Portugal, have no balanced sectors; they do well in certain highly-concentrated, labor-intensive traditional industries (e.g., clothing, wool/cotton manufacture, and wine) but show poor performance in high-tech, capital-intensive industries.

In order to obtain an overall assessment of how these countries are performing in the sectors that will be most affected by the completion of the single market, we have reduced these profiles to a single nation-level indicator. The proportion of industrial employment in each sector is weighted by that sector's performance score; 1 if weak, 2 if balanced, and 3 if strong. The results are then summed across the sectors and divided by the overall share of industrial employment in the sensitive sectors.[14] According to this indicator a "perfect" score would be 3.0, implying that all of a state's sensitive sectors are strong. Alternatively, if they are all weak, the composite score would be 1.0.

The results are shown in Figure 21.2. We have here a "snapshot" indicating how well each of the member states is doing relative to the rest of the Community in those sectors that will be most affected by the 1992 Project. One can easily identify four groups: (1) Germany; (2) Belgium, the Nether-

Figure 21.2 National Performance in the Sectors Most Affected by 1992

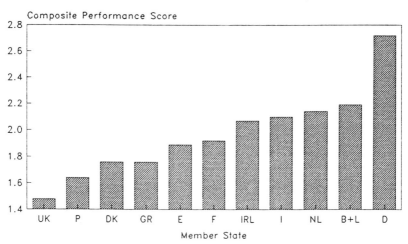

lands, Italy, and Ireland; (3) France and Spain; and (4) Greece, Denmark, Portugal, and the United Kingdom. That Germany has shown the strongest performance in these sensitive sectors is not surprising, but the gap between it and the other member states is impressive. The four states in the second group all have a majority of their sensitive sector employment in industries that have evidenced strong performance, and so their composite scores exceed 2.0. The proportion of strong sectors falls further in the third group—France and Spain—and the fact that their composite scores are below 2.0 indicates that the weak sectors are larger than the strong ones. In the fourth group— Greece, Denmark, Portugal, and the United Kingdom—employment in weak sectors accounts for more than half of the nations' sensitive sector employment. While Greece and Portugal do well almost exclusively in traditional or labor-intensive industries, Denmark does well in a mix of industry types from high-tech telecommunications to labor-intensive shipbuilding. Britain evidences reasonably strong performances in high-tech industries (with the exception of automobiles) but still has a large proportion of its industrial employment in labor-intensive industries where it does not fare well. It is useful to note that all of the original six members of the EC are in the top seven, based on our composite score. Ireland is the only latecomer that has managed to break into this group.

Crossnational Sectoral Comparisons: Demand Growth

Our composite score is a purely static measure based on past performance. It is useful because it provides an indication of how the countries lined up along the starting line as they prepared for the race to the single market. Germany began that race with a large lead, while the United Kingdom was standing well back of the line. However, to add a dynamic dimension to the analyses, we examine in this section how these sensitive sectors grew during the 1980s. Demand growth in a particular sector is an important element to success, and any state would obviously prefer to be concentrated in those sectors that are growing rather than in those that are either declining or stagnant.

Figure 21.3 presents the proportions of sensitive sector employment found in high, moderate, and low growth sectors. To measure growth, the average level of Community-wide production in a given sector during the 1980 to 1982 period is compared with average production in that sector during 1985 to 1987. If sectoral growth is less than 2 percent per annum it is labeled weak; if it is between 2 percent and 5 percent it is considered moderate; and if it is over 5 percent then it is judged strong.[14] The states have been ordered in Figure 21.3 based on the proportion of high growth sectors, and some significant differences can be seen when comparing this ordering with that in Figures 21.1 or 21.2. The biggest differences are that France and the United Kingdom jump from the middle and bottom of the pack, respectively, to the top. Relative to other types of sectors, capital- and R&D-intensive industries exhibited stronger growth during the 1980s, and they are typically concentrated in the northern member states. With the exception of Denmark, Figure 21.3 also clearly distinguishes between the more developed economies of the north and the less developed economies in the south.

While being concentrated in sectors that have grown well in the past is important, it is equally important to be performing well in those sectors. In order to analyze which states have been performing strongly in high growth sectors versus poorly in low growth industries, we have linked our indicators of performance from the previous section with the measures of growth to produce Figure 21.4. The proportion of industrial employment in sectors characterized by high growth *and* strong performance is plotted against the proportion of industrial employment in sectors exhibiting low growth *and* weak performance. A position in the lower right corner of the figure would be most desirable, while the upper left corner represents the least beneficial configuration.

Once again, Germany appears in a league of its own, highly concentrated in sectors that have been growing and performing strongly. In our analysis based on past performance (see figures 21.1 and 21.2), we identified a group composed of Belgium, the Netherlands, Italy, and Ireland, all of which

Figure 21.3 Demand Growth in the Economic Sectors Most Affected by 1992

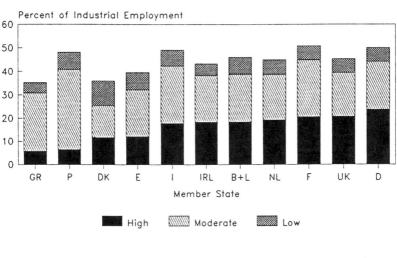

B+L:	Belgium-Luxembourg	E:	Spain	I:	Italy	P:	Portugal
D:	Germany	F:	France	IRL:	Ireland	UK:	United Kingdom
DK:	Denmark	GR:	Greece	NL:	Netherlands		

Figure 21.4 Performance and Growth in the Sectors Most Affected by 1992

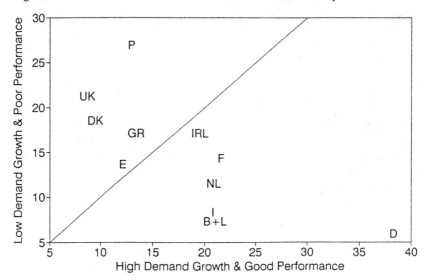

seemed to be performing at about the same level. However, Figure 21.4 illustrates some important distinctions among them. The four have roughly the same proportion of employment in sectors with good performance and high demand growth, but Belgium and Italy have less of their sensitive sector employment in poorly performing, low demand sectors. Ireland, in particular, has a much larger percentage of its employment in these less desirable sectors. While France and Spain produced almost identical results in terms of our composite score (see Figure 21.2), here we see a marked difference between them. They have essentially the same percentage of employment in low growth, poor performance sectors, but France has almost twice as much of its employment in high growth, strong performance sectors. Of the three newest members, Greece, Spain, and Portugal, it is clearly Portugal that faces the worst prospects, given a 2-to-1 ratio between the two types of sectors. Denmark has a ratio very similar to that of Portugal, and the UK, despite being highly concentrated in strong and moderate growth sectors (see Figure 21.3), has only 8.7 percent of its industrial employment in sectors with high growth and good performance, while over 22 percent is in low growth, poor performance sectors.

In terms of the consequences for one's economy, the effect of a strong sectoral performance is multiplied when EC-level growth in that sector has been relatively rapid. Therefore, Germany's strong performance profile is even more impressive given that it is highly concentrated in high growth sectors. In Figure 21.4 the distinction between the EC's founding members and the newer states is even more dramatic than in Figure 21.2. All of the original member states are well below the forty-five degree line, indicating that they are substantially more concentrated in sectors that are performing and growing well than in low growth, poor performance sectors. All the newer members, with the exception of Ireland, lie above the forty-five degree line.

Crossnational Sectoral Comparisons: Adjusting to the Single Market

In the previous two sections, our focus was on who might be able to take advantage of the completion of the single market. Equally important, however, is the question: who is vulnerable to these changes? Which sectors, in which countries, are likely to suffer negative consequences from the 1992 changes? We know what those changes will be, and in this section we use that information to investigate further the adjustments that the member states will face in specific types of sectors.

The 1992 program was a massive economic liberalization and deregulation plan. Its goal was to remove all barriers that distorted the efficient allocation of the factors of production and create a single, unified market. Traditional theories of international trade would argue that once all these noneconomic distortions are removed, the underlying comparative advantages of the member states become increasingly important. High-tech, capital-intensive industries (e.g., telecommunications) in countries that have an underlying comparative advantage in labor-intensive industries will probably shrink as the nontariff barriers and public procurement regulations that have protected them in the past are removed. The opposite argument holds for labor-intensive industries (e.g., footwear or clothing) in states with a comparative advantage in capital-intensive sectors. Therefore, if we let ourselves be guided by traditional trade theory, we would predict that as these barriers and distortions are removed, the underlying comparative advantages of the member states will become increasingly important in determining production profiles and trading patterns.

However, modern approaches to trade theory differentiate between interindustry and intraindustry trade. The more traditional form, interindustry trade, is still seen to be largely determined by comparative advantage as explained above. Intraindustry trade, in which there exists two-way trade in similar products, is explained not by comparative advantage, but rather by differences in tastes, technology, and rates of innovation, as well as economies of scale.[15] In the first case, entire industrial sectors could be reduced, if not eliminated, because they are no longer able to compete in this new unprotected environment. In the second case, the economic adjustments are less dramatic, as specialization occurs *within* industrial sectors. The distinction is important because many economists have noted that intra-EC trade, at least in the past, has been dominated by intraindustry trade.[16] As long as the members of the Community are relatively homogeneous in terms of their economic structures, the removal of barriers fosters intraindustry, rather than interindustry, trade, and increases in this form of trade produce fewer adjustment problems in terms of economic restructuring and unemployment. As Paul Krugman points out in reference to the expansion of EC trade in the 1960s:

> the specialization that took place as trade in manufactured goods grew tended to involve concentration on different niches within sectors rather than wholesale concentration of different countries on different industries. . . . In part due to the relatively benign character of the trade expansion it produced, the EEC in its years of rapid trade growth aroused fewer complaints about problems of adjustment than many had expected.[17]

With the growth of intraindustry trade within the Community, there were no big winners and no big losers, and so any changes in the distribution of costs and benefits were relatively subtle. These were the types of economic adjustments that resulted from the last important round of economic liberalization in the 1960s and will be a major part of the 1992 changes.[18] Therefore, in this section we want to identify empirically those national sectors characterized by interindustry trade, for it is in these sectors where economic gains and losses could be greatest. Comparative advantage will become more important as barriers are lifted, and if countries are not already specialized in sectors in which they have a comparative advantage, adjustments, in terms of losses of output and employment, could be significant.

The first step is to identify those national sectors that are characterized by intraindustry trade versus those that exhibit interindustry trade. To measure this we rely on the widely-used Grubel and Lloyd[19] coefficient, defined for sector k in country i as:

$B_{ik} = 1 - [|X_{ik} - M_{ik}| / (X_{ik} + M_{ik})]$
where
X_{ik} = exports in sector k by country i to the EC
M_{ik} = imports in sector k by country i from the EC
$| |$ = absolute value operator.

If bilateral exports and imports in a given sector are equal, then the Grubel and Lloyd (G-L) index will be 1.0, indicating complete intraindustry trade in that sector. However, if a country's imports or exports are zero, then the G-L coefficient will be zero, indicating complete interindustry trade. Ranging from 0 to 1, this coefficient provides a summary statistic for the degree of intraindustry trade, with high values indicating intraindustry trade and low values indicating interindustry trade.

In Figure 21.5 we show how the member states compare in terms of the proportion of industrial employment in those sectors characterized by either intra- or interindustry trade. We have defined as interindustry trade those

Figure 21.5 Intra- and Interindustry Trade in the Economic Sectors Most Affected by 1992

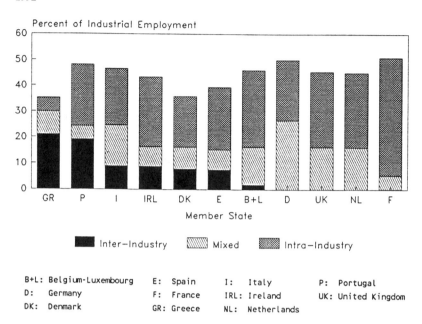

B+L: Belgium-Luxembourg   E: Spain   I: Italy   P: Portugal

D: Germany   F: France   IRL: Ireland   UK: United Kingdom

DK: Denmark   GR: Greece   NL: Netherlands

sectors in which the G-L coefficient is between 0.0 and 0.33, while intraindustry trade is found in sectors with G-L values over 0.67.[20] For instance, in Greece, 21 percent of industrial employment is in sectors characterized by interindustry trade, 8.9 percent is in an indeterminate middle range, and only 5.3 percent of industrial employment is in sectors typified by intraindustry trade. This can be compared with France, where there are no sectors characterized by interindustry trade, and employment in the sensitive sectors is almost completely concentrated in those industries exhibiting intraindustry trade.

In terms of the type of industrial trade, Figure 21.5 clearly illustrates the existence of three groups within the EC. In the first group, we find the core northern countries: France, the Netherlands, the United Kingdom, Germany, and Belgium. This group is characterized by no (or negligible) interindustry trade in the sensitive sectors. The states in this group are very similar in terms of factor proportions and, for the most part, exchange similar products. Except for Italy, all of the original six members of the Community are in this group. The second group—Spain, Denmark, Ireland, and Italy—have 8 to 9 percent of their industrial employment in sectors dominated by interindustry trade, while the two poorest countries—Portugal and Greece—compose the final group, with about

20 percent of their industrial employment in such sectors.

Since sectors dominated by intraindustry trade are likely to have fewer and less severe adjustment problems with the completion of the single market, we will focus the remainder of our analysis on those states that have significant levels of industrial employment in sectors typified by interindustry trade. It is these states that will be most vulnerable to the 1992 changes.

While the states in the second group all have about the same proportion of their industrial employment in sectors dominated by interindustry trade, a closer look reveals some important differences among them. In Italy, the sectors with low G-L values (i.e., low interindustry trade) have traditionally been strong performers; they include clothing, footwear, pasta, and wine. Clearly, the Italians are already concentrated in those sectors that one would expect based on their comparative advantage. Despite being one of the least developed economies within the Community, the 8.7 percent of Irish industrial employment in sectors characterized by interindustry trade is concentrated (6.5 percent) in capital- and R&D-intensive industries. While one might expect this to be a problem, these industries have performed very well in Ireland because foreign multinational corporations dominate the high-technology sectors, and these multinationals have a comparative advantage in such industries. Spain has performed strongly in only two sectors, wine and footwear, that evidence interindustry trade. Most of Spain's industrial employment that one finds in the other interindustry sectors is in areas where Spain could not claim a comparative advantage relative to the economies of the north. Finally, Denmark, the only "developed" northern economy in this group, has 7.8 percent of its industrial employment in sectors dominated by interindustry trade. It is in the unusual position of having half of that employment in the labor-intensive industry of shipbuilding. Though this sector has performed strongly in the past, pressures will likely increase as it is forced after 1992 to compete more directly with shipbuilding industries in the labor-rich countries of the south. All of the other Danish sectors characterized by interindustry trade have performed poorly in the past. To summarize, within this group of countries we can distinguish between Italy and Ireland, which already appear to be concentrated in sectors in which they have a comparative advantage, versus Spain and Denmark, which have significant levels of employment in sectors in which they do not appear to have a comparative advantage and could face sharp adjustments with the completion of the single market.

Greece and Portugal are probably in the most exposed position post-1992. Greece has 21 percent of its industrial employment in sectors characterized by interindustry trade, but only 9 percent of that employment is in the labor-intensive sectors in which Greece has a clear comparative advantage relative to most other EC members. The remaining 12 percent is in sectors in which Greece does not have a comparative advantage—mainly capital- and R&D-intensive sectors such as telecommunications and pharmaceuticals.

Similar to Greece, Portugal has 19 percent of its industrial employment in sectors characterized by interindustry trade, but it is much more highly concentrated (14 percent) in the labor-intensive industries (e.g., clothing and footwear) in which it has a comparative advantage. Only 5 percent of its industrial employment in sectors exhibiting interindustry trade is in capital and R&D-intensive industries.

Summary of the Analyses: Who Wins, Who Loses

Based on our analyses, the nation that seems to be in the strongest position is Germany. The strong performance of its industrial sectors and the dominance of intraindustry trade make it likely that Germany will not only be able to exploit the advantages created by the single market but will also be able to avoid the negative adjustments some member states will face. Add to this the fact that it is highly concentrated in those sensitive sectors that in the past have exhibited high growth, and it would appear that Germany is in a dominant position.

These conclusions are based on data drawn from the pre-unification period, and it is worth briefly speculating about how the costs of unification might affect the German economy. Higher taxes, larger budget deficits, higher interest rates, less money for investment, lower rates of growth, and increased social conflict are a series of consequences that have already appeared in light of the massive financial burden of rebuilding East Germany. Given Germany's central role in the EC economy, these policies and their consequences have reverberated throughout the Community. As the speed of the locomotive slows, then all the cars that follow also slow down, and so the most direct effect of unification will be slower growth for the EC economy as a whole. However, Community-level effects have not been the focus of our analyses. Our interest has been in shifts in the distribution of costs and benefits, and even here some possible consequences can be discerned. In addition to the financial drain on the West German economy, new consumers in the east also increase the demand for both domestic and international goods. As the German economy turns inward to satisfy domestic demand and imports more from other states, the bilateral, sectoral trade ratios that are at the core of our analyses could shift against Germany. Repeating our analyses of performance in the sensitive sectors with trade data from the postunification period would probably not change the rank order of the countries in Figure 21.2 but could well reduce the large gap between Germany and the other member states. In the short term, therefore, unification will lead to some reduction in overall EC growth, as well as shifts in the relative gains away from Germany. However, over the longer term, the productivity, technology, research and development, and financial and human capital that make Germany the dominant economic power in Europe will most likely be, in large measure, retained.

France, the Netherlands, Belgium, and even Italy also seem to be in strong positions and have good prospects in the years following 1992. Italy is the outlier here because it has a much higher proportion of its sensitive sector employment in labor-intensive industries. However, whether it is the high-tech industries of northern Italy or the traditional, labor-intensive industries of the south, our analyses provide evidence of the strong performance of Italian industry relative to its EC competitors. In summary, the original six members seem to occupy the strongest positions in this new single market.

The other three northern member states—Ireland, Denmark, and the United Kingdom—may not "lose" with the implementation of the single market but are certainly not as well positioned as the top six. As with Italy, Ireland has a production profile that includes concentration in both capital- and R&D-intensive industries and labor-intensive sectors, and at least in the high-tech sectors, it has performed well. However, unlike Italy, Ireland's capital-intensive sectors are almost completely dominated by foreign multinationals, and its traditional sectors have performed poorly relative to their EC rivals. In Denmark, the performance of the sensitive sectors has been relatively weak. It is concentrated in sectors characterized by low to moderate growth, and some of the labor-intensive sectors that are dominated by inter-industry trade could be negatively affected by the 1992 changes. For the United Kingdom, the good news is that employment in the sensitive sectors is concentrated in industries that have exhibited high to moderate growth at the EC-level. However, in terms of performance, it does not seem to be able to compete with other members of the EC. In addition, it has a higher than expected proportion of its employment (9.0 percent) in labor-intensive industries that have performed relatively poorly in the past, and these will probably come under increased pressure from more efficient producers in southern Europe.

Of the new southern states, Spain is probably in the best position. It has exhibited strong performance in high-tech as well as labor-intensive industries. Some of the capital- and R&D-intensive sectors that have performed poorly will come under increasing pressure from northern competitors with the completion of the internal market, but Spain, like Italy, appears able to compete in a broad range of industries. In Portugal, the negative adjustments are likely to be more severe, with many of the high-tech sectors that it has protected in the past being unable to compete in the new single market. However, Portugal's employment is relatively concentrated in traditional sectors where it has a comparative advantage. Of all member states, Greece seems in the most vulnerable position: almost all of its high-tech, high-growth sectors are characterized by interindustry trade, which implies the possibility of sharp, negative adjustments following the removal of barriers. Strong performances are concentrated in a handful of traditional industries, such as clothing, footwear, and the wool manufacturing sectors.

For Greece and Portugal, we suspect that the high-tech industries they have protected in the past will, on the one hand, be hurt by competition from the northern member states, but on the other hand, their labor-intensive industries such as footwear and clothing have performed strongly in the past. If they can exploit their advantage in labor-intensive sectors relative to the northern members, the gains they make in these areas will help ameliorate losses in the high-tech sectors. The result of such a scenario, however, will not be the economic convergence that occurred during earlier rounds of economic liberalization in the 1960s, but a divergence between a relatively high-tech north and a labor-intensive south.

Conclusion

Both economic theory and empirical analyses indicate that significant economic benefits in terms of growth and employment will result *at the Community level* from the completion of the single market. There will certainly be costs from this program, but overall, on a Community-wide basis, there are widespread expectations that economic welfare will increase. However, there has been almost no attention paid to how those costs and benefits will be distributed among the member states. Who wins? Who loses?

In this chapter we have attempted to address these questions by examining the industrial sectors that will be most affected by the 1992 project. Using both indicators of past performance and analyses based on the underlying comparative advantages of each state, we can begin to understand how the costs and benefits that result from the completion of the single market might be distributed.

Our results indicate that relative gains are likely to accrue (with some exceptions) to the more advanced states, while the less developed members are likely to experience relative, if not absolute, losses. The development of poles of growth and poles of stagnation—a pattern that led to considerable conflict and disintegration within Third World regional integration efforts— is an increasingly probable outcome due to growing heterogeneity within the Community. Given that differences in levels of development and economic structure will not disappear, at least in the medium term, the Community will need instruments, in the form of adequate regional development and structural adjustment funds, to allow it to redress those inequities in the distribution of costs and benefits that are likely to develop from the completion of the internal market.

This is not an indictment of the 1992 project. The attainment of a true common market was an important step in the much larger process of economic and political integration, but it was only a step. If the completion of the single market is to be a stimulus, rather than a brake, to future integration efforts, then we must recognize that there will be both costs and benefits to this project and that their distribution will be asymmetrical. Some will gain, others will lose, or at least not gain as much. Unless these issues are recognized and addressed, the disgruntled "losers" could seriously disrupt plans for further integration.

Notes

1. Theories of regional integration by political scientists did include the process distributional consequences as is clearly illustrated in Nye's revision of the early neofunctionalist model. According to Joseph S. Nye "Comparing Common Markets: A Revised Neo-Functionalist Model," in *Regional Integration: Theory and Research,* Leon N. Lindberg and Stuart A. Scheingold, eds. (Cambridge, MA: Harvard University Press, 1971), the perceived equity of the distribution of costs and benefits affects the "integrative potential" of any regional community.

2. With respect to the consequences of EC membership for the United Kingdom, see, for example, William Wallace, ed., *Britain in Europe* (London: Heineman, 1980); Ali M. El-Agraa, ed., *Britain within the European Community: The Way Forward* (London: Macmillan, 1983); and E. L. Grinols, "A Thorn in the Lion's Paw: Has Britain Paid Too Much for Common Market Membership," *Journal of International Economics* 16 (1984):271–293. L. Alan Winters, "Britain in Europe: A Survey of Quantitative Trade Studies," *Journal of Common Market Studies* 25 (1987): 315–335, surveys analyses of trade-related effects of British membership, and Jacques Pelkmans and L. Alan Winters, *Europe's Domestic Market* (London: Routledge, 1988), provide a very early study of the possible consequences of 1992 for Britain. Economic analyses of the CAP are numerous and varied, though a useful survey of the literature is Dimitrios G. Demekas, et al., "The Effects of the Common Agricultural Policy of the European Community: A Survey of the Literature," *Journal of Common Market Studies* 27 (1988): 113–145. One of the most thorough analyses of the CAP on member states is A. E. Buckwell, et al., *The Costs of the Common Agricultural Policy* (London: Croom Helm, 1982). Recent analyses, however, have begun to examine the consequences of European integration and recognize the importance of distributional issues for the continuation of the process. See, for example, the analysis of the Single European Act's political costs and benefits in terms of its effects on institutional developments and policymaking dynamics in Geoffrey Garrett, "International Cooperation and Institutional Choice: The European Community's Internal Market," *International Organization* 46 (1992): 533–560. In a study of the consequences of Community policy on Italy, see Alberta Sbragia, "Italy in the European Community: The Overlooked Power," paper presented at the annual meetings of the Midwest Political Science Association, Chicago, 1991. Sbragia finds that participation in the customs union has benefited the industrialized north, while the agricultural south has suffered under the policies of the CAP. Studies have also investigated the effects of recent integration efforts on non-EC states, particularly EFTA; see Jan I. Haaland, "Assessing the Effects of EFTA-EC Integration on EFTA Countries: The Position of Norway and Sweden," *Journal of Common Market Studies* 28 (1990): 379–400. For analysis of effects on developing countries see Ad Koekkoek, Arie Kuyvenhoven, and Willem Molle, "Europe 1992 and the Developing Countries: An Overview," *Journal of Common Market Studies* 29 (1990): 111–132.

3. Nye, "Comparing Common Markets," op. cit., pp. 210–211.

4. W. Andrew Axline, "Underdevelopment, Dependence, and Integration: The Politics of Regionalism in the Third World," *International Organization* 31 (1977): 83–105.

5. Ibid., p. 86.

6. Paul Krugman, "European Economic Integration: Some Conceptual Issues," in

Tommaso Padoa-Schioppa, *Efficiency, Stability and Equity: A Strategy for the Evolution of the Economic System of the European Community* (Oxford: Oxford University Press, 1987) p. 124.

7. Paolo Cecchini, *The European Challenge, 1992: The Benefits of a Single Market* (Aldershot, UK: Gower, 1988) pp. 97–98; Michael Emerson, et al., *The Economics of 1992: The E.C. Commission's Assessment of the Economic Effects of Completing the Internal Market* (Oxford: Oxford University Press, 1988) p. 208.

8. While the Cecchini Report remains the most extensive study of the consequences of 1992, it has been criticized from both sides. Tony Cutler, et al., *1992—The Struggle for Europe: A Critical Evaluation of the European Community* (New York: Berg, 1989) argue that the Commission study overestimates the benefits of the single market program. Richard Baldwin, "The Growth Effects of 1992," *Economic Policy* 2 (1989): 247–281, finds that the report seriously underestimates the dynamic benefits that will accrue to the Community. In a simulation of ten EC industries, Alasdair Smith and Anthony J. Venables, "Completing the Internal Market in the European Community: Some Industry Simulations," *European Economic Review* 32 (1988): 1501–1525, find that the removal of barriers will lead to modest welfare gains, but more substantial gains can be achieved through qualitative changes in firms' behavior that eliminates price discrimination between national markets.

9. Pierre Buigues, F. Ilzkovitz, and J.-F. Lebrun, "The Impact of the Internal Market by Industrial Sector: The Challenge for the Member States," *European Economy* (*Social Europe*), special edition, (Brussels: Commission of the EC, 1990)

10. An example of a strong sector would be German motor vehicles, with a trade ratio of 2.8, while the British machine tools industry, with a trade ratio of 0.56, is an example of a poorly performing sector.

11. We are forced to categorize the trade ratios because of the very skewed distribution of the actual values. While 86 percent of these ratios are between 0 and 2.0, about 2 percent of the national sectors have ratios that exceed 10. For instance, Spain's trade ratio for wine is over 20. However, this cannot compare with Italy's dominance with respect to the manufacture of pasta where the trade ratio is 739. As we move to the quantitative analyses that follow, it will become clear why we could not use the actual trade ratios, but had to rely on some sort of categorization. While our choice is admittedly subjective, we experimented with several more finely grained cut-points (as well as one that was coarser) but found that when weighted and aggregated to the national level to obtain an overall measure of performance, there were no significant differences among them. The use of 0.9 and 1.1 to categorize weak, balanced, and strong sectors was suggested in Buigues, et al., "The Impact of the Internal Market."

12. Any reference to Belgium in the text of our chapter actually refers to the Belgium-Luxembourg Economic Union.

13. The composite score (ComScr) is defined as:

$CompScr_i = [\Sigma_k \text{ (SecScr}_{ik})^*(Emply_{ik})\ ]/[\Sigma_k \text{ (Emply}_{ik})\ ]$

where

$SecScr_{ik}$ = sectoral performance score (1,2,3) in sector k and

$Emply_{ik}$ = share of industrial employment in sector k

The last term is necessary because the share of industrial employment in the sensitive sectors ranges from a low of 35 percent for Greece to a high of 51 percent for France (see Figure 21.1), and failing to take account of these differences would bias our composite score in favor of those states with higher overall levels of employment in the sensitive sectors.

14. Buigues, et al., "The Impact of the Internal Market," p. 107.

15. See Bela Balassa and Luc Bauwens, "The Determinants of Intra-European Trade in Manufactured Goods," *European Economic Review* 32 (1988): 1421–1437, for an empirical analysis of the determinants of intra-European trade in manufactured

goods.

16. Willem Molle, *The Economics of European Integration* (Aldershot, UK: Dartmouth, 1990) p. 191.

17. Krugman, "European Economic Integration," op. cit., p. 124.

18. Though the consensus is that intraindustry trade will dominate, David Greenaway and Robert C. Hine, "Intra-Industry Specialization, Trade Expansion and Adjustment in European Economic Space," *Journal of Common Market Studies* 29 (1991): 603–622, present evidence that the growth of intraindustry trade among OECD countries has stabilized and that Europe may be entering a new phase that could result in further interindustry specialization.

19. H. G. Grubel and P. J. Lloyd, *Intra-Industry Trade: The Theory and Measurement of International Trade in Differentiated Products* (London: Macmillan, 1975).

20. There is no agreement in the economic literature as to how to divide the continuous G-L scale into the distinct categories of intra- and interindustry trade. Others have used a G-L value of 0.5 to distinguish between the two types of trade; (see, for example, P. K. M. Tharakan and Jacob Kol, eds., *Intra-Industry Trade: Theory, Evidence and Extensions* (London: Macmillan, 1989). Given the large middle range in our definition (0.34 to 0.66, denoted "mixed" in Figure 21.3), ours is a relatively conservative categorization.

22

The Community Budget
After Maastricht

Michael Shackleton

The end of 1992 heralded not just the arrival of the single market but also the expiry of the financial framework that had been negotiated at the Brussels summit in February 1988 and that for five years had contained the budgetary disagreements amongst member states and between them and the Community institutions in the run-up to the establishment of a Community without frontiers.[1] The detailed provisions governing this framework obliged the Commission to present proposals for future financing by the end of 1991. The response of the Commission came in February 1992 when President Delors presented the new budgetary package that became known as Delors II.

What made this package of proposals of special interest is that it came two months after the Community had completed negotiations on the Maastricht Treaty, a treaty that sets much more ambitious goals than the Single European Act, signed in 1986, and in particular provides for a three-stage move to Economic and Monetary Union (EMU) before the end of this decade. If it is ratified and the Community moves toward EMU in accordance with the conditions specified in the Treaty, the effect on the budgetary policy of the member states will be considerable. They will be obliged, in particular, to apply strict budgetary discipline on their own budgets, with the specific obligation to avoid excessive deficits. A protocol to the Treaty specifies those deficits very precisely by indicating reference values that are not to be exceeded: 3 percent for the ratio of government borrowing to GDP and 60 percent for the ratio of government debt to GDP.

What effect can these changes and proposed changes be expected to have on the budgetary policy of the Community itself? Two kinds of response could be envisaged: one that the effort required to meet the criteria laid down for entry into EMU makes it essential to minimize growth of the Community budget; or alternatively that the very fact that national expenditure has to be limited makes it essential that the Community help to make up the shortfall.

This chapter will examine the tension between these two points of view in relation to the Delors II package but will argue that it does not itself provide a full explanation of the process of negotiation on the future shape of the budget. Rather one needs to consider the way in which the existing structure of the budget together with the prospect of future changes in that structure combined to constrain and direct the bargaining that took place between the member states and the Community institutions. The outcome of that process is not one that can be derived simply by considering the extra functions allocated to the Community or by the extra burdens imposed on member states by the Maastricht Treaty.

The chapter is divided into four main parts, followed by a brief conclusion: the first considers the contents of the Delors II package, drawing particular attention to the differences and similarities between it and the budgetary settlement agreed in February 1988; the second looks at the debate on the revenue components of the package and argues that the room for maneuver was severely restricted given the impact of any change on the balance of advantage between member states; the third looks at the argument on the allocation of expenditure and identifies the limited level of agreement on the budgetary impact of specific Community functions; and the fourth part is devoted to the specific issue of redistribution as a goal of Community budgetary policy, suggesting that the precise form and content of this goal is likely to become increasingly difficult to agree upon as and when the Community moves toward closer Economic and Monetary Union.

The Delors II Package

The contents of the Delors II package were presented by the Commission president to the European Parliament on February 12, 1992, just five days after the Maastricht Treaty was formally signed by the twelve member states. The link between the two events in the eyes of the Commission was quite clear from the title of the document that accompanied the presentation by the president: "From the Single Act to Maastricht and Beyond: The Means to Match our Ambitions." In other words, the aims laid down in the new treaty could only hope to be achieved if the Community equipped itself with sufficient budgetary resources.

This argument was buttressed by precedent. After the Single Act was signed, at the beginning of 1987 the Commission had presented a document designed to provide a financial framework for the five-year period leading up to the completion of the single market.[2] That document had provided the basis for lengthy negotiations that were successfully concluded in February 1988 at the extraordinary European Council meeting held in Brussels.[3] The Commission now wished to follow that example.

Both in 1987–1988 and 1992, the basic aim of the Commission was to establish a medium-term financial framework that would assure financial security for the Community and give the member states a clear picture of the level of their liability for a five-year period. To achieve this it followed a similar pattern on both occasions: it divided up Community expenditure into a number of categories and proposed a certain level of increase for each category over the following five years. Together these categories constituted what is described as a "financial perspective," providing an overview of the anticipated development of all Community spending.

In 1992 the Commission summarized its proposals for the perspective in terms laid down in Table 22.1. The proposal was that total spending should increase by some ECU 20 billion from 1992 to 1997, rising over that period to come to represent some 1.37 percent of Community GNP. In making this proposal the Commission maintained a very important aspect of the 1988 settlement whereby the volume of revenue available should be calculated in terms of a percentage of overall Community GNP. This meant that spending was geared to the fortunes of the Community economy as a whole rather than to the vagaries that could affect individual elements of revenue, as had happened before 1988.

In terms of the components of revenue, the Commission proposed to retain the four existing "own resources": customs duties, agricultural levies, a VAT percentage, and a GNP-related contribution. However, it returned to a suggestion that it had made in 1987 in proposing to alter the balance between the third and fourth resource in favor of the latter. Specifically, it suggested that the VAT call-up rate be cut from 1.4 percent to 1 percent, the drop being compensated for by an increase in the relative share of the GNP resource. It estimated that the effect would be to reduce the importance of the VAT resource from 55 percent to 35 percent of the total, taking the GNP component to 40 percent.[4]

As for the distribution of the increase in expenditure, the Commission sought to concentrate it on three specific areas: structural spending, internal policies, and external actions. Together these would represent over 80 percent of the total growth in expenditure proposed. The pattern proposed can be usefully compared with that laid down in 1988.

The most obvious similarity was the importance accorded to structural spending, referred to more commonly in terms of economic and social cohesion. At the Brussels summit in 1988, it had been agreed to double the structural funds, and as a result structural spending increased substantially as a percentage of total Community spending: by 1992 it had reached 27 percent of the budget compared with 17 percent in 1987. Now the Commission proposed to reinforce substantially the provision for economic and social cohesion to enable it to reach one third of the total by the end of the next five-year period. This was to be achieved by a two-thirds increase in the allocation for the least prosperous regions (defined under the regulations as objective 1 regions), by a 50 percent rise in the amounts allocated to the other structural policy objectives, including the regions affected by industrial decline (objective 2 regions), and by the inclusion of the new Cohesion Fund

Table 22.1 Financial Perspective Commitment Appropriations (ECU million 1992 prices)

	1992	1993	1994	1995	1996	1997
1. Common Agricultural Policy	35,348	35,340	37,480	38,150	38,840	39,600
2. Structural Operations	18,559	21,270	22,740	24,930	27,120	29,300
Structural Funds	17,965	19,770	20,990	22,930	24,870	26,800
Cohesion Funds	1,500	1,750	2,000	2,250	2,500	
(IMPs/Pedip)	594					
3. Internal Policies[a]	3,991	4,500	5,035	5,610	6,230	6,900
4. External Action	3,645	4,070	4,540	5,060	5,650	6,300
5. Admin. Exp.	4,049	3,310	3,465	3,720	3,850	4,000
Commission						
Institutions	1,696	1,760	1,825	1,890	1,960	2,035
Other Institutions[b]	895	930	960	1,000	1,040	1,070
Pensions (all inst.)	249	290	325	380	400	445
Buildings	287	330	355	450	450	450
(Repayments)	922					
6. Reserves	1,000	1,500	1,600	1,200	1,300	1,400
Monetary Reserve	1,000	1,000	1,000	500	500	500
Exceptional Exp.	500	600	700	800	900	
Total in Commitments	66,592	69,990	74,860	78,670	82,990	87,500
Payments Required	63,241	67,005	71,650	75,110	79,060	83,200
Payments (% GNP)	1.15	1.19	1.24	1.27	1.30	1.34
Margin For Revision (% GNP)	0.05	0.03	0.03	0.03	0.03	0.03
Own Resources (% GNP)	1.20	1.22	1.27	1.30	1.33	1.37

[a]Indicative amounts
set for RTD policy: 2,448   2,730   3,040   3,380   3,770   4,200
[b]Subject to confirmation by the institutions concerned.

that was agreed at Maastricht.

Under the terms of the Maastricht Treaty, this fund was to be established before the end of 1993 to provide Community financial contributions for projects in the fields of the environment and trans-European networks in member states with a per capita GNP of less than 90 percent of the Community average that have a program leading to the fulfillment of the conditions for economic convergence. However, the Treaty gave no guidance as to the level to be entered for the fund; so it was the Commission that took advantage of its power of proposal to suggest that it be accorded ECU 10 billion over five years, with ECU 1.6 billion already allocated in 1993.

As for the second and third priorities, there was an essential difference with the situation in 1987–1988. Then, a distinction had been made between policies with multiannual allocations, essentially research and Integrated Mediterranean Programs (IMPs), which constituted category 3, and other policies, including both external and internal policies, which made up category 4. Now the Commission proposed to create a separate category for external policy and to merge all internal policies, bringing research into the same category as other internal activities of the Community.

What this reflected was the very large increase in one component of the old category 4, namely, spending on external policy. In 1988 the resources allocated to external expenditure, essentially on development cooperation, totalled some ECU 1.2 billion; by 1992 it had trebled to reach ECU 3.6 billion, with more than one-third of that total reserved for Central and Eastern Europe and the former Soviet Union. Now it was proposed that both internal and external policies should grow substantially between 1993 and 1997, category 3 by 53 percent and category 4 by 55 percent. These increases were not as great as those that had actually taken place in the old categories 3 and 4 between 1988 and 1992 (both had grown by more than 100 percent in real terms), but they were still larger than those proposed for any other category in percentage terms.

In absolute terms, not only were the increases in the structural funds greater, but so too were those relating to agricultural guarantee spending. The Commission proposed maintaining the guideline established in 1988 for managing CAP spending, but the amount allocated was still anticipated to grow by ECU 4.26 billion in real terms up to 1997. However, such growth included an amount of ECU 1.5 billion that the Commission felt was necessary to cover the estimated costs of the reforms that were in the process of being negotiated. Even so, the allocation for agriculture was destined to drop from 50 percent to 45 percent of the total by 1997.

Overall, the structure proposed by the Commission bore considerable resemblance to that which was agreed in Brussels in 1988. The components of revenue, the way of calculating the total level of revenue in terms of Community GNP, the use of a financial perspective divided into categories of expenditure, and, the stress on economic and social cohesion, all gave an aura of familiarity to the Commission proposals of 1992. However, these broad similarities concealed important differences that arose above all from the changes that had occurred in the Community and around it since 1988. The Community had given itself a very major set of tasks in the Maastricht Treaty at the same time as it was faced by significant challenges to its own image of itself, with economic prosperity under threat, political upheaval in many other parts of Europe, and a dramatic increase in the number of states expressing an interest in becoming members of the Community. All of these elements ensured that the negotiations proved to be just as difficult as they had been five years earlier, despite the superficial similarity of the exercise.

The Debate on Revenue

As indicated above, the Commission proposed that Community spending should be allowed to grow to 1.37 percent of Community GNP by 1997. This figure was one that had been the product of a lively debate inside the Commission and proved just as controversial once it was made public as the minimum figure that the Commission thought was necessary if the Community was to fulfill the ambitions it set itself in the Maastricht Treaty.

The figure was hardly a large one if one compares it with the amounts that had been discussed in the 1970s in the well-known MacDougall Report. It had spoken of the Community moving toward a "small public sector federation," devoting 5 to 10 percent of its GDP to the budget.[5] Now such figures were no longer part of the political debate. Indeed there was broad opposition among the member states to the 1.37 percent GNP figure when the package was first discussed in the Council at the beginning of March. Such a response was not one that should have been unduly surprising: It certainly could not be ascribed simply to the extra discipline required to meet the EMU targets. A similar process of reducing the Commission's suggested figures had taken place in 1987–1988 with Delors I when 1.4 percent was reduced to 1.2 percent. Indeed, the Commission showed how it recognized such retreats as part of the Community process when in June it indicated its willingness to spread the increase to 1.37 percent over a longer period of seven years, with the present ceiling remaining in force until 1995.

However, the attitude of the member states was not simply part of a bargaining process but also reflected a continuing unwillingness to perceive the Community budget in fundamentally different terms from the perspective that had prevailed before Maastricht. This was particularly obvious if one considers the nature of the debate about budgetary discipline and the relationship between the increase in Community and national spending.

The Commission argued that the Community budget could not be subject to the same strict limits applied to national expenditure, where increases in public expenditure are expected in some cases to be lower than the rate of growth. In its view, this would be "tantamount to ignoring the decisions taken at Maastricht and refusing to assume our international responsibilities."[6] Hence, it pressed for growth in Community expenditure amounting to more than 5 percent per year. Moreover, it claimed that such a stance was not contrary to the tenets of budgetary discipline. It noted that throughout the life of the financial perspective up to 1992, the budgets voted had remained within the limits imposed in 1988. This had been possible despite major changes prompted by the unification of Germany, the breakdown of communism in Central and Eastern Europe, and the breakup of the Soviet Union, all of which had prompted important increases in expenditure that were not envisaged in 1988. These increases had all been easily accommodated within the GNP limits laid down in 1988.[7]

These same elements prompted a very different response from most member states. They were not prepared to accept without demur the argument that the Community budget should increase at a more rapid rate than national ones. It was a claim that British Chancellor Norman Lamont included as the first point for discussion in the letter that he sent to all the other members of the Ecofin Council at the outset of the British presidency in July. In his view, it was inconsistent with the need to reduce budgetary deficits as provided for under EMU. In any case it was a hard principle to accept given the universal pressures on public spending. This was particularly true for Germany, where the expenditure prompted by unification made it difficult for it to contemplate major increases at the Community as well as the national level.

As for the fact that spending had respected the existing limits, this only served to confirm the view of many that in that case it was not necessary to increase those limits, or at least not yet. When they assumed the presidency in July 1992, the British made great play on the volume of headroom within the existing ceiling of 1.2 percent of Community GNP. In the letter of the British chancellor, referred to above, he argued that there was some ECU 13 billion to be called upon, thanks to the margin available within the ceiling (the 1992 budget was set at 1.16 percent of GNP), the impact of anticipated economic growth, and the fact that certain programs were coming to an end. The letter was accompanied by a questionnaire containing eighty-five questions, and the very first question invited the other delegations to indicate their views on the period that a new financing arrangement should cover: 1993–1997? 1993–1999? Some other period? There was little doubt that the British wished in this way to signal their preference for a longer rather than a shorter period.[8]

Why, though, did these states take such a negative view of the increases proposed by the Commission? One can claim that all governments were committed to limiting public spending and that this was now given a strong boost by the need to meet the criteria laid down at Maastricht. However, such sentiments were not new: a strict attitude toward public spending had become the hallmark of all national governments during the 1980s. Moreover, despite increases in the Community budget in the 1980s, it still represented in 1992 no more than 2.4 percent of public expenditure in member states.[9]

Rather, one needs to look, in narrower budgetary terms, at the balance between net contributors to and net beneficiaries from the Community budget. Throughout much of the 1980s, the net contributors were essentially limited to Germany and Britain. The former had more or less accepted the situation, the latter had objected strongly and been rewarded by the Fontainebleau Agreement in 1984 under which it receives as a reduction from its annual contribution two-thirds of the difference between its percentage contribution to revenue and its percentage receipts from allocated expenditure. This arrangement had been effectively maintained in 1988. Moreover, it was written into the decision on own resources and could not therefore be changed without unanimity. This in turn meant that the level of Community revenue could only be increased if the British were satisfied with the new arrangements relating to its rebate, a point that they did not fail to make during the negotiations.

However, the situation had changed markedly by the beginning of the 1990s. By that time not only had France joined Germany and Britain as a significant net contributor, but the level of benefit obtained by the other, wealthier countries was in sharp decline. Between 1984 and 1990, for example, all countries except Greece, Spain, Ireland, and Portugal saw their level of net contribution go up, even where, as in the case of Denmark, they remained net beneficiaries.[10] This meant that the Community budget was becoming more clearly redistributive in the sense that the most money flowed to the least prosperous countries. For the four states concerned the result was that a central feature of the negotiations consisted of ensuring that this situation was confirmed, not least through the establishment of the Cohesion Fund. The impact on the other states was rather different.

First, it meant that the wealthier states were more sensitive to any proposal that was likely to accentuate the tendency toward a reduction in their net benefits from the budget. Italy, for example, was strongly opposed to the Commission proposal that the volume of the GNP resource should be significantly increased at the expense of the third VAT resource in the name of taking greater account of contributive capacity. The Italians noted that according to the Commission's own figures, the impact of the introduction of the new revenue system on the 1992 budget would have been to increase the net Italian contribution by ECU 517 million, with no other state having to contribute more than ECU 56 million extra.[11]

Second, it also contributed to a much stronger challenge to the British rebate than had taken place in 1988 when there was little open resistance to the continuation of the Fontainebleau arrangements. By contrast, when the Council discussed the issue at its meeting on September 28, 1992, six delegations, including two important net contributors, Germany and France, formally challenged its continuation.[12] The states involved felt that the rebate was no longer appropriate, not least because agricultural spending, from which Britain had always benefitted much less proportionately than others, was going to continue dropping as a percentage of the whole. For the British presidency, this challenge posed an important choice as it had to calculate how much weight to give to this element in the search for an overall settlement.

In a situation of this kind where even relatively small-scale change to the existing arrangements was strongly resisted by one or another party, there was also little enthusiasm for major innovation. One way of extracting the Community from the difficulties it faced in relation to revenue was to propose that a fifth resource be established. The Belgian government urged that consideration be given to allocating the proceeds of a Community tax on CO^2 emissions or to creating a Community tax on savings income (a witholding tax), arguing that this would impose greater responsibility upon the structure of decisionmaking and help to reduce the elements of regressiveness in the system.[13] However, the Commission declined to introduce any specific proposal and thereby effectively acknowledged that a new tax constituted too major a step for anyone to contemplate seriously at this stage. Better to adapt the existing structure than set up something new whose economic and political impact could only be dimly discerned.

Allocating Expenditure

The general resistance to an increase in overall revenue and the individual objections to specific proposals for changes in the revenue system presented a formidable obstacle to gaining a settlement on a new financial perspective. However, although all resisted the Commission's proposals, no one resisted all of them; there was something for everyone. Indeed, had this not been the case, it is hard to see how any negotiation could have begun.

How far, though, was this support for increases in expenditure the result of a realization that the move to EMU meant increased pressure on spending at home and hence a desire to claim Community support for national expenditure? At first sight this view looks to have some strength. If we consider the major increase in spending proposed by the Commission, namely, in relation to structural spending, then it is clear that the context in which this spending was set had changed. The Cohesion Fund provided for in Maastricht was specifically linked to the presentation of an economic program designed to lead toward EMU. In principle, therefore, any finance from the fund could be withheld if the program were considered unsatisfactory. Hence, the opportunity had to exist for states to claim that they needed financial assistance to meet the targets set in the Treaty.

However, such an argument overlooks a central feature of the debate on Delors II, which is that it took place against the background of an existing allocation of advantage which no one could hope to alter dramatically. All states remained strongly committed to the existing pattern of expenditure where it benefitted them and sought to ensure that that pattern not be disturbed. All had gone through the same process of discussion in 1987–1988, and hence the contours of the debate were familiar, even if the specific circumstances had changed.

This broad stance can be seen in the responses to proposed changes in relation to agriculture. It was an area where there was much less disagreement than in 1988 when the issue of control of agricultural spending was at the center of the whole debate. At that time, budgetary rules were seen as no match for the guarantees written into Community legislation, and so an attempt was made to redress the balance by establishing a more effective system of control. The result was that there was a trade-off between those who sought to limit agricultural expenditure and those who wished to see an increase in the volume of revenue available to the Community, not least to finance a doubling of the structural funds. Neither could be successful without the other, and in the end both gained substantial satisfaction. The revenue ceiling was raised, but at the same time there were important changes in the structure of the CAP.

After 1988, agricultural spending did drop significantly at first, but this was essentially due to exogenous factors, in particular a fall in the value of the dollar, drought in the United States, and corresponding increases in world prices. Thereafter it became clear that the system devised in 1988 would not by itself contain spending: in 1991 it even looked as if the ceiling incorporated into the financial perspective might have to be revised upward. At the same time, there was a major debate on the reform of the CAP, which came to fruition in the spring of 1992. Although the precise details of the reform remained to be worked out, the very fact that the broad shape was laid down before the negotiations on future finance were very far advanced meant that this part of the package was subject to less argument than it had been five years previously.

However, there was still a major dispute about the value to be accorded to this policy, as reflected in its share of spending. The Commission argued that the rate of increase permissible under the guideline should be maintained but that it should be broadened to include "all measures directly linked to the reformed CAP" as well as the fisheries guarantee fund. At the same time, it called for an extra ECU 1.5 billion to be added to the guideline figure once the CAP reform was complete to cover the move from a system of guaranteed prices to one of direct aid to producers.

Loosening the guideline in this way was not welcomed by a number of states, including Britain. The British wanted to see it tightened still further, and they gained some satisfaction at the Lisbon summit when it was agreed that the financial means necessary for the execution of the CAP should be provided within the existing guideline. At the very least, this meant that the Commission's idea of adding ECU 1.5 billion was withdrawn; moreover, the possibility of further restriction remained open, although others (such as the French, themselves) strongly contested such an interpretation. Thus, although the existing arrangements were unlikely to be altered fundamentally, the idea of an *acquis communautaire* in this sector conceals an ongoing argument about how much the agricultural policy should cost, with the participants constantly trying to modify or maintain the contours of the policy in accordance with their differing interests.

Such disputes were just as keenly fought in areas where the *acquis* was not so firmly established. Thus the divide between those who wish to avoid as far as possible intervention in the economy and those who consider such intervention as both necessary and desirable was of major significance in the debate on the increase in internal policies. The Commission set the increases in this area under the banner of increased competitiveness, arguing that

European industry required a boost given its fragile position in relation to the United States and Japan. It linked its concerns directly to Maastricht, and to the new Article 130 which makes "industrial competitiveness in an open, competitive market a central issue."[14]

Of course, this does not acknowledge how very hotly the contents of Title XIII, entitled "Industry" and containing Article 130, had been contested in the negotiations on the Treaty. It had only been accepted after the inclusion of the phrase that the title "shall not provide a basis for the introduction by the Community of any measure which could lead to a distortion of competition." This reluctance to allow a broad definition of the article resurfaced in the debate on the Delors II package. Although the Commission (with the support of the European Parliament) maintained that such improved competitiveness required investment in research, transport networks, and telecommunications, it was this area of the package that was seen as most open to amendment by the member states. It was an area that did not benefit any countries in a very specific way, and so all could contemplate its reduction without undue anxiety.[15]

The fact that the category "Internal Policies" did not offer guaranteed financial advantage to specific countries or regions is not sufficient by itself to explain why it received such weak backing from the member states; otherwise it would not be possible to explain the very strong consensus in favor of the figures included by the Commission for external policy following the agreement at the Lisbon Summit in favor of "substantial increases" in this area. This apparent consensus reflected in part the broader role being assumed by the Community in the world, but it was also possible because the figures did not specify how the extra finance should be distributed between different parts of the world. There were at least three different interests that could be satisfied by what the Commission proposed: those seeking to provide further support in Central and Eastern Europe, those eager to increase traditional development assistance, and those wanting to develop Community assistance in hitherto relatively neglected parts of the world, such as Latin America or the Mediterranean. These three groups could merge their differences in an increased global figure for external policy.

Deferral of decision applied to other aspects of external spending as well. For example, Maastricht left uncertain how far the Community would go in financing a future common foreign and security policy. Article J.11 specifies that all administrative spending relating to such a policy should be borne by the Community but that operating expenditure should either be charged to the member states or to the Community if the Council decides so unanimously. This compromise between those wishing to bring foreign and security policy within the Community ambit and those preferring a more intergovernmental approach pushed into the future awkward issues such as the mechanism by which administrative and operational expenditure would be distinguished. No one in 1992 wanted to make it more difficult to reach agreement by trying to address them immediately.

The debate on the allocation of expenditure combined with an ongoing argument about the cost and value of the policies concerned. However, this argument went on inside a framework of expectations where all were aware of the susceptibilities of the others and where this served to dampen conflict and make it possible to move toward a settlement. Such a settlement would leave important issues unanswered, but this was a condition for any agreement to be made. It meant that the approach to finding solutions was fundamentally incremental in character, with the overarching issue of the move toward EMU only serving to act as part of the overall context rather than as a determining factor.

The Issue of Redistribution

One of the central features of the Maastricht Treaty is its stress on the need for economic convergence as a condition for enabling states to join in a single currency managed by a central bank. But what the Treaty does not specify is who is to assume the main responsibility in achieving such convergence. Is it the member states, or does the Community have a role? If the Community has a role, how far should it extend?

As with much of the Treaty, proponents of different views could refer to different parts of the text. Thus, the provisions relating to the need to limit national spending in the move toward EMU can be set against the inclusion in the protocol on economic and social cohesion of an explicit acceptance of the principle that the level of Community participation in structural spending should be varied to take account of the need to avoid excessive increases in spending in less prosperous states. How far this latter principle should be extended cannot be answered by any automatic formula but depends on divergent views on the importance of the Community budget as a redistributive mechanism.

That this purpose was broadly perceived as legitimate can be inferred by the inclusion, already in the Single Act, of the principle of economic and social cohesion and by the agreement to double the structural funds by 1993. Moreover, the importance of such cohesion was underlined at Maastricht with the agreement to establish a Cohesion Fund. Even though no figure was laid down, its inclusion gave an important legitimacy to the goal of aiding the four least prosperous states. Indeed those states could look back to their success in 1988 as proof that if placed under sufficient pressure, the others would eventually agree to an increase not so far from that which they were demanding.

However, the fact that the objective was widely seen as legitimate did not avert significant disagreement about how it should be achieved. There was a great divide between beneficiaries and contributors over the issues of what impact the funds had had and how those funds should be managed in the future. Where people stood on these issues depended very largely on where they sat.

The Commission argued that the funds had contributed to raising the GNP level of the poorer states, but this was not a view that the wealthier states were eager to accept. They challenged the methodology used in the calculations and maintained that the increases could just as well be attributed to the benefits of a single market. To agree to the contrary proposition would be to give further legitimacy to the goal of economic and social cohesion as achieved through the Community budget and would have severely limited the possibility of resisting the increases proposed for the structural funds. Rather, the richer states could and did use a special report of the Court of Auditors that pointed to the weakness of the funds in terms of their organization and the directed quality of their spending.[16]

One point that the Court stressed in its report was the inadequacy of the application of the principle of additionality.[17] It had always been a part of Community orthodoxy that structural spending should not be used by states to offset what governments had intended to spend anyway: it was supposed to be genuinely extra expenditure. At the same time, it had constantly proved very difficult to ensure that this principle was respected. Now the debate on the reinforcement of economic and social cohesion funds served to stretch the idea still further. Not only was there the specific provision that the levels of Community participation be modulated to avoid excessive increases in budgetary expenditure in the less prosperous states, but the nature of Community spending was being subtly modified through the creation of the Cohesion Fund. Whereas hitherto the purpose of structural spending was to assist particular regions or sectors of the economy, the new fund was directed at specific countries for environmental projects or ones relating to trans-European networks, with no restriction on where the expenditure should go. The only conditions laid down in the protocol (up to now no legislative framework exists) are that the country have a per capita GNP of less than 90 percent of the Community average and that it also have a program aimed at achieving economic convergence. As a result, the fund looked as much like a mechanism of financial equalization as a way of developing Community policies in the structural area.

At the very least, the argument was moving away from the specific functioning of the structural funds and toward the idea that funds should flow with limited conditions toward the poorer states with a view to bringing about convergence. The greater automaticity of spending was linked with the specific aim of equalizing the situation of the individual states as measured in terms of GNP. It was an implicit part of the argument that once a country had risen above the 90 percent threshold, the justification for payments from the fund would no longer apply. The logic of this position would be twofold. On the one hand, the Community would lose a hold over the operation of policy; it would cease to be able to argue in favor of the principle of additionality as the important question would no longer be whether the member states contributed their part, but rather whether the effect was to aid the move toward EMU. On the other hand, it would imply that the Community would assume responsibility for ensuring that this more developed form of redistribution actually took place and under what terms.

Such developments can be seen as healthy for the development of the Community. If the whole budget were reformed to become deliberately redistributive, and if, as a result, budgetary flows corresponded closely with contributive capacity, one could argue that anomalies such as the British rebate need not be maintained, and Community policies could be developed without constant reference to the distribution of gains and losses.[18] Certainly there is no shortage of technical devices available to bring about such a result.[19]

However, one can expect there to be strong resistance to such ideas. It would inevitably lead the Community into more difficult areas of choice, not least the trade-off between fiscal autonomy and interregional transfers. Could such a system of transfers work or even be established unless all parties were satisfied with the broader economic policy framework of the weaker states? The issue, for example, of contributive capacity would start to assume a much more contentious form than it does at present. For the time, it is limited to a static debate about relative levels of GNP with little stress on the dynamic forces that led to those levels being what they are. If the concept of capacity comes in for closer scrutiny, one could easily be drawn into a more delicate debate about the domestic choices that led to a particular level of GNP.

For the time being, the member states have sought to avoid such issues, concentrating instead on the level of the Cohesion Fund and the terms under which it would be paid out. Inevitably this pitched the four beneficiaries against the rest of the Community, with the former seeking to maximize their gain from the fund. Their bargaining position was not so different from that which had prevailed in 1987 when the poorer states had sought a doubling of the structural funds as compensation for the uncertain effects of the move toward a single market. They now could argue similarly that the move toward EMU would be particularly difficult for them and that the Cohesion Fund would go some way to cushioning the impact of that move. The fact that other states were also far from meeting the EMU criteria was not necessarily a reason for supposing that agreement could not be reached, but rather that the terms of the fund might in future be relaxed to assist others to reach EMU targets. In any case, the four least prosperous states had some support in wishing to see an increase in category 2 in that Germany wished to have its East German länder included in the list of objective 1 regions. This meant that it too had an interest in ensuring that the issue of structural provision be resolved in a satisfactory way. As with the rest of the package, there was reason to suppose a formula could be found to avoid more fundamental long-term dilemmas.

Conclusion

The Council of Ministers held wide-ranging discussions on the Delors II package in the spring of 1992, but there was not a sufficient consensus to reach an agreement at the Lisbon European Council in June. Instead, the heads of state and government passed the dossier on to the British presidency with the specific undertaking that they would reach decisions on the package at their meeting in Edinburgh in December.

Under any circumstances it would not have been easy to bring the issue to a conclusion, but the situation was made immeasurably more complicated by the no vote in the Danish referendum on June 3, by the turbulent monetary conditions which led to the British leaving the exchange rate mechanism in the middle of September, and by the narrow vote in favor of the Maastricht Treaty obtained in the French referendum on September 20.

In the event, the careful preparations made by the British presidency before the Edinburgh meeting (and skillful chairmanship during it) made it possible for the Community to avoid the high costs of a failure whose repercussions would have extended well beyond the budgetary arena. However, the nature of the deal served to confirm the significant features of the budgetary debate that had preceded it in terms of the development of the Community and the willingness of member states to adapt their positions on the issue of Community financing.

First, one can note that the definition of state interests took place in a broad framework where the scope for major change in the existing arrangements was extremely limited. The Delors I package had established a set of revenue and expenditure arrangements which no one wanted to alter fundamentally, despite the major decisions taken at Maastricht. The *acquis communautaire* weighed heavily in the calculations of everybody.

Second, and as a corollary of the first, there was a marked tendency to push into the future the resolution of highly contentious issues. There was occasional talk of radical ideas, such as the creation of a Community tax, but no one wanted to put a solution at risk by insisting on their inclusion in any settlement. More general issues, such as how far the EC should take charge of problems caused by EMU and the issue of redistribution, were sensed rather than directly addressed. The incremental approach to problem-solving was dominant.

Third, despite all differences of view, there remained a strong sense of obligation to find a joint solution. This need not be attributed to any sense of idealism but should be seen in the context of a Community where there is significant linkage between issues. For the British, for example, a satisfactory solution was not just something with which successfully to conclude the presidency but also a step toward the much sought-after goal of enlargement. Once the Lisbon summit had declared that official negotiations on such enlargement could only begin once the Maastricht Treaty was ratified and there was agreement on the Delors II package, the need for a solution was necessarily greater in the eyes of the presidency.

Fourth, in terms of the contents of an agreement, there was acceptance of the principle of an increased budget, but within strict limits. Net contributors to the budget took the strongest line against the growth of Community resources, but even those who stood to gain the most from a settlement were not concerned necessarily to increase the "own resources" ceiling quickly if their aims could be achieved without this happening. In both cases the weight of national economic imperatives made it impossible to perceive the role of the Community budget as a central focus of Economic and Monetary Union.

At the heart of the reluctance of states to look at the budget in this way lies an implicit realization of the longer-term implications of so doing. The result would be that they would have to consider a whole set of wider issues at the Community level. For the time being, the Community is seeking to move toward EMU as if it can be done without any effect on a broader budgetary agenda. On the other hand, perhaps it is recognition that this cannot be done that is making the prospects for such a union look less bright now than they did when the goal of EMU was incorporated into the Treaty.

Notes

The views expressed in this chapter are strictly personal.

1. For a discussion of the budgetary debate during part of that five-year period, see Michael Shackleton, "Budgetary Policy in Transition" in Leon Hurwitz and Christian Lequesne, eds., *The State of the European Community* (Boulder: Lynne Rienner, 1991).

2. Commission of the European Communities, *Report by the Commission to the Council and Parliament on the Financing of the Community Budget*, COM(87) 101 (Brussels, February 1987). This document provided the financial details relating to the more general material in Commission of the European Communities, *Making a Success of the Single Act*, COM(92)100 (Brussels, February 1987). The two documents bore the same relationship toward each other as did COM(92)2000 and 2001 in 1992.

3. For a discussion of these negotiations, see Michael Shackleton, *Financing the European Community* (New York: Council on Foreign Relations Press, 1990), pp.9–22.

4. Commission of the European Communities, *From the Single Act to Maastricht and Beyond: The Means to Match Our Ambitions*, COM(92)2000 (Brussels, February 1992), p.34.

5. Commission of the European Communities, *The Role of Public Finance in the European Communities*, (The MacDougall Report), volumes 1 and 2 (Brussels, 1977).

6. Commission of the European Communities, COM(92)2000, p. 5.

7. The budgets voted were below the ceilings set in 1988 by the following percentages of GNP: 0.03 percent in 1988, 0.15 percent in 1989, 0.19 percent in 1990, 0.10 percent in 1991, and 0.04 percent in 1992. This amounted in aggregate to some ECU 10 billion.

8. The chancellor's letter and the questionnaire were made available to the author by the British permanent representation in Brussels.

9. See Commission of the European Communities, *The Community Budget: The Facts in Figures*, SEC(92)950 (July 1992), p.17.

10. Court of Auditors, *Annual Report Concerning the Financial Year 1990 Together with the Institutions' Replies* (Luxembourg: Office for Official Publications, 1991), C 324, volume 2, pp.66–67.

11. Commission of the European Communities, *The Community's Finances between Now and 1997*, COM(92) 2001 final March 10, 1992, p.58.

12. *Agence Europe,* September 28–29, 1992, pp.7–8.

13. See *Agence Europe,* May 7, 1992, pp. 13–14.

14. Commission of the European Communities, COM(92)2000, p. 25

15. The French may be considered a partial exception to this general claim given their interest in particular projects such as high definition television, which could expect to benefit from such spending. Nevertheless, President Delors felt there was a "total lack of interest for the competitiveness section" shown by all delegations (*Agence Europe,* May 24/25, 1992, p.12).

16. Opinion no.2/92 of the Court of Auditors of the European Communities complementary to the annual reports on Community expenditure since 1988 on the EAGGF Guarantee Section, structural measures, research, and nonmember states.

17. Ibid., p.21.

18. This argument is persuasively put by Michael Franklin in *The EC Budget: Realism, Redistribution and Radical Reform* (London: Royal Institute of International Affairs, 1992).

19. See, for example, T. Padoa-Schioppa et al., *Efficiency, Stability and Equity: A Strategy for the Evolution of the Economic System of the European Community* (Brussels: EC Commission, 1987).

23

Structural Policy and Multilevel Governance in the EC

Gary Marks

The aim of this chapter is to analyze recent developments in the European Community's structural policy, asking two sets of questions that have implications for our understanding of the European Community in general: (1) How have institutional innovations come about, and which actors have been most responsible for shaping them? (2) What are the consequences of institutional innovation for existing institutions? What kind of political order is emerging in Europe, and what are the consequences of institutional innovation for the existing state system?

Two lines of theorizing have staked out the terrain of debate on these questions. On the one side, functionalists and neofunctionalists have conceived of the process of institutional innovation as one of "integration" in which supranational institutions compromise state autonomy and sovereignty by shaping institutional competencies, resources, and decisionmaking rules.[1] On the other side, realists, neorealists, and intergovernmental theorists have argued that member states and their executives continue to dominate decisionmaking in the European Community.[2] They emphasize the de jure supremacy of member states in the treaties that establish the institutional framework of the European Community; they note that member state executives are represented directly in the most powerful EC decisionmaking body, the European Council; and they stress the de facto subordination of supranational institutions to member state executives in major episodes of institutional innovation, including most recently, the Single European Act and the Maastricht Treaty.

While they differ substantively, these contending accounts share a fundamental assumption about how to conceptualize the European Community. Both view the defining features of the outcome in terms of the relative role of supranational versus national institutions. They share a conception of the outcome of institution building in the European Community as varying along a dimension characterized by intergovernmentalism at one extreme and a supranational state at the other. Hence, the debate between these accounts has been pursued by examining the relative influence of EC institutions vis-à-vis member state executives and by asking how supranational the EC institutions really are.

This chapter bears on this debate in two ways. First, I argue that a convincing analysis of institution building in the EC should go beyond the areas that are transparently dominated by member states: financial decisions, major pieces of legislation, and the treaties. Beyond and beneath the highly visible politics of member state bargaining lies a dimly lit process of institutional formation, and here the Commission has played a vital role.

Second, I argue that the debate between supranational and national conceptions of institutional formation in the European Community misses a critical element of the whole picture, namely, the increasing importance of subnational levels of decisionmaking and their myriad connections with other levels. I suggest that we are seeing the emergence of *multilevel governance,* a system of continuous negotiation among nested governments at several territorial tiers—supranational, national, regional, and local—as the result of a broad process of institutional creation and decisional reallocation that has pulled some previously centralized functions of the state up to the supranational level and some down to the local/regional level.

The Budget for Structural Policy

The Maastricht Treaty of December 1991 set the stage for a large increase in spending on structural policy, following on the heels of the doubling of the funds agreed to in 1988. Reaffirming the Community's commitment to reduce "disparities between the levels of development of the various regions and the backwardness of the least-favored regions, including rural areas," at Maastricht the member states agreed to set up a new Cohesion Fund to funnel money for meeting environmental standards and for building trans-European transportation networks to the four countries (Greece, Ireland, Portugal, and Spain) with a per capita GNP of less than 90 percent of the Community average.[3]

However, the Maastricht Treaty contained no figures on how much structural spending would increase nor on the size of the new Cohesion Fund. At the Edinburgh summit of December 1992, after several rounds of intense bargaining, the member states agreed to increase structural spending from its present ECU 18.6 billion to ECU 30 billion (in 1992 ECU) in 1999, of which ECU 2.6 billion will be devoted to the Cohesion Fund. That amounts to an increase of 61.3 percent in structural funding, which in absolute terms is even larger than the previous doubling between 1987 and 1993.[4] The share of structural operations in the total EC budget will rise from 28 percent in 1992 to more than one-third in 1999. Of the additional ECU 17.3 billion in EC spending agreed to at Edinburgh, ECU 11.4 billion is targeted for economic and social cohesion.

Structural aid will continue to be concentrated on the poorest countries and regions. At present, countries and regions with a per capita GDP of less than 75 percent of the EC average (objective 1 regions: Northern Ireland, Ireland, Portugal, large parts of Spain, Corsica and the French Overseas Departments, Southern Italy, Greece, and now the five eastern German länder) receive around two-thirds of structural funding.[5] Funding for these regions will double by 1999. The bulk (two-thirds) of this proposed increase will come not from the new and much reported Cohesion Fund, but from further expansion of the structural funds.

Funding is slated to increase by 50 percent for the remaining objectives (objective 2: converting regions seriously affected by industrial decline; objective 3: combatting long-term unemployment; objective 4: facilitating occupational integration of young people; objective 5a: speeding up adjustment in agricultural structures, particularly marketing and processing, across the EC; and objective 5b: rural development in selected regions, particularly those covered under objective 1). In addition, the Commission has stated that "there might be a case" for establishing a sixth objective, to aid regions particularly dependent on fishing.[6]

At both the Maastricht and Edinburgh summits, structural spending became high politics as Spain demanded—and eventually received—a new regional initiative on cohesion to offset its impending net revenue loss with the Community. The Spanish demand for a national cohesion fund for member states whose per capita GNP was less than 90 percent of the EC average was a cleverly calculated move, providing Spain both with the lion's share of the funding and allies in pushing the measure forward. Because the fund is directed to member states, not poor regions within member states, it cuts out the remaining two of the three most populous poorer regions in the Community, the Mezzogiorno and eastern Germany, because these are in relatively wealthy member states. Whereas Spain has just 7 percent of the population of all objective 1 regions, it encompasses more than 60 percent of the population of countries whose per capita GNP is less than 90 percent of the EC average, and Spain has already received informal endorsement for its claim on 55 percent of the Cohesion Fund.

The poorer countries argue that they should receive funding as a side payment for their agreement to market integration and monetary union, innovations that leave them economically vulnerable. These countries are in a double squeeze: they face the challenge of constraining public expenditure, reducing inflation, and balancing their external accounts to meet the criteria of convergence for European monetary integration while trying to meet competitive pressures that are intensifying as a result of market unification. This is not to say that they are bound to lose, either absolutely or even relative, to the richer member states over the next several years. Disparities in GDP per capita at the member state level narrowed slightly over the 1980s.[7] Of the countries whose per capita GDP was less than 90 percent of the EC average,

Spain, Portugal, and Ireland did better than average; Greece alone did worse.[8] While many, perhaps most, economists believe that in the absence of major fiscal redistribution, EMU will hurt the poorer countries, a Commission study of the distributional effects of EMU concluded that the overall effects on the Community's regions are not clear-cut.[9] On the one hand, poorer regions will lose the nominal exchange rate instrument and face stricter national budgetary discipline. On the other hand, they can take advantage of new economies of scale, lower transaction costs, and reduction of interest rates presently bearing exchange risk premiums.

Given their middling performance over the past decade, and the sensitivity of the poorer countries to factors that are difficult if not impossible to predict (such as the outcome of the Uruguay Round of GATT and the state of the world economy), it makes little sense to conceive structural policy as a side payment for expected losses. However, governments in the poorer societies make a convincing case that they face a particularly severe economic *risk* as a result of the twin pressures of Europe-wide economic competition and attempts to meet EMU convergence criteria. Further, it seems sensible to argue that an economic downturn stands to hurt a poorer country more than one that is richer, because the welfare safety net of a poor country is weaker.

The intense economic bargaining of the past year reveals just how imprecise is the Maastricht Treaty.[10] Despite the high emotions it has engendered among publics who were formerly content to let elites run European integration, the Treaty is an open-ended and ambiguous document. It is full of legalese and "Eurospeak" concerning an impressive range of policy areas but holds few hard commitments on the part of member states. The Maastricht Treaty has been the starting point, not the end point, for negotiation among interested parties. This is the case for most areas covered in the Treaty, including economic and monetary policy, the creation of a central bank, and social policy. In structural policy, the Treaty barely sets the parameters of negotiation. It contains no overall spending commitments nor even projections for planned expenditure. As noted above, the institutional innovation it does describe in some detail, the new Cohesion Fund, accounts for only a small part of the total increase agreed at Edinburgh. The Treaty calls for a "thorough evaluation of the operation and effectiveness of the Structural Funds," but provides minimal substantive guidance to the Commission on the task of institutional restructuring.

While it is sensible to view the Maastricht Treaty with a lens focused on bargaining among member states, to understand the process of institutional creation in the European Community one must go beyond the process of treatymaking. In the first place, the Treaty must be ratified in each of the member states; this has involved intense public scrutiny, party political mobilization, parliamentary votes, and, in Denmark, Ireland, and France, national referendums. European integration and approval or rejection of the Treaty are tied into diverse crosscutting issues—immigration, national identity, state sovereignty, anti-elite sentiment, dynamics of party competition, and above all, support or opposition to existing governments—that cloud the debate and make prediction of outcomes impossible. In sharp and entirely unexpected contrast to the previous round of institutional recasting, the Single European Act of 1986, the debate about the Treaty captured the political arenas of several member states, including Denmark, France, and the UK. Now that the genie of European integration has been released from the bottle of technocratic planning, quiet accommodation, and elite-driven bargains into the highly charged atmosphere of domestic party politics, it seems unlikely that national leaders will ever be able to coax it back.

Secondly, there is the less transparent, but very consequential, process of post-Treaty interpretation and institution building. The causal logic of this process varies across policy areas. In this and the next section, I argue that in budgetary matters member states are dominant. However, determining the size of the budget does not determine the manner in which it is spent, and in subsequent sections of this chapter, I show that the Commission has played an autonomous and powerful role in spending.

Principle of Structural Policy

When one examines the operation of structural policy, it is clear that the Commission has come to be a central actor. The Maastricht Treaty affirms the reform of the structural funds agreed to at the Brussels summit of February 1988. The current system is based on the principles of programming, partnership, and additionality, each of which provides the Commission wide latitude in formulating and implementing policy.

Programming

With the 1988 reform of the structural funds, the Commission has shifted from its previous role as hands-off financial manager to that of active participant in framing and monitoring regional development programs.[11] Rather than support individual "projects" proposed by member states that in all likelihood would have gone ahead in any case, the three funds responsible for structural policy (the European Regional Development Fund, the European Social Fund, and the Guidance Section of the Agricultural Guidance and Guarantee Fund) have increasingly combined their interventions in multifaceted "programs" budgeted for five-year periods. Whereas projects usually consist of straightforward infrastructural investment (such as road building) planned and carried out exclusively by member states themselves, programs generally include a mix of public and private activities designed by the Commission and subnational governments in conjunction with member states. Programs involve diverse measures such as direct investment in private industry, provision of consulting services, R&D, and technical and vocational training.

A Protocol on Economic and Social Cohesion annexed to the Maastricht Treaty suggests some changes in the administration of structural funds. While the changes have a technocratic justification—to increase "flexibility" in funding—they also enlarge the Commission's scope for autonomous decisionmaking. The Commission is currently drawing up a detailed recommendation based on these suggestions ("the reform of the reforms") that will be put to the Council in 1993.[12] The overall direction of these reforms will be as follows:

1. *Increased scope for structural intervention.* The Commission wishes to integrate aid for health and education, areas currently not covered by structural spending, into its development programs.

2. *Increased rates of Community assistance.* At present the Commission can decide to provide a maximum of 75 percent of the funding for a program in objective 1 regions. This rate will be increased so as to reduce the squeeze that the poorest member states face in cofunding extensive Community development programs while simultaneously having to reduce public spending to satisfy EMU convergence goals. The maximum rate for Community cofunding for the new Cohesion Fund is 90 percent.

3. *Greater emphasis on Community initiative programs.* The Commission will call for an increase in the share of total structural spending to be channeled into special sectoral programs designed by the Commission from the current 9 percent to about 15 percent. In using these funds, the Commission would be granted latitude to incorporate neighboring regions not included under existing objectives.

4. *Simplifying the planning process.* At present there are three stages: first the member state draws up a national development plan that sets out broad planning goals; then the Commission, in conjunction with representatives of local and regional authorities and member states, develops community support frameworks (CSFs) that set out funding priorities and outline the general means to achieve them; finally, the CSF is hammered down into a number of five-year operational programs that become the basis for Community funding. The Commission is now weighing the case for reducing the number of stages to two by cutting out the first stage, at least for smaller CSFs.

Partnership

Partnership, the participation of subnational governmental representatives alongside member state representatives and the Commission in preparing, implementing, and monitoring development programs, is now a guiding principle of Community structural policy.[13] In drawing up CSFs, Commission administrators visit the regions, consult, and (if necessary) actively mobilize input from local government administrators concerning the kinds of programs they want in their regions. Subnational representatives are involved alongside member state representatives in the biannual meetings of the monitoring committees for each CSF. Whereas the Commission used to deal exclusively with national governments, which articulated their own regional plans, since 1988 it has opened the process to regional and local governments.

The Commission cultivates regional contacts in several ways. Bruce Millan, the Commissioner for DG-16, the regional fund, has relied extensively on his contacts with subnational government representatives in developing new Community initiatives. For example, RECHAR, an EC initiative to aid economic adaption in coal-mining communities, was designed after consultation with representatives in the north of England and other affected regions. With the support of the Commission, both objective 1 and objective 2 regions have created supranational associations to mobilize their interests in Brussels and Strasbourg. In 1991, in the first of what is intended to be an ongoing series of meetings, DG-16 invited representatives from each of the sixty objective 2 regions to a conference in Brussels where they exchanged information on development strategies and sources of future funding.

In its proposals for reform of the reforms, the Commission intends to press for "enhancement of partnership on the basis of more clearly defined responsibilities: the division of responsibilities between the Commission and the regions should be more clear cut to make for more decentralization in the detailed definition of projects and in the implementation of programs, which should be handed over to those in charge of the operations on the spot."[14] This demand is consistent with "subsidiarity," the principle (discussed below) that decisions should be taken at the lowest feasible level of government. It is also consistent with the Commission's inability to administer programs directly in the regions, given its small staff. The Directorate General that has prime responsibility for the operation of programs in the field, DG 16, has a staff of less than 500 managers and field operatives to administer a budget in excess of ECU 6 billion spread over more than 200 programs.

Since 1990, the Commission has been elaborating an expanded conception of partnership ("social partnership") encompassing nongovernmental organizations, particularly regional labor and employer organizations.[15] While it lacks authority to enforce participation of the social partners in structural decisionmaking against the wishes of a member state and does not yet challenge the right of member states to determine the formal composition of the regional side of the partnership triangle, the Commission has served notice of its ambition that "the social partners must be more involved in the programming procedures than they were in the past."[16]

Additionality

The principle of additionality demands that financial contributions to structural funds are *additional* to what member states would otherwise spend. The justification for additionality is straightforward: to the extent that member states take account of EC structural funds in their own financial calculations, spending correspondingly less of their own money in the target regions, this defeats the very notion of a Community structural policy.

Despite the importance of the principle, it has proved extremely difficult to implement. One part of the problem is that it is ambiguous for member states (in particular, the United Kingdom) that have received no increase in EC structural funding. Article 9 of the Council regulation setting out the 1988 reform of the structural funds specifies that "the Commission and the Member States shall ensure that the *increase* in appropriations . . . has a genuine additional economic impact in the regions concerned."[17] Hence, the British government has maintained that it is under no legal obligation to provide additionality, and the bulk of EC structural aid is, at this time of writing, channeled through the Treasury.[18] Under the present UK system, local authorities are not allowed to borrow additional funds to match Community spending but must draw their share from existing planned expenditure.

A second, more general, and perhaps even more intractable problem is that it is very difficult for the Commission to ascertain additionality, even in cases where the member state is cooperative, because it is impossible to know how much would have been spent in a targeted region if there were no Community regional policy. Since 1990, the Commission's approach to this has been to press member states to create special budget lines for structural spending so that they can observe the flow of EC money to the regions concerned. In Eurojargon this is the demand for "transparency." The Commission has also sought to gauge additionality by evaluating how total regional spending in individual countries has increased over time as EC structural spending has increased. To this end, in August 1990 the Commission asked member states to provide (by November 30, 1990) statistical information on regional aid to targeted regions.[19] No member state complied; most pleaded for more time, invoking technical problems with breaking down the data by geographical units as required. The Commission extended the deadline to May 15, 1991. At the time of writing, the Commission still was not completely satisfied that the UK, Italy, or Spain were fulfilling additionality.

Financial Growth, Institutional
Formation, and Decisional Power

A notable characteristic of structural policy in the EC is that the dynamics of budgetary expansion are very different from those of institutional formation and policy practice. The driving force for change in all areas of structural policy has been the considerable growth in resources as a result of member state bargaining. The institutions and practices that govern how those resources are used, however, bear little relation to how they were gathered.

The Council of Ministers remains the key forum for innovations in structural policy funding.[20] The creation of a Regional Development Fund in 1975, the decision to double structural funding in 1988, and the current bargaining about further increases in structural funding at Edinburgh—all are the result of negotiation among member states. If one's vision were limited to highlights in the development of the EC's structural policy over the last seventeen years, one would conclude that this policy area is dominated by member states. From this perspective, the creation and expansion of regional funding reflects the need to find a financial instrument to pay off poorer member states to gain their assent to policies that they would otherwise reject.

This is a valid perspective, but it needs to be extended by examining the *practice* of structural policy, for it is obvious that the way an institution is funded does not tell us how it actually works and spends. An exclusive focus on key watersheds of institutional creativity—as critical as they are to the overall process of European integration—is not just partial, but seriously misleading. Both the Single European Act and the Treaty on European Union are exceptional institutional breakthroughs that tell us only a limited amount about other aspects of political life in the EC, in the same way that constitutional structuring and restructuring in a nation-state provide only one line of sight into its political dynamics. When one lifts the lid on the practice of structural policy, it is clear that the Commission has played a vital role in designing the institutional framework. Within that framework, the Commission is the key actor in the process of policymaking and implementation.

While the doubling of structural funding in 1988 at the Brussels summit resulted from member state bargaining, the institutional reforms that were agreed by the Council later that year were drawn up by the Commission. Apart from the concession of a watered-down clause concerning additionality to mollify the UK, the result reflected the Commission's wishes.

The reforms have given the Commission an impressive margin of latitude in allocating resources. A significant portion of total structural spending, ECU 5.5 billion, 9 percent of total spending during the funding period 1989 to 1993, has been allocated directly by the Commission in the form of Community initiatives.[21] These are programs originated and administered by the Regional Development Fund for specific problems, such as converting regions formerly dependent on steel, shipbuilding, or coal. The remainder of the structural budget is allocated among member states on the basis of broad ranges rather than fixed quotas.

The Commission's power of the purse can be used to apply intense pressure in disputes with member states, as was evident in the dispute with the UK concerning additionality. After several months of inconclusive posturing on both sides, in December 1989 Bruce Millan, the Commissioner of the Regional Fund, decided to create a new Community initiative that would highlight the policies of the offending ministries of the Thatcher government, the Department of Trade and Industry, and the Treasury and in the process encourage strong opposition to the government from political interests in the regions that stood to gain from the program. The Community initiative that Millan created, RECHAR, was designed to aid in the conversion of coal-mining regions. Funding criteria were such that qualifying regions in the UK were slated to receive 44 percent of the ECU 300 million allocated to the initiative.[22] In addition, Millan arranged for the European Coal and Steel Community to earmark ECU 120 million in potential loan rebates and ECU 40 million in supplementary funding for 1990, ECU 50 million for 1991, and further amounts in subsequent years. When the government continued to insist that Community structural funds would be channeled into the Treasury, leaving the target regions to raise the bulk of their matching funds by cutting expenditures elsewhere, Millan blocked the UK side of the program. Later in 1991, with the dispute still unresolved, Millan threatened to block the total structural allotment to the UK for 1992–93, amounting to around 900 million pounds.[23] Under intense political pressure, described in more detail below, the UK government was brought to the negotiating table, and in mid-February 1992 it formally accepted (but has not yet implemented) the Commission's demands concerning additionality, whereupon Millan released the RECHAR funds.[24]

The climb-down by the UK government in the dispute is all the more remarkable when one considers the diverse grounds of UK opposition to the Commission's position. The government's resistance to additionality was part of its overall strategy to control public spending. From the Treasury's standpoint, true additionality meant additional spending of about 130 million pounds. Opposition to additionality was reinforced by the perception that the UK receives no net benefit from EC structural funds; its receipts relative to those of all member states are smaller than its relative contribution to the Community budget. The government goes even further and opposes the principle of Commission interference in regional spending decisions on the grounds that they are an internal matter for the UK alone. In his testimony to a House of Lords select committee concerned with the structural funds, Peter Lilley, secretary of state for trade and industry, argued that the UK would prefer the abolition of the structural funds in favor of financial transfers from Brussels directly to Whitehall.[25] From a legal standpoint, the government continues to insist that it is under no formal obligation to enforce additionality under Article 9 because its structural funding has not increased since 1988.

As I detail in the next section, the Major government backed down for several reasons, including its sensitivity to opposition from Conservative local authorities and MPs in the run-up to a general election. Millan pursued a carefully orchestrated strategy that succeeded in gaining regional support for the Commission's position within the UK and diffusing the government's claim that the dispute pitted the country against intransigent and interventionist Eurocrats. While the Commission's control of spending was by no means sufficient for its political success, it was certainly a necessary condition.

How has the Commission managed to create an institutional framework in which it has such impressive control over resources? One important source of Commission power is its agenda-setting ability. The progressive expansion of structural spending has been driven by bargains involving financial transfers across member states, but these bargains have had virtually no institutional component. While the Council is the key arena for resolving basic issues of governance and finance in the Community, it has neither the cohesion nor the institutional capacity to act in detail. The Commission drew up the blueprint for the 1988 reform of the structural funds, and this blueprint, with only minor revisions, was approved by the Council.

The Commission's way was smoothed because the EC's structural policy was an innovation that supplemented rather than replaced existing efforts on the part of member states to provide regional aid. As a result, there was little resistance from member state bureaucracies entrenched in regional policy. Moreover, regional policy was very weakly developed in the poorest member states—Greece, Ireland, Portugal, and Spain—that had the most at stake in the institutionalization of funding. These countries welcomed an activist approach on the part of Brussels because they lacked not only money, but the expertise to spend it wisely. Conversely, those countries that had the most entrenched bureaucracies in the field of structural policy—the UK, West Germany, and France—believed that they would be least affected and were generally content to go along with the Commission's plans.

The Regional Dimension in the Emerging European Polity

With the exception of "Europe of the Regions" visionaries, whose ideas have had little impact on either the practice or the theory of institution building in the European Community, the dominant conception of possible outcomes has been a continuum between a system dominated by existing states at one extreme and a supranational European state at the other. While scholars' ideas about the causality of European integration vary sharply, as do their predictions, most share this conception of the range of alternative destinations.

The experience of structural policy compels us to reevaluate this conception of outcomes. Structural policy in the EC does not fit along a continuum running from continued national state predominance to the emergence of a Eurostate. Instead, it appears to be a two-sided process, involving *decentralization* of decisionmaking to subnational levels of government as well as centralization of new powers at the supranational level. If we encompass the experience of structural policy in our notion of the future European polity, it can be viewed as the leading edge of a system of *multilevel governance* in which supranational, national, regional, and local governments are enmeshed in territorially overarching policy networks. Instead of a *centripetal* process where decisionmaking is progressively centralized in Community institutions, in structural policy we see a *centrifugal* process in which decisionmaking is spun away from member states in two directions: up to supranational institutions, and down to diverse units of subnational government; instead of the unambiguous allocation of decisionmaking responsibility between national and supranational governments, we see the institutionalization of *contested spheres* of influence across *several tiers* of government.

Subnational governments have developed vertical linkages with the Commission that bypass member states and challenge their traditional role as sole intermediary between subnational and supranational levels of government. Direct contacts between the Commission and subnational governmental representatives take place on a daily basis both in the regions and in Brussels. Commission officials visit targeted regions and consult extensively with local and regional government representatives, and these representatives are active participants alongside Commission and member state officials in the tripartite CSF monitoring committees. About 240 committee meetings involving Commission, national, and subnational representatives to monitor CSFs and operations programs were held in the regions of the EC in 1992.[26] A large number, perhaps a majority, of regional or local governments in objective 1 and objective 2 areas have sought direct links with the Commission by opening offices in Brussels where they monitor EC regulations, lobby the Commission, and shepherd their proposals for funding through the Community process.[27] As noted above, subnational representatives have also played a critical role in designing and campaigning for new regional initiatives, sometimes, as in the case of RECHAR, quite independently of their member states.

The growth of direct links between subnational governments and the Commission opens up some interesting coalitional possibilities, pitting both ends against the middle (i.e., member states). In an earlier analysis of the 1988 reform of the structural funds and its consequences, I speculated about how existing states might be "outflanked on the one side by the transfer of authority to the EC and on the other by incentives for newly assertive and politically meaningful regional bodies," noting that it would not be surprising if "regional governments and Community institutions should regard each other as useful potential allies in bargaining with member states."[28] The recent clash between the Commission and the UK over additionality reveals the scope for such alliances even in a country where subnational government is relatively weak. The efforts of the Commission to put financial pressure on the UK government went hand in hand with the political mobilization of local authorities on the issue, led by a Barnsley-based organization, the Coalfield Communities Campaign (CCC), that represents ninety-seven local authorities in coal-mining areas in the UK and coordinates them with like regions in

Belgium, France, Germany, and Spain.[29] The CCC was instrumental in developing the RECHAR initiative in cooperation with the European Regional Development Fund and in alerting local authorities to the sources of the conflict between the UK government and the Commission by publishing pamphlets, organizing educational seminars for local government representatives, and informing the media.[30] The fact that some Conservative, as well as Labour and Liberal Democratic, local authorities were involved in the campaign to change the government's policy on additionality undermined the government's attempt to paint the conflict as one that pitted Britain against a meddlesome Eurocracy headed by a Labourite (Bruce Millan, former secretary of state for Scotland under a Labour government). By late 1991, when the conflict first hit the front pages of several UK newspapers, the campaign had gained the support of regional affiliates of the Confederation of British Industry as well as of the Trades Union Congress, the Yorkshire Chamber of Commerce, and Conservative members of parliament in constituencies that were being denied Community funding. All five national associations of local authorities opposed the government.

Several aspects of the conflict—the way in which local actors were mobilized, their alliance with the Commission, and the effectiveness of their efforts in shifting the government's position—confirm the claim that structural policy has provided subnational governments and the Commission with new political resources and opportunities in an emerging multilevel policy arena.

The conflict over additionality shows the scope for unintended consequences in the EC very clearly. In the previous section, I argued that treaties shape the process of institutional creation only in rough outline. A corollary of this is that member states do not know exactly what they are agreeing to when they sign on. In this case, the UK government fell into a trap of its own making, for it had agreed to reforms of the structural funds that included an ambiguous commitment to additionality and provided the Commission with the means to enforce its own interpretation. It is worth stressing, however, that the idea of unintended consequences is tricky in the context of ongoing political relationships where learning takes place. Having been at the sharp end of growing Commission power and subnational government assertiveness, the UK government is likely to pay more attention to institutional details in the future and be more willing to exert its veto power, or threaten to do so, to stave off future debacles.

Subnational Government and Transnational Networks

At Maastricht, the member states agreed in a protocol attached to the Treaty to expand the Consultative Council of Regional and Local Authorities, set up by the Commission in 1988 with consultative rights over the formulation and implementation of regional policies, into a Committee of the Regions on lines parallel to the existing Economic and Social Committee. The Committee of the Regions has a larger membership than the previous Consultative Council (189 against 42), and although the new body remains largely symbolic, it is given a wider consultative role.[31] The protocol directs the Council of Ministers and the Commission to consult with the Committee of the Regions on regional issues. In addition, the Committee can forward its opinion to the Council and Commission "in cases in which it considers such action appropriate."

This new chamber is merely the most visible of a diverse and growing number of mostly specialized transnational organizations representing subnational governments, including the Assembly of European Regions; the Conference of Peripheral Maritime Regions; the Association of Regions of Traditional Industry; the European Association of Border Regions; the Union of Capital Regions; associations covering the Western, Central, and Eastern Alps, the Jura, and the Pyrenees; the Association of Frontier Regions; and the Coalfields Communities Campaign.[32]

The creation of new networks of interaction, influence, and policymaking spanning subnational governments, member states, and the EC complicate institution building in the European Community. While the notion that member states intermediate between domestic pressures and supranational institutions, as illustrated in Figure 23.1, provides a useful theoretical starting point for the analysis of some policy areas, such an approach is not appropriate in structural policy. Instead we are seeing the emergence of a far more complex, open-textured, and fluid situation in which subnational governments interact both with the EC and crossnationally, as represented in Figure 23.2.[33]

Figure 23.2 is misleading in one important respect: it suggests homogeneous patterns of multilevel governance across the EC. In fact, there are wide variations across, and even within, member states. This is partly a reflection of the widely differing roles and powers of subnational governments across member states.[34] In Germany, a federal polity with an extremely strong regional tier of government, the länder dominate the role of subnational partner, occasionally to the exclusion of any local input from the two lower tiers of government, the Kreise and Bezirke. In the regionalized states of Spain and Italy, subnational governments have a strong constitutional position, though they usually find themselves financially dependent on the central government, and their autonomy is constrained by national framework legislation. Ireland, Portugal, Greece, and the UK, at the other extreme, have no regional tier. In these countries, the interlocutors of the Commission are representatives of weak, financially dependent local authorities. The effectiveness of local authorities in these countries as voices independent of the national state depends upon their resources and ability to create region-wide coalitions. For example, local governments in the Azores and Madeira Islands are far more effective than those on the Portuguese mainland, and especially

Figure 23.1 Territorial Policy Networks Pre-1992

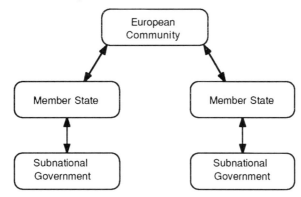

Figure 23.2 Territorial Policy Networks Post-1992

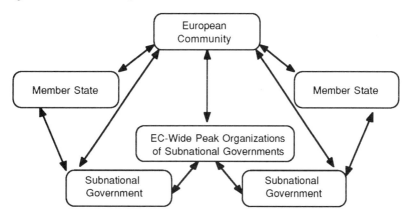

in the Algarve, because they are far more cohesive. For the same reason, partnership is more balanced in northeastern England, where there is a stronger sense of local identity than in the western Midlands.

Diversity is also an integral feature of the operation of the structural funds themselves. In the first place, the influence of the funds is felt only in the targeted regions, which contain around 43 percent of the total population of the EC.[35] However, there are also important differences across the targeted regions. Countries that qualify in their entirety for structural funding, i.e., the very poorest countries eligible for objective 1 funding, are covered by nationwide CSFs, whereas countries that quality for objective 2 funding have regional CSFs.[36] The operational programs that make up both types of CSFs have a regional slant, though even here there is a difference: projects in the poorer countries are frequently sectoral rather than regional in focus. As a result, it is often difficult for subnational governments in the poorer regions to present the case for regional priorities against central government assertion of national priorities.

The Commission has framed its demand for extensive regional participation in structural policy in terms of "partnership," a new buzz word that may have a significant future in debates about Community institution building. Partnership shares with subsidiarity the notion that, to quote from the opening paragraph of the Treaty on European Union, "decisions are taken as closely as possible to the citizen."[37] However, partnership conceives the relationship between levels of government as being one of interaction rather than autonomy. Instead of giving independence to subnational governments within a defined framework of powers and duties in which certain issues are deemed to be exclusively handled at the subnational level, partnership involves governments at local, regional, national, and supranational levels in complex patterns of mutual influence.[38]

One of the achievements of Maastricht was to raise such issues formally for the first time. However, the gap between exhortation and practice remains very large. If member states were to take seriously the admonition to make decisions as closely as possible to their citizens, this would demand nothing less for most of them than their reconstitution. The debate about how subnational tiers of government fit into the multilevel governance of the European Union has only just begun. The notion of subsidiarity surfaces in the Treaty just three times, in each case as a general principle without specific application.[39] In this case, as in many others in the development of the EC, unanimous consent was achieved by a combination of caution and ambiguity. Member states have not committed themselves to specific policies actually to implement subsidiarity, and the meaning of the term remains open to conflicting interpretations. The United Kingdom, for example, interprets subsidiarity to mean that internal political arrangements—however centralized—are not subject to Community influence because they form part of the member state's exclusive subsidiary responsibilities!

Conclusion

Successive treaties provide the basic outline of institutional formation in the European Community. National executives dominate the process of treaty creation. Treatymaking is "high" politics, and "high" politics continues to be the preserve of national executives. Although ratification has now shifted beyond the predictable control of national executives to legislatures and mass publics, member states remain the sovereign participants in the treaty process. The highly politicized debates that have taken place in the wake of Maastricht have been carried out in definitively national political arenas, not in the EC as a whole. Treaties have implicitly enshrined states as the ultimate constitutional units of institutional formation. In this chapter, however, I have endeavored to show that treaties are not representative of the ongoing process of institution building. In this sense, the creation of the European Community, like the formation of nation-states, is an interstitial process. The treaties, including the Maastricht Treaty, have been ambiguous and open-ended, and the European Council, the organ of member states, has neither the coherence nor the organizational capability to press member state concerns directly into institutional practice. Structural policy provides an extreme case of the disjuncture between the Treaty and the institutional outcome, and of the vital role of the Commission in mediating these.

In this respect, I interpret the evidence on structural policy as a critique of intergovernmentalism, which has perhaps all too easily won the day in the wake of the recent infusions of life into the European Community as a result of interstate bargaining.[40] To put this positively, my conclusion is congruent with the emphasis of neofunctionalism on the autonomous role of supranational institutions, and in particular, the Commission.

However, there is a second conclusion to be drawn from the experience of structural policy that compels us to reevaluate the character of the European Community in a more fundamental way. My discussion of the role of subnational governments suggests that intergovernmental and neofunctional theories of the EC are inadequate because they are too narrow in one important respect: they conceive the systemic outcome of institution building in the EC in terms of a single dimension ranging from national state domination at the one extreme to a supranational polity at the other. From the standpoint of the case I have described, the debate between intergovernmentalism and neofunctionalism is sterile because it cannot come to grips with the most salient and novel characteristic of that case, the mobilization and empowerment of subnational governments. I believe we are witnessing the emergence of *multilevel governance* in the European Community, characterized by co-decisionmaking across several nested tiers of government, ill-defined and shifting spheres of competence (creating a consequent potential for conflicts about competencies), and an ongoing search for principles of decisional distribution that might be applied to this emerging polity. To put this more speculatively, the experience of structural policy suggests that it might be fruitful to describe the process of decisional reallocation to European Community institutions merely as one aspect of a centrifugal process in which some decisional powers are shifted down to municipal, local, and regional governments, some are transferred from states to the EC, and (as in the case of structural policy) some are shifted in both directions simultaneously.

Notes

I could not have written this chapter without the help of several administrators in DG-16 and DG-22 of the EC Commission, the Department of Trade and Industry, the Local

Government International Bureau, and the Coalfield Communities Campaign in the UK, who gave generously of their time in explaining their versions of events over the past two years. I cannot name them, but I hope they gain some pleasure in recognizing their own stories. I would also like to thank my fellow collaborators on "The Consortium for 1992" for their comments and criticisms on drafts of earlier, related papers that dealt with the 1988 reforms of the structural funds and with European integration and state building. Participants in the Comparative Politics Discussion Group in the Department of Political Science at UNC-Chapel Hill gave freely of advice and criticism. Jenna Bednar, Leonard Ray, and Kermit Blank provided useful editorial and research assistance. This chapter was researched while I was a fellow at the Center for Advanced Study in the Behavioral Sciences at Stanford. I am grateful for financial support provided by National Science Foundation Grant #BNS-8700864, as well as a grant from the Social Science Research Council to "The Consortium for 1992."

1. See Ernst B. Haas, *The Uniting of Europe: Political, Social and Economic Forces 1950–1957* (London: Stevens and Son, 1958); the essays, particularly Haas's, in Leon N. Lindberg and Stuart A. Scheingold, eds., *Regional Integration: Theory and Research* (Cambridge, Mass.: Harvard University Press, 1971); Leon N. Lindberg and Stuart A. Scheingold, *Europe's Would-Be Polity: Patterns of Change in the European Community* (New York: Prentice Hall, 1970); and Donald J. Puchala, "Of Blind Men, Elephants and International Integration," *Journal Of Common Market Studies* 10 (1972).

2. See, for example, Geoffrey Garrett, "International Cooperation and Institutional Choice," *International Organization* 46 (1992); and Andrew Moravscik, "Negotiating the Single European Act," in Robert O. Keohane and Stanley Hoffmann, eds., *The New European Community: Decisionmaking and Institutional Change* (Boulder: Westview, 1991).

3. Commission of the European Communities, *Treaty on European Union* (Brussels: Commission of the European Communities, 1992), Article 130a and Protocol on Economic and Social Cohesion.

4. Commission of the European Communities, *From the Single Act to Maastricht and Beyond: The Means to Match Our Ambitions,* Com(92) 2000 final (Brussels: Commission of the European Communities, 1992). Hereafter cited as *Maastricht and Beyond.*

5. Commission of the European Communities, *Second Annual Report on the Implementation of the Reform of Structural Funds* (Brussels/Luxembourg: Commission of the European Communities, 1992). Hereafter cited as *Second Annual Report on Implementation.*

6. Commission of the European Communities, *Maastricht and Beyond,* p. 23.

7. Commission of the European Communities, *Community Structural Policies: Assessment and Outlook,* Com(92) 84 final (Brussels: Commission of the European Communities, 1992), Graph 1.

8. Per capita gross national product at market prices in Greece decreased from 60.0 percent of the EC average in 1980 to 52.6 percent in 1990. In Spain, Portugal, and Ireland the increases were from 73.5 to 77.4 percent, 53.5 to 55.5 percent, and from 61.5 to 61.7 percent, respectively, over the same period. Commission of the European Communities, *Community Structural Policies,* Table 1a.

9. Commission of the European Communities, *The Regions in the 1990s: Fourth Periodic Report on the Social and Economic Situation and Development of the Regions of the Community,* Chapter 1.

10. This point is made forcefully by Philippe Schmitter in "Interests, Powers and Functions: Emergent Properties and Unintended Consequences in the European Polity," paper prepared for a meeting of "The Consortium for 1992" at the Center for Advanced Study in the Behavioral Sciences, Stanford University, May 23–25, 1992.

11. Commission of the European Communities, *Guide to the Reform of the*

Community's Structural Funds (Luxembourg: Commission of the European Communities, 1989). Hereafter cited as *Guide to Reform.*

12. This information is derived partly from interviews and from EC documents, particularly, Commission of the European Communities, *Maastricht and Beyond* and Commission of the European Communities, *Treaty on European Union.*

13. For an interesting overview of the rise of regional identity that discusses "partnership," see James G. Kellas, "European Integration and the Regions," *Parliamentary Affairs* 44 (1991).

14. Commission of the European Communities, *Maastricht and Beyond,* p. 20.

15. Commission of the European Communities, *Amélioration des Mécanismes et des Procédures de Mise en Oeuvre de la Réforme des Fonds Structurels* (Brussels: Commission of the European Communities, 1991). Hereafter cited as *Amélioration des Mécanismes.*

16. Commission of the European Communities, *Community Structural Policies,* p. 41.

17. Commission of the European Communities, *Guide to Reform,* p. 77, emphasis added.

18. House of Lords, Select Committee on the European Communities, *EEC Regional Development Policy* (London: HMSO, 1991), p. 27ff.

19. Commission of the European Communities, *Amélioration des Mécanismes.*

20. Gary Marks, "Structural Policy in the European Community," in Alberta Sbragia, ed., *Europolitics: Institutions and Policymaking in the "New" European Community* (Washington: The Brookings Institution, 1992).

21. Commission of the European Communities, *Annual Report on the Implementation of the Reform of the Structural Funds 1990,* Com(91) 400 final, (Brussels: Commission of the European Communities, 1991).

22. Stephen Fothergill, "The New Alliance of Mining Areas," unpublished, 1992.

23. "How to Grab the EC Money," *Financial Times,* February 7, 1992; Alison Smith and David Gardner, "UK Split over EC Funds for Mining Rejuvenation," *Financial Times,* December 18, 1992.

24. As explained to me in interviews with officials in the Department of Trade and Industry and the European Commission. The best written source is the *Financial Times;* for example, see the two articles just cited, as well as Philip Stephens and David Gardner, "UK, EC Agree on Regional Funds," February 18, 1992.

25. House of Lords, Select Committee on the European Communities, *EEC Regional Development Policy,* p. 54.

26. Commission of the European Communities, *Second Annual Report on Implementation.*

27. There is at present little literature on this. For an overview of British interest group activity see Sonia P. Mazey and Jeremy J. Richardson, "British Pressure Groups in the European Community: The Challenge of Brussels," *Parliamentary Affairs* 45 (1992).

28. Gary Marks, "Structural Policy in the European Community,"op. cit., pp. 212 and 218.

29. Stephen Fothergill, "The New Alliance of Mining Areas."

30. *The Additionality Problem* (Barnsley: Coalfield Communities Campaign, 1991); *Rechar and the Case for Additionality* (Barnsley: Coalfield Communities Campaign, 1991).

31. Commission of the European Communities, *Treaty on European Union,* Articles 189a, 189b, and 189c.

32. Paul N. Bongers, *Local Government and 1992* (Harlow, UK: Longman Industry and Public Service Management, 1990).

33. See Shari Garmise, Jürgen Grote, and Robert Leonardi, "Regional Governance

in a European Environment: The Increasing Role of the Region for Functional and Territorial Interest Intermediation," presented at the IPSA-SOG conference on Levels of Government and 1992, Montpellier, France, 1992, for an earlier representation of multilevel governance in the European Community.

34. See Jeffrey J. Anderson, "Skeptical Reflections on a 'Europe of Regions': Britain, Germany, and the European Regional Development Fund," *Journal of Public Policy* (1992); Richard Batley, "Comparisons and Lessons," in Richard Batley and Gerry Stoker, eds., *Local Government in Europe: Trends and Developments* (London: MacMillan Education Ltd, 1991); "The Regions in the EC: Legislative Diversity and the Search for an Integrated Political Role," Final Report (Bonn: Institute for European Policy, 1991); Edward C. Page and Michael J. Goldsmith, "Centre and Locality: Explaining Crossnational Variation," in Page and Goldsmith, eds., *Central and Local Government Relations: A Comparative Analysis of West European Unitary States* (Beverly Hills: Sage Publications, 1987).

35. Objective 1 areas encompass 21.7 percent of the population of the EC, objective 2 areas encompass 16.4 percent, and objective 5b areas encompass 5.0 percent. Commission of the European Communities, *First Annual Report on the Implementation of the Reform of the Structural Funds* (Brussels/Luxembourg: Commission of the European Communities, 1990).

36. Commission of the European Communities: Directorate-General for the Co-ordination of Structural Policies, *The Community's Structural Interventions,* Statistical Bulletin no. 1 (Brussels: 1991); Commission of the European Communities, Director-ate-General for Regional Policy, *The ERDF in 1989* (Brussels/Luxembourg: 1991).

37. Commission of the European Communities, *Treaty on European Union,* Article A.

38. For a suggestive discussion of networks in the EC, see Robert O. Keohane and Stanley Hoffmann, "Institutional Change in Europe in the 1980s," in Keohane and Hoffmann, *The New European Community,* op. cit.

39. See Commission of the European Communities, *Treaty on European Union,* Article A, Article B, and Article 3b.

40. For a "Commission-centric" perspective that runs against this tide, see George Ross, "Confronting the New Europe," *New Left Review* 191 (1992).

Acronyms

ARRC	Ace rapid reaction corps
ASEAN	Association of South East Asian Nations
BRITE	Basic Research in Industrial Technologies for Europe
CAP	Common Agricultural Policy
CEEP	European Center for Public Enterprises
CFSP	Common Foreign and Security Policy
CIS	Commonwealth of Independent States
CMEA	Council for Mutual Economic Assistance
COPA	Committee of Professional Agricultural Organizations
COREPER	Committee of Permanent Representatives
CS	Collective security
DG	Directorate-General
DM	deutschemark
EC	European Community
ECSC	European Coal and Steel Community
ECU	European Currency Unit
EDI	European Defense Identity
EEA	European Economic Area
EEC	European Economic Community
EFTA	European Free Trade Area
EIC	European Industry Committee
EMI	European Monetary Institute
EMS	European Monetary System
EMU	Economic and Monetary Union
EP	European Parliament
EPC	European Political Cooperation
EPU	European Political Union
ERM	Exchange rate mechanism
ESC	Economic and Social Committee
ESCB	European System of Central Banks

ESPRIT	European Strategic Program in Information Technology
ETUC	European Trade Union Confederation
ETUI	European Trade Union Institute
EWC	European works councils
FEBI	Fédérations Européennes par Branch d'Industrie
FRG	Federal Republic of Germany
FTA	Free trade agreement
GATS	General Agreement on Trade and Services
GATT	General Agreement on Tariffs and Trade
GDR	German Democratic Republic
GMP	Global Mediterranean Policy
IEPG	Independent European Programme Group
IGC	Intergovernmental Conference
IMF	International Monetary Fund
JESSI	Joint European Submicron Silicon Initiative
MFN	Most favored nation
MNC	Multinational corporation
MTO	Multilateral Trading Organization
NAC	North Atlantic Council
NAFTA	North American Free Trade Agreement
NATO	North Atlantic Treaty Organization
OMA	Orderly marketing arrangement
RACE	R&D in Advanced Communications Technologies for Europe
RRF	Rapid reaction force
SEA	Single European Act
SPP	Social Policy Protocol
TNC	Trade Negotiation Committee
TRIM	Trade-related investment measure
TRIP	Trade-related intellectual property
UNICE	Union of Industry and Employer Confederations of Europe
VER	Voluntary export restraint
WEU	Western European Union
WPM	Workers' participation in management

The Contributors

David M.
ANDREWS

Assistant Professor
Center for German and European Studies
Georgetown University
Washington, DC, USA

Hans-Georg
BETZ

Assistant Professor
Loyola University of Chicago
Chicago, IL, USA

Timothy J.
BIRCH

Doctoral Candidate
University of Missouri-Columbia
Columbia, MO, USA

Alan W.
CAFRUNY

Henry Bristol Associate Professor
of International Affairs
Hamilton College
Clinton, NY, USA and
Visiting Professor
European University Institute
Florence, Italy

John H.
CROTTS II

Doctoral Candidate
University of Missouri-Columbia
Columbia, MO, USA

Françoise
DE LA SERRE

Senior Research Fellow
Center for International Studies and Research (CERI)
Fondation Nationale des Sciences Politiques
Paris, France

413

Wilson P.
DIZARD

Senior Associate
Center for Strategic and International Studies
Washington, DC, USA

Robert
GEYER

Doctoral Candidate
Department of Political Science
University of Wisconsin
Madison, Wisconsin, USA

Stephen
GEORGE

Reader
Department of Politics
University of Sheffield
Sheffield, United Kingdom

Walter
GOLDSTEIN

Professor of Political Science
State University of New York at Albany
Albany, NY, USA

Michael J.
GORGES

Doctoral Candidate
Department of Political Science
University of California at Berkeley
Berkeley, CA, USA

Brigid
LAFFAN

Jean Monnet Professor of European Politics
Department of Politics
University College Dublin
Belfield, Dublin, Ireland

Finn
LAURSEN

Professor of International Politics
European Institute of Public Administration
Maastricht, Netherlands

Christian
LEQUESNE

Research Fellow
Center for International Studies and Research (CERI)
Fondation Nationale des Sciences Politiques
Paris, France

Wolfgang
LUTHARDT

Professor of Political Science
Department of Social Sciences
Universität Osnabrück
Osnabrück,Germany

Gary MARKS	Associate Professor of Political Science University of North Carolina Chapel Hill, NC, USA
Sir William NICOLL	Director General(Ret.), Secretariat General Council of the European Communities Brussels, Belgium
Daniel G. PARTAN	Professor of Law and R. Gordon Butler Scholar-in-Law Boston University School of Law Boston, MA, USA
John REDMOND	Professor of International Studies and Director Graduate School of International Studies University of Birmingham Birmingham, United Kingdom
Glenda G. ROSENTHAL	Adjunct Associate Professor of Political Science and Research Scholar, Institute on Western Europe Columbia University Institute on Western Europe New York, NY, USA
Wayne SANDHOLTZ	Assistant Professor Department of Politics and Society School of Social Sciences, University of California, Irvine Irvine, CA, USA
Alberta SBRAGIA	Director, West European Studies Program University Center for International Studies University of Pittsburgh Pittsburgh, PA, USA
Michael SHACKLETON	Principal Administrator Division for Relations with National Parliaments European Parliament Secretariat Brussels, Belgium
Dale L. SMITH	Assistant Professor of Political Science Department of Political Science Florida State University Tallahassee, FL, USA

Jürgen   Doctoral Candidate
WANKE   Florida State University
                        Tallahassee, FL, USA

Paul J.J.   Faculty of Economics
WELFENS   Universität Münster
                        Münster, Germany

Pia Christina   Assistant Professor
WOOD   Department of Political Science and Geography
                        Old Dominion University
                        Norfolk, VA, USA

Index

About the Book

The second volume in the European Community Studies Association's biennial series, this book reviews developments in the EC—with special attention to general theories and concepts—in the critical 1991–1992 period. The authors cover the evolving contours of the Community in the post-Maastricht era, details of the internal market, and the ongoing debates about the implications of the EC, both for its member states and in a global context.